Benito Pérez Galdós:

A Selective Annotated Bibliography

compiled by

Hensley C. Woodbridge

The Scarecrow Press, Inc.

Metuchen, N. J.   1975

Library of Congress Cataloging in Publication Data

Woodbridge, Hensley Charles, 1923-
    Benito Perez Galdos: a selective annotated bibliography.

    Includes indexes.
    1. Pérez Galdós, Benito, 1843-1920--Bibliography.
Z8672. 95. W66   016. 863'5   75-2045
ISBN 0-8108-0800-5

Manufactured in the United States of America

Copyright 1975 by The American Association of
Teachers of Spanish and Portuguese

DEDICATED

TO

JOSE SIMON DIAZ, JOSEFINA SIMON DE PALMER AND
THEIR CHILDREN: MARY CARMEN, PEPE AND
PALOMA

in memory of their inexhaustible friendship
and hospitality to Annie and
Hensley Woodbridge

iii

TABLE OF CONTENTS

ACKNOWLEDGMENTS

Bibliographers build upon each other's work. I have carefully explored the works by Theodore Sackett and Leo Hoar, Jr. mentioned in the text. Much material would have been inaccessible to me had it not been for assistance received from the photoduplication departments of the Biblioteca nacional (Madrid), the Library of Congress, the New York Public Library and the library of the University of Illinois.

Jack Emory Davis, Arnold Chapman, Charles King, Richard Reeve, Vernon Chamberlin, Joseph Schraibman, Warren Meinhardt, Carlos Márquez-Sterling, David Zubatsky and Charles McBride have been of great help. James Chatham, while in Madrid during the first five months of 1970, helped to keep me informed of what was being published concerning Galdós during this period in Spain.

In Santiago, Chile, Arístides Bocaz Concha provided me with a Chilean bibliography of more than one hundred items concerning Galdós.

In Argentina, Fernando García Cambeiro sent me clippings from the Buenos Aires newspapers concerning Galdós.

In Venezuela, Soberbia, C. A. has sent me references to Galdós found in Venezuelan sources.

Much of the French material concerning Nazarín was reproduced for me by the Bibliothèque nationale.

In Great Britain I am grateful to the University of London Library and to Mrs. Vera Colin who allowed this library to microfilm for my use a copy of her thesis. Mrs. Colin also has provided me with data concerning M. A. and Ph. D. theses and dissertations accepted in the universities of Great Britain.

The Biblioteca Menéndez y Pelayo reproduced for me the text of Pedro Núñez Peña's Juicio crítico de 'Fortunata y Jacinta' novela contemporánea, a volume which was not in the University of Valladolid's library, and no copy of which could be found through running an advertisement in El Norte of this city. José Simón Díaz was kind enough to tell me that it could be found in the Santander library.

I am also indebted to Pilar Corrales, director of the Biblioteca de la Facultad de Medicina in Barcelona, for her assistance.

My students over the years have stimulated my thoughts along critical, bibliographical and pedagogical directions.

To the above mentioned and to all other librarians, teachers and scholars who took time off from their busy day to answer my inquiries or who sent reprints, I desire to express my gratitude. Such errors as exist in this bibliography, I can claim as my own. However, had it not been for a network of friends and correspondents in both hemispheres, many an interesting study might not have been mentioned and the over-all value of this bibliographical study would have been greatly diminished.

Hensley C. Woodbridge

INTRODUCTION

This bibliography is intended for graduate students in the field and for the non-Galdosian Spanish teacher who may have good reasons for wanting to know what has been published on a given subject or work by Galdós. The Galdós expert will necessarily find the comprehensive forthcoming bibliography by Hernández Suárez of greater use to him than this selective bibliography of approximately 500 items.

In view of the fact that both Sackett and Hoar provide data on contemporary reviews and criticism of Galdós' Novelas contemporáneas españolas, no attempt has been made in this bibliography to cover this material, for it is my opinion that needless duplication is neither useful nor scholarly.

All items that could be included in a bibliography are not of equal value. I have, therefore, selected those that seemed to be the best-written and the most scholarly for inclusion. Only a sampling of reviews of the Episodios nacionales and of Galdós' plays have been mentioned. Within the classification system, the works discussed have been arranged in alphabetical order. I would agree that a more scholarly arrangement would have been one of chronology; however, I am convinced that an alphabetical arrangement is the easiest to work with.

The length of the annotation has little to do with the over-all quality of the entry. Some critics are quite careful to state in a few words both their purpose and their conclusions. Other critical articles defy ready condensation. It is regrettable that this could not be a critical essay on Galdós criticism, so that the differences between the critics could be brought out in sharper relief. Such an essay would have had to be several times the present length of this book.

In view of the fact that new data are constantly being found to replace older information, it is obvious that most of the material discussed here has appeared in the last twenty-five to forty years.

Important books and reviews are discussed; at times, important book reviews are quoted from. Doctoral dissertations which have been accepted at universities of the United States have been noted. No M. A. theses accepted at U. S. universities have been noted. With the kind assistance of Mrs. Vera Colin of London, two M. A. theses and one Ph. D. dissertation written in universities of Great Britain have been annotated and included in this bibliography. Two theses from Chile have also been included. It had been my hope to deal with dissertations written on Galdós in Spanish universities, but I have still found no way to get around the fact that permission for their reproduction must be obtained from their authors. Several newspaper articles have been included. No attempt has been made to comment upon unpublished French theses or to list them in this bibliography. Galdós has fascinated the French Hispanist as he has those in the United States. For example, Anuario de estudios atlánticos, 12 (1966), 610-615, provides bibliographical data on seven theses written at the University of Paris, most of which were directed by Robert Ricard.

It might be expected that prologues to editions of Galdós' works would be useful and helpful. On the whole, I have found this true only with text editions. Thus bibliographers speak of Rafael Alberti's prologue to the Editorial Pleamar edition (Buenos Aires, 1945) of Cádiz. This two-page "Canción a las Cortés de Cádiz" is of much greater value to students of Alberti than to those of Galdós. On the whole, then, introductions, prefaces and prologues to reprints and translations of Galdós' works have been purposefully omitted.

The compiler hopes that this bibliography can serve as a guide to the student interested in discovering the most important criticism written about Galdós and his works. The student perhaps should start with this guide, then go to Sackett's important bibliography and, if still more data are needed, he should go to Hoar and then to Hernández Suárez.

The compiler's linguistic competence is such that he is capable of annotating material only if it is in English, Spanish or French. He realizes that important material on Galdós has appeared in German, Portuguese and Italian, and occasional items in these languages have been included when I have been able to determine their value to the student of Galdós through reviews or the critical comments of other Galdós students.

Several works of Galdós have been made into movies. [1] These notes will deal only with those made of Nazarín, Tristana and Fortunata y Jacinta.

Approximately half-a-dozen starred items have not been personally examined.

BIBLIOGRAPHIES

The scholarly world has waited with interest the appearance of what will become the standard bibliography by Hernández Suárez. In early September 1973, there were various news stories in the Madrid newspapers that this bibliography was immediately forthcoming. However, as of November 1974 I have had no word of its appearance.

Anales galdosianos, 3 (1968), 191 writes of the "gran volumen bibliográfico recopilado y ordenado por nuestro bibliógrafo Manuel Hernández Suárez que incluirá toda la obra de y sobre Galdós hasta 1965."

Manuel Hernández Suárez has continued his bibliography in Anales galdosianos, 3:191-212 (1968) (1-296 entries), 4:127-152 (1969) (297-586), 6:139-162 (1971) (587-950), and 7:145-165 (1972) (951-1245). This comprehensive current classified bibliography on Galdós should be consulted by all students for recent publications on this author. It includes books, book reviews, articles in newspapers and periodicals, and unpublished material in the form of theses and dissertations. Accounts of lectures and radio programs on Galdós are listed when they have been the subject of news stories.

J. E. Varey, "Galdós in the light of recent criticism," Galdós studies, pp. 1-35, is a fascinating bibliographical study of recent criticism. It is the work of one of Great Britain's leading scholars on this author and Varey shows himself to be thoroughly conversant with both Galdós' works and with the criticisms written about them. It is considerably fuller than T. A. Sackett's "The history of Galdosian criticism," pp. viii-xi of his Pérez Galdós: an annotated bibliography.

Luciano E. García Lorenzo, "Bibliografía galdosiana," Cuadernos hispanoamericanos, nos. 250-252 (1970-71), 758-797, provides an extensive bibliography divided into two parts: I. Obras de don Benito Pérez Galdós, and II. Estudios sobre don Benito Pérez Galdós.

Enrique Ruiz-Fornells, "Benito Pérez Galdós y la
crítica norteamericana, " Cuadernos hispanoamericanos, nos.
250-252 (1970-71), 712-719, is a brief discussion of Galdosian
studies in the United States. His concluding paragraph follows: "Resumiendo, Benito Pérez Galdós tiene un puesto
en la enseñanza del español en Norteamérica atestiguado por
los estudios aparecidos, las ediciones escolares, los artículos de crítica literaria y con esa base, sin duda, lo seguiré
teniendo como pruebas las tesis doctorales escritas y en
preparación, y todo ello en un ambiente de comprensión para
su obra y para su vida y, lo que es más importante, para
sus ideas" (p. 719).

For the study of the Novelas españolas contemporáneas
the following two bibliographies are indispensable: Leo
Jerome Hoar, "Pérez Galdós and his critics. Galdós and
the Novelas contemporáneas as seen in the Spanish press of
his day" (Ph.D. dissertation, Harvard University, 1965, ix,
445 leaves) and Theodore A. Sackett, Pérez Galdós: an annotated bibliography (Albuquerque, New Mexico, University
of New Mexico Press, 1968, xiv, 130pp.).

Hoar's dissertation is a study of Galdós' reputation as
seen through criticism found in the Spanish press of his day,
as critics and journalists comment on his Novelas contemporáneas. The novels are discussed in chronological order
of their publication. Lengthy summaries and quotations are
provided from all important reviews.

The appendix, leaves 419-423, lists the novels or selections from the novels that were published in Spanish newspapers. Hoar notes that "Many of these secondary publications or fragments were often published in the press to coincide with the publication of, and create interest in, the novel
from which they were taken, or, in order to celebrate some
event directly related to Galdós and his career" (ℓ. 419).
The secondary bibliography of works consulted and cited is
found on leaves 424-428. Leaves 429-445, "Reviews and
articles, " "include ... all of the reviews and articles ever
published in Spain on the 'novelas contemporáneas'.... It
also contains a certain number of the articles most pertinent
to this study, dealing with different aspects of Galdós' biography, career and criticism of related works in other genres"
(ℓ. 429).

The first paragraph of Sackett's introduction is reproduced to show the compiler's purpose. He writes: "A desire

to collect and examine the largest possible portion of the
literary criticism of the non-historical novels of Pérez
Galdós has led to the compilation of this annotated bibliography; the desire to assist scholars in the increasingly difficult task of appraising a growing list of Galdosian studies
has led to its publication. The usefulness of this study may
include the following aspects: the compilation in one location of a bibliography of greater length than anything concerning Galdós yet in print, the annotated form of the majority
of the entries, the division of entries into books--major
studies of Galdós, and articles--chapters on his works, a
subject index with which the scholar may locate studies on
various topics related to Galdosian studies, and finally,
some considerations on the history of Galdosian literary criticism based on specific materials and statistics" (p. vii).

The most important reviews of the Sackett bibliography are: Gilbert Smith, Modern Language Notes, 85 (1970),
312-314; Robert Ricard, Bulletin hispanique 71 (1969), 416-
417; Ricardo Gullón, Comparative Literature Studies, 7
(1970), 403-404; Shirley A. Orsag, "An appraisal of Sackett's
annotated bibliography on Galdós," Anales galdosianos, 4
(1969), 123-125; and Hensley C. Woodbridge, La torre, no.
63 (1969), 172-175.

Smith states that "Mr. Sackett's publication should
not be a complete bibliography, and not even a complete
listing of important studies.... This publication will, however, serve as a useful reference work, for it does supply
the reader with the means for locating quickly most of the
important studies on Galdós and it does describe the content
of most of these studies, thus eliminating much fruitless
searching on the part of the scholar" (p. 314).

Ricard writes that "D'une façon plus générale, cette
bibliographie présente le gran avantage de mettre un com-
mencement de clarté dans une production qui devient de plus
en plus foisonnante et qui est restée longtemps d'une extrême
inégalité. Mais, limitée comme elle l'a été, elle semble
fournir une base insuffisante pour permettre de dégager la
'courbe' de ce que l'auteur appelle le 'Galdosian criticism' "
(p. 417).

Gullón finds the volume so useful that he utters not
one word of adverse criticism. He finds it an "obra que
merece ser acogida con interés y gratitud por los críticos
literarios interesados en el estudio de la novela y particularmente en el de la novela española" (p. 403).

He has special praise for the index and in his last
paragraph (p. 404) he notes the "... ha sido feliz idea la de
detenerse a inventariar cuando hasta la fecha se ha hecho en
materia de estudios galdosianos.... El profesor Sackett ha
realizado su tarẹa con meticulosidad y modestia, y a la
previsible objección de que faltan algunos items en su compilación, se podrá contestar con la sencilla afirmación de que
no existe tal cosa como una bibliografía completa."

Orsag feels that "the fact that future Galdosian bibliographies are in preparation dictates that this book be thoroughly evaluated.... I gained the impression that the effec-
tiveness of the book is reduced by editorial inconsistencies,
not only respecting the accuracy of the entries and index,
but also the general format" (p. 123).

About eighty per cent of the review is adverse criticism. The reviewer feels that Sackett should not have neglected the Episodios nacionales and that the index could have
been greatly improved. The last paragraph states that "In
spite of the defective numerical system, and omission of
entries and subjects, Sackett has made a definite contribution
to bringing together so many materials" (p. 125).

I am, however, completely baffled by the following
remarks: "The two main divisions ["Books on Pérez Galdós"
and "Studies on Galdós"] are entirely too broad. In the first
place they do not cover original works written by Galdós"
(p. 123). Nowhere does Sackett state that he is interested
in producing a bibliography of Galdós' works. Surely the
critic's job is to determine how successful Sackett was within his self-imposed limitations. While it is true that Orsag
speaks of "omissions of entries ...," nowhere in his review
does he provide a list of what he considers important publications omitted. He writes concerning this point: "Two
areas still require thorough investigation by future Galdosian
bibliographers: the publication of foreign editions of Galdós'
works, and doctoral theses published in the United States.
It is time to expand our bibliography to include all the significant publications of and on Galdós throughout the world.
Doctoral theses, too, represent an invaluable source of
Galdosian criticism" (p. 124).

Little would seem to exist concerning the location
of Galdosian manuscripts. Carmen Bravo Villasante, "Los
manuscritos de Galdós en la Biblioteca nacional," Cuadernos
hispanoamericanos, nos. 250-252 (1970-71), 703-05, lists

sixty manuscripts recently acquired by this library and which were exhibited there.

BIOGRAPHY

H. Chonon Berkowitz, Pérez Galdós, Spanish liberal crusader (Madison, University of Wisconsin Press, 1948, xi, 499pp.) "consists of twenty highly readable chapters followed by a substantial section of 'Notes and references' and an index.... The text is at times amusing and racy, reminiscent of an earlier humorismo of the author, perhaps occasionally purple and flamboyant, but never dull" (William H. Shoemaker, Hispanic Review, 18 [1950], 79). Shoemaker also states that this volume is "an awe-inspiring and overwhelming one.... It is hardly necessary to say that all previous biographical studies have been fully utilized and may now be considered singly or together, completely superseded" (ibid., p. 78).

This volume is the fullest biographical study that has appeared in any language. It appeared posthumously and the author was unable to see his work through the press. Shoemaker "found that indubitable errors of factual statements are remarkably few and insignificant" (ibid.). He found "errors in the rich and compact bibliographical detail of the twenty pages of Notes and References (463-82) to be "so few and so relatively insignificant that they will remain unmentioned here" (ibid., p. 83).

This bibliography will therefore list no biographical studies prior to this one. Material of a biographical nature published after 1948 has done little to expand our knowledge of Galdós' life except in the area of his relations with his contemporaries. Numerous collections of letters published in the last two decades add greatly to our knowledge and these are listed in a separate section.

The Shoemaker review, Hispanic Review, 18 (1950), 78-86; reprinted in his Estudios sobre Galdós (Madrid, Castalia, 1970) pp. 73-84, should be carefully examined by all those interested in both the work's strong points and the few weaknesses pointed out by the reviewer. The views of L. B. Walton, Modern Language Review, 44 (1949), 580-581, are not as generous as those of Shoemaker. He faults

Berkowitz' attempts at literary criticism. In Spain, the
Boletín de la Biblioteca Menéndez Pelayo, 26 (1950), 394-
396, published a review by E. Sánchez Reyes.

In 1970 there were published two biographical studies:
Carmen Bravo-Villasante, Galdós visto por si mismo (Madrid,
Editorial Magisterio Español), 316pp. (Colección novelas y
cuentos) and Federico Carlos Sáinz de Robles, Pérez Galdós:
vida, obra y época (Madrid, Vassallo de Mumbert), 305pp.
(Biblioteca literaria "Tomás Borrás").

Both must be considered as popular biographies,
neither has any footnotes, and only Bravo-Villasante provides
a bibliography. Of the two, I prefer that by Bravo-Villasante. The numerous illustrations, the reproduction of unpublished letters, and the bibliography of Galdós' works and
of material about him make this volume superior to that of
Sainz de Robles.

José Luis Cano, Insula, no. 287 (Oct. 1970), 8-9,
notes that "Otro aspecto que aborda Carmen Bravo en su
excelente libro es el de la estética galdosiana. No intenta
la autora defenderla, pero si justificar por qué Galdós se
preocupó más del plan de su obra novelesca que del estilo"
(p. 8). He finds of great interest the publication of letters
between Pereda and Galdós upon the publication of Gloria.
His one bit of adverse criticism notes that "Lastima que
Carmen Bravo pase como sobre ascuas por esos amores que
insinúa, pero que no aclara. Es un reproche que tenemos
que hacer a su libro, tan lleno, por otra parte, de novedades
y de atisbos certeros sobre la personalidad del novelista"
(p. 9). He comments on her treatment of "el femenismo de
Galdós" and of his "evolución política." He finds that this
is a "libro sugestivo, vivaz, penetrante" (p. 9).

Two other full-length biographical studies are: Domingo Navarro Navarro, Enaltecedores y detractores de
Pérez Galdós (Madrid, 1965), 350pp. and Francisco Rodríguez Batllori, Galdós en su tiempo [Estampas de una vida],
prólogo de Federico Carlos Sáinz de Robles (Las Palmas,
Litografía Saavedra, 1968), 173pp.

Navarro's volume is well illustrated. It is extraordinary to see Berkowitz referred to as a Lithuanian (article by F. Serrano Anguita in Madrid, reprinted in pp. 341-
342). The volume has no footnotes and no bibliography.
The author has adapted both Clavellina and Un joven de

provecho for the stage. Among the essays are: "Recuerdos
de infancia y juventud," pp. 21-26; "En casa de Galdós,"
pp. 45-63; "El destino manda," pp. 65-69; "En una tarde
tranquila...," pp. 71-78; "El museo galdosiano," pp. 79-
116; "Monumento a Pérez Galdós," pp. 117-121; "La fontana
de oro y Clavellina," pp. 123-137; "Deseo nacional: derrota
de Galdós en la Real Academia," pp. 139-152; "Moret y el
viaje del rey a Canarias," pp. 153-166; "Generosa iniciativa
del rey Alfonso XIII en favor de Galdós," pp. 191-193; "Y
volví a ver al abuelo ..." pp. 195-203; and "Pérez Galdós
fue amortajado con la bandera española," pp. 205-214.

The volume by Rodríguez, which has a section, "Palabras finales" by Juan Antonio Cabezas, is a collection of
twenty-three essays which "aspiran a satisfacer un propósito
de divulgación, sin exigencias eruditas ni profundidades
críticas que, en el mejor de los casos, estarán de más"
(p. 17). The essays are too short to deal with their topics.
Chapter XI, "Espíritu religioso," pp. 89-92, can hardly do
justice to its subject. "¿Galdós político?," pp. 95-98, leaves
more questions unanswered than dealt with adequately. Even
where documentation is given, it is too sketchy to be useful.
The illustrations would appear to be the most useful portion
of the volume.

Parentage and Early Life in the Canary Islands

Enrique Ruiz de la Serna and Sebastián Cruz Quintana,
Prehistoria y protohistoria de Benito Pérez Galdós: contri-
bución a una biografía ([Las Palmas] Ediciones del Excmo.
Cabildo insular de Gran Canaria [1973]), xxviii, 474pp., contains a prologue by Alfonso Armas Ayala. Armas Ayala
notes that "Estudian estos biógrafos galdosianos una faceta del
Galdós poco conocida, precisamente sus años juveniles en
Las Palmas. Concretamente, el libro concluye en 1864, año
en que Galdós realiza su primer regreso a la isla, después
de haber marchado a Madrid en 1862 para iniciar sus estudios universitarios" (ix).

He also states that "Han conseguido los autores del
libro reunir una muy rica y desconocida documentación
galdosiana encontrada en los archivos parroquiales, particulares y aun oficiales de Tenerife y Las Palmas. Gracias a
ella es posible conocer nuevos ángulos de la vida del novelista. Para ser más exactos, del entorno familiar del escritor" (ix).

These biographers correct a good number of errors found in previous biographies; they reproduce a variety of documents that they transcribe, and they provide a reader with the texts of "La Emilianada," "Un viage redondo," "El sol" and "Un viage de impresiones."

This then is the most important work yet produced concerning Galdós' ancestors and the first twenty-one years of his life.

Until the appearance of the above volume, the most thorough account of his youth was that of José Pérez Vidal, Galdós en Canarias (1843-1862) (Madrid, El museo canario, 1952), 146pp., which was divided into three parts: I. El ambiente; II. La infancia y los primeros brotes literarios; III. La vocación literaria se acentúa. The footnotes occupy pp. 137-144; references are made to publications of the Canary Islands and to newspaper articles published in Spain.

Juan Antonio de Zunzunegui, "Galdós y la tierra vascongada," Punta Europa, nos. 70-71 (1961), 38-50, and Guillermo Camacho y Pérez Galdós, "La familia de Galdós (Carta abierta a Zunzunegui)," Punta Europa, no. 73 (1962), 30-32, deal with Galdós and the Basque country. The last article presents data on Galdós' genealogy.

Education

Josette Blanquat, "Lecturas de juventud," Cuadernos hispanoamericanos, nos. 250-252 (1970-71), 161-220, has the following parts: I. Las Palmas, el Colegio San Agustín; II. Madrid, El curso de Camus. The second part is especially valuable for its discussion of Galdós' courses with Alfredo Adolfo Camus, professor of Latin literature at the University of Madrid. Many of the themes and ideas that Galdós later used in his fiction are shown to have had their origin in reading done for this professor's classes. Blanquat concludes her article with this paragraph: "El estudio de los años que presenciaron el fin de los reinados de Isabel II y Napoleón III es apasionante. Hemos tratado hoy de definir lo que pudo ser el papel de Camus en la formación de Galdós, 'moralista experimental,' durante el curso de los años en los que el Naturalismo es encontraba en gestación, intentaremos pronto evaluar la influencia de Castelar sobre el joven escritor.... Diremos, pues, que el profesor de Literatura latina contribuyó a transmitir los arquetipos del pensamiento huma-

nista que son reconocibes en la obra de un autor naturalista
que nunca estuvo animado por el espíritu de sistema.   La
huella fue duradera.   El lector la aprecia como una señal de
originalidad en las novelas naturalistas españolas, bien sea
porque el escritor estigmatiza la sociedad de su tiempo o
porque celebra la vida creadora de bondad e inteligencia.   Y
es, sin ninguna duda, un timbre de gloria para Alfredo
Adolfo Camus" (pp. 219-220).

Santander

Jos‚ Sim˘n Cabarga, "Santander en la biografía y
bibliografía de Galdós," Boletín de la Biblioteca Menéndez
Pelayo, 36 (1960), 393-395, is a discussion of Galdós'
visits to Santander and of his home there as well as the
importance of this city on his writing.   The following is a
list of the article's divisions: "Un personaje singular," i.e.
the last Spanish survivor of the battle of Trafalgar; "Co-
mienzan las estancias santanderinas"; "Polemistas y amigos";
"Viajes a Portugal, Italia e Inglaterra"; "San Quentín, un
banquete"; "Primera obra en San Quintín: La loca de la
casa"; "Galdós y la Condesa de Pardo Bazán"; "René Bazan";
"San Quentín y la obra galdosiana"; "Los últimos años."
The article concludes with three appendices.

José Maria de Cossio, "Galdós en Santander," Ruta
literarias de La Montaña (Santander, Diputación provincial,
1960), pp.   324-332, shows the influence of Santander, La
Montaña, and the writers of the area on Galdós.   Marianela
and Gloria are both said to have a Montaña setting.   The
author also discusses aspects of Galdós' life in Santander.

Carmen Bravo-Villasante, "Polemicas en torno a
Caldós en la prensa de Santander ("La Atalaya" contra "El
Atlántico" en 1893.   "La Atalaya" contra "El Cantábrico"
en 1901)," Cuadernos hispanoamericanos, nos. 250-252
(1970-71), 694-703, discusses: a) the polemic that arose in
1893 between the anti-Galdós newspaper La Atalaya and El
Atlántico, his defender, concerning a banquet given Galdós
in Santander on March 9, 1893, and b) La Atalaya and El
Cantábrico's battle in 1900 over the reception given to his
play, Electra.   Pp. 701-3 reproduce a letter by Galdós
which was published in El Cantábrico of June 26, 1900.

Death

Pablo Beltrán de Heredia, "España en la muerte de Galdós," Anales galdosianos, 5 (1970), 89-101; reprinted in Benito Pérez Galdós (1973), pp. 89-109, notes that "Los españoles recibieron la noticia de la muerte de Galdós con un cierto sentimiento de sorpresa. Para muchos era una realidad inexistente hacía tiempo. Para otros, un elemento de la naturaleza que podía hacer frente incluso a la muerte" (p. 89). This article discusses Spanish reactions, as seen chiefly through the press, to Galdós' death.

Galdós died in 1920. No. 128 (1920) of Nosotros (Buenos Aires) was devoted to him. Ciudad de Dios ran a series of articles entitled "Pérez Galdós" that year. In Caracas, there appeared Julio C. Salas' "Carta de España: don Benito Pérez Galdós," Cultura venezolana, 4:321-323. Carmen Lira's brief tribute, "Don Benito," is found in Repertorio americano, 1 (1920), 193-194.

Juventud, revista mensual editada por la Federación de estudiantes de Chile, año 2, núm. 9 (mayo de 1920), published Armando Donoso, "Al margen de Pérez Galdós," pp. 1-13, 15, and Eduardo Marquina, "Antes el cadáver de Pérez Galdós," pp. 17-20. Especially valuable as an evaluation written for the English-speaking world is Salvador de Madariaga, "Benito Pérez Galdós," Contemporary Review, 117 (April, 1920), 508-516. The Mercure de France, 137 (1920), 855-856, is an obituary; whereas this same journal, 138 (1920), 238-243, published Marcel Robin, "Lettres espagnoles. Benito Pérez Galdós (1846-1920). I. Les romans espagnols contemporains."

The two Jesuit discussions of his life summarized below show the attitude of the religiously conservative.

Constancio Eguía Ruiz, "El españolismo de Pérez Galdós," Razón y fe, 56 (1920), 437-450, and 57 (1920), 41-62, is a bitter attack on Galdós. The author is astonished at the great honors paid Galdós upon his death. He finds that Galdós "no encaja ni perfecta ni imperfectamente en la verdadera gloria de los héroes patriotas, de los autores y genios populares españoles" (p. 444). He attacks him for not showing any love towards his "patria chica." The first article ends with this sentence: "Veamos, en efecto, como su obra no tiene nada de españolista" (p. 450). The second article is an attack on Galdós' politics as seen in his

Episodios nacionales and a violent attack against Galdós'
portrayal of religious figures in his fiction.   The series concludes with this sentence: "Pero, en fin, dado que viva en
la común patria, nada le deberá la terrena mientras no se
quemen muchas de sus obras a mano del verdugo" (p. 62).

Pierre Lhande, "Benito Pérez Galdós (1843-1920),"
Etudes, 162 (Feb. 5, 1920), 281-295, and 162 (Feb. 20,
1920), 452-470, is divided into "L'homme" and "L'oeuvre."
This Jesuit account discusses his life from a purely conservative point of view.   On p. 294 it is stated that "Ni son
patriotisme ni son talent, ni même la pénible situation de
ses derniers jours ne doivent pourtant nous aveugler sur
les méfaits de son oeuvre politique et littéraire."   The section devoted to the study of his works is "du point de vue
littéraire, moral et religieux" (p. 295).   While Devlin states
that Galdós did not die a Catholic, Lhande writes "L'écrivain
est mort en chrétien" (p. 294).   The second article is a
bitter attack on Galdós' work: "Galdós a l'inconcevable
pauvreté d'idées et la naive suffisance des affirmations"
(p. 462).   It is stated on p. 468 that "L'auteur de _Gloria_ est
un mauvais maître dans l'art d'écrire."   The numerous
quotations from the Spanish press cited throughout the two
articles contain bibliographical data of value.

Library

According to Shoemaker, H. Chonon Berkowitz, _La
biblioteca de Benito Pérez Galdós._ Catálogo razonado, pre-
cidido de un estudio (Ediciones El Museo Canario [C. S. I. C.],
1951), 227pp., "makes available for the first time the classified lists of the near 4, 000 volumes in the Madrid and
Santander libraries of Benito Pérez Galdós which the late
Professor Berkowitz compiled and submitted, together with
his brief analysis and study, to the Santander institution
[i. e. Biblioteca de Menéndez Pelayo] for publication in its
Boletín in 1932" (p. 125; the William H. Shoemaker review
of this volume can be found either in the _Hispanic Review_,
21 [1953], 353-355, or in his _Estudios sobre Galdós_, pp.
125-127).   Shoemaker also notes that "The great value of this
catalogue, with all its mistakes of detail, is that it is possible now for the first time, to know what books Galdós
possessed and which ones he may be presumed to have read
or with which he must surely, in part at least, have been
acquainted" (p. 126).

Centennial of 1943

Galdós in 1943 was not particularly persona grata in Spain and the centennial of his birth appears to have been celebrated more outside Spain than inside.

In Chile, Atenea devoted a special number to him. Many of the studies in this issue are commented upon separately. In addition to these, this issue published "El centenario de Galdós," 72 (1943), 89-91, which served as an introduction to this special number; Rodrigo Soriano, "Don Benito," 93-98, memoirs by a friend; and Antonio R. Romera, "Estampa de Galdós," 108-120, an article which argues after a rather long physical description of Galdós that, "su literatura deriva de una manera lógica, como el lento fluir de un arroyo, de todo lo que caracteriza fisicamente a su autor" (p. 113).

In Argentina, an issue of vol. 24 of Cursos y conferencias was devoted to his memory. Among the articles in this issue not to be otherwise noted are: Roberto F. Giusti, "Prefacio. La obra galdosiana," 3-12, a brief comment on the author and his works; Angel Ossorio, "El sentido popular de Galdós," 113-128, which has the following parts: El tipo humilde, Las pinturas del pueblo, Contra la masoneria, La república de 1873, El liberalismo, Las novelas llamadas sectarias, ¿Qué es Galdós? and La estatua; and Guillermo de Torre, "Nueva estimativa de las novelas de Galdós," 25-37, which discusses changes that have occurred in the evaluation of Galdós' works. He comments briefly on La desheredada, Fortunata y Jacinta, Angel Guerra, Nazarín and Halma.

In Mexico, the most important articles published to commemorate this centennial would appear to be José Carner, "La España de Pérez Galdós," Filosofía y letras, 5, 9 (1943), 75-84, and 5, 10 (1943), 215-222; and several in Cuadernos americanos: Alfonso Reyes, "Sobre Galdós," 10, 4 (1943), 234-239; Julio Torri, "Una nota sobre Galdós," 10, 4 (1943), 240-241; and Agustín Yáñez, "Traza de la novela galdosiana," 10, 5 (1943), 222-240,

In the United States, it would seem that only the Revista hispánica moderna, 9 (1943) remembered the occasion to any extent. This journal published the following short articles: Francisco García Lorca, "El realismo de Galdós," 289-290; Angel del Río, "Los ideales de Galdós," 290-292; Tomás Navarro, "La lengua de Galdós," 292-293;

and Federico de Onís, "En humorismo de Galdós," 293-294.

In Venezuela, Pedro de Repide, "Pérez Galdós," Revista nacional de cultura, no. 41 (1943), 116-159, is worthy of mention.

It should be noted that the publications of the Spanish Republicans in Chile, Argentina and other parts of the hemisphere also devoted articles to this occasion.

Fiftieth Anniversary of Galdós' Death

In 1943 when celebrations occurred in several countries on the centenary of Galdós' birth, he seemed hardly in favor in Spain. The same cannot be said of 1970, for the 50th anniversary of the writer's death was commemorated in Spain with homenajes, books, articles, etc. Thus, ABC, Feb. 6, 1970, p. 45, carried a news story on Guillermo Díaz-Plaja's lecture "Galdós y la literatura." ABC, Jan. 29, 1970, p. [110], is a news story concerning the publication of the correspondence of Galdós and Tolosa Latour. ABC, Feb. 8, 1970, p. 65, notes the recent appearance of film versions of both Fortunata y Jacinta and Tristana. Ya, Jan. 27, 1970, p. 32, carried a photograph of the "Homenaje a Galdós en el Retiro" at which Federico Carlos Sáinz de Robles spoke on Jan. 25, 1970. For detailed data on 1970 publications on Galdós, see the bibliographical section of Anales galdosianos.

Cuadernos hispanoamericanos, nos. 250-252 (1970-71) was completely devoted to articles on Galdós' life and works. Most of these are discussed in this bibliography.

Francisco Ayala, "Commemoración galdosiana," Los ensayos (Madrid, Aguilar, 1970), pp. 1017-1022, is also of interest.

In Buenos Aires, La razón, Jan. 7, 1970, p. 9, published "Hace 50 que murió Benito Pérez Galdós" in which it is stated that "A medio siglo de su desaparición, hoy está en el pináculo de la gloria literaria." La Nación, Jan. 18, 1970, p. 2, contains Guillermo de Torre's "En el cincuentenario de Galdós: vicisitudes de su fama," which is a brief study of Galdós' reputation since his death.

In Chile, there appeared Angel Lazaro, "Don Benito, en bronce," El Mercurio (Santiago), Feb. 1, 1970, p. 6.

In the United States, issues of <u>Symposium</u> and <u>Hispa-</u>
<u>nia</u> were devoted to studies on Galdós.

In Guatemala, Enrique Hidalgo de Bizkarronde published in <u>El Imparcial,</u> "Patriarca de las letras hispanas:
Don Benito <u>Pérez Galdós,</u>" Feb. 28, March 2, March 3,
1970.

<u>Congreso internacional galdosiano</u>

The first Congreso internacional galdosiano (Las
Palmas, Aug. 29-Sept. 5, 1973) is discussed in two stories
in <u>La Estafeta literaria,</u> no. 524 (Sept. 15, 1973), 28, 47.
The first is Manuel Gómez Ortiz, "Quincena de la cultura:
El congreso galdosiano y don Benito visto por Unamuno's, "
which discusses three essays on Galdós found in Miguel de
Unamuno's <u>Libros y autores españoles contemporáneos.</u>[3]
The second is entitled simply "I Congreso internacional
galdosiano. "

"El Congreso galdosiano de Las Palmas," <u>Insula,</u>
no. 324 (Nov. 1973), p. 2, provides valuable data concerning the speakers and their subjects.

Vernon A. Chamberlin, "Primer congreso interna-
cional galdosiano," <u>Hispania,</u> 57 (1974), 157, would seem to
be the first account of this conference published in the United
States.

"I Congreso internacional de Pérez Galdós, 28 agosto-
5 septiembre," <u>Letras de Deusto,</u> 3, no. 6 (julio-diciembre
1973), 187-190, is a general commentary on the Congress
with a list of speakers and their topics.

GALDOS AND HIS CONTEMPORARIES

Much has been published concerning Galdós and the writers who lived at approximately the same time. This section deals briefly with material on Galdós and the Generation of 1898, then indicates studies on individual authors and their relationship to Galdós, and ends with a section which lists two volumes that have published letters to Galdós.

Several articles deal with Galdós' relationship to the Generation of 1898 rather than with individual authors. Among the more important of these are José Angeles, "Galdós, precursor del noventa y ocho," Hispania, 46 (1963), 265-73; H. Chonon Berkowitz, "Galdós and the Generation of 1898," Philological Quarterly, 21 (1942), 107-20; and José María Monner Sans, "Galdós y la generación de 1898," Cursos y conferencias, 24 (1943), 57-85.

Angeles speaks of "las diferencias ... de pensamiento, entre Galdós y los hombres del Noventa y Ocho son de tal magnitud que no sólo les alejan, sino que les contraponen" (p. 265). His table on p. 271 summarizes what he finds to be the differences between Galdós and writers of the generation of '98. He speaks of "la, á nuestro juicio equivocadamente, pretendida influencia de Galdós sobre el Noventa y Ocho" (p. 271).

Berkowitz shows the reactions of such authors as Martínez Sierra, Benavente, Azorín, Baroja and Unamuno to Galdós both as an individual and as an artist.

Monner Sans discusses "los juicios" on Galdós of Ganivet, Maeztu, Baroja, Azorín, Benavente and Unamuno. He feels that "La falla de los del 98 frente a Galdós-- exclúyase a Benavente--ha consistido en lo haber aquilatado, con elemental equidad restrospectiva, la integra obra del maestro, esa obra cuyas porciones ofrecen algunos flancos vulnerables, pero que, sopesada en conjunto, revela maciza estructura" (p. 85).

Claire Olson Szoke, "Anticipation of the noventayochista

analysis of the problem of Spain in the work of Galdós prior
to 1898" (Ph.D. dissertation, University of Illinois, 1969,
2 vols., xi, 791pp.) (Dissertation Abstracts, 31 [1970] 769A),
is the fullest discussion of its topic yet produced. In her
introduction, the author notes that "This study is a systematic
analysis of the relationship to be found in the work of Benito
Pérez Galdós prior to 1898 and that of members of the Generation of 98" (p. 1). She feels that "In spite of differences
in personal temperament, aesthetic values and certain thematic
considerations there was a definite ideological affinity between
the approach of Galdós and that of the noventayochistas re-
garding their profound concern for the Spanish nation and the
problem of the individual" (p. 1). Her dissertation is an
"analytic study involving a considerable portion of the work
of Galdós" (p. 3), i.e., works written before 1898. In her
conclusions, pp. 727-64, she discusses Disparity of style,
Affinity of ideas and the Generation of 98's attitude toward
Galdós.

LEOPOLDO ALAS ("CLARIN"). The chief studies on
the relationship of these two individuals are: Albert Brent,
Leopoldo Alas and La Regenta, University of Missouri Studies, 24, ii (1951), 135pp.; Sergio Beser, Leopoldo Alas,
crítico literario (Madrid: Gredos, 1968 [Estudios y ensayos
117]), with eighty references to Galdós listed in its index;
W.E. Bull, "The naturalistic theories of Leopoldo Alas,"
PMLA, 57 (1942), 535-51; Juan Antonio Cabezas, 'Clarín' el
provinciano universal (Madrid: Espasa-Calpe, 1936, 224pp.;
1962, 229pp.), and W.E. Bull and V.A. Chamberlin, "Clarín's
treatment of Pérez Galdós," in Clarín: the critic in action
(Stillwater, Oklahoma: Oklahoma State University, University Publication, vol. 60, no. 9 [March 20, 1963], pp. 26-
40. It is to be noted that Galdós wrote a prologue to Alas'
La regenta which was published in the 1901, 1908 and 1946
editions of this novel. Few contemporary critics wrote
more on Galdós than did Alas. For a bibliography of Alas,
see Marino Gómez-Santos, Leopoldo Alas "Clarín": Ensayo
bio-bibliografico; prólogo de D. Gregorio Marañón (Oviedo:
Instituto de estudios asturianos, 1952), pp. 222-53.

The chapter by Bull and Chamberlin is an excellent
evaluation of Clarín as a critic of Galdós. They note that
when Clarín deals with Galdós he "appears as a highly
sensitive but calm, serene, even humble soul earnestly dedicated to art and the task of serious literary criticism"
(p. 27). They found that "There are two phases in the development of Alas's attitude toward Galdós" (p. 29). Their

final paragraph to this chapter follows: "The emphasis which
Clarín puts upon the enduring features of the Galdosian novel
and the manner in which he glosses over the weaknesses in
craftsmanship stand in sharp contrast with his treatment of
the writers who were not admitted to the ranks of his literary aristocracy" (p. 40). This study deserves a most careful reading, for the authors have both read and interpreted
Clarín well.

Fernando Ibarra, "Clarín-Galdós: una amisted,"
Archivum, 21 (1971), 65-76, is an excellent summary of the
relationship of the two authors based chiefly on Clarín's
letters to Galdós, for practically no letters by Galdós to
Clarín have survived. Ibarra feels that "La relación personal Clarín-Galdós ... se nos muestra como un interesante
aspecto de la personalidad del crítico asturiano" (p. 65).

AZORIN. A brief comment by Azorín on Pérez
Galdós is found in Azorín's Obras completas (Madrid: Aguilar, 1947), vol. 3, 1215-19.

PIO BAROJA. There are scattered references to
Galdós and his works in Baroja's Obras completas (Madrid:
Biblioteca Nueva, 1948). Vol. 5 (1948), includes his "Pérez
Galdós y la novela histórica española," pp. 498-99, Baroja
here denies that he has been influenced by Galdós and ranks
him among "hombres de segunda fila" (p. 498). He further
denies that Galdós has provided "una innovación al escribir
la novela histórica contemporánea" (p. 498). On p. 1331 he
briefly comments on El terror de 1824 with these cutting remarks: "Como siempre, en Galdós, los datos son poco exactos y la interpretación un tanto mediocre...." On p. 1150,
there are a few comments on España trágica. On p. 1172
there is a paragraph of comment on El 7 de julio. Here
Baroja accuses Galdós of writing "para un público de buenos
burgueses, un poco lerdos e incapaces de mirar un libro y
de tener una idea propria sobre algo, en lo cual quizá tu-
viera razón."

Baroja explains why "sus [Galdós'] libros históricos
y los míos tengan más que un parecido externo: el que
les da la época y el asunto." While the passage on p. 1074
of vol. 7 (1949) is very brief, it is a revealing example of
self-analysis and of his opinions concerning some of his own
works and Galdós' Episodios Nacionales. These remarks
were first published in Memorias desde la última vuelta del
caminos, V. La intuición y el estilo.

José Angeles, "Baroja y Galdós: un ensayo de dife-renciación," Revista de literatura, 23 (1963), 49-64, has an introduction and then a discussion under these headings: El amor, El personaje, El paisaje and El estilo. He concludes that "sus creaciones surgen de raices distintas y son, no sólo independientes, sino en lo fundamental, opuestas" (p. 64). He continues: "Porque si la influencia técnica, estilística de Galdós sobre Baroja sólo puede enunciarse de manera poco pensada, las diferencias de sensibilidad, de actitud ante la vida, de temple humano, de talento anímico, que es precisa-mente, lo que hay que buscar en un novelista, debieran ser suficientes para impedir, la asimiliación del gigantesco esfuerzo de objetivación que es Galdós, al portentoso esfuerzo de subjetivación que es Baroja" (p. 64).

Julio Caro Baroja, "Confrontación literaria o las re-laciones de dos novelistas: Galdós y Baroja," Cuadernos hispanoamericanos, nos. 265-267:160-168 (julio-septiembre 1972), is a discussion by Baroja's nephew of the way the relationship between the two novelists varied from period to period in their lives.

MIGUEL H. DE LA CAMARA. Alfonso Armas Ayala, "Galdós editor," Asomante, 19, 1 (1963), 37-51, reproduces six letters to Don Miguel H. de la Camara written in 1880 with a useful introduction and the following parts: El escri-tor y el hombre, Don Ignacio Pérez Galdós, Comandante militar de Canaria and Exito familiar. The author finds that "Asimismo demuestra el epistolario, que no fué Galdós ni tan solitario, ni tan egoista, ni tan poco comunicativo" (p. 38) as he is often said to be.

JOAQUIN COSTA. G. J. G. Cheyne, "From Galdós to Costa in 1901," Anales galdosianos, 3 (1968), 95-98, re-produces the text of two letters from Galdós to Joaquín Costa. Cheyne suggests that a study of Costa's influence on Galdós might be fruitful.

ANGEL GANIVET. Robert Ricard, "Deux romanicers: Ganivet et Galdós. Affinités et oppositions," Bulletin hispa-nique, 60 (1960), 484-99, shows "Que Ganivet ait éprouvé pour Galdós une admiration clair-voyante, mais profonde, il suffit pour s'en convaincre de consulter son Epistolario" (p. 486). Pages 486-91 provide evidence based on Ganivet's correspondence that "c'est assez pour nous donner la certi-tude que Ganivet lisait Galdós et le lisait avec soin" (p. 491). Ricard's purpose is to point out "certain aspects de la

production romanesque de Ganivet et certains aspects de
l'oeuvre de Galdós" (p. 491) which show differences or similarities.   He notes that Galdós has completely ignored Ganivet (p. 498).   He writes: "on ne trouve pas la moindre
trace d'une curiosité ou d'un interêt pour le createur de Pío
Cid et l'essayiste de l'Idearium.... Le nom de Ganivet n'est
jamais prononcé" (p. 498).

FRANCISCO GINER DE LOS RIOS.   William H. Shoemaker, "Sol y sombra de Giner en Galdós," Homenaje a
Rodríguez-Moñino (Madrid: Castalia), 1967, 2:213-25 (reprinted in Shoemaker's Estudios sobre Galdós, pp. 259-75);
H. Chonon Berkowitz, "Galdós and Giner: a literary friendship," Spanish Review, 1 (1934), 64-68; and Vicente Cacho
Viu, La Institucuión Libre de Enseñanza, (Madrid, Rialp,
1962), 1:507-512, are the most important discussions of Giner
and Galdos.

    Shoemaker publishes the text of Giner's letter to Pérez
Galdós, pp. 224-25.   He writes: "Como se verá, la carta no
nos defrauda en las esperanzas primeramente expresadas por
Cossío.   Con su ayuda ha sido posible: (1) hacer otra pe-
queña búsqueda, con todo lo cual se despejan las tres incógni-
tas; (2) establecer una cronología y algo de cronometría de
importancia crítica en la obra creadora de Galdós; y (3) como resultado, sacar de cierta oscuridad causas o motivos
de aparentes vaivenes de su novelística desde La familia de
León Roch hasta El doctor Centeno, pasado por La desheredada y El amigo Manso, que se explicarán, según nuestra
interpretación, en la influencia de Giner en el ánimo de
Galdós" (p. 214).

    Berkowitz notes that Giner reviewed La familia de
León Roch and La fontana de oro.   Giner also wrote Galdós
on March 20, 1881 his favorable opinion of La desheredada,
to which Galdós replied in a letter dated April 12, 1882.
Both of these letters are reproduced.   Berkowitz provides
bibliographical data and commentary on the reviews.

    LEON Y CASTILLO.   Alfonso de Armas Ayala,
"Galdós y León y Castillo," Homenaje al Excm. Sr. Dr.
D. Emilio Alarcos Garcia (Valladolid, 1965-1967) 2:169-181
(Universidad de Valladolid, Facultad de filosofía y letras),
discusses the relationship of the two individuals, "unidos
por una profunda amistad y por un conjunto de ideas com-
munes" (p. 169).

ANTONIO MAURA Y MONTAMER. Marcos Guimerá
Peraza, Maura y Galdós (Las Palmas: Edicines del Excmo.
Cabildo insular de Gran Canaria, 1967, 158pp.) (Geografía
e historia 3) has the following chapters: I. Preliminar.
II. Esquema biográfico. III. Su común dedicación a la
pintura. IV. La Academia. V. La política y los políticos.
VI. La crítica literaria. VII. El caso de la Srta. Uboa y
la "tempestuosa Electra." VIII. El abogado y el cliente,
and Documentos. Guimerá Peraza notes that "Las relaciones
entre don Antonio Maura y Montaner (1853-1925) y don Benito
Pérez Galdós (1843-1920) presentan aspectos interesantisimos
para los que se acerquen a conocer cualquiera de ambas
figuras. Iniciadas--seguramente--en 1886, al ser ambos elegidos diputados a Cortes por el partido liberal, habrían de
perdurar hasta la muerte de don Benito. Si bien con una
línea que, ascendente al final descendiendo, también por mo-
tivaciones políticas. En medio: amistad, comunes aficiones
artísticas, elecciones, academicas, envío de producciones
con la crítica consiguiente, relaciones de abogado a cliente.
Una gama rica, según puede verse a la simple enumeración"
(p. 9). The author had made use of Galdós correspondence
as well as published sources.

Angel González Araúzo, "Relaciones epistolares entre
Maura y Galdós," Anales galdosianos, 4 (1969), 113-117, is
an extremely critical evaluation of this volume. The reviewer states that "En general, el tema promete y el libro
decepciona" (p. 114) and he speaks of "la ausencia de una
estricta objetividad en los juicios del señor Guimerá" and
notes that "Como ilustración del defecto principal de que
adolece este libro puede servir la consideración detenida de
la forma en que nos es presentada esta correspondencia"
(p. 115).

Marcos Guimerá Peraza, "Algunas precisiones a la
reseña del libro Maura y Galdós," Anales galdosianos,
6 (1971), 133-137, is a ten-point reply to the González review. He writes "Como en la misma se abren interrogantes
y se formulan juicios que reputo inexactos, he aquí mis
respuestas y precisiones...." (p. 133).

MARCELINO MENENDEZ Y PELAYO. Of the several
bibliographies concerning Menéndez y Pelayo, one may mention José Simón Diaz, "Bibliografá de estudios sobre Menéndez y Pelayo," in Estudios sobre Menéndez Pelayo (Madrid:
Editora Nacional, 1956), pp. 480-581. Items 193-95 and 202
deal with the proposal that Galdós be nominated for the Nobel

Prize for Literature. Item 274 is a brief newspaper discussion of the relationship of the two men.

There are numerous references to Galdós in Epistolario de Pereda y Menéndez Pelayo; prólogo y notas de María Fernanda de Pereda y Torres Quevedo y Enrique Sánchez Reyes (Santander, 1953).

MESONERO ROMANOS. H. C. Berkowitz, "Galdós and Mesonero Romanos," Romanic Review, 23 (1932), 201-05, is an early treatment of the relationship of these two men. The fullest discussion is that found in Eulogio Varela Hervias, Cartas de Pérez Galdós a Mesonero Romanos (Madrid: Artes Gráficas Municipales, 1943), 59pp.

FRANCISCO NAVARRO LEDESMA. Carmen de Zulueta, Navarro Ledesma: el hombre y su tiempo (Madrid and Barcelona, Alfaguara, 1968) (Estudios de literatura contemporánea, I) is the most important source for the study of the relationship of these two authors. Of special interest are the following sections: "La amistad con Galdós," pp. 85-100, and "Documentos galdosianos," pp. 279-326. In the latter section are presented the texts of 23 letters and 15 cards as well as "El humano sainete," "Estreno de La de San Quintín," and "Notas sobre Galdós de Francisco Navarro Ledesma. Utilizadas probablemente para su artículo en Nuestro tiempo."

ANTONIO NUNO DE LA ROSA. R. Cardona, "Un olvidado texto de Galdós," Anales galdosianos, 3 (1968), 151-61, reproduces "Ciudades viejas: El Toboso," pp. 155-61, as well as four letters to Galdós from Antonio Nuño de la Rosa, three written in 1909 and one in 1915. These letters provided data that Galdós found useful when writing this piece.

NARCISO OLLER. William H. Shoemaker, "Una amistad literaria: la correspondencia epistolar entre Galdós y Narciso Oller," Boletín de la Real Academia de Buenas Letras, 30 (1963-1964), 247-306 (the preface has been reprinted in Shoemaker's Estudios sobre Galdós, pp. 201-22), is a collection of 54 letters written between 1884 and 1915. Oller is identified as "el fundador y el venerable padre de la novela catalana moderna" (p. 248). Shoemaker finds that "las relaciones entre los dos señores eran casi por completo epistolares o por medio del intercambio de cartas; que esas relaciones versaban mayormente si no en su totalidad, sobre

materias literarias y que la índole de las relaciones era
sincera, cándida, cordial, de una calurosa franqueza de
amigos verdaderos y hasta íntimos" (p. 247). Eight of the
letters deal with Fortunata y Jacinta.

Also of interest is Francisco Madria, "En el centena-
ri de Pérez Galdós: Les novelles de Narcís Oller i 'Don
Benito,'" Catalunya (Buenos Aires), 14, no. 150 (1943), 22-
23, which emphasizes that "Pérez Galdós fou un amic de
Cataluny a la manera castellana" (p. 22). The author comments briefly on Gerona. Most of the last page is a long
quotation by Pérez Galdós from an article on Oller which was
published in a Buenos Aires daily.

JOSE ORTEGA MUNILLA. Ruth A. Schmidt, "José
Ortega Munilla: friend, critic and disciple of Galdós," Anales
galdosianos, 6 (1971), 107-111, presents much data that show
that the friendship of these two men "extended over a period
of many years and involved numerous personal and professional contacts" (p. 107). The article's last paragraph notes
that "Thus, in addition to being over a long period of time a
warm friend of Galdós and a faithful promoter and sympathetic critic of his Novelas españolas contemporáneas, José
Ortega Munilla, in his own novelistic production, reflects the
influence of Benito Pérez Galdós, even well into the twentieth
century" (p. 110). The notes provide data on Ortega Munilla's
review of Galdós' works in Los Lunes de El Imparcial.

JOSE ORTEGA Y GASSET. Ciriaco M. Arroyo,
"Galdós y Ortega y Gasset: historia de un silencio," Anales
galdosianos, 1 (1966), 143-50, is a discussion of the four
places in Ortega's works that mention Galdós. The article
studies the reasons for the almost perpetual silence on
Ortega's part concerning Galdós.

RICARDO PALMA. Joseph Schraibman, "An unpublished letter from Galdós to Ricardo Palma," Hispanic Review, 32 (1964), 65-68, provides the text of a letter dated
Oct. 12, 1901. Schraibman discusses the letter's importance.
"It is Galdós' first published letter to a Latin American
writer and as such opens the way for further investigation
of the mutual relations, often mentioned but seldom sub-
stantiated, between Galdós and Latin American authors"
(p. 65).

Robert Ricard, "Otra vez Galdós y Ricardo Palma,"
Anales galdosianos, 7 (1973), 135-136, discusses briefly

24   Benito Pérez Galdós

their relationship as seen through correspondence. Galdós
never wrote a play based on any of Palma's Tradiciones
peruanas.

EMILIA PARDO BAZAN. Carmen Bravo-Villasante,
Vida y obra de Emilia Pardo Bazán (Madrid, Magisterio
Español, 1973), 313pp. (Colección novelas y cuentos), provides correspondence between the two writers, described by
José López Martinez, La Estafeta literaria, no. 524 (Sept.
15, 1973), 1464-1465, as follows: "La correspondencia
mantenida con don Benito evidencia una pasión apenas conocida, el gran amor y la admiración que reciprocamente se
profesaron los dos novelistas. Amor que habría de repercu-
tir en varias obras, tanto de Pérez Galdós como de la condesa. Cada cual quiso mostrar la raiz de sus sentimientos,
el alcance humano y moral de sus actitudes, valiéndose de
sus medios mas idóneos: la literatura...." (p. 1465).

PEREDA. The fullest discussion is Henry Addy
Bradley, "Pereda and Galdós: a comparison of their political, religious and social ideas" (Ph.D. dissertation, University of Southern California, 1966, 274pp.; Dissertation Abstracts, 27 [1967], 2145-46A). Bradley states that "This is
the first comparison of a comprehensive nature that has, as
yet, been made of the ideas of Pereda and Galdós." He
notes that "The first chapter, entitled 'The Two Spains,' is
devoted to a description of the political, religious and social
situation of the Spain of Pereda and Galdós.... Chapters II
and III deal respectively with the lives of the two authors,
insofar as their ideological development and participation in
national affairs is concerned. Chapters IV and V discuss
the political, religious and social ideas of each writer as
they are reflected in their novels, plays, articles, short
stories, and cuadros de costumbres.... The last chapter
summarizes the differences and similarities in the thinking
of Pereda and Galdós and discusses the two writers in the
context of the 'two Spains.'"

See also José María Cossío, "Pereda y Galdós en
Portugal," Revista de historia, 13 (1924), 72-74, which reproduces the partial text of a letter by Pereda to Aurelio
de la Revilla dated May 11, 1885. The published text discusses, with but little mention of Galdós, the trip that the
two authors made to Portugal in the spring of 1885.

Jose Montero, "Pereda y Galdós," Revista chilena,
año 3, IX, 26 (Oct., 1919), 519-25, is a brief account of
the friendship of the two authors.

C. F. Cordero Azorín edits sixty-eight "Cartas de Pereda a José María y Sinforoso Quintanilla," Boletín de la Biblioteca de Menéndez Pelayo, 44 (1968), 169-327. These contain numerous references to Galdós both in the text and the footnotes.

Of interest, too, is William H. Shoemaker, "Cartas de Pereda a Galdós y ocho borradores," Boletín de la Biblioteca Menéndez Pelayo, 42 (1966), 131-72 (the preface is reprinted in Shoemaker's Estudios sobre Galdos, pp. 277-81).

Carmen Bravo-Villasante, "Veintiocho cartas de Galdós a Pereda," Cuadernos hispanoamericanos, nos. 250-252 (1970-71), 9-51, finds that the publication of these letters can "aclarar muchas dudas acerca de la situación espiritual de Galdós en determinados años" (p. 9).

RAMON PEREZ DE AYALA. José Schraibman, " "Cartas inéditas de Pérez de Ayala a Galdos," Hispanófila, no. 17 (1963), 83-103, reproduces 26 letters from Pérez de Ayala to Galdós written between 1905 and 1917. A brief introduction discusses the personal relationship between the two men.

Pierre E. Sallenave, "Notas sobre una lectura política de Galdós," Cuadernos hispanoamericanos, nos. 250-252 (1970-71), 109-116, writes that "Ramón Pérez de Ayala es a la vez el escritor que probablemente debe más a Galdós y el admirador más incondicional del maestro. En este breve trabajo nos proponemos definir el alcance y los límites del parentesco que existe entre estos dos grandes escritores" (p. 109). He finds that, "Con excepción de unas cuantas loas hiperbólicas y redundancia de tipo general, todo lo que escribió sobre el insigne canario se relaciona con preocupaciones de orden estrictamente politico" (p. 109).

RICARDO RUIZ ORSATTI. Robert Ricard, "Cartas de Ricardo Ruiz Orsatti a Galdós acerca de Marruecos (1901-1910)," Anales galdosianos, 3 (1968), 99-117, reproduces the text of eighteen letters. Data from these letters were used by Galdós in writing Aita Tettauen and Carlos VI en la Rápita.

MANUEL TOLOSA LATOUR. Ruth Schmidt, Cartas entre dos amigos del teatro: Manuel Tolosa Latour y Benito Pérez Galdós (Ediciones del Excm. Cabildo Insular de Gran

Canaria, 1969), 181pp. (Lengua y literatura, no. 11), contains an introduction, pp. 11-26, which discusses "la estrecha
amistad" between these two men. Tolosa's first known letter is dated Jan. 28, 1882; his last is dated Aug. 8, 1916.
While the publication of the letters in chronological order occupies the most space in this volume, there are undated letters and postcards from Galdós to Tolosa Latour, undated
letter from Tolosa Latour to Galdós, and undated calling
cards from Tolosa Latour to Galdós. This is a valuable collection of letters which have been well annotated.

    Joseph Schraibman is the editor of "Cartas inéditas de
Manuel Tolosa Latour a D. Benito Pérez Galdós," Insula,
no. 179 (Oct., 1961), 3, and "Cartas de Tolosa Latour a
Galdós," El museo canario, nos. 77-84 (1961-62), 171-86.
The original of all of these letters is found in the Museo
canario. The Insula article reproduces 11 letters. The
Museo canario article reproduces 30 letters written between
1883 and 1895 on a variety of subjects.

    Anales galdosianos, 3 (1968), contains two articles
concerning Galdós and Manuel Tolosa Latour. They are:
Ruth Schmidt, "Manuel Tolosa Latour: prototype of Augusto
Miquis," 91-94, and Robert Ricard, "Tolosa Latour, el
P. Lerchundi y La loca de la casa," pp. 87-90. Schmidt
declares that "The external evidence from letters and the
internal one from novels confirm that Manuel Tolosa Latour
was the chief inspiration for Augusto Miquis. In addition to
their common profession of medicine which they both exercise
wisely and with kindness, Tolosa and Miquis share an interest
in the arts of music and the theater and perhaps more importantly, a flair for extravagant and overly-rhetorical language which is the vehicle for their sense of humor" (p. 93).
Ricard states that "No parece temario, pues, suponer que,
en La loca de la casa, el personaje de don Manuel Jordana,
fundador de un hospital-asilo y tocayo de Manuel Tolosa
Latour, nació en parte--solo en parte, desde luego--del
conocimiento que tuvo Galdós de la fundación del sanatario
de Chipiona" (p. 89).

    MIGUEL DE UNAMUNO. H. Chonon Berkowitz,
"Unamuno's relations with Galdós," Hispanic Review, 8
(1940), 321-38, and José Schraibman, "Galdós and Unamuno,"
Spanish Thought and Letters in the Twentieth Century (Nash-
ville: Vanderbilt University Press, 1966), pp. 451-82,
should be read in conjunction. Also see pp. 530-35, "Unamuno y Galdós," of Segundo Serrano Poncela, "Unamuno
y los clásicos," La Torre, 9 (1961), 505-35.

Berkowitz based his article on "casual and brief references to Galdós made by Unamuno in several essays; a few speeches reported in the Madrid and provincial press; and excerpts from his correspondence carried on with the novelist between 1898 and 1912" (p. 321). He notes that Unamuno's "critical norm with reference to this author" was "a curious mixture of stinted praise, outright condemnation and helpful suggestions" (p. 321). He finds that much of their differences can be attributed to Unamuno's "fierce independence of temperament and supreme egotism" (p. 321).

Schraibman notes that the Berkowitz article portrays Unamuno as "injusto, envidioso, y contradictorio en sus relaciones con Galdós," (p. 452). Pages 460-82 are an appendix which includes "la carta anteriormente citada de Unamuno a Berkowitz, las de Unamuno a Galdós, hasta ahora inéditas, y las que don Ramón Castañyra tuvo la gentil amabilidad de dejarme copiar de los originales que conservaba" (p. 460).

RAMON DE VALLE-INCLAN. Francisco Ynduráin, "De Valle-Inclán a Galdós (variaciones sobre técnica novelesca)," Papeles de Son Armadans, no. 101 (1968), 13-30, is a study of "las imágenes" used by the two authors. "Entiendo por 'imagen,' simplemente la representación de algo evocado por medio de la imaginación" (p. 13). The rather long footnote on pp. 18-19 discusses Valle-Inclán's animosity towards Galdós. He states on p. 28 that "No se me ocultan las dificultades que hay para aceptar mi tesis arriba apuntada de la posible sugestión galdosiana en Valle-Inclán, incluso enunciada con tanta cautela" and on p. 29 he writes that "Sería curioso apurar los antecedentes de la novela de Valle en la de Galdós...."

MARGARITA XIRGU. Edgardo Garrido Merino, "Margarita Xirgu y Pérez Galdós," El Mercurio (Santiago de Chile), May 11, 1969, p. 7, notes that the famous actress often came to read or recite to Galdós.

The following articles reproduce other Galdosian letters: Ada M. Coe, "An unpublished letter from Pérez Galdós," Hispanic Review, 14 (1946), 340-42; Joseph Schraibman, " "Cartas inéditas de Galdós," Symposium, 16 (1962), 115-21; Felipe Ximénez de Sandoval, "Seis cartas de Galdós," Arriba, Feb. 24, 1960, p. 17, and Ventura Doreste, "Una carta inédita de Galdós," Supplemento de la Revista Telde, 1 (1957), 4.

Coe publishes the text of a letter dated April 18, 1908 to Alice H. Bushee. In it Galdós states that little has changed in Spain in regard to intolerance and bigotismo since the publication of Doña Perfecta.

The Symposium article reproduces eight letters by Galdós to Teófilo Fernández, Agustín Millares, Gregorio Chil, Vicente Boada, Luis and Agustín Millares Cubas.

Arriba publishes six letters written in 1908 to his daughter María.

Two book-length collections have been published recently. They are Cartas a Galdos presentados por Soledad Ortega (Madrid: Revista de Occidente, n. d.) 454pp., and Cartas del Archivo de Galdós edited by Sebastian de la Nuez y José Schraibman (Madrid: Taurus, 1967), 382pp. The first contains letters to Galdós from Mesonero Romanos, José María de Pereda, Leopoldo Alas, Francisco Navarro y Ledesma, Emilio Mario, Antonio Vico, Juan Valera, Joaquín Costa, Marcelino Menéndez Pelayo as well as "Cartas de Galdós a Ramón Pérez de Ayala." The second volume is a collection of letters written to Galdós by Azorín, Baroja, Valle-Inclan, Ramiro de Maeztu, Unamuno, Pérez de Ayala, Armando Palacio Valdés, Blasco Ibañez, Ricardo León, Amada Nervo, Jacinto Octavio Picón, Ortega Munilla, Martínez Sierra, Gómez de Baquero, Gomez Carrillo, Francisco de Grandmontage, Joaquín Costa, Tolosa Latour and Salvador Rueda. These letters present interesting data concerning his life and works as seen by his contemporaries.

H. Chonon Berkowitz, "Gleanings from Galdós' Correspondence," Hispania, 16 (1933), 249-90, and Alfonso Armas, "Galdós y sus cartas," Papeles de Son Armadans, 40 (1966), 9-36, deal with Galdós as a correspondent and discuss the importance of his letters.

Berkowitz discusses the types of letters found in Galdós' Archivo epistolar. On p. 290 he concludes with these sentences: "It is in this sense that the letters which have been summed up, interpreted, quoted and reproduced above constitute an indispensable biographical document, because, just as Galdós revealed Spain to itself in a series of books, so Spain revealed Galdós to himself in an interesting collection of genuine and spontaneous letters. If, as the consecrated evaluation of Galdós has it, he was extremely impersonal in his works, the popular correspondence becomes

an even more valuable source of information about the personality of the great novelist, because it does sketch his
likeness as reliably and as authentically as he sketched the
image of the Spaniard in his monumental gallery of modern
Spain."

The Armas article has the following parts: La bandera de la realidad, El Episodio y las cartas, Dualidad epistolar.   The author notes that "Sus cartas, páginas vivas de la
más viva y minúscula realidad, nos ofrece el envés de
muchos de los libros galdosianos, de muchas páginas de su
vida, de muchos desvanes de su interior más inexcrutable.
Galdós, sin querer, está escribiendo, como a contrapelo
algo, de lo mucho que estaba llevando a las galeradas de
sus novelas" (pp. 22-23).

GENERAL BOOK-LENGTH CRITICAL STUDIES

Criticism is constantly changing, so that a volume
that might have been considered an outstanding one in 1920
will be considered of little value today. The three titles
most recommended are all publications of the 1960's. They
are: José F. Montesinos, Galdós (Madrid, Castalia, 1968-
1973), 3 vols. (Estudios sobre la novela española del siglo
xix, VII-IX); Joaquín Casalduero, Vida y obra de Galdós
(1843-1920), tercera edición revisada y aumentado (Madrid,
Gredos, 1973), 374pp. (Biblioteca románica hispánica.
Estudios y ensayos, 94), 294pp.; and Ricardo Gullón, Galdós,
novelista moderno (Madrid, Taurus, 1960), 299pp.; (Madrid,
Gredos, 1966), 326pp.; (tercera edición revisada y aumentada
(Madrid, Gredos, 1973; Biblioteca románica hispánica, Estudios y ensayos, 94), 374pp. The Gullón study originally appeared in a slightly different form as the "Estudio preliminar" to his edition of Miau (Madrid, Ediciones de la Universidad de Puerto Rico and Revista de Occidente, 1957), pp. 11-
302.

The individual interested in a more complete listing
of books on Pérez Galdós is referred to Theodore A. Sackett,
Pérez Galdós: An Annotated Bibliography, especially items
1-46, though references are made throughout this bibliography
to other book-length discussions of his works.

It is to be noticed that almost none of the above three
titles deals at any length with Galdós' theater or miscellaneous writings, i.e., poetry, journalism, short stories, etc.
They deal with him essentially as a novelist.

The student interested in an over-all view of Galdós'
work would probably be wise to begin with the set by Montesinos. These volumes are a series of notes for students
and readers of the novelist. On p. x, Montesinos writes:
"Habiendo tratado de guiar a mis alumnos por las vastas
construcciones novelescas de Galdós, esto ha venido a resul-
tar el libro que ahora ofrezco: una guía de los lectores
del novelista." In view of his audience, "haya prescindido
con frecuencia de muchos detalles eruditos y haya recurrido

a notas y citas con parquedad...." (p. x). Certain of the
remarks found in the Nota preliminar are of great interest.
He laments the fact that no good edition of Galdós' works
exists and notes numerous examples of poor proofreading
and textual changes in the various editions and printings of
Galdós' works.

This study of Galdós' fiction holds the reader's attention. Montesinos shows a knowledge of what other critics
have said about a given novel and does not hesitate to disagree with them, sometimes in quite bitter and sarcastic
tones.

The first volume contains a Nota preliminar, Nota
adicional, an author-subject index and nine chapters: Prehistoria y primeras tenativas, Escritos menores, Las
primeras novelas, Los Episodios nacionales, La segunda
serie, Doña Perfecta, Gloria, Marianela and La familia de
León Roch.

The second volume contains an introductory section,
"La 'segunda manera' and discussions of "Las novelas peda-
gógicas," i.e., La desheredada and El amigo Manso, Las
novelas de la locura crematística, i.e., El doctor Centeno,
Tormento, La de Bringas and Lo prohibido; the third chapter
is a seventy-page discussion of Fortunata y Jacinta. The
appendix reproduces the text of a letter from Castro y Serrano to Galdós dated July 22, 1884. This volume concludes
with an "Indice onomástico y de materias."

The third volume has the following sections: Nota
preliminar by the publishers; I. Los nuevos episidios;
Tercera serie: La carlistada y las dos regencias; II. La
cuarta serie: Epoca Isabelina; and III. La serie final:
Revolución y restauración. There is an "Indice onomástico
y de materias."

To my way of thinking it is regrettable that a work
of such value should appear without the usual scholarly apparatus. It is true that certain references are worked into
the text. The work seems to pride itself on its lack of
notes and bibliography. Were it not for Montesinos' un-
doubted mastery of the field of the 19th-century Spanish
novel, one would have the feeling that he expects the reader
to accept too much on faith. Yet the quality of the work is
so high that the student of Galdós would be wise first to discover what his opinions are on a given work and then go on
to other critics.

Andrés Amorós has reviewed these volumes in Revista de Occidente, no. 71 (Feb., 1969), 256-57, and no.
81 (Dec., 1969), 391-93.   He notes that "El libro de Montesinos pone en constante relación las novelas de Galdós con
los problemas más agudos de la sociedad española de la
segunda mitad del xix; literariamente, subraya sus cercanías
y diferencias respecto de la novela romántica, el costumbrismo y el folletín.   Insiste especialmente en la profundísi-
ma influencia de Cervantes y el mundo quijotesco sobre
Galdós" (p. 256).   He finds that the author "Se limita a
hacer una excelente crítica literaria con sólida base erudita
pero de vuelos muy amplios, que tiene su origen en una
lectura fervorosa, y su objectivo más humilde en servir de
guía al lector" (p. 256).   He finds that Montesinos' is one
of the most important works of Spanish literary criticism
published in the last ten years.   Amorós finds "su visión
crítica es irreprochablemente certera" (p. 391).   "No deja
de atender a los aspectos técnicos y lingüísticos.   Tiene muy
en cuenta las ideas, pero pone por encima de todas ellas
ese 'infinto replanteamiento del insoluble problema de la
realidad humana que, según él, caracteriza a todo gran novelista" (pp. 391-92).   He calls it "magistral" (p. 393).

Josette Blanquat, Bulletin hispanique, 71 (1969), 633-
46, is the most scholarly review yet to appear concerning
the first volume of this set.   She describes the set as "une
grande étude, la plus vaste, certainement, qu'un érudit ait
jamais entreprise sur Galdós, qui embrassera la vie et
l'oeuvre du romancier en suivant leur déroulement dans le
temps" (p. 633).   One rarely finds so completely laudatory
a review of this length.   What I would consider defects, she
praises.   For example, she writes that "J. F. Montesinos a
l'élégance de ne citer personne et de ne jamias parler sur
un ton doctoral ou dogmatique" (p. 645).   She praises him
because he "a délaissé la sociologie de la littérature ou,
plutôt, il ne s'y réfère qu'en passant" (p. 645).   She writes
that, "En étudiant l'oeuvre littéraire en elle-même sans
établir de distinction entre les Episodios et les autres romans, J. F. Montesinos a comblé une immense lacune.   Il
a prouvé que les Episodios peuvent être considérés comme
une oeuvre d'art et non, seulement, comme un témoignage
historique sur la société du XIXéme siècle" (p. 645).   This
evaluation by an outstanding contemporary French scholar on
Galdós contains many interesting and provocative insights into Galdós and his works and should also be required reading
for those interested in an evaluation of this set by Montesinos.

S. Beser, "J. F. Montesinos crítico de Pérez Galdós," Anales galdosianos, 4 (1969), 89-97, is an extremely favorable and flattering review of the first volume of this critical study and of Montesinos as a critic.

J. E. Varey, Modern Language Review, 65 (1971), 922-924, is, on the whole, favorably impressed by the first two volumes. He believes, however, that "it would have been interesting to have the reactions of Montesinos to recent critical articles, and to discuss what approaches he considers to be the most unrewarding" (p. 922). Varey states that "we are offered in these two volumes a panoramic view of Galdós' novelistic production which goes far beyond the modestly stated aim of introducing the novelist to university students who have no previous knowledge of the author and for whom he is a writer in a foreign language" (p. 924). He also calls it "a basic study" (p. 924).

Casalduero writes that "Este estudio se propone mostrar la unidad interior de la obra galdosiana y el desarrollo orgánico del mundo de Galdós, que va de la Historia a la Mitología, de la Materia al Espíritu, de España a la Humanidad. Desarrollo que no es una evolución, sino una formación, un depurado crecimiento, en el cual cada etapa creadora no anula la anterior: la incorpora a una realización necesario de su mundo" (p. 7). He writes on this same page that "En este trabajo no se encontrará ni un análisis de las obras de Galdós, ni un estudio de los temas que constituyen el mundo galdosiano. Obras y temas se han tenido en cuenta en tanto que nos mostraban el significado de la Obra y sólo en el grado que ayudaban a ello."

The eight chapters have the following titles: I. La vida de Galdós. II. Historia y abstracción. III. El naturalismo. IV. La materia y el espíritu. V. El espiritualismo. VI. La libertad. VII. Mitología. Extratemporalidad. VIII. La obra galdosiana en su total integración.

The seven appendices are: "La sombra," "Marianela y De l'intelligence de Taine," "Auguste Comte y Marianela." "El amigo Manso." "Significado y forma de Misericordia," "Sobre El abuelo" and "Galdós y la Edad Media." The notes are worked into the text; pp. 271-83 is a bibliography. There is an index of proper names.

The back of the book-cover of Gullón's states that "podemos recorrer con fruto la vida y la obra novelesca del

gran autor canario, seguir paso a paso sus tanteos, su ple-
nitud, su superación de todas las escuelas, comprender ese
realismo trascendente en que estriba su secreto. Gullon
alumbra valores y hace hincapié en la modernidad del arte
galdosiano, con sus seres y mundos extraordinarios (no todo
ha de ser pintura de la mesocracia madrileña), su hondura
de visión, su poder de caracterización psicológica."

The various sections of this volume have the following
titles: Vida, Situación de Galdós, Un mundo novelesco, Los
supuestos de la creación, Los ámbitos oscuros, Personajes
anormales, Lenguaje y técnica, La burocracis, mundo absurdo
and Bibliography.

Geoffrey Ribbans, "Ricardo Gullón and the novels of
Galdós," Anales galdosianos, 3 (1968), 163-68, is an extremely adverse criticism of this volume. He writes that "My
first criticism of his study, then, is that at no point does he
attempt to come to grips with any single novel (other than
Miau) in a systematic or coherent way. The very structure
he has adopted precludes any detailed analysis" (p. 163). On
p. 164, he notes that his "second main criticism of Gullón's
interpretation is that his vision is dominated by an outdated
concept of 'real characters.'" Pages 165-66 discuss his
treatment of Lo prohibido, while the rest of the review deals
with Miau. He cites differences in the three versions of
this study and feels that they "represent a successive advance in interpretation and analysis" (p. 164). On the whole,
Ribbans is of the opinion that "Until much more spade work
has been done on individual novels ... general studies will
almost inevitably be at best cautious and groping and at
worst woolly and misleading" (p. 163).

Of earlier studies, Leopoldo Alas (Clarín), Obras
completas, tomo primero: Galdós (Madrid: Renacimiento,
1912, 366pp.), should be of interest in view of Clarín's outstanding reputation as a critic. This volume reproduces
almost all of his reviews and critical studies on Galdós.
This volume contains material on Gloria, Marianela, La
familia de León Roch, La desheredada, Tormento, La prohibido, Miau, Angel Guerra, Tristana, the Torquemada
series, Nazarín, Halma; there is an article on the Episodios
Nacionales and individual ones on Mendizábal, Luchana, La
campaña del Maestrazgo, La estafeta romántica, Vergara,
Montes de Oca, Los Ayacuchos and Bodas reales. Of the
plays, he discusses Realidad, La loca de la casa and El
abuelo.

In 1934, there appeared Emilio Gutiérrez Gamero y
de Laiglesia, Galdós y su obra (Madrid: Blas, 3 vols.).
Both his fiction and his theatre are dealt with in this set,
the lengthiest discussion of Galdós' works that had yet appeared.

Robert Ricard, Aspects de Galdós (Paris: Presses
Universitaires de France, 1963), 104pp., and his Galdos
et ses romans (Paris: L'Institut de'Etudes Hispaniques,
1961), 89pp.; Alfredo Rodríguez, Aspectos de la novela
de Galdós (Almeria: Estudios literarios, 1967), 150pp.;
Angel del Río, Estudios galdosianos (New York: Las Américas Publishing Co., 1969), 139pp.; and William E. Shoemaker, Estudios sobre Galdós (Madrid: Castalia, 1970),
295pp., are important collections of previously published essays devoted to the study of Galdós. Important portions of
these volumes appear under the novels or topics with which
they deal.

The earliest important critical study on Pérez Galdós
in English is Leslie Bannister Walton, Pérez Galdós and the
Spanish novel of the nineteenth century (New York, E.P.
Dutton; London and Toronto, J.M. Dent, 1927), xi, 250pp.
A long paragraph from p. viii shows how the author describes
his purpose: "The present work is an endeavour to estimate
the significance of Benito Pérez Galdós in the history of
modern Spanish fiction and to show that he may justly be regarded as the creator of the modern novel in Spain. After a
brief survey of the development of Spanish fiction prior to
the appearance of Galdós' first novel, La fontana de oro, we
have attempted, in an analysis of his principal books, to
trace the evolution of his genius through the various stages
of its development. Then, in a final chapter, we have called
attention to those elements in his work which distinguish it
from that of his predecessors; endeavouring also to estimate
the influence which he has exercised upon those who succeeded him. We cannot claim to have done more than clear
the ground for those who may wish to undertake more detailed studies, and although exigencies of space account for
some notable lacunae, there are several aspects of Galdós'
genius which have been almost ignored for the reason that,
if they are to be dealt with adequately, they demand treatment apart. This applies especially to his work in the
drama, and to the Episodios nacionales, for the latter really
constitute a separate genre. We have here confined our attention to those works which entitle Galdós to a place among
European novelists of importance, and this study makes no
claim to be exhaustive."

Galdós: papers read at the Modern Foreign Language
Department Symposium: Nineteenth Century Spanish Literature ... Mary Washington College of the University of Virginia, Fredericksburg, Virginia, April 21-22, 1967, 122pp.,
contains the text of eight papers, each of which is discussed
in this bibliography.

GENERAL SHORT STUDIES

There are numerous short studies on Galdos. Many
of these are too brief to be of much use, and many are rep-
etitious and bring nothing new to bear on the subject either
of his life or his works.

This section discusses three early French studies on
him in an attempt to show Galdós' reputation in France at
that given time, and presents data on a handful of Spanish
studies.

Among the early French studies on the works of Benito Pérez Galdós are: Leo M. Quesnel, "Littérature
espagnole contemporaine: M. Benito Pérez Galdós," Revue
politique et littéraire, 9 (May 9, 1885), 598-602; Count M.
Toulouse-Lautrec, "Un romancier espagnol contemporain:
Pérez Galdós," Le Correspondant, 132 (Aug. 10, 1883), 518-
43; and A. de Tréverret, "La littérature espagnole contempo-
raire: le roman et le réalisme, III.   M. Pérez Galdós,"
Le Correspondant, 139 (April, 1885), 150-67.

The article by A. de Tréverret is a French discussion of La desheredada, Marianela, and El amigo Manso.
He has little but praise for Galdós' works and feels that his
best works lie ahead.

Count Toulouse-Lautrec's long article deals almost
entirely with Marianela.   However, before his discussion of
this novel, he makes a few comments on Spain, Spanish literature, and Galdós in particular, and two pages are devoted to Gerona.   He translates several passages from the
novels, discusses the plot and the characters and speaks of
"le charme du récit" (p. 542).   He also notes that "Le
payage sobre, mais bien caractérisé, l'observation sagace
et minutieuse des caractères, le dialogue vivement mené ...
Ces saillies imprévues, jaillisant tout d'un coup au milieu
de scènes mélancoliques, reposent et refraichissent l'espirt,
détendent un moment l'émotion" (p. 543).   He states that
"Il a fait pour l'histoire contemporaine de son pays ce
qu'Alexandre Dumas a tenté chez nous avec tant de succès

pour plusieurs époques de nos annales" (p. 543). He praises
the novel with these words: "Le drame d'une simplicité extrême, se joue entre quatre personnages sont si soigneuse-
ment étudiés, les caractères si fouillés, l'analyse si subtile,
que le défaut d'évenements ne nuit pas à l'intérêt" (p. 523).

Quesnel's article has three parts: an introduction,
a discussion of Tormento and of La de Bringas. He finds
Galdós to be an original author, different from many Spanish
authors of his period who copy French models or imitate
Charles Dickens. He is called Spain's "vrai romancier"
(pp. 598-99) and "c'est humoriste par excellence" (p. 599).

Andrenio, "La generación de 1898. El momento del
renacimiento de la novela. Pérez Galdós," El renacimiento
de la novela española en el siglo XIX (Madrid: Mundo Lati-
no, 1924), 51-67, is a brief study by an author who considers
Galdós "el fundador de la nueva novela y su primera figura"
(p. 67).

Joaquín Casalduero, "Conjunción y divergencia de
vida y arte en Galdós," Hispania, 53 (1970), 828-835, is annotated by Chamberlin, Hispania, 53 (1970), 822-823, as
follows: "Casalduero ... gives us a panoramic view of
Galdós' works and demonstrates how the relationship between
the character-forming events in the author's own life and the
personalities he created for many of his personages. Specif-
ically, Professor Casalduero examines the influence of
Galdós' mother on the author's life, the reasons he chose
not to marry, and the fictional reflection of these factors in
the variety of ways his characters react to the mother and/
or mother-wife figure throughout the more important novels."

The speeches of the first Galdós congress will be
published in the Actas del primer congreso galdosiano.
Vernon Chamberlin has graciously sent me the text of his
"El interés sovético por los Episodios y novelas de Galdós
(1935-1940)" which will appear in these Actas. He notes
that in the Soviet Union "... los años 1935 a 1940 sobresalen
como una de las épocas de mayor entusiasmo por las obras
de Galdós. He comments on Russian translations of the
following novels by Galdós: Doña Perfecta (1935), La fontana de oro (1937), Zaragoza (1938), Cádiz (1938) and Juan
Martín, el empecinado (1940). Chamberlin studies "el
enfoque de tales introducciones y reseñas," i.e., to those
translations. His last two sentences follow: "Aunque los
ensayos en ruso que hemos comentado están a veces cargados

de propaganda oficial y con la jerga del partido, (características especialmente típicas de esa era stalinista), Galdós
brilla, aun en ellos, como un historiador efectivo, como un
luchador inspirado en la causa de la justicia social y como
un maestro que enseña grandes lecciones. Además se le
estima como humanista sincero y como creador de novelas
de gran interés para el lector de cualquier ideología."

Joaquín de Entrambasaguas provides an interesting
biographical-critical sketch as a preface to Misericordia
that appears in Las mejores novelas contemporáneas, tomo
1 (1895-99), (Barcelona: Editorial Planeta, 1962), pp. 757-
866, with a bibliography, pp. 867-77.

Alberto Ghiraldo, "Don Benito Pérez Galdós," Atenea,
72 (1943), 165-77 has the following outline: "Diálogo sugestivo con el maestro. Porqué fuí yo su albacea literario. Su
'obra inédita.' Diez años de labor para América. Galdós
y el teatro argentino. Galdós, los hermanos Alvarez Quintero y Marianela. Galdós periodista y reportero. Su labor
primigenia. El 'estilo' de Galdós. Otra lección del maestro."

Angel Lázaro, "España en su novelística: Galdós,"
Revista cubana, 19 (1945), 42-65, reprinted in Semblanzas
y ensayos (San Juan, 1963), pp. 14-44, is a general study
concerning Galdós' style, language, and subject matter.
Among the sections are: España en su novelistica, Galdós
y su concepto de la patria, El pícaro y el héroe, Estatismo
y picarismo, Rojo y negro, El guerrillero, El español y su
clima, Lección de tolerancia and Galdós y Pereda.

Vicente Marrero, Historia de una amistad (Madrid,
Editorial Magisterio Español, 1971), contains an interesting
section entitled "1871. Galdós en Santander," pp. 41-61.
This section has the following parts: Su encuentro con
Pereda, Galdós, el hombre, Galdós en la calle and Galdós
literario. This volume also contains the following parts
that deal with Galdós: "Galdós y el problema de la moderna
España," pp. 122-125; "Galdós en San Quintín," pp. 187-194
"Los discursos en la Real Academia (1897)," pp. 217-232;
and "Galdós (1920)," pp. 286-297.

Ramón Pérez de Ayala, Amistades y recuerdos (Barcelona, Aedos, 1961), contains the following four articles reprinted from newspapers: "La cabeza de Galdós," pp. 35-
40; "Valera y Galdós. La incógnita y realidad," pp. 40-46;
"El censo galdosiano. Biología, biografía, biometría,

psicología y cura de almas," pp. 46-50; and "Galdós o la
fecundidad creadora," pp. 50-54. His Divagaciones literarias
(Madrid: Biblioteca Nueva, 1958), contains "Letanía galdosiana," pp. 125-42, and "Auto de fe con Galdós," pp. 143-
55.

Domingo Pérez Minik, "Libre plática con Galdós,"
Novelistas españoles de los siglos XIX y XX (Madrid:
Guadarrama, 1957), pp. 67-106, is of value for its discussion of Galdós' style and for his comments on a revival
of interest in him after the Spanish Civil War. He writes:
"Se le volvió a leer como si se tratase de un novelista contemporáneo. En realidad, él se nos apareció sobre un plano
capaz de aglutinar una nación muy dolorida" (p. 103).

Milton Rossel, "Valoración de Galdós," Atenea, 72
(1943), 121-35, is more biographical than an attempt at a
critical evaluation of his works. Rossel finds that critics
have gone from one extreme to the other; that some of
Galdós' works have become dated and that the reader of today
is no longer interested in some of the problems that his
novels discuss. Yet, he finds that "tales reparos no amino-
ran en nada el valor intrínesco de sus obras, porque están
estremecidas de humanidad y llenas de ese espíritu del
pueblo que en medio de sus derrotas no pierde la fe un
destino superior" (p. 134).

Emile Sosa López, "Itinerario de Galdós," Razón
y fábula, no. 13 (mayo-junio de 1969), 49-59, besides an
introduction, has the following sections: 1. El fondo histórico; 2. Verdad de lo novelesco; 3. La sociedad contemporánea; 4. La dialéctica de lo real; 5. Enfrentamiento de una
crisis; 6. La búsqueda de un nuevo principio; 7. Una voluntad
de catarsis. This article deals briefly with about a dozen
novels. In his concluding paragraph the author finds that
Galdós' "arte novelístico fue un arte puro, incontaminado,
trasparente, equilibrado y de notable fidelidad con la realidad
inmediata ... Sólo que el arte de Galdós se distingue, por
sí mismo, como un arte de incomparable perfección en el
manejo de las situaciones, en la interiorización de los personajes, y si no se extralimitó en presunciones metafísicas,
como muchos autores de su tiempo, fue porque con sobriedad
se mantuvo dentro de la pureza del género, sin que llegaría
a ser en sus manos ensayo ni tratado del alma" (p. 59).

Guillermo de Torre, "Redescubrimiento de Galdós,"
Insula, no. 136 (1958), 1-2, is a comment on the renewed

interest in Galdós, with special emphasis on Gullón's volume on Galdós.

Jaime Torres Bodet, Tres inventores de realidad: Stendhal, Dostoyevski, Pérez Galdós ([Madrid]: Ediciones de la Revista de Occidente, 1969), pp. 169-247 (Cimas de América; earlier edition, México: Universitaria, 1955, pp. 203-87), an outstanding study by a Mexican critic, has the following sections: ¿Por qué Galdós? Galdós y la historia, Galdós y la realidad and Cuatro ejemplos. The second section should be of interest to students of the Episodios Nacionales, while the last section deals with Doña Perfecta, El amigo Manso, Fortunata y Jacinta and Angel Guerra.

Manuel Tuñon de Lara, "La España de Pérez Galdos," La palabra y el hombre, no. 21 (enero-marzo de 1961), 91-103, is of interest for its references to "el caciquismo y el clericalismo" in the works of Galdós. The author believes that, "En efecto, decir la España de Galdós, equivale a decir la España del siglo XIX. Y en Galdós no hay mera coincidencia cronológica con el vivir español, sino que su obra entera es fiel trasunto de la España decimonónica" (p. 91).

Francesco Vian, "La Spagna di Galdós," Aevum, 24 (1950), 515-27, and 25 (1951), 1-19, begins by quoting Altamira's lament over the lack of any "obra de conjunto sobre la España del siglo xix" and concludes with this paragraph: "Nessun filosofo di professione, nessun ideologo, nessum poeta o letterato puro poteva comprendere e rendere in tutta la sua integrità la vita stessa dell'Ottocento spagnolo, quel gran fiotto di sangue che sgorgava da un grande corpo ferito. Chi osó proporsi l'arduo e umanissimo assunto, tessendo con tutti gli elementi dell'essere ispanico un gigantesco 'corpus' narrativo di ventimila pagine, fu un romanziere, o piuttosto il romanziere di quella nazione e di quell'età: Benito Pérez Galdós."

OBRAS COMPLETAS

The most recent attempt at the publication of Galdós' complete works is Obras completas de Don Benito Pérez Galdós. Introducción, biografía, bibliografía, notas y censo de personajes galdosianos, por Federico Carlos Sáinz de Robles (Madrid: Aguilar, 1941-42), 6 vols. (other so-called ediciones would appear to be reprints). It must be noted that this set does not provide the user with a truly complete set of his works; that it is not a critical edition, that the editor nowhere discusses his choice of text. The editor, on the whole, takes a most uncritical attitude towards both the author and his works.

The first volume contains an introduction, "Don Benito Pérez Galdós: su vida. Su obra. Su época," pp. 9-191. The bibliography contains "Obras de Pérez Galdós," pp. 195-98, which is a listing, not always accurate, of his published books. The editor is no bibliographer. The dates he gives are those when Galdós wrote rather than published the book. The compiler states that except in one or two instances the year in which he wrote a given book coincides with the date of publication. The dates given for theatrical pieces are those of the years in which they were staged. Thus, the user is provided with no data concerning place and publisher. No data appear concerning reprints or translations and no data are given concerning Galdós' works in newspapers and periodicals. Pages 198-202 consist of a listing of 120 items of "Obras acerca de Pérez Galdós." This too could have been many times more extensive and the data presented more complete. The most scholarly, unbiased, and for this reason all the more damaging and penetrating review of this set is by William Shoemaker, Hispanic Review, 12 (1944), 258-64; reprinted in Estudios sobre Galdós, pp. 17-25.

Ricardo A. Latcham's review of Doña Perfecta in La Nación, Jan. 10, 1943, p. 5, is of interest for its attack on this set. He attacks the set's prologue in these words: "Merecería comentario aparte el estudio del escritor falangista, desconocido del público americano e inspirado en el más absurdo espíritu." He feels that this deluxe edition makes Galdós' works "inaccesible al lector medio" and he has nothing but praise for the Editorial Losada which is reprinting Galdós' works in a form accessible to all.

Ricard, Galdós et ses romans, p. 77, writes: "mais une bonne édition des romans de Galdós nous fait cruellement défaut."

Yet, this set is very widely used and referred to because nothing better exists.

GENERAL SOURCES

This section will discuss general studies on the influence of foreign and Spanish authors on Galdós. Source studies on individual works will be presented when these are discussed.

Josette Blanquat, "Los annotations marginales des livres de Galdós," Etudes ibériques et latino-américaines (IVème Congrès des hispanistes français [Poitiers, 18-20 mars 1967]) (Paris, Presses universitaires de France, 1968) (Publications de la Faculté des lettres et sciences humaines de Poitiers), pp. 23-43, has the following parts: Introduction, Galdós et Tolède, Galdós et le "De Oratore," Minuta de un testamento and Galdós et Erasme, Le thème de la richesse. "Galdós et Tolède" discusses Angel Guerra and Sixto Ramón Parro's Toledo en la mano and Amador de los Ríos' Toledo pintoresca. "Galdós et le 'De oratore'" by Cicero suggests that Galdós read this volume around 1880-1881. The next small essay deals with Minuta de un testamento by Gumersindo de Azcárate with special mention of Doña Perfecta and La familia de León Roch. The last section of this article deals with The praise of folly by Erasmus and its relation to Galdós' works. Her concluding paragraph is: "Nous ne ferons pas, évidemment, de Galdós un humaniste, bien que son oeuvre nous ramène au grand courant qui se trouve à l'origine de la libre pensée. Mais il a senti la nécessité de revenir aux sources vives, aux grands livres que ont marqué des étapes dans le développement de l'esprit humain. Ils lui ont conseillé de vivre dans le présent, d'observer le réel et la Nature et ils ont éveillé en lui les grands rêves créatures sans lesquels il n'est pas d'oeuvre d'art authentique" (p. 43).

The Bible

Alfred R. Saez, "La influencia de la Biblia en las novelas de Galdós" (Ph.D. dissertation, Northwestern University, 1966, 255 leaves; Dissertation Abstracts, 27A

[1967] 2160), is the fullest treatment of Biblical influence
on the Novelas contemporáneas. Besides a preface, introduction, conclusion and bibliography, its five chapters deal with
the Bible in Galdós, Biblical quotations and characters in the
novels of Galdós, Charity in his works, and Biblical allusions
found in his novels. The dissertation shows that Galdós "sólo se sirvió de Scío para las citas latinas y para la traduc-
ción inmediata del latín. Las citas en español, incluso
aquellas previamente marcadas en Scío, las tomo el autor de
Reina-Valera, la versión protestante de la Biblia" (p. 2160A).
These remarks must modify those that Pattison made in regard to use of Scío in the composition of Gloria.

English Influence

        Antonio Mejía, "Galdós e Inglaterra," Insula, no. 82
(Oct. 15, 1952), 8; Esteban Salazar Chapala, "Galdós e
Inglaterra," Cuadernos (Paris), no. 15 (Nov.-Dec. 1955),
97-100; Effie L. Erickson, "The influence of Charles Dickens
on the novels of Benito Pérez Galdós," Hispania, 19 (1936),
421-30; Antonio Regalada García, "Galdós y Walter Scott,"
in Benito Pérez Galdós y la novela histórica española:
1868-1912, pp. 133-57; Walter T. Pattison, "How well did
Galdós know English?" Symposium, 24 (1970), 148-57;
Doireann MacDermott, "Inglaterra y los ingleses en la obra
de Pérez Galdós," Filología moderna, nos. 21-22 (1965),
43-58; and Hope K. Goodale, "Allusions to Shakespeare in
Galdós," Hispanic Review, 39 (1971), 249-60, would appear
to be the most important sources for the study of the influence of England and English literature on Galdós.

        Mejía studies the references to England and English
authors in Galdós' works and seeks to show that "Inglaterra
como nación estuvo y está muy presente en la producción
galdosiana."

        Salazar Chapala's articles attempt to show Galdós'
knowledge of England and its literature. He points out reflec-
tions of these in his works. Unfortunately, there are several either debatable or false statements which mar this discussion. Thus, speaking of translations of Galdós works into English, he writes: "Al francés, que yo sepa, sólo se
tradujo una novela en vida del autor; al inglés, al menos en
Inglaterra, creo que nada" (p. 99). This statement is most
inaccurate in regard to English translations.

Erickson analyzes what previous writers such as
Menéndez y Pelayo, Alas, Walton and Madariaga have written
concerning Galdós' indebtedness to Dickens. She notes Galdós'
own views on this subject and then shows certain Dickensian
influences on several of Galdós' novels. She feels that "In
social doctrines, these two writers may be said to agree almost entirely, although many of Galdós' ideas rose out of experience rather than through his contact with Dickens" (p.
430).

Regalada García is the first critic to study the Scott-
Pérez Galdós relationship. According to this author, direct
influence is difficult to prove. Scott was influenced by both
Cervantes and Balzac, who influenced Galdós in a much more
direct way.

Pattison's article is a thoroughly documented study
that disproves the idea that Galdós learned "English as a
child" (p. 155). Pattison shows that Galdós read Dickens
in French translation rather than the English original. "After
several trips to England he still did not speak the language
fluently; in fact, he had only those phrases which permitted
him to satisfy the prime necessities of a traveller" (p. 155).

MacDermott's study is a discussion less of the influence of English literature on Galdós' works than of how
Galdós presents England and the English in such works as
Cádiz, La batalla de los Arapiles, Gloria, Lo prohibido,
Fortunata y Jacinta and Halma. Pages 53-57, "Galdós en
Inglaterra," note that Galdós, when he wrote of his visits
to England, "nos explica ciudades y monumentos con la
frialdad de un Baedeker" (p. 53). Pages 57-58 deal briefly
with Galdós and Dickens. The article's last sentence states
that "En Galdós, las figuras inglesas y las alusiones a
Inglaterra nos ponen en contacto más o menos directo con
su vida de colegial, con la participación inglesa en la guerra
de la Independencia; son testimonío de unos viajes a aquel
país y de una admiración fervorosa hacia su más importante
novelista; pero se mantienen siempre como meras y lejanas
referencias, sin alcanzar nunca decisivo relieve en el vastí-
simo friso humano puesto en movimiento por la maravillosa
imaginación de Galdós" (p. 58).

Goodale's article is the most extensive study yet produced on Galdós and Shakespeare.

French Influence

Francisco C. Lacosta "Galdós y Balzac,"[4] Cuadernos hispanoamericanos, nos. 224-25 (ago.-sept. 1968), 345-74, has an introduction and then discusses the two authors under the following headings: Escenario, Personajes, Significado, Estilo, Clasificación. He concludes with the remark "Más que influencia se nota la protesta propia de cada autor por la irregularidad del clima en la vida de sus tiempos...." (p. 374).

Mary B. MacDonald, "The influence of Emile Zola in the novels of Benito Pérez Galdós produced during the years 1881-1885" (Ph.D. dissertation, University of Minnesota, 1959, 341 leaves; Dissertation Abstracts, 20 [1960], 1194), states that "The plan followed in this study was first, to sketch in the background, proving that Galdós had a knowledge of Zola by 1881, and second, to show that Galdós was influenced by Zola in these novels, by specific comparisons on various points: general techniques or general prose-fiction devices; specific techniques or naturalistic-fiction devices; similar descriptions, occasionally showing verbal borrowings or echoings, character portrayals, plot situations" (p. 2294).

Robert Ricard, "Galdós devant Flaubert et Alphonse Daudet," Galdós et ses romans, pp. 37-48 (reprinted from Les lettres romanes, 13 [1959], 3-18, and Bulletin de l'Institut francais en Espagne, no. 102 [1958], 24-33; translated by Douglass Rogers as "Galdós ante Flaubert y Alphonse Daudet," Benito Pérez Galdós (1973), pp. 195-08), notes that Flaubert and Daudet are rarely considered to have influenced Galdós. Ricard believes "que cette omission fréquente [ne] soit entièrement justifiée. C'est ainsi qu'il m'a été donné de constater qu'un épisode de La familia de León Roch évoque fortement certain passage de L'éducation sentimentale et que les dernières pages de Miau font semblablement penser à un chapitre du Nabab. Ce sont ces rapports que je voudrais mettre ici en lumière" (p. 37).

German Influence

George F. Kussky, "Galdós' acquaintance with German literature as revealed in his Novelas españolas con-

temporáneas," Modern Language Forum, 29 (1944), 41-55,
and Denah Lida, "Sobre el 'krausismo' de Galdós," Anales
galdosianos, 2 (1967), 1-27, are the only articles of any con-
sequence that deal with German influences of his works.

Kussky concludes that "first, Galdós was better acquainted with German literature than is usually assumed;
second, that he did not study the older periods of German
literature, but began his study of it with the works of the
middle of the eighteenth century; finally, that Goethe was his
favorite author and that his Faust interested him especially"
(p. 55).

José F. Montesinos, Galdós (1968), p. 49 refers to
Kussky's study with the words "deplorable trabajo." He
feels that critics have ignored the influence of Hoffmann on
Galdós.

Lida's article is the fullest recent discussion devoted
exclusively to the study of Krause and Galdós. It discusses
La familia de León Roch, La desheredada, El doctor Centeno,
El amigo Manso. The footnotes, pp. 21-27, present an
elaborate bibliographical apparatus which should be of great
value to the individual who wishes to pursue this matter in
more detail.

Greek Influence

Gustavo Correa, "Galdós y el platonismo," Anales
galdosianos, 7 (1972) 3-17, finds that "Platón influyó desde
muy temprano en la obra novelística de Galdós. Las influencias del filósofo griego son en algunas ocasiones de
carácter específico. En general, puede hablarse más propiamente de una influencia difusa, aunque no por ello menos
efectiva y persistente. Ante todo, la lectura de los diálogos
de Platón debió prestar al novelista ciertas direcciones fundamentales que iban a ser decisivas en su concepción del hombre y de la sociedad...." (pp. 12-13).

Norwegian Influence

The most important commentary on Galdós and Ibsen is
found in Halfdan Gregorsen, Ibsen and Spain: A Study in
Comparative Drama (Cambridge: Harvard University Press,
1936 [Harvard Studies in Romance Languages 10]), pp. 130-
39 and scattered references. Gregorsen discusses the pros

and cons of the Ibsenian influence; the question of direct indebtedness is not settled, and perhaps can never be. He
finds that the "spiritual outlook" of the two men is related.
He writes that Galdós, when he replied to the review by F.
Fernández Villegas of Los condenados (La época, Jan. 10,
1895), stated that "ningún autor ha influído en mi menos
que Ibsen...." (p. 133).

Russian Influences

        The most scholarly treatment of Tolstoy's influence on
Galdós is Vera Colin, "The influence of Tolstoy on Galdós"
(M.A. thesis, University of London, 1962, 215, xliii leaves).
This thesis has an abstract, introduction and the following
chapters: Tolstoy in France and Spain; Tolstoy and Galdós;
The first probability of influence: Angel Guerra, Zumalacárregui, Narváez, Aita Tettauen, Torquemada, Nazarín, and
Halma; The last group of novels: Misericordia, El abuelo,
La razón de la sinrazón; Conclusion. There are 43 leaves
of appendices which provide lists of Tolstoy's works in French,
English and Spanish which would have been available to Galdós
during his lifetime; reproductions of Spanish articles which
dealt with Tolstoy and a selected bibliography of the two authors. She explores carefully all that has been written in the
past on the matter of Tolstoy's influence on Galdós. On p. 3
she writes: "The purpose of this thesis therefore is to widen
and deepen what up to now has been said in a general way by
these writers and to prove that Tolstoy's religious doctrine
had been known to Galdós and had influenced him in a direct
way." So far only one article has appeared that has been
based on her thesis. Her "A note on Tolstoy and Galdós,"
Anales galdosianos, 2 (1967), 155-68, has the following sections. Tolstoy in Spain, the foundation of Tolstoy's teaching,
Tolstoy's influence on Galdós, Nazarín and Halma, and El
abuelo. Mrs. Colin is a native of Russia who has lived most
of her life in England. Parker calls her thesis "the fullest
treatment of this subject" (Anales galdosianos, 2 [1967], 100).
Her facts and conclusions have not been sufficiently noticed,
so that the question of Tolstoy's influence on Galdós is still
a debated one.

        Apparently the first serious attempt to study Tolstoy's
influence on Galdós is George Portnoff, La literatura rusa
en España (New York: Instituto de las Españas, 1932).
Chapter IV, Influencia de Tolstoy en Galdós, and Chapter V,
Influencia religiosa de Tolstoy en Nazarín y Halma, pp. 123-
205, are of special interest.

José Bergamín, "Tolstoy y Galdós," in La corteza de
letra (Buenos Aires: Losada, 1957), pp. 93-102, is a study
by a well-known author rather than by a scholar in the field.
Bergamín writes, it would seem, from intuition rather than
exact facts. The first part of this essay presents some interesting views comparing the religious philosophy of the two
writers. Bergamín states: "la religiosidad que en ellos se
manifesta tiene muy diverso, y aun contrario sentido, aunque
ambos coincidan en una idéntica afirmación de la vida, de la
verdad, de lo que ahora digo humanismo íntegro, pleno: de
la razón y pasión de ser la vida humana, individual y social"
(p. 97). He compares Galdós' first series of Episodios
Nacionales to Tolstoy's War and Peace and Anna Karenina.

William Donald Mills, "La influencia de Tolstoi en tres
novelas de Galdós: Nazarín-Halma y Misericordia," Revista
de la Universidad de Madrid, 13 (1964), 596-97, shows the
influence on these three novels of Tolstoy's Mi religión. According to Mills, "se nota un gran cambio de estilo en
Galdós al escribir Nazarín-Halma, porque sus esfuerzos
propagandistas le llevaron a adoptar una tecnovelística comparable con la utilizada en sus primeras novelas de tesis"
(p. 597). He finds that "al final de Halma ya ha rechazado
en parte la doctrina cristiana propuesta en Mi religión, para
acercarse mas a lo humano" (p. 597). In regard to Misericordia, Mills states that "Las ideas de Mi religión ahora
están tan fundidas con la forma que sin un análisis detallado
es casi imposible reconocerlas. Al mismo tiempo, Galdós
supera aún más su fuente rusa, haciendo hincapié en la
caridad y misericordia humanas y rechazando todo obstáculo
que se oponga a esta finalidad" (p. 597).

A. Zviguilsky, "Tourguéniev et Galdós," Revue de
littérature comparée, 41 (1967), 117-20, notes the disap-
pearance of Turgenev's two letters to Galdós. The article
notes that at the beginning of his career "Galdós se consi-
derait, ... come le disciple de Tourguéniev" (p. 119). As
for influence, the author feels that "On peut dire en tout cas
que les deux écrivains se ressemblent par leur constant
souci de vérité et de justice, par la clarté et la netteté de
leur style" (p. 119).

Spanish Influence

The discussion of the influence of Spanish literature on
Galdós is presented chronologically.

Joaquín Casalduero, "Galdós y la Edad Media," Asomante, 9, 2 (1953), 13-27, states that "Las ideas del novelista sobre la Edad Media son las de España en la segunda
mitad del siglo XIX; mejor dicho, son las de parte de España. Su contacto con las obras y las figuras medievales,
como era de suponer, revelan no la Edad Media, sino lo que
naturalmente encontraba Galdós: la nota humana individual
opuesta a la tiranía (Mío Cid), la explicación psicológica de la
alucinación colectiva (Santiago de Clavijo), una característica
muy antigua de la vida social española (Arcipreste de Hita),
la imaginación del tormento y del dolor excepcionales (Dante)"
(p. 27). He also notes Galdós' knowledge of La Celestina as
seen through his works.

Gustavo Correa, "Tradición mística y cervantismo en
las novelas de Galdós," Hispania, 53 (1970), 842-851, develops the theme that "...la vida y obra de Santa Teresa
y de San Juan de la Cruz debieron de proporcionarle aspectos
importantes de la conformación espiritual de ciertos personajes y en la determinación de numerosos detalles y situaciones
que se encuentran en estas novelas" (p. 843). Correa notes
that "...creemos que fundamentalmente Galdós llega a esta
etapa de espiritualización por una exigencia interna de su
mundo novelístico que lo lleva a utilizar en este momento de
su evolución fuentes diversas, entre las cuales se encuentran
la Biblia, Tolstoy, y, de manera especial, una veta de misticismo hispánico que no ha sido lo suficientemente puntalizada
por la crítica" (p. 842). He also states that "Esta ver de
raigambre que encontramos en este ciclode la novela galdosiana se funde, por otra parte, con la fundamental perspective
cervantina, característica de la obra total de Galdós y que
en estas novelas adquiere especial intensidad" (p. 848).

Gustavo Correa, "Pérez Galdós y la tradición calde-
roniana," Cuadernos hispanoamericanos, nos. 250-252 (1970-
1971), 221-241, shows that "Galdós ha recorrido así una
gama de matices diversos del mundo calderoniano que se revelan como maneras de ser arcáicas de la cultura hispánica
y que, en calidad de tales, se encuentran sometidos a un
sostenido examen a lo largo de su obra novelística. Los
fundamentos de la nueva sociedad requieren transformaciones
a fondo que den una nueva dirección y sentido a la España
del futuro" (p. 241).

Of all Spanish authors, Galdós was the most influenced
by Miguel de Cervantes. The period since 1933 has seen the
appearance of numerous articles and three dissertations
written in American universities concerning this influence.

The scholarly studies on this subject begin with J. Warshaw,
"Galdós' Indebtedness to Cervantes," Hispania, 16 (1933), 127-
42. Warshaw seems to be correct in saying that until his
study "most of the literary critics and historians are silent
on this important element," i. e., the Cervantes influence, "in
Galdos' writings." Shoemaker calls this study "admirable"
yet goes on to declare that Warshaw fails "to probe deeply
and disclose the deep neo-Cervantian character of Galdós
thought, especially, for example, in the novels from Fortunata y Jacinta to Misericordia" (Crónica de la quincena,
p. 52).

M. Latorre, "Cervantes y Galdós," Atenea, 88 (Oct.,
1947), 11-40, has the following divisions: Novelistas y
novelas representativas, Dos hombres, dos épocas, Similitudes y contrastes, El paisaje en Cervantes y en Galdós,
Humorismo, personajes afines, técnica narrativa.

César Rodríguez Ch., "La huella del Quijote en las
novelas de Galdos," La palabra y el hombre, no. 38 (1966),
223-63, is of interest despite the author's not citing most
of the previous studies on this subject. "Estudio aquí--lo
intento--dos aspectos en los cuales la huella del Quijote es
evidente en la obra de Galdós: el estructural y el lingüístico" (p. 223). He studies Cervantes' influence as found in
eighteen novels.

Three doctoral dissertations exist on this subject.
They are: J.C. Herman, "Don Quijote and the novels of
Pérez Galdós" (University of Kansas, 1950, 203 leaves);
A.H. Obaid, "El Quijote en los Episodios Nacionales"
(University of Minnesota, 1953, 330 leaves); and Betty Jean
Zeidner, "Cervantine aspects of the novelistic art of Benito
Pérez Galdós" (University of California, 1957, 230 leaves).

Herman has published a volume with the same title as
his dissertation (Ada: Oklahoma State College, 1955, 68pp.)
as well as "Galdós' expressed appreciation for Don Quijote,"
Modern Language Journal, 36 (1952), 31-34, and "Quotations
and locutions from Don Quijote in Galdós novels," Hispania,
36 (1953), 177-81.

Obaid states in Dissertation Abstracts, 13 (1953), 1187-
88, that he has produced "an analysis of the influence of El
Quijote in the composition of Galdós five series of Episodios
Nacionales." It "attempts to offer a comprehensive and systematic study of the extent, degree and nature of these in-

fluences and the specific passages where they can be found.
Every effort has also been made to point out the passages of
El Quijote which Galdós used for his inspiration." He notes
that "There are evident signs of Cervantine influences in at
least forty-two of the forty-six novels of the Episodios, for
which Galdós utilized material taken from no less than thirty-
eight chapters of the first part and forty-two chapters of the
second part of El Quijote" (p. 1187).

Hispania published the following articles based on this
dissertation: "Galdós y Cervantes," 41 (1958), 42-47, and
"Sancho Panza en los Episodios Nacionales, 42 (1959), 199-
204.

The Zeidner dissertation contains an introduction, conclusion, notes and list of works consulted. Its nine chapters
are: Galdós and Cervantes, Galdós' concept of the social
novel, The historical novel, The novels of the first epoch:
Doña Perfecta and La familia de León Roch, La desheredada,
El doctor Centeno and Tormento, Fortunata y Jacinta, The
Torquemada tetralogy, Angel Guerra, Realidad, La incógnita,
and Miau, Nazarín, Halma and Misericordia, and El caballero encantado. She writes: "The purpose of this investigation
is an attempt to discover the influence which the writings of
Cervantes had in the development of the former's novelistic
art" (1.1). She also states that "In this study the influence
of Cervantes will be traced according to the appearance of
the following elements within the novels in question: (1) the
creation of the unique, independent novelistic personage whose
life is motivated by an incitement, the desire to fulfill a
dream or illusion; (2) the relationship of the author to his
created character; (3) the problem of the confusion between
illusion and reality" (1.3).

Critics have pointed to certain elements of the picaresque in some of Galdós novels, especially in Lo prohibido
(q. v.). Some have also suggested that Quevedo may have had
an influence on them.

Pablo Cabañas, "Moratín en las obras de Galdós,"
Actas del Segundo Congreso Internacional de Hispanistas
(Nijmegen: Instituto Español de la Universidad de Nimega,
1967), 217-26, shows that "la presencia de Moratín en la
obra de Galdós es importante y quizá sólo ceda, entre los
escritores españoles, a la ejercida por Cervantes y Mesonero Romanos. La influencia de Moratín en Galdós es honda
y decisiva" (p. 226). He shows the influence of Moratín on

both the fiction and drama of Galdós. He notes the use by
Galdós of "una serie de frases humorísticas moratinianas"
(p. 220). "Galdós hereda de Moratín una serie de temas
capitales en la España de los siglos XVIII y XIX como la
educación de las mujeres y la mortalidad infantil" (p. 222).
He also notes that "La obra de Galdós ... refleja especialmente en El sí de las niñas, en el siglo XIX" (p. 225).

For the influence of Ramón de la Cruz on Galdós one
should consult Ernesto Enrique Moreno, "Influencia de los
sainetes de don Ramón de la Cruz en las primeras obras de
Benito Pérez Galdós" (Ph. D. dissertation, University of
Minnesota, 1966: 146 leaves; Dissertation Abstracts, 28
[1967], 2215A). The abstract concludes with this paragraph:
"Por los materiales encontrados al estudiar sus obras, y
por lo que Galdós dice en sus referencias a Cruz, llegamos
a la conclusión de que hubo influencia de éste sobre aquél,
en la selección de temas costumbristas, en tipos y escenas
populares, en la manera de tratar el lenguaje del pueblo y
de expresar las emociones del mismo. Y que ambos autores
coinciden en sus simpatías por el pueblo y en criticar certe-
ramente las costumbres y vicios generales."

Robert Kirsner, "Galdós and Larra," Modern Language
Journal, 25 (1961), 210-13, feels that "Larra is in many
aspects a precursor of Galdós.... In addition to paralleling
Larra, Galdós also complements him" (p. 212).

Jose Bergamín, "Galdós y Goya," in La corteza de la
letra, pp. 103-108, is a comparison of the artist's Desastres
de la guerra and Caprichos with the first series of the Episodios nacionales. Bergamín notes: "Lo que Goya pintaba,
porque lo veía, contemporáneamente, Galdós lo evocaba,
históricamente, en su creación novelesca de la primera parte
de los Episodios" (p. 104).

NOVELAS CONTEMPORANEAS ESPAÑOLAS

Studies on Individual Works

For the purposes of this bibliography novelas de la primera época and the Novelas españolas contemporáneas are treated as a unit and discussed alphabetically by their title.

The compiler is aware of such works as Joaquín Casalduero, "El desarrollo de la obra de Galdós," Hispanic Review, 10 (1942), 244-50, and of Robert Ricard, "La classification des romans de Galdós," Les lettres romanes, 14 (1960), 143-58 (reprinted in Galdós et ses romans, pp. 10-17), which attempt to classify and categorize either the novels or the periods of Galdós creative existence. Casalduero's article attempts to analyze and characterize the four main periods into which he divides Galdós works. According to Ricard, "Le seul fait indiscutable, c'est qu'il a indiqué dans la classification de ses oeuvres l'importance qu'il attachait au changement de 1879-1881, et qu'en revanche il n'a pas cru devoir mettre en lumière celui qui marque le passage de Misericordia (1897) à Electra (1901)."

El abuelo

Outside of contemporary reviews, no important Spanish criticism has been found of this novel. Ephrem Vincent, "Lettres espagnoles," Mercure de France, 25 (1883), 966-68, in reviewing this novel quotes from Galdós' prologue especially in regard to its form. He presents a brief plot survey and praises "la poésie de cette oeuvre...." (p. 967). He notes that the Italian actor Novelli has asked Galdós' permission to dramatize the volume.

El amigo Manso

Important studies on this novel are the following: Monroe Z. Hafter, "Le crime de Sylvestre Bonnard, a

56   Benito Pérez Galdós

possible source for El amigo Manso," Symposium, 17 (1963),
123-29; Walter T. Pattison, "El amigo Manso and El amigo
Galdós," Anales galdosianos, 2 (1967), 136-53; Josette
Blanquat, "Le naturalisme espagnol en 1882: El amigo
Manso de Galdós," Bulletin hispanique, 54 bis (Mélanges
offerts à Marcel Bataillon), (1962), 318-25; G.A. Davies,
"Galdós' El amigo Manso: an experiment in didactic method,"
Bulletin of Hispanic Studies, 39 (1962), 16-30; Ricardo Gul-
lón, "La invención del personaje en El amigo Manso," Insula,
no. 148 (1959), 1-2, and his "El amigo Manso entre Galdós
y Unamuno," Mundo nuevo, 4 (oct. 1966), 32-9 (see also his
"El amigo Manso, nivola galdosiana," Técnicas de Galdós,
pp. 59-102); Robert Kirsner, "Sobre el amigo Manso de
Galdós," Cuadernos de literatura, 8 (1950), 180-99; Nancy A.
Newton, "El amigo Manso and the relativity of reality," Revista de estudios hispánicos, 7 (1973), 113-25; Francisco
Pina, "El humanismo de Galdós; reencuentro afortunado con
El amigo Manso," El Valle Inclán que yo conocí (México:
UNAM, 1969), pp. 182-91; R.M. Price, "The five padrotes
in Pérez Galdós' El amigo Manso," Philological Quarterly,
48 (1969), 234-46; Eamonn Rodgers, "Realismo y mito en
El amigo Manso," Cuadernos hispanoamericanos, nos. 250-
52 (1970-1971), 430-44; María de Villarino, "Un extraño
caso de sinfronismo literario," Revista Buenos Aires, no. 1
(1961), 155-60; and Arnold M. Penuel, "The influence of
Galdós' El amigo Manso on Dolores Medio's El diario de
una maestra," Revista de estudios hispánicos, 7 (1973), 91-
96.

   Monroe Z. Hafter states "Anatole France should be
added to the number of French authors on whom Benito Pérez
Galdós drew for inspiration" (p. 123). The article discusses
"the basic likeness between the two novels" (p. 123).

   The autobiographical elements of the novel are stressed
by Pattison who shows that "the autobiographical elements
in the novel and its protagonist are even greater than heretofore suspected. In order to sustain this belief I must first
call attention to some neglected details of Galdós' biography"
(p. 136). The article has the following sections: Parallels
in biography and fiction, Galdós and Manso in love, Immanuel
Kant and daily routine, Philosophy and natural law, The background of Manso's intellectual development. He concludes:
"there is little doubt that Don Benito himself was one of the
principal models. His problems during his personal crisis
of 1879-1880 are reflected in Manso's dilemma, and his re-
orientation towards a new concept of realism, a compromise

form of French naturalism, is revealed in Manso's new
awareness of reality" (pp. 148-49). The extensive documentation of the author's views include one hundred footnotes
(pp. 149-53).

Kirsner discusses the work's critical neglect and notes
that it "presenta la lucha de un individuo incapaz de armoni-
zar dentro de sí mismo su existencia interior y su existencia
exterior" (p. 196). On p. 199 he compares this novel with
Unamuno's Amor y pedagogia.

Davies finds that the society described by Galdós in
this novel "is essentially infinite" and that he presents us
"with an imagined world which merges at its fartherest edges
into the infinity of the real world" (p. 17). He disagrees
with Kirsner's interpretation of novel, for he feels that
Kirsner "fails to take into account Galdós' didactic purpose
in the novel" (p. 20). Davies discusses the ideological issues
raised in the novel as well as Galdós' "new way ... of com-
bining ideological criticism with the novel-form" (p. 20). He
concludes with these remarks: "The book's success is largely to be explained by the way in which Galdós has chosen at
significant points to draw our attention to the lessons he
wishes to teach, and thus make us more aware of the didactic
significance of certain other episodes. The result is a novel
much superior to Doña Perfecta in its social analysis and
study of human character, but which subtly and profoundly
examines at the same time a problem as fundamental to
human society as that with which the author was concerned
in the earlier novel" (p. 30).

Gullón's "La invención ..." notes that one can analyze
this novel on three distinct levels. "En el plano moral hay
en esta novela una lección de liberalismo y tolerancia" (p. 1).
"En el piano social Manso, es, según ya indiqué, el hombre
frente a la sociedad" (p. 1). "En el plano artístico la novela es de ritmo lento" (p. 2). Gullón discusses the novel
and the development of the character of Manso vis-à-vis the
reader. "Esa proximidad sitúa al personaje a nuestro nivel,
en comunicación con el lector, en relación acentuada por la
impresión de normalidad que produce to trivial del episodio
y lo verosímil del incidente" (p. 1).

Gullón's "El amigo Manso ..." has the following parts:
Mundo real y mundo imaginario, Del querer ser al ser, El
ideal perdido en el aburguesamiento, El amigo Manso, nivola.
Though the discussion of the character of Manso and of the

novel's style are excellent, the last part may be of greater
interest, for it is a commentary on Unamuno's Niebla and
El amigo Manso. Gullón writes: "Los elementos de El
amigo Manso que permiten considerarlo como antecedente
de Niebla se refieren a la materia novelesca, a la relación
autopersonaje, a la de los personajes entre sí y a los temas"
(p. 37).

"El amigo Manso, nivola galdosiana" contains (pp. 59-
82) the same sections as the Mundo nuevo article. In addition, there are the following sections: Procesos mentales,
El narrador-testigo, Estructura novelesca and Tiempo y
espacio.

Blanquat's article is an extremely interesting critical
study of this novel. Both the character of Manso and the
novel itself are well analyzed. The article's last sentence
is: "Expression de l'idéologie libérale, mais indépendant de
tout système, ce roman si caractéristique du Naturalisme
dans l'Espagne de 1882 affirme son indépendance par l'humour
qui n'affaiblit en rien la vigueur d'une pensée qui s'inscrit
dans la lignée spirituelle de l'humanisme platonicien" (p. 335).

Newton develops the theme that "An awareness of the
method by which Galdós creates his protagonist affords a
more complete understanding of the novel's thematic import,
for in El amigo Manso the author's handling of form is at
the service of the work's problematic [sic] in a most deliberate way" (p. 113).

Price finds that the four busts mentioned in chapter
three "represent oratory, literary and other satire, active
stoic philosophy, and drama and these are important elements
in the novel. The four padrotes are in Manso's study, and
he, as we shall see, is the fifth padrote. What the padrotes
represent deserved some consideration since they illustrate
aspects of the chief character, Manso, and throw light upon
the technique and sources of the novels" (p. 234). The author feels that "The four padrotes are therefore a device
which illuminates the character of Manso and the complex
texture of the whole novel" (p. 245).

Pina's brief essay discusses the author's rereading of
the novel. Pages 189-91 attack Los precursores de la fa-
lange, "en el cual figuran como antecedentes ideológicos del
franquismo, entre otros, algunos escritores como Mariano
José de Larra, Pío Baroja y ... Galdós!" (p. 189). He

finds the novel to be "una profunda lección de vida" (p. 188).
He notes that Galdós "intentó más innovaciones y tuvo muchas
más inquietudes estilísticas y preocupaciones literarias de lo
que generalmente se supone" (pp. 187-88). This essay is
full of polemic spirit and makes for exciting reading even
when one does not agree 100 per cent with the critic.

Rodgers feels that previous critics have not dealt sufficiently with it as a realistic novel. On p. 432, he writes
that "Siendo todo esto así, El amigo Manso tiene un interés
especial para los lectores de Galdós, porque es la primera
novela en que el autor se abstiene deliberadamente de adoptar
posiciones simplistas, y por eso mismo, como intentaré de-
mostrar, la primera que podemos calificar de plenamente
realista."

Rodgers discusses the novel's style and characterization.
His concluding paragraph (pp. 443-44) follows: "Ya dijimos
al principio que la actitud del autor en El amigo Manso es
ambigua: esta hondamente identificado con el mundo que
crea, pero al mismo tiempo mantiene su imparcialidad artística. De un modo más general, podemos ver que la calidad de
está relacionada con toda una serie de dualidades análogas.
El amigo Manso refleja las realidades materiales de la vida,
pero al mismo tiempo afirma valores espirituales. Evoca
auténticamente un período histórico determinado, pero, al
elevarse al nivel mítico, logra superar la dimensión temporal. No rehuye el mostrar el egoísmo y la estupidez humanos tales como son; pero, al captar la complejidad de la
personalidad humana, hace difícil censurar al individuo.
Finalmente--y esto es quizá lo más importante--, es una
obra maestra del realismo objetivo, lograda a través de las
limitaciones de una visión subjetiva."

José Varela Zequeira reviewed El amigo Manso in the
Revista de Cuba, 12 (1882), 305-12. As a portion of this
novel's action takes place in Cuba, the views of a Cuban reviewer are of interest. In regard to the Cuban element in
the novel, the reviewer feels that Galdós "no ha estado igualmente feliz en la elección de personajes cubanos que intervienen en la fábula, ni en la pintura de su carácter y costumbres, que nos parece de brocha gorda y con un tono cari-
caturesco muy subido" (p. 310). He finds that Galdós' knowledge of Cuban Spanish does not ring true and that his knowledge of Cuba and the Cuban character is second-hand (p. 311).

Penuel develops the theme that "The similarities

between the two novels with regard to situations, plot,
themes, and characterization are too close and numerous
to be mere affinities or unrelated coincidences" (p. 91).

   Maria de,Villarino discusses El amigo Manso and Memorias póstumas de Bras Cubas by J.M. Machado de Assis.
Parallel passages are arranged under these headings: Tratamiento y proceso de la narración intelectual, Estado, el
amor y las mujeres amadas, Afectos interesados and Afectos
reales. The author notes that "Las similitudes asombran
tanto más por la contemporaneidad de los dos autores, de
tan lejanos continentes y diferente habla, como por su ubica-
ción estética" (p. 159).

Angel Guerra

   This novel can best be studied through Francisco Ruiz
Ramón, Tres personajes galdosianos: ensayo de aproximacion a un mundo religioso y moral, (Madrid: Revista de
Occidente, 1964), 270pp.; Gustavo Correa, "El misterio de
la vocación en Angel Guerra," in El simbolismo religioso...,
pp. 146-65; Josette Blanquat, "Tolède medievale et l'Eglise
de l'avenir dans Angel Guerra," Actes du Septième Congrès
National: Société Française de Littérature Comparée, vol.
53 of Etudes de littérature étrangère et comparée, 1967,
pp. 150-67; Victor M. Valenzuela, "Comentario crítico sobre
la novela Angel Guerra de Benito Pérez Galdós," in Ensayos
sobre literatura española [Bethlehem, Pa.]: Lehigh University, 1967), pp. 55-108; Robert Ricard, "Galdós, Tolède et
la Nouvelle-Castille," in Aspects de Galdós, pp. 86-98; Vera
Colin, "Tolstoy and Angel Guerra," Galdós Studies, pp. 114-
35; Monroe Z. Hafter, "Bálsamo contra bálsamo' in Angel
Guerra," Anales galdosianos, 4 (1969), 39-48; Matías Montes
Huidobro, "Benito Pérez Galdós: variedad estilística en la
expresion de los planos de la realidad," XIX: Superficie y
fondo del estilo (University of North Carolina, Department of
Romance Languages, 1971), pp. 53-68 (Estudios de Hispanófi-
la, 17); Kathleen M. Sayers, "El sentido de la tragedia en
Angel Guerra," Anales galdosianos, 5 (1970), 81-85; Francis
Donahue, "Hacia una solución galdosiano del problema relio-
gioso español: Angel Guerra," Sin Nombre, 2 (1971), 58-
63; and Medardo Fraile, "La atracción por Angel Guerra,"
Samuel Ros (1904-1945) hacia una generación sin crítica
(Madrid, Editorial Prensa española, 1972), pp. 93-100 (El
Soto 19).   A contemporary review by Ramón del Valle-
Inclán, which was first published in El Globo (Madrid), Aug.

13, 1891, can now be readily found in Publicaciones periodísticas de don Ramón del Valle-Inclán anteriores a 1895, edición, estudio preliminar y notas de William L. Fichter (México: El Colegio de México, 1952), pp. 56-59, and in Benito Pérez Galdós (1973), pp. 317-319.

The volume by Ruiz Ramón is a revision of a University of Madrid doctoral dissertation. In the volume's introduction he writes: "Como el subtítulo de este estudio indica, mi propósito ha sido escribir un simple ensayo de aproximación al mundo religioso y moral de algunos personajes galdosianos. He tomado como 'base de operación' la novela Angel Guerra no porque me parezca la de mayor calidad, sino porque a ella vienen a confluir caminos iniciados en anteriores obras y de ella parten otros que serán prolongados posteriormente. Angel Guerra es, en este sentido, una novela de encrucijada, tanto de temas y de propósitos, como de personajes" (p. 11).

The volume has an introduction, a bibliography and three main divisions. The first chapter, "Angel Guerra, Aspectos de un proceso espiritual," has the following sections: La profunda huella de la infancia, Los factores de la crisis, Mística Toledo, La ruta de Don Quijote. The second chapter, "Los clérigos toledanos," is divided into El clérigo de 1870 a 1891, El clérigo de 1891 a 1918, La cuestión del anticlericalismo galdosiano. The third chapter, "En torno al misticismo de Leré," has two sections: De doña Paulita Porreño a Leré and El misticismo de Leré. This volume then presents great interest not only as a study of Angel Guerra but as a study of many of Galdós' religious ideas.

Blanquat writes: "C'est la force créatrice de ce rêve tolédan, si cher aux libéraux espagnols, que nous voudrions montrer en étudiant, l'une après l'autre, deux oeuvres très inégales: tout d'abord la série d'essais consacrés à Tolède, publiés en 1870; puis, un grand roman, Angel Guerra, chef-d'oeuvre du Naturalisme spiritualiste, écrit en 1890" (pp. 150-51). The influence of Dante, Zola and Tolstoy are mentioned. The author notes that "Avec Angel Guerra, le thème de l'amour platonique est repris, mais associé cette fois aux valeurs religieuses du catholicisme, tel que Dante avait pu le concevoir" (p. 157). This study of Toledo and its symbolic meaning in this novel is one of the finest that exists on Angel Guerra.

Colin states her purpose in these words: "As will be demonstrated in the following brief summary of Tolstoy's

work, the pages of Ma religion [i. e., in Galdós' library]
which are turned down contain significant passages. The
purpose of the present article is to suggest that these passages are crucial to an understanding of Galdós' novel,
Angel Guerra, and, indeed provide a key to the interpretation
of that work" (p. 114).

She finds that "The following points represent the Tolstoyan elements in the rules laid down for Guerra's new foundation: 1) The decision not to appeal to law-courts" (p. 127)....
2) The refusal to use violence even in self-defense" (p. 128
.... and 3) The annulment of personality" (p. 129).

Mrs. Colin finds that "Guerra's profound conviction that
by putting his theory into practice, by practicing charity as
preached by Christ, the existing order of things could be al-
tered peacefully" (p. 124) and "The absence of armies and politicians in Guerra's new utopian state" (p. 125) "are clearly
of Tolstoyan origin" (p. 124).

Her last sentence is: "The tragic end of Angel Guerra
proves what Galdós set out to prove, namely that the creation
of a new society based on non-resistance to evil, as preached
by Tolstoy, is inconceivable" (p. 135).

The chapter from Correa's volume has an introduction
and three sections: La vocación de Leré, El amor de Angel
por Leré, and La transformación de Angel. According to
Correa, "La novela Angel Guerra (1890-1891) plantea el
problema de la vocación en relación con el amor humano y
el amor divino. Es decir, trata de encontrar una respuesta
a la particular forma de vida personal frente a la inclinación
hacia lo sobrenatural o a un destino puramente humano"
(p. 146). He states that "La novela se halla dividida en tres
partes que corresponden a tres etapas en la trayectoria ascen-
sional de protagonista" (p. 148). He finds that "Leré representa el tipo de vocación religiosa pura, sin rodeos, dudas
ni vacilaciones" (p. 151). On p. 165 he writes: "La vocación de Angel fue, asi, un amor irreductible a la monja
Leré, el cual dio frutos fecundos en su espíritu, en virtud
de su misma incapacidad de realización. A través de este
gran amor humano no realizado, Angel experimentó una transformación fundamental en su personalidad y logró presentir
el secreto del amor de Dios que se hallaba fuera de su
alcance."

Hafter notes that Doña Emilia Pardo Bazán believed the

volume's worst fault was "the distracting nature of so many
subordinate characters and episodes" (p. 39). However,
Hafter's view is that "Galdós' narrative, therefore, does not
depart from the main plot line when it develops secondary
characters and scenes. Apparent digressions can be shown
to conform to an orderly construction. Galdós makes use of
all his material to shade and color in the story of the central
protagonists. What might have been a sentimental tale of
spiritual regeneration is given extraordinary depth by the
author's affective separation from his character's progress
to salvation. Galdós never fails to let the reader perceive
that the narrator has a perspective on the events of the novel" (p. 46).

Montes Huidobro states that "Angel Guerra es una de
las novelas galdosianas donde realiza el autor, con el máximo
de eficacia, la fusión entre la realidad y el delirante mundo
del subconsciente" (p. 53). The whole point of the article,
which is developed in detail, is summarized in the last paragraph: "Sólo a través del más efectivo manejo del idioma
se puede alcanzar tanta variedad estilística en la presentación
de los múltiples planos de la realidad" (p. 68).

Sayers' article contains numerous interesting references
and comparisons to Fortunata y Jacinta. The final paragraph
is of great interest: "Galdós desarrolla el sentido de la
tragedia en Fortunata y Jacinta y en Angel Guerra a base de
un estudio psicológico profundo. En ambas novelas los personajes se ven obligados a renunciar algo exigido por su
propia naturaleza. El énfasis en la afectividad y la psicología del personaje es típico de la novela de Galdós y de la
novela de la última mitad del siglo XIX. Lo que cambian
es la manera de enfocar los problemas humanos. El punto
de vista del estudio es distinto en las dos obras. En Fortunata y Jacinta es colectivo, en Angel Guerra, individual. El
interés de Galdós por la realidad exterior y la interrelación
de los personajes en Fortunata y Jacinta refleja una actitud
naturalista. El enfoque en Angel Guerra del conflicto espiritual interior y la lucha del personaje por conocerse refleja
la corriente espiritualista de fines del siglo" (p. 85).

Donahue notes that "En la segunda mitad del siglo XIX,
descubrió Galdós que lo medular del 'problema español'
quedaba plasmado en la cuestión religiosa. Es decir, esa
cuestión revestía el punto de mayor divergencia entre los
liberales y los conservadores. Y, según Galdós, fue producto de esta divergencia el atraso politico y social en que

se encontraba la sociedad española con respecto a otras socieda-
des europeas" (p. 58). His thesis in this article is that "Angel
Guerra (1890-1891) refleja la clase de solución a esta cuestión
que el novelista español, durante una época, anhelaba para España. Y esa solución viene a ser la aplicación de la pura doctrina
evangélica del Cristianismo primitivo a la vida actual" (p. 58).

Medardo Fraile compares the ideas of Galdós as found
in Angel Guerra with those found in the works of Ros. Fraile
notes, for example, that "Las ideas de Samuel Ros y Angel
Guerra sobre la mujer--tan entusiastas y cálidas como cor-
rientes--, concuerdan casi al pie de la letra" (p. 98). He
concludes his brief study with these words: "Es el 'horizonte'
de Guerra, la realidad radical del personaje, lo que fascina
a Ros, sin importarle si el 'género' se sirve con impurezas
y con libertad" (p. 100).

Ricard finds that Angel Guerra "est un de ceux où le
grand écrivain s'est le plus rapproché au catholicisme de son
enfance" (p. 86). He notes that after Madrid no city plays a
greater role in Galdós' novels than Toledo and that in two of
the three parts of this novel this city "est évoquée et décrite
de façon magistrale" (p. 92). Ricard quotes several passages
from the novel that could be interpreted as favoring a more
or less independent Catholic Church and discusses the position
that Toledo has had in Spanish history and religion. He believes that "la fréquentation de quelques amis krausistes n'a
pu que fortifier l'attachment de Galdós pour Tolède" (p. 96)
and that "Le lien tolédan entre Galdós et les krausistes est
donc établi avec certitude" (p. 97).

Valenzuela states that "Es nuestro propósito hacer un
análisis crítico de Angel Guerra, personaje que sin duda
alguna descolla entre el resto de la galería galdosiana como
uno de los tipos mejor estudiados y el que más se asemeja
por su ideologia a su propio creador" (p. 59). This article
has a brief introduction and sections entitled "Angel Guerra,"
"Resumen de Angel Guerra," "Personajes," pp. 69-101, "El
lenguaje," pp. 102-06, and a conclusion. This critic finds
that "Don Benito Pérez Galdós usó en Angel Guerra un lenguaje familiar y corriente, de expresión cálida y espontánea
dándonos asila sensación de lenguaje hablado, lleno de realismo, sencillez y humanidad" (p. 102). In the conclusion it is
emphasized that "Angel Guerra, es en esta novela el personaje creado por Galdós que simboliza y encarna la idea liberal y el sentimiento del amor; sentimiento e idea que el

novelista usará para conciliar conflictos ideológicos y que
además servirán para llegar a obtener la comprensión y el
mejoramiento espiritual del individuo y de la sociedad"
(p. 106).

El audaz

    This novel has been little studied. One can recommend
Leonel Antonio de la Cuesta, "La audaz de Benito Pérez
Galdós: edición critica con introducción, texto y notas"
(Ph. D. dissertation, The Johns Hopkins University, 1971),
832 leaves; Dissertation Abstracts International, 32 [1971],
2681A), who notes in the abstract that "The introduction is
divided into six parts: the first four are principally concerned with the formal analysis of the novel (date of publication, sources, influences, classification, themes, structure,
point of view, narrative technique, characters, plots, and
setting as well as a summary of the novel); the fifth deals
with the identification and analysis of the work which became
characteristic of the Galdosian style. The sixth part is
meant to inform the reader about the various editions of El
audaz and the way in which some of these editions were used
in the preparation of mine."

    The fullest published discussion of this novel is Fran-
cisco Yndurain, Galdós entre la novela y el folletin (Madrid,
Taurus, 1970), 82pp. (Cuadernos Taurus 98); reprinted in
his De lector a lector (Madrid, 1973), pp. 93-135 (Bibliotica
Estudios Escelicer I: Estudios de crítica literatura 1). The
author writes that "... voy a tratar de exponer mi opinión
sobre una obra de Galdós, El audaz, que he tomado no tanto
por haber sido menos estudiada, sino por tratar de ver algo
más en una fase germinal de su oficio y arte de escritor"
(pp. 8-9).

    On p. 48 he notes that "Dentro de la economia del
organismo que es la novela--hablo de El audaz--hay motivos
que actúan en distintos niveles y con varia frecuencia, por
ejemplo que ahora me interesa analizar, la descripción sea
de paisaje, de personas, de objetos, de lo visto y percibido
como escenario de la acción. De lejos le viene a la novela
el alternar con varia proporción diálogo, narración y descrip-
ción--sin otros modos que ahora no cuentan--, y Galdós,
tanto por sus lecturas de escritores nacionales como extranje-
ras, no opera de modo nuevo."

It is noted that "El folletín dominaba los gustos de
los años en que Galdós iba a comenzar su carrera de novelista, y bien lo hizo notar él mismo" (p. 56). He finds in
this novel "tipos de catadura netamente folletinesca" (p.
60) and shows that it is "truco folletinesco el terminar los capítulos en un punto crítico de la acción" (p. 61). Yndurain
states that "El movimiento y entonación interrogativos son
usados con profusión en la novela folletinesca, sin duda como
excitantes de la curiosidad y tensión emotiva en los lectores"
(p. 61).

This is an extremely interesting critical study and is
worth the attention of everyone who desires to explore in
depth one of Galdós' early novels.

Alberto Míguez provides a very brief introduction to
his edition of this novel (Andorra and Barcelona, Editorial
Andorra, 1972), pp. 7-10.

El caballero encantado

Gustavo Correa, "El sentido de lo hispánico en El
caballero encantado de Pérez Galdós y la generación del
98," Thesaurus, 18 (1963), 14-28, notes that "la novela
constituye un llamamiento a la conciencia de la nación para
superar los males del momento y representaría la immersión
más profunda del arte de Galdós en esta inquietud fundamental"
(p. 15). The character and importance of Tarsis are discussed in detail. It is noted that this is one of three of
Galdós' novels which deal with agricultural reforms. The author believes that this novel "plantea en forma artística las
inquietudes de una problemática que se halló siempre latente
en la obra de Galdós, al mismo tiempo que indica una solución. Tal actitud pone de relieve las afinidades y diferencias
del autor con la generación del 98" (pp. 27-28).

Eduardo Gómez de Baquero, "El caballero encantado,"
Novelas y novelistas (Madrid: Calleja, 1918), pp. 102-07, is
a discussion of the plot, style, characters and language of
this novel, which the critic states "es un libro maravilloso y
singular. El encanto que reza su título no es metáfora;
verdad es la mezcla de lo real y lo inverosimil con que el
subtítulo define la índole del relato. Empieza, pues, este
libro con los caracteres de una novela contemporánea, ob-
servadora de las costumbres que forman el ambiente social;
mas luego se introduce en la fábula el elemento maravilloso

y la conduce por fantásticas sendas, desde las cuales se
siguen contemplando los paisajes de la realidad" (p. 102).

Julio Rodríguez Puértolas, "Galdós y El caballero
encantado," Anales galdosianos, 7 (1972) 117-32, desires to
show that this novel "no es ... ni 'un curioso capricho de
Galdós' ni tampoco su 'último sueño romántico'" (p. 117).
The article is divided into El condicionamiento histórico,
Novela social, novela política, Regeneracionismo y 98, El
futuro.

José Antonio Gómez Marín, "Sobre el realismo mági-
co de Galdós," serves as a prologue to El Caballero encantado (Madrid, Miguel Castellote, 1972), pp. 7-17. It is a pity
that it is so short. Gómez Marín comments on the symbolism found in the novel and how it deals with the Spanish problem.

Cassandra

This novel has been practically ignored by the critics.
Eduardo Gómez de Baquero, "Cassandra," Novelas y novelistas (Madrid: Calleja, 1918), pp. 87-101, has the following
parts: El género, el asunto, El tono de la novela, La acción.
Las psicosis en la obra de Galdós. He finds that "hay en
esta obra aciertos y bellezas que reconozco, siquiera la
impresión general que me ha dejado su lectura es la de ser
una obra de decadencia de desmayo de un espíritu creador"
(p. 89).

Of the more recent critics, Gustavo Correa has briefly studied this novel in his El simbolismo religioso...,
pp. 216-25. This chapter is entitled "La búsqueda del Dios
verdadero en Cassandra." Correa states that "La oposición
entre ángel y monstruo, ejemplificada en los dos personajes
de Rosaura y doña Juana, pone de manifiesto el mundo religioso de la novela que se caracteriza por la presencia del
Dios verdadero y su ocultamiento entre los demonios y los
dioses falsos" (p. 220). He also notes that "El pacto de los
herederos con estos diablos curialescos revela el otro aspecto
demoniológico del mundo social en que se mueven los personajes de la novela, o sea, el de los dioses falsos" (p. 222).

La desheredada

Important studies on this novel are: Carmen Bravo

Villasante, "El naturalismo de Galdós y el mundo de La desheredada," Cuadernos hispanoamericanos, no. 230 (febrero de
1969), 479-86; Kay Engler, "Linguistic determination of point
of view: La desheredada," Anales galdosianos, 5 (1970), 67-
73; M. Gordon, "The medical background to Galdós' La desheredada," Anales galdosianos, 7 (1972), 67-77; Monroe Z.
Hafter, "Galdós' presentation of Isidora in La desheredada,"
Modern Philology, 60 (1962-1963), 22-30; Jennifer Lowe,
"Galdós' skill in La desheredada," Ibero-romania, 3 (1971),
142-51; Marie-Claire Petit, "La desheredada, ou le procès
du rêve," Romance Notes, 9 (1968), 235-43, and his "La
folie et la mort dans La desheredada," Cahiers du monde
hispanique et luso-brésilien (Caravelle), 11 (1968), 193-204;
Robert Ricard, "La desheredada (1881) et l'oeuvre romanesque de Galdós," Aspects de Galdós, pp. 21-43; Eamonn
Rodgers, "Galdós' La desheredada and naturalism," Bulletin
of Hispanic Studies, 45 (1968), 285-98; Carlos Rovetta, "El
naturalismo de Galdós en La desheredada," Nosotros second
series, no. 84 (1943), 275-84; Antonio Ruiz Salvador, "La
función del trasfondo histórico en La desheredada," Anales
galdosianos, 1 (1966), 53-62; Robert H. Russell, "The structure of La desheredada," Modern Language Notes, 76 (1961),
794-800; and Chad G. Wright, "The representational qualities
of Isidora Rufete's house and her son Riquin in Benito Pérez
Galdós' novel La desheredada," Romanische Forschungen, 83
(1971), 230-45.

Bravo Villasante reviews at length the 1967 Alianza
Editorial edition of this novel. Her review is full of interesting remarks which unfortunately cannot be quoted at length.
She suggests that "Si la copia de los grandes cuadros de
Goya es de una total evidencia, no sucede lo mismo con
otras manifestaciones pictórico-literarias de Galdós, que
están por estudiar" (p. 485). The reviewer dwells on the
novel as one belonging to the naturalist school and comments
upon Zola's influence. Yet she notes "En los cuadros del
más terrible realismo o del más crudo naturalismo, hay una
nota divertida, y mas que sarcasmo hay alegría de la vida
y esperanza el fondo" (p. 484). The reviewer also comments
on style and characters.

Engler concludes her study with these remarks:
"...we have examined the relationship between language and
point of view in one of Galdós' novels. We have seen how
the narrator's mimetic language creates the illusion of external reality; we have seen how expressive language estab-
lishes the presence of a perceiving consciousness and iden-

tifies the point of view from which the external reality is perceived. Finally, we have seen how language itself, in all its functions, creates the interrelationship of perceiving consciousness and external reality which in fact is the very psychological and aesthetic basis of Galdós' fiction" (p. 73).

Gordon writes: "An examination of the medical background to La desheredada, however, suggests that much of Galdós' medical documentation for the novel was drawn from Spanish sources. The nature of some of this source material gives it a certain minor interest in itself. However, since much of it relates to the characterisation of Mariano Rufete, generally considered to be the most Zolaesque element in the novel, it also has a bearing on the whole question of naturalism in La desheredada and may perhaps help to explain why in so many important respects Galdós' naturalism is different from that of his French contemporary" (p. 67). This article notes the influence of Manuel Tolosa Latour and José María Esquerdo, "the most prominent Spanish psychiatrists of the day" (p. 68).

Hafter concludes his discussion of Isidora with these sentences: "Dignity and foolishness, aspiration and irresponsibility, ideals and obsessions, Galdós has multiplied the points of view from which to judge and to observe his heroine. Anticipating the achievement of his next novel, El amigo Manso, he at the same time breaks down the generic forms of the novel and contributes to his protagonist's autonomy. One chapter may give way to the next with no apparent transition, but the continuing commentary on Isidora connects one to another. It is in this way that Galdós gives to a wide social spectrum his coherent artistic expression of a woman's folly and tragedy" (pp. 29-30).

Lowe hopes "to show that both subtlety and artistic skill are often shown in the way in which aspects of her [i. e., Isidora's] character are conceived and developed and also in the preparation which is made for her disillusion and eventual decision" (p. 142). Her concluding paragraph follows: "Thus, although we can certainly find numerous examples of clumsy execution in La desheredada, the way in which Isidora's character and behaviour are conceived can be considered a clear indication of the penetration we are to find in Galdós' later novels. 'Transitional' La desheredada may be but much of Galdós' insight and skill are already maturing here. Moreover, the meaningful structure, the continual play on the vida muerte concept, the all-revealing word or phrase apparently casually introduced and the possibilities for reader-participation provide further evidence of Galdós grasp on the aspects which contribute to a good novel" (p. 151).

Petit concludes her article with this paragraph: "C'est pas par hasard que La desheredada commence dans un asile où un fou attaque ses contemporains en termes si convainquants que leur déraison parait plus grande que la sienne. La confusion est voulue: elle montre l'interpénétration de deux univers que des murs ne sauraient séparer. Derrière Isidora, la porte de Leganés ne se ferme qu'en apparence. Les rêves de Tomás Rufete et de Canencia à l'asile, ceux d'Isidora et de don José dans les rues de Madrid, ceux des Carlistes et des libéraux dans toute l'Espagne, tissent une trame de folie qui enserre le pays et l'immobilise. Galdós, conscient de ce danger, fait de La desheredada un symbole et un avertissement. Isidora perd son procès, mais l'échec est à la fois celui du rêve et de l'Espagne" (p. 243).

The second study by Petit is one of the few that finds Pérez Galdós "comparable à Poe par le choix des thèmes et la perception des rapports qui existent entre la vie et la mort," yet the author finds that "Galdós s'en éloigne sur certains points" (p. 203). She notes that "La mort, pour Galdós, est nécessaire et juste, et elle est avant tout delivrance" (p. 200), and on the same page she speaks of the "aspect positif de la mort." Her analysis of madness as found in the novel and as seen through the character of Rufete is worth extended study. In her last paragraph she writes: "...Vivement intéressé par la richesse de l'inconscient et sensible au mystère de la mort, Galdós part toujours du réel pour mieux le dépasser ensuite et suggérer l'inexplicable. La réalité du monde visible n'est pas plus grande, à nos yeux, que celle du monde invisible. Tous deux méritent que s'exercent sur eux l'observation et l'analyse réservées par Zola au premier, et si Galdós utilise constamment les instruments du Naturaliste, il élargit beaucoup le champ de l'expérience. C'est la conscience de cette dualité qui fait la richesse de son univers, doté de ce qui manque à celui du Zola: la dimension surnaturelle" (p. 204).

Ricard states that "Isidora Rufete est le prototype de ces grandes amoureuses qui forment une des galeries les plus riches parmi les personnages de Galdós" (p. 21). "Elle est aussi le prototype de ces visionnaires et de ces mythomanes qui pullulent dans les classes de la société" (p. 23). In regard to Galdós' descriptions of illness this novel

"n'innove rien" (p. 29). However, Ricard qualifies this by
saying "Mais elle innove sur deux points précis. On voit
surgir en effet dans La desheredada deux formes patholo-
giques nouvelles ... La première, ces sont les monstruosi-
tés tératologiques, la second les affections épileptiques ou
épileptformes" (p. 30). In regard to style, this novel "nous
apporte à la fois une consolidation et une innovation: consolidation d'un procédé qui prendra une place croissante dans les
romans de Galdós: le monologue intérieur; innovation dans la
présentation du dialogue" (p. 35).

Rodgers states that "It is generally agreed that if
Galdós is a Naturalist, it is only in this broad and peculiarly
Spanish sense. This article takes this view as its starting-
point and attempts to carry the discussion further. I shall
try to establish the extent of naturalist influence in La desheredada, and to examine whether there are any elements in
the novel which arise out of earlier, possibly romantic attitudes. I shall also say something about the particular
strengths and weaknesses to which Galdós' understanding of
Naturalism gives rise at this stage in his career, and attempt a general assessment of the importance of La desheredada in the context of the development of Galdós' work"
(p. 286).

Rovetta and Rodgers also discuss the novel as a piece
of naturalistic fiction. Rovetta states that this novel "mostra-
ba la intención, que ya no abandonaría Galdós hasta Miau, de
examinar la vida de la sociedad--clase media para abajo--
con instrumentos análogos a los empleados por Zola y sus
discípulos" (p. 279).

The article by Ruiz Salvador concludes with the sentence, "Con ello el diagnóstico optimista del pasado pasa a
ser en La desheredada una autopsia del presente" (p. 61).
The author discusses the various types of symbolism that he
finds in the novel and shows how the historical background
portrayed in the novel affects style, plot and characters.

Russell finds the novel to be "an artistic experiment
and a moral lesson; it is not primarily a scientific demonstra-
tion. It draws freely on the techniques and structures of
naturalism, but cannot go the whole way. Neither can it be
satisfied with the aesthetic poverty implicit in naturalistic
theory. It reserves to human personality a self-determina-
tion, which, for good or ill, is the secret of the novelist's
illusion" (p. 800).

Wright states that "Two of the most important symbols
... are Isidora Rufete's house on Hortaleza Street and her
macrocephalic son, Riquín. These two important facets of
La desheredada will be discussed in this brief study" (p. 230).

He finds that "In La desheredada Galdós attempts to
show through his 'house' symbol that the facade aspect of life
is indeed important to the Spaniard. His central character,
Isidora Rufete, is interested in surface appearances and superficial pleasures. Her house exemplifies this basic tenet of
her personality" (p. 232).

He states that "Galdós, however, did not intend for
Riquín to serve only a Naturalistic role; the deformed child
is also a political representation of the Restoration. Like the
Rufete line, Galdós indicates that the present generation of
political leaders has inherited the evils of the past" (p. 242).

His concluding paragraph follows: "In conclusion, it
can be said that Galdós has adapted the Naturalism of Zola
to a representational, allegorical vision. In La desheredada
he utilizes the Zolaesque doctrines of heredity and environment to show the tragic downfall of Spain. This 'representational Naturalism' serves as an important experiment for
Galdós, as well as a warning from a gentle patriot who loved
his country and did not wish to see it become a victim of
self-prostitution to the degree that it would have no other
course but national suicide. La desheredada, according to
Galdós himself, should be considered an 'historia de verdad
y análisis' (LD, 1020) from which all may benefit. As Ruíz
Salvador has said, Galdós intended La desheredada to be 'una
autopsia del presente' and a prescription for Spain's future"
(p. 245).

Robert M. Fedorchek, "Social reprehension in La
desheredada," Revista de estudios hispánicos, 8 (1974), 43-
59, concludes with this paragraph: "Much of what Galdós
sees as injurious in La desheredada is ultimately the result
of pretentiousness or the absence of sincere human exchange
in which falseness is prescribed. Whether it be a disingenu-
ous dealing, as in Melchor, or public nonchalance, as in the
aborted reforms discussed after Mariano's crime, forms of
honesty work against the fundamental truthfulness needed to
overcome deception and apathy. What is amiss in a society
is traceable to the short-comings of its members, a notion
that Galdós continues to explore with poignancy and unstinting
humanity in all the novelas españolas contemporáneas"
(pp. 58-59).

El doctor Centeno

German Gullón, "Unidad de El doctor Centeno," Cuadernos hispanoamericanos, nos. 250-52 (1970-1971), 579-585, states that to study this novel, the following questions must be dealt with: "¿Es El doctor Centeno una sola novela o son dos?, ¿necesitamos conocer todo el grupo (1) para comprenderla totalmente?, ¿por qué se titula esta novela El doctor Centeno siendo Cento, aunque siempre presente, un muy modesto comparsa en ella? (2) Si examinamos detenidamente los problemas planteados en estas preguntas, en seguida notamos que coinciden en referirse de una o de otra manera a la unidad de la obra, y que alrededor de esta cuestión básica giran las demás. En este trabajo nos proponemos hallar esa unidad, si es que existe, examinando primeramente el tema de la novela, y su estructura, que es lo que en definitiva concede entidad a una obra" (p. 579).

Doña Perfecta

J.E. Varey, Doña Perfecta (London, Grant and Cutler in association with Tamesis Books, 1971) 84pp. (Critical guides to Spanish texts, 1), is the fullest discussion yet written on this novel. The ten chapters are: Introduction; The opening chapters; Motives and attitudes; The development of the situation; The characters; The conflict: social criticism; The conflict: moral aspects; The conflict: political issues; Stylistic features; Conclusion. There is a brief bibliographical note, pp. 82-84.

Varey finds that "Doña Perfecta is, then, a novel which reflects the political and ideological struggles of its day; to use a modern phrase, it can be described as 'littérature engagée.'" At the same time, it is the product of a young writer who is still endeavouring to find his own style, not completely sure of himself, and yet a work which foreshadows in many respects the great novels of Galdós' mature period" (p. 9).

Little has been written concerning the sources of this novel. Alexander Haggerty Krappe, "The sources of B. Pérez Galdós, Doña Perfecta, cap. vi," Philological Quarterly, 7 (1928), 303-06, finds that Heine's essay Zur Geschichte der Religion und Philosophie in Deutschland and Lucretius' De rerum natura are sources for D. José de Rey's speech in chapter six of this novel.

Vernon A. Chamberlin and Jack Weiner, "Galdos'
Doña Perfecta and Turgenev's Fathers and Sons: two inter-
pretations of the conflict between generations," PMLA, 86
(1971), 19-24 (translated by Felipe Díaz Jimeno as "Doña
Perfecta, de Galdós, y Padres e hijos, de Turgueneff: dos
interpretaciones del conflicto entre generaciones," Benito
Pérez Galdós [1973], pp. 231-243), indicate that "Scholars
have long noted the influence of Russian writers, particularly
Tolstoy and Dostoevsky, in the novels of Benito Pérez Galdós.
However, in an interview granted to the Russian journalist
Ia. Pavlovskii in 1884 (only recently published in the West),
Galdós acknowledges an indebtedness to an earlier Russian
master, Ivan Turgenev, referring to him as 'my great teacher.' A close reading of Turgenev's Fathers and Sons and
Galdós' Doña Perfecta suggests that the Russian masterpiece
may have inspired the well-known Spanish work. The novels
share a common theme (the conflict between generations),
and in each the hero is a young man trained in science who
makes an extended visit to the provinces. In both works the
protagonist dies a tragic, untimely death. There are other
important similarities between the two books, but significant
differences as well, particularly in the authors' attitudes
toward the conflict itself. Galdós believed completely in
Pepe Rey's cause, while Turgenev was ambivalent about the
forces his hero represented; in tone and structure each novel
reflects its author's feelings. There appears to be no doubt
that Galdós knew Fathers and Sons and made use of certain
of its ideas in creating his own independent and highly personal interpretation of the conflict between generations" (abstract).

Several critics discuss whether or not the novel
should be considered a melodrama. Roberto G. Sánchez,
"Doña Perfecta and the histrionic projection of character,"
Revista de estudios hispánicos, 3 (1969), 175-90, and
Rodolfo Cardona in his introduction to Doña Perfecta (New
York: Dell Publishing Co. 1965), pp. 11-130, present
arguments on this point.

Sánchez notes that numerous critics consider Doña
Perfecta's dramatic quality to be among its most striking
features (pp. 175-76). According to him, "The present
study proposes to examine the nature of this dramatic
quality from somewhat different premises: that the dramatic
force acknowledged by all resides primarily in the title
character, that of Doña Perfecta, and that the novel does
not manage to avoid melodrama but rather glories in it"
(p. 176).

He finds the novel "melodramatic in intent" (p. 177)
and further states that "indeed, melodrama is the guiding
spirit of the novel. It is there in the suspense with which
Galdós works toward a confrontation of the two antagonistic
forces" (p. 177). His views, based on several portions of
the novels, are ably argued.

Cardona's introduction is an excellent and useful
one and is intended primarily for students who are reading
this novel. He finds that the novel "smacks of melodrama"
(p. 18) and elsewhere he speaks of "the danger of a melodramatic situation" being "avoided" (p. 22). His introduction presents the student with a summary of recent criticism
of the novel.

Josette Blanquat, "De l'histoire au roman Doña Perfecta: approche méthodologique," Actes du VIe Congrès
national des hispanistes francais de l'Enseignement supérieur
(Annales littéraires de l'Université de Besançon, 126, 1971),
pp. 59-71, is interested in the data provided by novels on
"l'état social, psychologique, moral, de l'époque; de juger ce
témoignage et de reconnaître souvent l'état d'esprit de
l'artiste au moment de la création" (p. 60). She reviews in
special detail various journals of the time that discussed
religious ideas (pp. 62-66). She calls the novel "un document
sociologique" (p. 66). Yet it is even more, "C'est l'oeuvre
d'un visionnaire dont l'imagination est de nature mythique"
(p. 68). In her last paragraph she notes that "En nous
permettant de retrouver le point de départ du romancier et de
confronter deux images, celle du roman et celle de la presse,
la méthode historique ne nous met pas seulement en mesure
de juger Galdós historien et mythographe de son temps. Loin
de nous enfermer dans un passé clos, elle nous a mis en bon
chemin pour juger l'oeuvre littéraire en elle-même, rectifier,
parfois, les erreurs de la critique à son sujet et découvrir,
avec la structure du roman, de nouveaux aspects du génie du
romancier...." (p. 71).

Richard A. Cardwell, "Galdós' Doña Perfecta: art or
argument?" Anales galdosianos, 7 (1972), 29-47, finds many
reasons to disagree with previous interpretations of the novel.
He writes: "From what follows, it becomes increasingly obvious that Galdós is far from concerned to present 'una interpretación simbólica de la vida española' as Gullón has observed (op. cit., p. 62). The novel is no simple confrontation of liberalism with reactionary orthodoxy, of tolerance
with intolerance or materialism with spiritualism. Nor does
it attempt to portray exclusively fictionalised 'attitudes' as

Gullón suggests in his judgement that Rey 'es el representante
de otra España, de la clase de hombre a quién el autor mira
con esperanza, porque le considera capaz de traer al país
espíritu de comprensión y libertad' (62). It outlines a network of complex human relationships wherein the author is
aware that he is only just beginning to apprehend the essentials and that more subtle and intangible factors must for the
moment elude his immature grasp. It is these subtle relationships and interactions and not the partisan interests that
feed them which provide the substance of tragedy. The
'oculta fuente' is revealed as Maria Remedios. The twin
impulses of material ambition and a sense of inferiority
interact, complicate and nourish one another; they set up a
chain reaction of behaviour patterns that travel outwards
through each character in turn. The conflict is not rooted
in ideology alone. As Galdós further develops the narrative
intrigues and the personality of Remedios, it is increasingly
obvious that the widespread antagonism to Rey is not based
on provincial obscuranist mistrust or ideological difference.
It stems from the all too human source of an ambitious
mother whose plans have been thwarted. The tale of how
Remedios intimidates, emotionally blackmails and finally
wears down the resistance of her uncle so that he capitulates
to her demands to use force against Rey illustrates the power
of an unbridled resolve" (p. 37).

Vernon A. Chamberlin, "Doña Perfecta: Light and
Darkness, Good and Evil," in Galdós..., (Mary Washington
College...), pp. 57-70, is of interest not only because of
Chamberlin's discussion of his idea that "the contrasting
interplay of light and darkness, as well as the use of animal
imagery constitute two of the most forceful and effective
techniques which Galdós uses to work on the subconscious"
(p. 57), but for his comments on how to teach the novel
(p. 67); he states that it "should be taught as a didactic
novelistic adaptation of classical tragedy." He feels that
the students should be told ahead of time that they are dealing with a tragedy, "so that they concentrate on, appreciate,
and learn from the consummate technical skills which Galdós
employs and, very importantly, also understand the didactic
social message with its positive and negative value systems."

Vernon A. Chamberlin, "The significance and artistry
of the sound effects in Galdós' Doña Perfecta," Homenaje a
Sherman H. Eoff (Madrid, Castalia, 1970), pp. 79-85, concludes with these two paragraphs:

"Consequently, we may reasonably hypothesize that when Galdós was creating Doña Perfecta as a novelized adaptation of classical tragedy, he knew well that emotive sound effects would properly accompany his narration if it were written in pure dramatic form. However, since he was not writing a drama to be seen and heard (but rather a highly dramatic novel to be read), he, perforce, dispensed with off-scene special effects and musical instrumentation.

"Galdós also did not have the benefit of a tonal language or rhythmically emotive poetry. Consequently, he chose to work with selected realistic elements, which not only introduce the reader into the ambiance and mood of the tragic conflict between liberalism and Carlism in nineteenth-century Spain, but which also well symbolize and vivify the struggle: church bells, trumpet blasts, horses hoofs, and gunfire. These and other sounds Galdós wove purposefully into his tragic narrative, achieving thereby a heightening and intensification of the dramatic conflicts, suspense, and emotional involvement of his reader" (pp. 84-85).

Vernon A. Chamberlin's "A Soviet introduction to Doña Perfecta (1964)" will be published in a forthcoming issue of Anales galdosianos. The brief introduction by Chamberlin is followed by an English translation by Chamberlin of the Russian prologue by K.V. Taurinov to the Soviet edition of Doña Perfecta (Moscow, Editorial "Enseñanza Superior," 1964). The translated prologue is entitled "Benito Pérez Galdós and his novel Doña Perfecta." Chamberlin desires that the "readers of Anales galdosianos may have the clearest understanding possible of how Galdós is viewed by an official government commentator and, more importantly, how the Soviet youth of today is introduced to Don Benito."

The prologue is an extremely interesting Soviet commentary on Galdós as a whole; only about a third of it is devoted to an interpretation of the novel itself.

Gustavo Correa, "El arquetipo de Orbajosa en Doña Perfecta," La Torre, no. 26 (1959), 121-36, reprinted in El simbolismo religioso..., pp. 35-48, examines "el arquetipo de Orbajosa con su diversidad de perspectivas a la luz de los rasgos que constituyen un ámbito artístico y cultural, y en relación con el dramatismo de la acción" (p. 36). On

p. 48, Correa writes: "Su doble dimensión en el espacio
y en el tiempo incorpora aspectos peculiares de la geografía
y la historia de España a la sustancia novelística. Su cambio
de sentido, de signo positivo en negativo, abarca todas las
categorías novelísticas y marca la dirección fatalista y catas-
trófica de la acción. El entrecruzamiento de las dos maneras
de visión corresponde a la antinomia Orbajosa-Madrid, y nos
muestra la manera como opera un sistema cultural, tradicional y autónomo, frente a otro de características disímiles
y absorbentes. El ángulo de la perspectiva externa (Madrid)
descubre un plano de visión irónica y trágica sobre el mundo
interno de Orbajosa. Pero este último revela su densidad
emocional al conferir una dimensión religiosa a su sistema
cultural cerrado."

John V. Falconieri, "Un capítulo de Galdós que no se
le olvidó a Cervantes," Revista de estudios hispanicos, 6
(1972), 145-51, notes the influence of Cervantes on Doña
Perfecta and concentrates his remarks on the second chapter
of the novel. He finds that "Este-capítulometáfora constituía
para Galdós una clave con la cual entraba en los dos mundos
psíquicos de la novela y con la cual esperaba que entrase
también el lector" (p. 150). He writes that "Por eso, Galdós
evoca una simpatía por su Orbajosa-España, irremediable-
mente fundidas en su mente. Lo importante entonces no son
las convenciones y las instituciones ni la reforma de éstas,
sono cómo penetra la civilización dentro de cada uno de
nosotros y cómo nos sirve en nuestros pasos por el mundo"
(pp. 150-51).

Luciano E. García Lorenzo, "Sobre la técnica drama-
tica de Galdós: Doña Perfecta de la novela a la obra teatral,"
Cuadernos hispanoamericanos, nos. 250-52 (1970-1971), 445-
71, writes that "El método que seguiremos en este trabajo
será precisamente el de tomar intriga, personajes, tiempo,
espacio y lengua en la novela y en el drama de Galdós titu-
lados Doña Perfecta y extraer del análisis comparativo de
esos cinco puntos una serie de conclusiones que esperamos
puedan ayudar a un mejor conocimiento de la génesis de la
obra dramática galdosiana" (pp. 446-47).

Stephen Gilman, "Las referencias clásicas de Doña
Perfecta. Tema y estructura de la novela," Nueva revista
de filología hispánica, 3 (1949), 353-62, desires "volver
a Doña Perfecta en un intento de comprender algo en su
relación novelística con la totalidad de la obra de Galdós.
Espero que de esta manera se haga luz en torno a la con-

tradictoria posición de Doña Perfecta como novela" (p. 353).
Gilman "compares the structure of this novel to that of a
Greek tragedy" (Cardona, p. 262).

Ricardo Gullón, "Doña Perfecta: invención y mito,"
Cuadernos hispanoamericanos, nos. 250-52 (1970-1971), 393-
414; Explicación de textos literarios, 1 (1972), 14-28, and
Técnicas de Galdós, pp. 23-56, has the following sections:
La creación del personaje, Estructura, El personaje en su
lenguaje, El antagonista, Mitologías, Función de la imagen.
El ritmo y el tono. This is an outstanding stylistic study
of the novel.

C.A. Jones, "Galdós's second thoughts on Doña
Perfecta," Modern Language Review, 54 (1959), 570-73, is
a study of the variants in two 1876 editions of this novel.
He concludes that "The broad-minded tolerance of Galdós'
later work is glimpsed much more in the later version of
this novel, which would be interpreted as a plea for modera-
tion on the part of both the conservative and the progressive
despite the survival of the cryptic final chapter. Certainly
the later version gives evidence of very much better taste,
and of a greater artistic sense" (p. 573).

Jennifer Lowe, "Theme, imagery and dramatic irony
in Doña Perfecta," Anales galdosianos, 4 (1969), 49-53, concludes with this paragraph: "The story of Doña Perfecta
with all its exaggerations and unlikely situations is a mecha-
nism by which much of the theme is conveyed to us. The
conflict between Madrid and the provinces, between enlightened
progressive thought and reactionary obscurantism is presented
in terms of a struggle between life and death, light and darkness. Pepe is killed, a dark cloud descends. Incidents and
comments must often be interpreted figuratively, the significance of the images and their frequent independence need to
be analysed, the dramatic irony to be understood. When this
has been done, although story and theme are still far from
having the artistically satisfying integration which we find in
Galdós' later works, the impact which they make on us and
our reaction to them are considerably strengthened" (p. 53).

Matías Montes Huidobro, "Benito Pérez Galdós: el
lenguaje como fuerza destructiva," XIX: Superficie y fondo
del estilo [Estudios de Hispanófila, 17, 1971], pp. 23-35, is
a stylistic study of the novel. Montes states that "En el
presente trabajo vamos a limitarnos a hacer un breve análisis comparativo del lenguaje de tres personajes de Doña

Perfecta y de algunos detalles complementarios utilizados por
Galdós en la presentación de sus diálogos. De ahí surgirán
tres direcciónes diferentes:

"1. Una dirección representada por Pepe Rey. El
lenguaje que se proyecta en una sola dirección, expresión
directa y sin recovecos de los sentimientos y de la razón.

"2. Otra dirección representada por don Inocencio.
El lenguaje se proyecta con un doble juego. Este doble
juego de don Inocencio, junto a su enloquecedora prolijidad,
llevarán a Pepe Rey, representante de la forma directa del
lenguaje, a perderse dentro del laberinto verbal.

"3. Una tercera dirección representada por Doña
Perfecta. En ella el lenguaje se hace más rico y variado.
Tiene multitud de facetas destinadas a aniquilar la primera
dirección de la palabra. No representa el lenguaje ni siquiera a una mujer, sino a toda una unidad social y política
que requiere esa multitud de direcciónes para ejercer su
dominio y lograr la destrucción en caso necesario" (p. 23).

Jorge Arturo Ojeda, "El siglo XIX on Doña Perfecta,"
Comunidad, 3 (1968), 688-90, attempts too much in too little
space. He finds that Galdós "no se immiscuye en los personajes ni en las ideas. Hay una especie de vida preponderante-
mente exterior, porque los hechos se imponen en la narración.... Pero con su prosa llena de ángel y a diversos tonos,
Benito Pérez Galdós dibuja magistralmente, como en trasfondo
siniestro y submarino, el carácter de doña Perfecta.... Doña Perfecta es una novela que resplandece por su creación
de mundo, ajena a las narraciones de aconteceres sin antes
ni después, ajena a personas y objetos dichos escuetamente;
es ajena también a las intimidades arbitrarias del escritor"
(p. 690).

William H. Shoemaker, "Cara y cruz de la novelística
galdosiana," Hispanic Studies in Honor of Nicholson B. Adams,
edited by John Esten Keller and Karl-Ludwig Selig (Chapel
Hill: University of North Carolina Press, 1966), pp. 151-66
(reprinted in Shoemaker's Estudios sobre Galdós, pp. 241-57),
is a study of Doña Perfecta and Misericordia. Shoemaker
states that the two novels have many points in common as
well as a few differences. "Me he de limitar en este ensayo
a algunos de tema y contenido, otros de actitud e intención
o tendencia del autor, y varios de forma en cuanto a estructura y procedimientos--esto último casi nunca tocado por los
críticos" (p. 152).

Robert J. Weber, "Galdos and Orbajosa," Hispanic
Review, 21 (1953), 348-49, reprints a letter from Apuntes
of April 5, 1896 "in which Galdós clearly states his opinion
about the state of Spain in terms of the fictional Orbajosa"
(p. 348). Weber feels that "The theatre was a powerful
agent which I believe Galdós intended to utilize at the height
of his popularity as a novelist in order to push Spaniards
into what he believed was the right course, toward an enlightened, secular yet truly Christian Spain" (p. 349).

Claire-Nicole Kerék, "Le personnage de Pepe Rey
dans Doña Perfecta de Pérez Galdós," in Hommage à Georges
Fourrier (Paris, Les Belles Lettres, 1973), pp. 209-33
(Annales littéraires de l'Université de Besançon, 142), is the
fullest treatment that has yet appeared on the character of
Pepe Rey. The author carefully analyzes the text to see
what it shows concerning Pepe Rey and reaches the conclusion that he is "donc un homme profondément simple, il
représente comme un juste équilibre des différentes qualites
désirables chez un homme du XIXe siècle, sans qu'aucune,
sauf son amour pour la science, l'emporte sur les autres.
Mais nous verrons aussi que, pour le propos de Galdós, il
importait peu de la caractériser davantage: l'essentiel était
qu'il possédât his traits qui pouvaient opposer Madrid à la
province" (pp. 216-17). Her view is contrary to that of
many critics who see Pepe Rey as Galdós' mouthpiece. She
writes: "Il est bien évident que Pepe Rey n'eest pas on
porte-parole, mais un pion qu'il déplace pour prouver une
idée" (p. 225). This article contains much of interest concerning Doña Perfecta, its ideology and its place in Galdós'
overall work.

David Hannay, "Doña Perfecta: A Spanish Novel,"
Temple Bar, 58 (March 1880), 326-42, is still, despite its
age, one of the longest accounts of this novel in English;
It consists almost entirely of a summary of the plot and a
discussion of the characters.

William Dean Howells was one of those responsible
for introducing this novel to the reading public of the United
States. His review first appeared in Harper's Bazaar, 28
(Nov. 2, 1895), 886; it was then published as an introduction
to the translation of the novel, v-xiii, and can now be easily
found in his Prefaces to Contemporaries (1882-1920, facsim-
ile reproductions with an introduction and bibliographical note
by George Arms, William M. Gibson, Frederic C. Marston,
Jr., Gainesville, Florida: Scholars' Facsimiles and Reprints, 1957), pp. 53-61.

Doña Perfecta, translated by Robert Marrast, introduction by María Pérez Galdós (Paris: Les Editeurs français
réunis, [1965]), reproduces the prologue in a French translation that Max Aub first published in his Mexican edition to the
novel, pp. 13-16. It is a pity that this critic's study is not
longer. Aub's "Prólogo para una edición popular de Doña
Perfecta" has also been published in his Pruebas (Madrid:
Editorial Ciencia nueva, 1967), pp. 163-85.

Pauline Marshall reviewed Harriet de Onfs' translation and introduction to her translation of this novel (Great
Neck, N.Y.: Barron's Educational Series, 1960, 235pp.)
in Hispania, 43 (1960), 634. The introduction, she states,
is "of value particularly to those unfamiliar with the work
of Pérez Galdós."

Jaroslav Rosendorfsky, "Algunas observaciones sobre
Doña Perfecta de B. Pérez Galdós y La Casa de Bernarda
Alba de F. Garcia Lorca," Etudes romanes de Brno, 2, 114
(1966), 181-210, discusses in pp. 182-200 "la contextura
ideológica y social de doña Perfecta en atención especial a
algunas figuras más salientes, cuya fisionomia puede intere-
sarnos por cuanto tengan alguna relación con el ambiente y
los personajes respectivos de La casa de Bernarda Alba"
(p. 200). Pages 200-09 discuss the Lorca play, while the
last two pages develop the comparison that the author wishes
to make between the novel and the play. He writes that "Es
en primer lugar el ambiente de un pronunciado color local
que enlaza Doña Perfecta con La casa de Bernarda Alba....
También las dos protagonistas principales resultan condi-
cionadas por este ambiente en su modalidad geográfica (clima,
áspero, población escasa), histórica (behetría rural, tendencias centralistas) y económica (falta de industrias, una mayoría aplastante del elemento campesino" (pp. 209-10). He
feels that "Nos muestran estas dos figuras una vez mas la
necesidad de radicales reformas en la estructura básica de
España--reformas cuya necesidad se hace cada vez más
urgente e inevitable" (p. 210).

Emma Susana Speratti Piñero, "Paralelo entre Doña
Perfecta y La casa de Bernarda Alba," Revista de la Universidad de Buenos Aires, 4 (1959), 369-78, declares that
"quizá parezca disparatado establecer un paralelo entre Doña
Perfecta y La casa de Bernarda Alba" (p. 369). She then
states: "Pero con todo, tipos y situaciones como los que
aparecen en Doña Perfecta y en La casa de Bernarda Alba,
no son tan infrecuentes como para que Lorca no pudiera
crear su personaje y su obra sin tener en cuanta los de

Galdós. Hay coincidencia, sin embargo" (p. 371) and these
"coincidencias" are discussed for the rest of the article.

Its influence on foreign literatures. Few 19th-century
Spanish novels have had greater influence on authors in other
countries.

Two articles discuss Doña Barbara and Doña Perfecta.
They are: David T. Sisto, "Doña Perfecta and Doña Barbara," Hispania, 37 (1954), 167-70, and Leo Ulrich, "Doña
Perfecta y Doña Barbara. Un caso de ramificación literaria,"
Revista iberoamericana, 16 (1950), 13-29. Sisto finds "an
interesting psychological parallel" (p. 167) between the two
novels and some of their major and minor characters. Ulrich
writes "de la semejanza incontestable de ciertos motivos,
existentes entre ambos libros; pero dichos motivos se desarrollan en sentido opuesto, resultando el libro de Gallegos
algo como una 'palinodia' del de Pérez Galdós. Tratamos,
no de encontrar dependencia positiva, sino de estudiar la
morfologia inmanente de un motivo literario, y sus razones"
(p. 14).

Sisto is also the author of "Pérez Galdós' Doña
Perfecta and Louis Bromfield's A Good Woman," Symposium,
11 (1957), 273-80, in which he points to parallels between
the two novels. He concludes that "Implications of direct
influence remain moot.... The basic similarities between
the two women and between other personages of the two
stories, as well as between the two provincial backgrounds
are nevertheless of interest to observers of creative perception and the literary process" (p. 279).

Donald F. Brown, "An Argentine Doña Perfecta:
Galdós and Manuel Gálvez," Hispania, 47 (1964), 282-87,
finds that Graciana in Gálvez' Perdido en su noche should
be considered as among the "literary progeny" of Doña
Perfecta.

Francis S. Heck, "Dos mujeres sin alma (La phari-
seienne y Doña Perfecta)," Duquesne Hispanic Review, 4
(1965), 79-89, arrives at no definite answer to the question
"¿es posible que Doña Perfecta ejerciese influencia sobre La
Pharisienne? ¿Conocía François Mauriac la obra de Galdós?"
(p. 89). Heck states that "La literatura española del siglo
diez y nueve y la literatura francesa del siglo veinte nos
ofrecen dos mujeres que poseen una misma personalidad.
Doña Perfecta y Brigitte Pian hacen uso de la religión y de
su posición social para marchar como conquistadores hollando

a su paso a cunatos se interponen en su camino. A los
ojos de las dos mujeres la busca de la felicidad es un
crimen contra Dios, el Dios cuya ley ellas interpretan es
Orbajosa y Larjuzon. Sus vidas son estériles y austeras
en las que falta el amor" (pp. 88-89).

La familia de León Roch

Alfredo Rodríguez, "Aspectos de la elaboración de
La familia de León Roch," in Aspectos de la novela de
Galdós, pp. 35-65, was first published as "Algunos aspectos
de la elaboración literaria de La familia de León Roch,"
PMLA, 72 (1967), 121-27. Rodríguez believes that Galdós'
source for this volume could have been Jules Michelet's Le
prêtre, la famille et la femme. He notes "que la actitud
galdosiana que se proyecta en todo este grupo de novelas
de temática religiosa se asemeja muchísimo al ataque frontal
contra la religion décimonona conque Michelet produjo, una
treintena de años, toda una controversia religiosa en Francia"
(p. 46). The article presents both "paralelos anotados" and
"algunas afinidades menos precisas entre los dos autores"
(p. 57). It shows how Galdós took his source material and
made of the subject matter a novel.

Juan López-Morillas, "Galdós y el krausismo: La
familia de León Roch," Revista de Occidente, no. 60 (1968),
331-57; reprinted in his Hacia el 98: literatura, sociedad,
ideología (Barcelona, Ariel, 1972), pp. 81-119 (Letras e
ideas: minor, 2), states that "es la novela de mayor grava-
men ideológico que ha salido de la pluma de Galdós" (p. 351).
This article has seven parts: I. El cultivo del hombre;
II. Disciplina e intransigencia; III. Hubris racionalista;
IV. Amor y pedagogía; V. A mis soledades voy...; VI. El
ruedo ibérico; and VII. La tiranía de la vida.

The article demonstrates the author's belief in the
importance of Minuta de un testamento (1876) by Gumersindo
de Azcarate. On p. 334, López-Morillas writes that "no
cabe duda alguna que el librito de Azcárate sugiere a Galdos
La familia de León Roch Galdós se propone mostrar lo que
le sucede a la 'idea pura' cuando abandona su empíreo y
baja a la plazuela pública para convertirse en 'ideología
aplicada.' Y, de paso, retrata con viva compasión la congo-
ja del hombre de noble espíritu que no puede resignarse a
que el mundo no sea mejor de lo que es."

Gustavo Correa, "Las configuraciones religiosas en La familia de León Roch de Pérez Galdós," Revista hispánica moderna, 26 (1960), 85-95, was reprinted as "La pasión mística de María Egipciaca en La familia de León Roch," in El simbolismo religioso..., pp. 63-79.

There are an introduction and sections entitled "La superestructura novelística" and "La estructura interna." Correa notes that his analysis "nos ha representada que se extiende a los personajes, a las instituciones religiosas y sociales y a las situaciones de todo orden dentro del contexto de la obra. Esta índole caricaturesca de la superestructura novelística obedece, sin embargo, a una desfiguración de caracter interno en la interrelación de los varios personajes y en el juego de las pasiones humanas" (p. 68). He states on p. 64 that "la superstructura novelística se revela artísticamente a través de esquemas desfigurativos de la realidad representada. El misticismo aberrante de María Egipciaca constituye, en sí, una deformación de la beatería en los hogares españoles." He notes that "En su estructura interna la novela muestra la interrelación de cuatro personajes principales: León Roch, María Egipciaca, Luis Gonzaga Tellería y Pepa Fúcar" (p. 68). On p. 69 he writes: "El desarrollo novelístico nos presenta a los personajes distribuidos en las dos parejas siguientes: a) León Roch--María Egipciaca, b) Pepa Fúcar--Federico Cimarra. Estas últimas son verdaderas desfiguraciones de la unión matrimonial y conducen inexorablemente a la catástrofe."

La fontana de oro

The fullest discussion of this novel is that of Marie-Claire Petit, Galdós et La fontana de oro: genèse de l'ouevre d'un romancier (Paris, Ediciones hispano-americanas, 1972), pp. 1-105. This volume contains an introduction, a conclusion and the following six chapters: Structure du roman, Interprétation de l'Histoire, Les personnages secondaires, Les personnages principaux, Les grands thèmes galdosiens (Imagination et pathologie), and Le double rôle du monde matériel.

Jacques Beyrie, "Résurgences galdosiennes dans La Casa de Bernarda Alba," Caravelle, no. 13 (1969), 97-108, first discusses the Speratti Piñero article (see p. 83) and then suggests that there are similarities between the García

Lorca play and La fontana de oro.   Themes and characters
are compared.   He notes, for example, "Certes, l'humour
bonhomme, l'ironie de Galdós, ne saurainet se confondre
avec le lyrisme brûlant de Lorca.   Malgré cette différence
de ton, le thème avec toutes ses incidences et les situations
demeurent cependant les mêmes" (p. 102).

Albert Dérozier, "El 'pueblo' de Pérez Galdós en La
fontana de oro," Cuadernos hispanoamericanos, nos. 250-52
(1970-1971), 285-311 has an introduction and the following
parts: I. Historia y creación literaria; II.   ¿Pueblo y afronta-
miento de clases? III.   Lázaro y Pérez Galdós a la hora de
la alternativa política.   Dérozier states that "Examinaré,
pues, La fontana de oro con respecto a la atmósfera política
que la suscitó; esto es, relacionándola con el liberalismo,
con la nocion de 'pueblo' y con las clases sociales en el
siglo XIX, entre 1820 y 1870.   Y trataré, al mismo tiempo,
de mostrar cuál es la consecuencia de esta 'circunstancia
histórica' sobre la creación literaria misma" (p. 285).

Albert Dérozier, "Le 'peuple' de Pérez Galdos dans
La fontana de oro," Affrontements de classes et création
littéraire, 1971 (Annales littéraires de l'Université de Besançon, 129), pp. 108-30, discussion, pp. 131-42, writes
that "J'étudierai donc La fontana de oro à la lumière de
l'atmosphère politique qui l'a vue naître, c'est-à-dire en
liaison avec le libéralisme, la notion du 'peuple' et le rapport des classes sociales au XIXe siècle 9entre 1820 et
1870).   Et j'essayerai, dans le même temps, de montrer
quelle est la répercussion de cette 'circonstance historique'
sur la création littéraire elle-même" (p. 108).   After a brief
introductory section, the article proper is divided into three
sections: 1. Histoire et creation littéraire; 2. "Peuple" et
affrontement de classes? and 3. Lazaro et Pérez Galdós à
l'heure du choix politique.   Dérozier insists that "La pré-
occupation de Pérez Galdós est donc essentiellement politique..." (p. 121) and that "c'est que c'est un roman fondé
sur une atmosphère exclusivement politique, ou à peu près:
c'est le premier essai en Espagne dans le genre" (p. 108).

Joaquín Gimeno Casalduero, "Una novela y dos
enlances: La fontana de oro," Ateneo, no. 88 (Sept. 15,
1955), 6-8, is a discussion of the differences in the two
versions of this novel.   After a brief introduction, there is
a discussion of the 1870 version and then one of the 1883
version.   The author notes that "Una profunda diferencia,
cargada de significado, se observa entre una y otra edición,

diferencia que radica precisamente en el desenlace, el cual,
en 1883, adopta una solución nueva y extraña, totalmente
distinta de la anterior." In his conclusion, he notes that
"No es de extrañar que la version de 1883 no alcanzara exito y se olvidara rápidamente.... No es de extrañar, repito:
los lectores preferían resbalar sobre la comodidad del primer
desenlace, ajenos a toda amargura de trasfondo, olvidando con
la solución feliz lo desastroso de la politica" (p. 8).

Angel González Palencia, "Para la historia de La
fontana de oro," Entre dos siglos (Madrid, 1943), pp. 103-
14 (publicado, en parte, en Revista de la Biblioteca, Archivo y Museo del Ayuntamiento de Madrid, 3 [1926], 110-13),
has the following sections: 1. Traspaso de "La Fontana de
Oro" en 1760; 2. Inventario de la botillería; 3. Información
testifical sobre el nuevo dueño; 4. Examen de cocinero del
nuevo dueño; 5. Licencia para ejercer la industria de hoste-
lero a Barbarán, y condiciones de ella; 6. Comparación de la
botillería de La Fontana, descrita en el protocolo notarial,
con la imaginada por Pérez Galdós. This article emphasizes
"la historicidad de las novelas históricas de Pérez Galdós"
(p. 112).

Monroe Z. Hafter, "The hero in Galdós' La fontana de
oro," Modern Philology, 57 (1959), 36-43, "has two purposes:
to show textually how Galdós presents Lázaro and to explain
his vision of the hero through an examination of the novelist's
earlier and contemporary writings" (p. 37).

Carroll B. Johnson, "The café in Galdós' La fontana
de oro," Bulletin of Hispanic Studies, 44 (1965), 112-17,
shows that the "description of the interior of the café" presents in this novel a "vital function as an integral part of an
artistic whole. An intimate relationship exists here between
setting, character and action, and an awareness of this relationship is essential to the comprehension of the artistic
structure of the novel" (pp. 112-13). Johnson shows "how
the setting of the Fontana de oro functions on the plot level,
in relation to the great political events of the novel. In addition, the café and its atmosphere function in direct relation
to the principal character, Lázaro" (pp. 114-15). He concludes that "the café in this novel, because from the first it
was conceived and created artistically and not historically, is
a vital, functioning part of an integrated artistic unit, La
fontana de oro" (p. 118).

Juan López-Morillas, "Historia y novela en el Galdós

primerizo: en torno a La fontana de oro," Revista hispánica
moderna, 31 (1965), 273-85; revised and enlarged text published
in his Hacia el 98: literatura, sociedad, ideologia (Barcelona, Ariel, 1972), pp. 45-77 (Letras e ideas: minor, 2) shows
that "la lectura de La fontana de oro revela que muchos de
los afanes ideológicos, objetivos estéticos, temas, símbolos,
tópicos y recursos técnicos que se echan de ver en el Galdós
maduro están ya sustancialmente presentes en esta su primi-
cia novelística.   Y ello es, a nuestro entender, testimonio
de la unidad y cohesión de una labor literaria que abarca
cerca de medio siglo" (p. 285).   He mentions the novel's defects only on the last page.   These he finds to be "la falta
de economía en el estilo, la inseguridad con que se manejan
ciertos recursos estructurales, la afición a detalles imperti-
nentes, la fácil y transparente simbología."

Most of López-Morillas' first chapter, "La revolución
de septiembre y la novela española," of Hacia el 98: literature, sociedad, ideología deals with this novel.

Florian Smeija, "Alternative ending to La fontana de
oro," Modern Language Review, 61 (1966), 426-33, discusses
the ending to this novel as found in the second edition of 1871
published by José Noguera and reprinted by Brockhaus.   This
ending is not that found in the Madrid edition of 1870, nor in
the third edition, Madrid, La Guirnalda, 1885.   Pages 426-
29 reprint this changed ending.   Smeija concludes his remarks with this sentence: "By returning to his original ending which 'se avenía mejor que nada a las condiciones
artísticas que quiso dar a su libro,' Galdós the artist proved
he was capable of substituting an inferior one, but that he
also had the good sense, and the courage, to restore his
first idea" (p. 433).

Marie A. Wellington, "The awakening of Galdós'
Lazaro," Hispania, 55 (1972), 463-70, feels that the character of Lázaro in La fontana de oro has been misjudged by
previous critics.   She writes: "While it poses no problem
to marshall evidence of Lázaro's ineptness, it is, in my
judgment, a mistake to consider him an inveterate bungler
meant to fail.   I contend, on the contrary, that Galdós intends him to be a new kind of hero worthy of imitation.
Dealing with a period of liberal revolt in Spain, La fontana
de oro focuses on forces of the past which militate against
forces of the contemporary age to produce social tensions.
The counterbalancing of these forces creates in Lázaro conflicts which he must ultimately resolve in accord with his

own nature and his own conscience, and I find Galdós' portrayal of him neither superficial nor wanting in the 'psychological design' which Prof. Eoff sees principally in the author's later works'' (pp. 463-64; text of two footnotes omitted).

Benito Varela Jacome, "Realismo y romanticismo en
La fontana de oro," Eidos, no. 33 (1970), 55-71, has an introduction and the following sections: Estructura novelística,
Tensiones de la acción, Peregrinaje por el Madrid nocturno,
Doble desenlace, Comportamiento de los personajes, Relaciones sociométricas, Textura deformante, Historicidad de la
novela and Bipolarización ideológica.

Fortunata y Jacinta

Two books, Pedro Muñoz Peña, Juicio crítico de
"Fortunata y Jacinta" novela contemporanéa ... (Valladolid:
Imprenta y Librería nacional y extranjera de H. Rodríguez,
1888), 88pp., and Juan Menéndez y Arranz, Un aspecto de
la novela "Fortunata y Jacinta" (Madrid: Martín Villagroy,
1952), 74pp., discuss this most studied of Galdós' novels.

The rare little volume by Muñoz Peña (it would appear to exist in no library in the United States) is a reprinting of a series of reviews of the novel published in Lunes
literarios, a section of La Libertad (Valladolid), Nov. 21,
28, Dec. 5, 19, 1887. The various sections of the study
are: (1) Consideraciones generales, pp. 7-28; (2) Los caracteres, pp. 29-63; (3) La novela, pp. 64-88. It is an extraordinarily complete contemporary appraisal of the novel.

In chapter I, the reviewer states: "es decir que en
Fortunata y Jacinta, Galdós se presenta francamente naturalista y sigue sin imitación servil, sino con propia y personal
individualidad a Zola, a Daudet, a Goncourt y a los mejores
novelistas franceses" (p. 8).

In chapter II, he writes: "Desde luego puede asegu-
rarse que en pocas producciones de este género se encontra-
rán personajes tan bien delineados y tan interesantes como
los que aparecen en esta novela, no sólo por su valor in-
trínsico como creación artística, cuanto por ser figuras y
caracteres que parecen arrancados de la realidad misma,
que se mueven, obran y hablan como el común de las gentes,
participando todos ellos del sentido naturalista de que está
impregnada la novela" (pp. 30-31). On p. 62, he speaks of

"la fuerza creadora de la fantasía de Galdós, su maestría
artística y su profundo conocimiento del corazón humano al
par que el de las costumbres y vida española, pues todo lo
y todo lo analiza con exquisita perspecacia y acierto." No
one dealt in Galdós' lifetime with the characters of this
novel more than did this reviewer.

In chapter III, the reviewer emphasizes "el maravilloso análisis psicológico de los personajes, y ... la exacta y
viva pintura de las costumbres de nuestra sociedad" (p. 66).
After praising the novel for more than 80 pages, he has
some adverse criticism of three pages. He elaborates on
the fact that "El principal inconveniente de Fortunata y Jacinta está en la amplificación que Galdós ha dado a la doble
acción de la fábula, perjudicando el interés por la bifurca-
ción del argumento de la novela" (p. 85). He feels that
Galdós has overdone his use of "los cuadros de costumbres"
and "al estudio psicológico de los caracteres" (p. 85). He
comments on Galdós' language by declaring that some may
be critical of his use of some words, but he feels that "estos
vocablos y modismos, manejados por un escritor de buen
gusto, sirven para dar a la producción novelesca carácter de
obra y creación espontánea, de expresión real de la vida y
de la sociedad, y no ficción amanerada, convencional y falsa"
(p. 87).

The volume's last paragraph follows: "No queremos
continuar la tarea poco grata de señalar más reparos en una
obra tan excelente como Fortunata y Jacinta; y si alguién nos
tachara de haber sido nosotros también demasiado latos y
extensos en la apreciación y juicio de esta novela, responde-
remos, que mucho más merece, y no sólo juicios, apre-
ciaciones y alabanzas de nuestra modesta pluma, sino de
otras que tengan mayor lucidez, mayor notoriedad y mayores
alcances que la nuestra" (pp. 87-88).

Menéndez y Arranz states that upon his latest reading
of this novel, "me interesó, ante todo, lo que en las almas
de Jacinta y Fortunata, heroínas de la fábula, y de Guillermina Pacheco y Mauricia 'la Dura,' compañeras suyas en trabajos y afanes, pasaba. Galdós nos dice por medio de la
esposa de Santa Cruz y de la de Rubín, y sirviéndose también
de Guillermina lo fuerte que en la mujer es el instinto de
maternidad" (p. 7). "Si no estoy mal informado, este aspecto
de la obra, que la coloca en lugar aparte de cuantas novelas
se escribieron el siglo XIX, no siempre ha sido lo suficientemente destacado, a mi parecer, por la crítica ni ahora ni

antes" (p. 8). This volume has the following parts: (1)
Galdosianos, (2) De morfología novelística, (3) Peculiarida-
des galdosianas, (4) Fortunata y Jacinta, (5) El hilo de la
novela, (6) La vida, (7-9) Dramatis personae, (10) La pasión de maternidad, (11) El estilo, (12) La crítica de Clarín
y de Menéndez y Pelayo and (13) El patriotismo de Galdós.
The introduction is entitled "Es difícil."

The fullest discussion of this novel would seem to be
that of Thomas Clarke Meehan, "A formal analysis of Fortunata y Jacinta (a study in the long novel form)," (Ph.D. dissertation, University of Michigan, 1965, 835 leaves; Dissertation Abstracts, 26 [1966], 7321-22). Part One, chapters 1-
4, presents a discussion of the theory concerning this type of
novel. Part Two, chapters 5-11 applies the theory to an
analysis of Fortunata y Jacinta. Chapter V "is an introduction and treats the external qualities of Fortunata y Jacinta
which justify its classification as a representative of the
form. Chapter VI treats the genesis of the work and the
antecedents of Galdós' literary career leading up to his masterpiece. Chapter VII is a plot summary ... and Chapter
VIII is a view of the historical background of the work, its
secondary structural level.... Chapter IX studies its long
encompassed fictional time span, investigates Galdós' plotting
techniques and extracts the aesthetic 'design' or 'pattern' of
the novel. Having separated 'the canvas' (history) from 'the
weave' (fiction), Chapter X now put the two back together
to see 'the tapestry embroidered' (the artistic interweaving of
fiction and history, which contributes considerably to the illusion of a larger reality emanating from this epic novel.
The final chapter treats the remaining internal characteristics
of Fortunata y Jacinta established in the theoretical part of
the study which further justify its inclusion as a Spanish representative of the long, 'wide-angle' novel" (p. 7321).

Marie-Claire Petit, "Les sources balzaciennes de
Fortuna y Jacinta," Galdós et La fontana de oro..., (Paris:
Editiones Hispano-americanas, 1972), pp. 106-18, states
that "Mais, si l'on cherche la structure romanesque sur
laquelle repose le déroulement de cette fresque sociale, on
trouve une présence étrangère qui loin de gêner Galdós,
l'aide dans sa tâche créatrice au point qu'il faut, pour la
découvrir, une étude attentive des textes: c'est celle de
Balzac dans Béatrix, roman écrit en 1838 à 1844 et inclus
parmi les "Scènes de la vie privée" (p. 107).

The two novels are compared. Her final paragraph

follows: "Ainsi, Béatrix et Fortunata y Jacinta donnent
l'exemple d'une de ces rencontres où deux inspirations se
rejoignent et où, sur un canevas commun, deux tempéraments
différents, mais d'une puissance créatrice comparable, dé-
veloppent un thème fondamental dont 1 l'expression la plus
frappante dans sa concision revient à Balzac: 'L'être le
moins imparfait serait donce alors la femme, malgré ses
fautes et ses déraisons'" (Béatrix, p. 546).

S. Bacarisse, "The realism of Galdós: some reflec-
tions on language and the perception of reality," Bulletin of
Hispanic Studies, 42 (1965), 239-50, states the belief "that
a greater insight into the nature of literature will be gained
from the convergence upon language of both philosophy and
literary criticism" (p. 239). He declares on p. 246 that
"We shall go a long way towards realizing the extent of the
achievement of writers like Galdós if we take what they have
to say as they say it. The content of a novel is not an absolute entity immediately available to us, as, perhaps under-
standably, we have often assumed. To make any progress
we must begin to treat language as MATERIAL SUBSTANCE."
His last sentence is: "Reality retains its oracular character
because Galdós found means of offsetting the conceptualization
and logic of language." The article is a philosophical-critical
discussion and analysis of one passage from Fortunata y Jacinta (Obras completas, 3rd ed., V [Madrid, 1961], 536).

Ricardo Baeza, "Fortunata y Jacinta," Cursos y conferencias, 24 (1943), 129-38, believes that Galdós "no sólo
es el menos nacionalista de los grandes escritores, sino que
incluso es el menos nacional" (p. 130). He considers Fortunata y Jacinta his masterpiece and laments the fact that what
he considers Galdós' worst works have been those that have
been translated. On the whole, this article has more to do
with Galdós' reputation than with the novel that it supposedly
was discussing.

Lucille Virginia Braun, "Problems of literary creation
in five characters of Galdós' Fortunata y Jacinta" (Ph.D.
dissertation, University of Wisconsin, 1962, 316 leaves; Dissertation Abstracts, 22 [1962], 4011) is a study of Fortunata,
Juanito Santa Cruz, Guillermo Pacheco, Maximiliano Rubín
and Mauricia La Dura. The author writes that her "intent
is ... to illustrate in the principal characters important
perspectives of Galdós creative vision--how he viewed reality;
how he adapted the real world to the requirements of fiction;
by what means he achieved objectivity and why he occasionally

failed to do so; and what personal factors affected his vision" (p. 4011).

Lucille V. Braun, "Galdós' re-creation of Ernestina Manuel de Villena as Guillermina Pacheco," Hispanic Review, 38 (1970), 32-55, is an extraordinarily interesting discussion "based on new materials which enable us to analyze in some detail how Galdós went about the task of adapting a character taken from reality to the requirements of a fictional world" (p. 33). Guillermina Pacheco "was patterned after Ernestina Manual de Villena" (p. 32). This article reviews available biographical data, notes that Galdós "eulogized doña Ernestina in his 'Santos modernos,' written shortly after her death, at the very time he was beginning Fortunata y Jacinta" (p. 32). Braun states that "the final concern of the present article is Guillermina's role in the changing relationship of Fortunata and Jacinta" (p. 32).

J. L. Brooks, "The character of Doña Guillermina Pacheco in Galdós' novel, Fortunata y Jacinta," Bulletin of Hispanic Studies, 38 (1961), 86-94, takes issue with the opinions of Gullón, Eoff and Casalduero concerning Guillermina Pacheco's character. These authors, according to Brooks, who bases his opinions on quotations from their works, are "uncritical adulators" (p. 86). Brooks' aim "will be to show that, while Guillermina herself, her friends, and the recipients of her bounty, were quite convinced that she was truly charitable, the author had considerable doubts about the efficacy of a charity exercised in this way, and by such a person" (p. 86). His remarks are based on a careful reading of the novel. He feels that "she is hampered in her efforts to be truly charitable by the unbreakable bonds which bind her background by her oversimplification of religious doctrines" (p. 94).

Sherman H. Eoff, "The deification of conscious process. Benito Pérez Galdós, Fortunata y Jacinta (1886-1887)," in The Modern Spanish Novel (New York: New York University Press, 1961), pp. 120-47, is a study of the psychological development that takes place in the leading character and then to the "attendant implications of a moral-philosophical nature" (p. 138). Pages 141-44 compare the ideas of Galdós and the German Wundt to show "how the novelist reflected in creative art a major contemporaneous development in psychology" (p. 141). Eoff finds the novel to be "a high mark of the 'spiritual naturalism' which was very much a part of the public consciousness in Europe in the 1880's" (p. 146).

Sherman H. Eoff, "The treatment of individual personality in Fortunata y Jacinta," Hispanic Review, 17 (1949),
269-89, is a profound study of the relationship between the
novel's technique and the psychology of the characters. Eoff
writes: "Fortunata y Jacinta, perhaps the novelist's most
vigorous treatment of individual personality, is an excellent
example of Galdós' study of the individual's adjustment to
social and physical circumstances. In it the adjustmental
problem centers upon the individual's effort to satisfy his
self-esteem. Our purpose is to study the novel by an analysis of this theme, primarily as it is manifest in the psychological plot involving the two main characters" (pp. 269-70).
Eoff notes that "the course of the developing psychology in
the two main characters is presented ... in some detail"
(p. 271). He contends that "Now the important consideration
with respect to Galdós method is not merely his view of
personality formation nor the fact that his characters change.
The most Galdosian feature is the patient observation of the
change and the clear perspective with which the author views
the whole of the personality process" (p. 280).

España libre, suplemento de literatura y arte (Santiago
de Chile) has published three articles on this novel. They
are: Antonio R. Romera, "Fortunata y Jacinta: el monólogo
silente y Conan Doyle," Aug. 24, 1943, p. 27; Eleazar Huerta,
"Releyendo a Galdós. Fortunata y Jacinta. El estilo galdo-
siano--Lenguaje hablado, July 24, 1943, pp. 19-20; and
Huerta's "Fortunata y Jacinta," July 10, 1943, p. 11.

Of these, Romera's article would appear to be the
most useful to the critic. He states that "Quisiera compa-
rarla con la novela de James Joyce. Ulises, por estimar
que Galdós es, con Stendhal, el precursor del talento más
fuerte que el siglo XX hadado a la novelística europea."
He finds that "La segunda parte del relato abunda en él"
[es decir, "el monólogo silente"]. Y este monólogo es, como en Ulises, una serie de reflexíones inconexas a veces,
atravesadas por relámpagos de incidencias y otros recuerdos
que nada tienen que ver con el hilo del soliloquio." He believes "que la construcción física--si se me permite la ex-
presión--del monólogo, su realización en el plano de la
técnica se debe a Galdós."

The July 24, 1943 Huerta article has two parts:
"Humorismo y estilo" and "La locura de Maximiliano
Rubén."

Maximiliano is studied from the psychoanalytical viewpoint in Angel Garma, "Jacqueca, suedo--oligofrenia y delirio en una personaje de Galdós," Acta neuropsiquíatrico
argentina, 3 (1957), 143-54; reprinted in Ficción, no. 14
(1958), 84-102. Garma states that "El contenido psicolopató-
logico de la novela, especialmente la jaqueca, la seudo-oli-
gofrenia y el delirio psicótico de Maxmiliano, la hacen va-
liosa para un estudio psicoanalítico" (p. 85). His concluding
paragraph follows: "Las explicaciones de Maxmiliano no son
completas, pero señalan una interpretación psicológicamente
perfecta del tipo de las que suele hacer un psicoanalista en
delirios parecidos. Toda esta obra de Galdós merece ser
estudiada con gran detención. Entonces rasaltan en ella
méritos grandes de intuición y compresión psicológicas; son
los que permiten a un escritor genial adelantarse a los
descubrimientos científicos" (pp. 101-02).

Stephen Gilman, "The birth of Fortunata," Anales
galdosianos, 1 (1966) 71-83, notes that this novel "is a world
of interlaced streets, professions, and classes, perhaps the
most complex world ever to be constructed within the fron-
tiers of a single book" (p. 71). This article is an elaborate
discussion of the significance of the fact that Fortunata "is
... the only major character whose birth is ignored or rather
dismissed in one casual sentence...." (p. 76). Various types
and forms of symbolism in the novel are studied, with special
emphasis placed on the novel's first part.

Carlos Blanco-Aguinaga, "On 'The birth of Fortunata',"
Anales galdosianos, 3 (1968), 13-24, is a reply to Gilman's
article which Blanco-Aguinaga feels "offers a radically mistaken interpretation both of Fortunata as a character and of
the novel--Fortunata y Jacinta--as a whole" (p. 13). This
article and Gilman's should be read together, for they attempt to reply to each other's ideas.

Stephen Gilman, "Narrative presentation in Fortunata
y Jacinta," Revista hispánica moderna, 36 (1969), 288-301,
should be read in conjunction with his "The birth of Fortunata" and an article by Carlos Blanco Aguinaga to which this
may be considered a partial reply. Gilman notes that "The
present essay is at best only a tentative and partial answer
to these questions," i.e., "how does the narrator transform
raw material that is profoundly historical and social in origin
into a lasting work of art? Why are the Naturalistic novels
that are still worth reading anything but 'documents humains'?"
(p. 288). Part three of the article develops the theme that

this novel is "a virtual archetype of 19th century narrative
presentation" (p. 292). This extremely thought-provoking
article defies ready summarization. It is, however, one of
the most important critical studies on the novel.

Stephen Gilman, "The consciousness of Fortunata,"
Anales galdosianos, 5 (1970), 55-65, is also difficult to summarize. Gilman finds that "Fortunata's consciousness must
have been taken from life. Otherwise we should have to
claim not just that he was a precursor of Freud but that he
invented independently major portions of contemporary psychoanalytical theory" (p. 65). He notes that "In Fortunata's
case, however, Galdós set out to explore a completely healthy
consciousness, impervious to education, immune to society,
without ambition, resistant to history--a consciousness which,
in spite of passionate excess and gross errors of judgment,
grows, flourishes, exercises freedom, creates values, and
radiates truth" (p. 65).

Ricardo Gullón, "Estructura y diseño en Fortunata
y Jacinta," Papeles de Son Armadans, nos. 143-44 (1968),
223-316; reprinted in his Técnicas de Galdós, pp. 135-220,
must surely rank as among the best stylistic studies on this
novel. According to Gullón, "La estructura de Fortunata y
Jacinta pudiera describirse sumariamente como la superpo-
sición de dos figuras geométricas: una línea, en cuyos
extremos, a modo de polos, vibrasen las encarnaciones del
bien y el mal, y un triángulo o triángulos superpuestos a la
polaridad mencionada" (p. 223). I shall refrain from the
temptation of lengthy citations from this article and indicate
that its main divisions are: Estructura: triángulos cam-
biantes; Figuras del triángulo: (1) Fortunata, (2) Jacinta,
(3) Juanito, (4) Maxi, (5) Feijóo; Estructura: la polaridad
complementaria; Espacio y tiempo; Estratos espaciales;
Espacio y sus ámbitos; Ambitos novelescos: (1) Historia y
vida privada, (2) Negocios, comercia, (3) El continente de
la pobreza, (4) Tertulias; El tiempo: (1) Rectilíneo y circular, (2) Cronológico e interior (3) Conexión y dilatación;
Función del personaje: (1) Duplicación interior, (2) Enlaces,
(3) Confirmación y oposición; El autor como personaje; Elu-
sión como técnica, and notes.

Olga Kattan, "Madrid en Fortunata y Jacinta y en
La lucha por la vida: dos posturas," Cuadernos hispanoamericanos, nos. 250-51 (1970-1971), 546-78, has the following parts: Galdós y Madrid, Madrid en Fortunata y
Jacinta, Baroja y Galdós, intérpretes de Madrid and Madrid

en La lucha por la vida. It is a rather extensive study of
how Madrid is portrayed in this novel and what it symbolizes.
The article also compares the role that Madrid plays in this
novel with its role in Baroja's novel. The author notes that
Galdós "nos ofrece una precisa descripcion de las calles de
Madrid y su 'ambiente'" (p. 551). She declares that "Galdos
es un formidable paisajista urbano" (p. 551). She also states
that "El lector de Fortunata y Jacinta tiene la suerte de encontrarse con la descripción del paisaje físico de Madrid--
admitida su elaboración artística--y ademas con una serie
de relaciones individuales e interracciones sociales que le
procuran el conocimiento del discurrir diario de la vida en
Madrid" (p. 557).

Robert Kirsner, "Galdos' attitude towards Spain as
seen in the characters of Fortunata y Jacinta," PMLA, 66
(1951), 124-37, concludes with this paragraph: "Through the
imaginary reliving of individual lives in Fortunata y Jacinta
Galdós treats Spain artistically. He no longer reports on it,
as he had in the early novel; instead, he recreates his nation
with artistic insight and understanding. Galdós expresses
the spirit of Spain intuitively, not logically. His relationship
to his country is analogous to his relationship to his literary
creations. He is sympathetically objective. Just as he
strives to express the total lives of his characters, so he
dedicates himself to expressing the livingness of Spain. Consequently, in Fortunata y Jacinta Spain appears as a living
image which, like the characters of this novel, inspires a
sympathetic appreciation" (p. 137).

John William O'Neill, "Un estudio del psiquismo fe-
minino en el analisis estructural de Fortunata y Jacinta y
Madame Bovary," Revista de la Universidad de Madrid, 16
(1967), 33-37, notes that both of these novels are "desta-
cadas en su género, son raras mezclas de penetración
psicológica y de genio artístico. Ademas de abordarlas
como obras independientes, ha tratado el autor de esta tesis,
de hacer patente y ejemplificar las similitudes de construcción, apuntando hacia una influencia de Flaubert en el arte
novelístico de Galdós" (pp. 33-34).

Suzanne Raphaël, "Un extraño viaje de novios,"
Anales galdosianos, 3 (1968), 35-49, is an analysis of "Viaje
de novios," a chapter of the book's first part. The two
parts of the article are: Estructura del capítulo and El
capítulo V: génesis de la novela. The author feels that
this chapter "es el punto de arranque de Fortunata y Jacinta"

(p. 43). She also states: "Sobre todo, la estructura de
aquellas páginas contiene el germen e incluso determina el
ritmo de la novela entera...." (p. 43).

Geoffrey Ribbans, "Contemporary history in the structure and characterization of Fortunata y Jacinta," in Galdós
studies, pp. 90-113, shows in pertinent detail "that political
references play a considerable and deliberate part in the
characterization of Fortunata y Jacinta, within the structure
of which they have a clear and coherent purpose" (p. 91).
He takes issue with Eoff, who wrote that "Politics sometimes
forms the topic of conversation--usually among minor charac-
ters--but nowhere, after the semisocial novel El audaz, does
it become a major force in the treatment of personality"
(quoted from The novels of Pérez Galdós, p. 102, on pp. 90-
91).

Douglass Rogers, "The descriptive simile in Galdós
and Blasco Ibañez: a study in contrasts," Hispania, 53
(1970), 864-69, compares the use of similes as found in La
barraca and in Fortunata and Jacinta. Rogers finds that
"...a comparative analysis confirms that: (1) the intrinsic
nature and the function of the simile are more fundamentally
antipoded than similar in the two authors; (2) the simile
throws new light on specific aspects of the markedly divergent
modes of novel-writing" (p. 864).

Joseph Schraibman, "Releyendo Fortunata y Jacinta:
los primeros cinco capítulos," Galdós ... Mary Washington
College, pp. 41-56, shows in some detail "cuán cuidadosamente teje Galdós su novela desde los primeros capítulos"
(p. 55). Schraibman provides the reader with a structural
and stylistic analysis of the first five chapters.

Schraibman is also the author of "Los sueños en
Fortunata y Jacinta," Insula, no. 166 (1960), 1, 18 (reproduced in Ediciones de la Cátedra de literatura española
moderna, serie D, no. 3, Facultad de filosofía y educación,
Universidad de Chile, Santiago, 1961 and in Benito Pérez
Galdós [1973], pp. 161-68). He concluded that dreams are
used in this novel "presentar o mostrar el desarrollo del
rasgo esencial de sus personajes en Jacinta, la maternidad
frustrada en Mauricia, la dualidad, en Maxi, un grave
complejo de inferioridad, en Fortunata, el ansia de pertene-
cer a Juanito" (p. 18).

Paul C. Smith, "Cervantes and Galdós: The Duques

and Ido del Sagrario," Romance Notes, 8 (1966), 47-50,
notes that "We offer here an interpretation of two mutually
illuminating episodes that exemplify this similarity [i. e.,
between these two authors]. One is from the second part of
the Quijote (1615); the other is from Galdós' Fortunata y
Jacinta (1886-1887). The first treats the misadventures
of Don Quijote and Sancho as guests of the Duques; the
second deals with the seller of periodicals, José Ido del
Sagrario, and the amusement he provides rich, bored Juanito
Santa Cruz. These passages, alike in over all implication
and specific details, merit juxtaposition because they place
in sharper perspective the authors' similar attitudes towards
humanity and certain social types" (p. 47).

Fernando Uriarte, "El comercio en la obra de Galdós,"
Atenea, 72 (1943), 136-40, rather than dealing with the subject of its title, is a discussion of Thomas Mann's Budden-
brooks and Galdós' Fortunata y Jacinta. Uriarte notes that
Galdós' Spanish middle class were businessmen and that
"Galdós aborda con firmeza al tema sumergiéndose en el
lenguaje y psicología de los personajes con morosidad certera y deleitosa hasta rematar el asunto exhaustivamente" (p. 137).

Anthony Zahareas, "The tragic sense in Fortunata y
Jacinta," Symposium, 19 (1965), 38-49, finds that this novel
is "above all an important statement about tragedy that is
crucial to an evaluation of Galdós' achievement. ... What is
remarkable about the novel is the artistry with which Galdós
has woven various distinct tragedies--psychological, moral,
social into one ... Galdós captures the tragic implications
of humanity not through archetypical themes such as virtue,
pride and sin, which are property of political, moral and
religious philosophies, but through man's everyday psychological performance" (p. 38).

This article has been published in Spanish as "El
sentido de la tragedia en Fortunata y Jacinta," Anales
galdosianos, 3 (1968), 25-34.

Two extremely different linguistic studies exist on this
novel. They are: Graciela Andrade, "Las expresiones del
lenguaje familiar de Pérez Galdós en Fortunata y Jacinta,"
(Ph.D. dissertation, State University of Iowa, 1957, 207
leaves; Dissertation Abstracts, 17 [1957], 3008-09), and
Stephen Gilman, "La palabra hablada y Fortunata y Jacinta,"
Nueva revista de filología hispánica, 15 (1961), 542-60;
reprinted in Benito Pérez Galdós (1973), pp. 293-315.

A glossary "constitutes the main part of the [Andrade] study." This dissertation "is devoted to a clarification of the popular expressions which appear in Fortunata y Jacinta and which are repeated in seven other novels of Galdós."

The penetrating article by Gilman defies ready summarization. He writes that "Tomado en su conjunto, el lenguaje de la novela es, pues, el lenguaje de la sobremesa, de la 'peña' y de la tertulia. Es un lenguaje semi-público y social, situado en algún punto intermedio entre la oratoria y las intimidades verbales de un diálogo interior" (p. 548). In a footnote on this same page he comments that "La estructura oral de la novela se basa en la separación de los hablantes en compartimientos estancos (tertulias, profesiones, clases sociales, etc.), también en la unidad lingüística del mundo de Madrid en su conjunto. El lenguaje tópico es la savia vital de todo el organismo novelístico y fluye por sus diversos órganos y partes de tal modo, que el lector se da cuenta de que existe allí una especie de unanimismo avant la lettre. Dicho en otras palabras, el principal hablante de Fortunata y Jacinta es Madrid, en perpetuo diálogo consigo mismo."

Carlos Clavería, Estudio sobre los gitanismos del español (Madrid: Revista de filología española, 1951 [Anejo 53]), pp. 41-42, deals briefly with the "vocabulario vulgar de Juanito" (Schraibman, "Releyendo Fortunata y Jacinta...," p. 56).

Dolores M. Comas de Guembe, La función del monólogo de Benito Pérez Galdós y Miguel de Unamuno (Mendoza: Universidad nacional de Cuyo [1969]; Trabajos de alumnos, no. 2, dated 1967), 39pp., is an interesting stylistic study whose purpose is "analizar la técnica del monólogo en B. P. Galdos y en M. de Unamuno en sus novelas claves: Fortunata y Jacinta y Niebla, partiendo de la concepción de la creación novelesca y la materia novelable. Señalaremos además las diferencias y puntos de contacto entre ambos escritores. Coinciden en un mismo afán indagador, pero difieren en la fundamentación: agónico-religioso-reflexiva de Unamuno, y el intento de captación vital de Galdós. Estableceremos paralelismos en el empleo de recursos técnicos y en la presentación de las formas dramáticas como tales, diálogo y monólogo. Frente a este paralelismo de la forma dramática existe una profunda diferencia en cuanto al fondo, ya que Unamuno parte de una visión poética de la existencia, desde sí mismo, y Galdós de la observación minuciosa de la realidad de su mundo novelesco" (p. 1).

Andrés Avelino Diez-Alonso, "Estructuralismo y reali-
so crítico en Fortunata y Jacinta," (Ph.D. dissertation,
Indiana University, 1971, 359pp.; Dissertation Abstracts International, 32 [1971], 2681-82A), notes that "This dissertation
is an attempt to analyze this novel ... by employing two
critical methods: structuralism and critical realism" (p.
2681A).

Kay Engler, "Notes on the narrative structure of
Fortunata y Jacinta," Symposium, 24 (1970), 111-27, is an
analysis of the novel's "four basic elements of the narrative
situation (the narrator, the narrative, the reader, and the
implied author who conceived and executed the imaginary narrative)" (p. 112). Engler finds that this novel's "structure
is highly complex, and it offers a wealth of narrative techniques, some of great originality for the period when they
were introduced. As such, the novel is ideally suited to a
study of the narrative structure" (p. 112). She believes that
"Through identification with the narrator as the reliable me-
diator of novelistic reality, the reader duplicates within the
world of the novel the multifaceted relationship with reality
which he had known in his own experience. It is this mirroring in the world of the novel of the reader's experience of
reality in the 'real' world which constitutes the basis of
Galdós' realism" (p. 127).

Manuel C. Lassaletta, "Algunas coloquialismos en el
lenguaje de Galdós: un estudio del verbo 'hablar' en Fortunata y Jacinta," Hispania, 54 (1971), 907-14, shows that "En
lugar del verbo hablar Galdós emplea numerosos sinonimos
familiares y locuciones formadas con un verbo en sentido
figurado seguido de su complemento directo o preposicional.
Seleccionamos el verbo hablar, pues es precisamente éste
uno de los campos donde el genio de la lengua se ha mostra-
do más exuberante en la creación de coloquialismos. Observador meticuloso de los giros y habla familiares, conoce
Galdós el valor estílistico y sensación inmediatez que se uso
confiere a la novela y, por lo mismo, no se retrae de in-
sertarlos profusamente en las suyas" (p. 908). The 73 terms
studied are divided into the following groups: comenzar a
hablar, continuar hablando, hablar solemnemente, hablar ve-
ladamente, hablar claramente, hablar acerca de cosas de-
sagradables, hablar airadamente, hablar mal del projimo,
hablar entrometiéndose and dejar de hablar.

José María Ribas Bonet, "Estudio estilístico de la
novela Fortunata y Jacinta de don Benito Pérez Galdos,"

Revista de la Universidad de Madrid, 16 (1968), 41-43, is
an abstract of a dissertation accepted on July 5, 1967.
"Consta de introducción y 16 capítulos. En la Introducción
se exponen las razones de haber escogido la novela de Galdós
para objeto del trabajo; se accompañan pormenores de la
apreciación de Fortunata y Jacinta por la crítica, y se hace
alusión a la deficiencia de estudios estilisticos sobre Galdós
y al metodo seguido (Vossler-Spitzer con recuentos) en la
presente investigación estilistica" (p. 41). The dissertation
has two parts: "La primera está dedicada a los recursos
morfosintácticos y léxicos" (p. 41) and "La segunda parte
de la tesis se ocupa de las facetas de técnica estilística y
de temática en relación con la estructura de la novela"
(p. 43).

James Whiston, "Language and situation in Part I of
Fortunata y Jacinta," Anales galdosianos, 7 (1972), 73-91,
"attempts to study some of the language of Fortunata y Jacinta, in particular Galdós' use of imagery, sentence structure and linguistic decorum" (p. 73).

Lester Clark provides an introduction, "Benito Pérez
Galdós (1843-1920)," to his Fortunata and Jacinta (Baltimore,
Maryland, Penguin Books, 1973), pp. 18-30. This introduction pays almost no attention to the novel that is translated
and is based on Berkowitz' biography. It is probably a pity
that Clark, who spent several years providing the contemporary reader with the first English translation of this novel,
does not present us with his views and the various critical
opinions that have arisen concerning it.

Monique Marazé provides a most interesting short introduction, pp. 7-15, to the French translation by Robert
Marrast, Fortunata et Jacinta: histoire de deux femmes
mariées (Lausanne: Editions Rencontre, 1970, 3 vols.).
These attractively bound and well-printed volumes provide
the French-speaking world with a translation of a work that
Marazé calls "un des sommets de l'oeuvre littéraire de Pérez
Galdós, comme d'ailleurs de l'histoire du roman dans tout
l'Occident" (p. 7). I find myself in complete agreement with
the anonymous reviewer of the ABC, May 5, 1970, p. 50,
who writes that "La presentación o prólogo no tiene más defecto que su brevedad, pues se siente que la autora se deja
mucho y muy bueno en el tintero, pudiendo decir que se lee
más entre lineas que en el texto."

Florence Delay reviews the French translation in La

nouvelle revue française, no. 218 (Feb. 1971), 86-93. The reviewer comments on the Morazé preface, noting that she "tourne délibérément le dos à l'histoire littéraire, choisit d'attacher plus de signification à l'environnemet de Galdós qu'aux événements personnels, et recrée le décor politique et madrilène sur lequel promena son miroir un grand écrivain modeste dont elle ne retient que les mouvements" (p. 86). This is one of the fullest French treatments of Fortunata y Jacinta, a work little examined by the French students of Galdós. The reviewer comments both on the plot and the characters and has high praise for the quality of the translation.

Fortunata y Jacinta (movie): The film based on this novel was released in 1969 and on the whole was not greatly acclaimed by the critics.

José Manuel Alonso Ibarrola, "Don Benito Galdós y el cine: tres mujeres, dos peliculas y un cincuentenario," Cuadernos hispanoamericanos, nos. 250-52 (1970-1971), 650-55, presents an overview of film versions based on Galdós' novels and options that have been granted on his works. He then discusses the film versions of Fortunata y Jacinta and Tristana. His opinion of the first movie is very low. He discusses the controversy aroused by Tristana. He writes that "... la Tristana de Buñuel es una cosa completamente diversa a la novela, y uno llega a preguntarse por qué los realizadores cinematográficos se molestan en adquirir opciones de obras literarias, cuando después tan pronto las abandonan para seguir sus propios impulsos creacionales" (p. 654).

Luis Urbez, Reseña de literature, arte y espectáculos, 7, 36 (junio 1970), 358-60, is apparently the fullest discussion of this film. The reviewer claims that "la película tiene el sabor de lo añejo, ya que no se han intentado en ningún momento rejuvencer la historia de amor y de pasiones que narra Galdós ... El respeto con el que la cámara presenta la portada de una vieja edición de la novela, que sirve de fondo a los títulos de crédito, se mantiene como atmósfera enrarecida a lo largo de todo el film" (p. 358). He finds that "se acerca al melodrama" (p. 359) and that it should have given a "más amplia entrada al madrileñismo de Galdós" (p. 359). The reviewer praises "el cuidado dibujo de los personajes secundarios" (p. 359). He notes that this film "ha acarparado varios de los premios nacionales para 1969 de cinematografía" (p. 360).

Gloria

Of interest for the study of this novel are: Paula
Ovadia de Bernardete, "La estructura operística de Gloria,"
Studies in Honor of M. J. Bernardete (New York, Las Ame-
ricas Publishing Co., 1965), pp. 143-65; Gustavo Correa,
"Los elementos bíblicos en la novela Gloria de Pérez Galdós,"
Quaderni ibero-americani, no. 25 (1960), 1-8, reprinted in
his El simbolismo religioso..., pp. 49-62; José María Cos-
sio, "De tal palo, tal astilla: Origen y polémica de la nove-
la de Pereda," Cruz y raya, 12 (1904), 7-31; Walter T.
Pattison, "The genesis of Gloria," Benito Pérez Galdós and
the Creative Process, pp. 18-113; Walter T. Pattison, "The
Manuscript of Gloria," Anales galdosianos, 4 (1969), 55-61;
E. J. Rodgers, "Religious conflict and didacticism in Gloria,"
Anales galdosianos, 1 (1966), 39-51; Charles A. Zamora,
"Tiempo ciclico: estructura temporal en Gloria de Galdós,"
Hispania, 46 (1963), 465-70; and B. Sicot, "Contribution à
l'étude de Gloria," Les langues néo-latines, no. 202 (1972),
45-55.

Sicot's article develops the theme that there exists an
"étonnante similitude" between Galdós' Gloria and Octave
Feuillet's Histoire de Sibylle (p. 49). He states that "En ce
qui concerne les personnages, les deux oeuvres présentent
un parallélisme presque parfait. Ils se ressemblent physi-
quement, psychologiquement et ils ont les mêmes rôles"
(p. 50). He discusses six points of similarity and concludes
that "Gloria, par ses qualités littéraires, par la profondeur,
pour l'époque, des problèmes posés, laisse loin derrière
elle les innombrables mièvreries de Sibylle" (p. 55).

Pattison's article discusses the first two versions of
this novel, the final manuscript and the novel's second part.
The study of the manuscript shows that "Galdós was not an
improvisor but rather a careful literary artisan, conscien-
tiously working over his materials in various drafts until the
final product met with his satisfaction" (p. 60). Pattison
feels that "The creation of Gloria was a slow and laborious
process; the admiration we now feel for Galdós is that which
is due a conscientious literary workman who sees a long
task through to successful completion" (p. 61). The article
is interesting also for showing changes in both plot and character in the "three stages, or even four, if we count the
changes made in the proofs" (p. 60) through which the novel
passed.

The chapter on Gloria in Pattison's book is the fullest study yet made of this novel. He is chiefly interested in Galdós' sources and how he took these and fashioned them into a work of art. His material has the following parts: Introduction, Topography, The ambiente moral, Religion and religions, Krausismo in other novels, Shipwrecks, Priests --French and Spanish, Gloria and Sibylle, Love for a heretic, The Bible and a banquet, Ivanhoe, The Jewish hero, More about characters, The creative process. This study is buttressed with 382 footnotes.

Correa shows that "En el 'plano' externo algunos de los personajes encarnan paradigmas del Antiguo y Nuevo Testamentos" (p. 1). He also states that "En un plano de más honda significación se hallan los protagonistas Gloria Lantigua y Daniel Morton, cuya identificación con arquetipos y situaciones bíblicas es evidente en la estructuración de la novela" (p. 4).

Bernardete states that "El propósito de este ensayo es mostrar que Gloria, a diferencia de las otras novelas galdosianas, se caracteriza por sus escenas, sus personajes y su tema central, por aquel mismo espíritu que se echa de ver en algunas de las óperas más famosas del siglo XIX ... Para defender este tesis este ensayo tratará de la historia de la ópera italiana en España y de la estructura de las y nombradas obras, y, finalmente, para cerrar el argumento, se darán los elementos operísticos de Gloria, teniendo en vista la Juive y el Fausto" (p. 143).

Rodgers attempts "to discern the nature of the religious conflict which Galdós has chosen to treat in this novel, and to trace the way in which he shows this conflict through the relationships between the main character. I hope it will emerge in the course of this article that Galdós, though he treats his subject for the most of the time with real mastery and insight, still lacks experience as a novelist, and that at times his interest in the didactic purpose of his work takes precedence over plausibility of character and situation" (p. 39).

Zamora states that "En el análisis que hemos hecho se revela, de una manera patente, el calculado empleo del tiempo cíclico que hace Galdós. En toda la obra jamás se menciona una fecha determinada y específica, pues para el autor esto menoscabaría el valor prototípico y por lo tanto

universal que aspira a dar a su creación. Este valor lo
consigue, como hemos dicho, empleando como artificio clave
de su realidad novelesca el tiempo cíclico" (p. 470).

José María Cossío states that "En el ambiente apasionado de aquellos días la publicación de Gloria ... cayó como
una bomba. No era posible la serenidad, y así la crítica
desde los opuestos campos perdió del todo la noción de su
destino, y cada artículo, cada reseña que aparecía, era más
bien munición de guerra religiosa, en la que la literatura y
el arte tenían poco que ver" (p. 9). Pereda discusses his
views on this novel in two letters to Galdós; the opinions of
Menéndez Pelayo are given. A discussion of the "génesis
polémica" and "antecedentes" of Pereda's De tal palo, tal
astilla is presented along with a summary of the volume's
critical reception.

La de Bringas

        Important recent discussions of this novel would in-
clude: William H. Shoemaker, "Galdós' classical scene in La
de Bringas," Hispanic Review, 27 (1959), 423-34 (reprinted in
his Estudios sobre Galdós, pp. 145-58; translated by Paul P.
Rogers as "La 'escena clásica' de Galdós, en La de Bringas,"
Benito Pérez Galdós [1973], pp. 279-91); Ricardo Gullón, "Introducción" to La de Bringas (Englewood Cliffs, Prentice-Hall,
1967), especially pp. 12-26; Ricardo Gullón, "Claves de
Galdós," Insula, nos. 284-85 (jul.-ago. 1970), 8 (both of the
Gullón items are reprinted in his "La de Bringas," Técnicas
de Galdós, pp. 105-34); Gregorio Marañón, "El mundo por la
claraboya," Insula, no. 82 (1952), 1-2; J.E. Varey, "Francisco Bringas: nuestro buen Thiers," Anales galdosianos, 1
(1966), 63-69 (also found in Actas del Segundo Congreso Internacional de Hispanistas ... [Nijmegen: Instituto Espanol de
la Universidad de Nimega, 1967], pp. 679-87); V.S. Pritchett,
"Galdós," in Books in General (London, Chatto and Windus,
1953), pp. 31-36, translated by Miguel Luis Gil as "Galdos
(sobre La de Bringas)," Benito Pérez Galdós (1973), pp. 273-
78; Andrés Amorós, "El ambiente de La de Bringas, novela
de Galdós," Reales sitios, no. 6 (1965), 61-68; Julian Palley,
"Aspectos de La de Bringas," Kentucky Romance Quarterly,
16, 4 (1969), 339-48; and Nicholas G. Round, "Rosalía
Bringas' children," Anales galdosianos, 6 (1971), 43-50.

        The introduction to the textbook edition of this novel
has the following parts: La de Bringas, which provides the

historical background needed for an understanding of the novel,
El maleficio mesocrático, Caos y laberinto, El autor-persona-
je, La verdad en el sueño, and El lenguaje.

Amorós elaborates in this paragraph: "Como es
bien sabido, los protagonistas de esta historia vivían en el
piso alto del Palacio Real madrileño. Debemos apresurarnos
a añadir que no se trata de una decoración artificiosamente
añadida a la trama, sino que el escenario es escencial en
esta novela, determina en gran medida los sentimientos, los
costumbres y la mentalidad de sus protagonistas. Así suele
suceder, en efecto, en las novelas decimonónicas de técnica
realista. Pero, en este caso concreto, el escenario juega
un papel especialmente interesante. Los pisos altos de Palacio formaban un mundo pintoresco, insólito, que adquiría su
verdadera fisonomía en cuanto formaba parte de otros mundos
mas amplios: el Palacio Real y Madrid. Galdós percibe con
gran sensibilidad las múltiples relaciones que existen entre
estos tres mundos. En este artículo intentamos recogerlas
ordenadamente y captar su íntimo significado" (p. 61).

Gullón's "Claves de Galdós" has two parts: "Estructura" and "Espacio." Gullón notes that the novel's structure
"es muy sencilla y se base ... en una polaridad representada
por la protagonista y su marido, encarnaciones del derroche
y la avaricia, respectivamente. Es la polaridad adecuada
para poner de relieve el tema novelesco: el dinero, obsesión
de los personajes...." The last fourth of the article elaborates on the idea that "La mejor ocurrencia del autor ...
fue la invención de un espacio que no es mero escenario,
sino ambito con sustantividad propia."

Marañón finds that this novel is "una de las representativas del genio de su autor. Porque la acción de su historia
de trágica y commovedora vulgaridad es un símbolo del autor
y de su obra" (p. 2).

Palley states that "En este ensayo intento destacar
various aspectos tematicos y estructurales de esta novela de
Pérez Galdós. En general, la ironía y la ambigüedad son
las cualidades que mejor caracterizan esta obra, sobre todo,
esa ironía con la cual Galdós disfraza su compasión" (p. 339).

This article has the following sections: La obra de
pelo, El punto de vista, Burocracia y laberinto, La de
Bringas y Madame Bovary, La glorisoa y la ceguera, La
comida de los pobres, La crisis: Rosalia y Refugio, El
laberinto, paraleismo e ironía.

The chapter in Pritchett's book is a reproduction of
his New Statesman and Nation review of The Spendthrifts.
He claims that "Pérez Galdós is the only novelist who es-
capes to some extent from Spanish provincialism and can be
compared with the European figures" (p. 31).   According to
Pritchett, "Galdós is deep in Spanish egoism.   But he was
sufficiently a European to explore that; he wrote at the time
of intellectual revival; he is free from that 'typical' region-
alism which travels so poorly in literature.   He has the certainty, sharpness and power of the novelist who is saturated
with his subject.   If, as they say, everything in Spain is
personal, then Galdós is the novelist of this kind of society
which destroys every idea and issue by the thickly involved
personal concern" (p. 36).

Round notes that "The contrasting natures of the
Bringas children and of their parents thus imply a division
of the characters which, in its turn, underlines the way in
which political and psychological themes converged in the
closing chapters" (p. 48).   He feels that "Unrealism is the
unifying theme of the book.   The diversity of the forms such
unrealism may take and of the spheres in which it may op-
erate gives La de Bringas its depth and richness as a novel.
The imaginative ordering of that diversity is a major aspect
of Galdós' art, and the shrewd differentiation of the book's
population of characters is one of the means by which that
ordering is achieved" (p. 49).

Shoemaker, after an exhaustive survey of the evidence
concerning the source of a scene that runs through chapters
45-48, concludes that "It would seem, therefore, that Galdós
could hardly have known Torres Naharro's Comedia Aquilana
in 1884 ... But the points of resemblance between the scene
in his novel and that of the Aquilana are so compellingly
significant that we cannot completely abandon the sixteenth-
century model.   Our suspicion is that Galdós saw the scene
in the performance of a play and that what he saw he later
adapted or recreated in his own Rosalía-Refugio scene; that
the scene was a lineal descendant of Plautus, Asinaria, through
either the Aquilana or some other hereditary line, Spanish of
foreign, that incorporated the salient features contained in the
Aquilana and perhaps even other features as well; and that
some day, deo volente, this play and its mistress-turned-
servant scene will be identified" (p. 434).

Varey shows the significance of such expressions as
"el buen Thiers," "el gran economista," etc. found in this

novel. The reference is to the Frenchman Louis Adolphe
Thiers and to his book De la propriété, which Galdós possessed in a Spanish translation. "Evidentemente la transfe-
rencia del apellido del ilustre economista francés al humilde
y ahorrativo oficial de Palacio es irónica, pero ha de preguntarse uno si encumbra también significado más hondo"
(p. 66). After a discussion of some of Thiers' political,
social and economic ideas, Varey notes that "Bringas recha-
zaría el mundo de Thiers, así como rechaza la revolución
liberal; representa un modo de vida que la marcha de la
civilización, según la entiende Thiers, va a suprimir totalmente" (p. 67).

P. A. Bly, "The use of distance in Galdos's 'La de
Bringas,'" Modern Language Review, 69 (1974), 88-97, states
that "a careful examination of the use of physical space and
distance in La de Bringas, supposedly one of the most representative novels of this realist style, will show, I hope, that
Galdós goes beyond a simple objective photograph of the material world. He is constantly breaking down what one would
expect to be the normal spatial relationship between various
points to produce a picture of disorder, confusion, and re-
pulsion. He even disrupts the normal literary 'distance' between the novel and its reader. The conscious manipulation
will appear inevitable, if he is to expose without ambiguity
the true moral fibre of his character" (p. 88). The article
develops in detail the ideas mentioned in the just quoted
sentences.

Jennifer Lowe, "Galdós' presentation of Rosalía in
La de Bringas," Hispanofila, no. 50:49-65 (1974), "examines
the actual way in which Galdós presents Rosalía: that is,
how he transmits her attitudes and actions to the readers"
(p. 49). The article's last paragraph follows: "The progression of Rosalía's behaviour has been very carefully presented
by Galdós. The various stages of her actions and attitudes
are clearly marked. However, although this is so and although Galdós often openly states or analyses in detail her
opinions or motives, the complex picture of Rosalía can be
obtained only if close attention is paid to Galdós' choice of
words and images, to the purpose behind his exaggeration,
to the order of events or reactions and to their frequently
meaningful repetition. Even when we come to understand the
reasons for Rosalía's behaviour it is highly unlikely that we
approve of it. Despite this we may still feel sympathetically
disposed towards her. This is due partly to the fact that we
know so much about her and her motivation and partly to the

various redeeming features that Galdós has included in his
portrayal of her. For all her vanity and her errors she is
a devoted mother, and although her feelings towards Bringas
fluctuate, she does care for him assiduously during his ill-
nesses. She is, in many ways, a pathetic figure, caught up
in the society in which she lives, unable to resist temptation.
The circumstances may be restricted and her behaviour extreme but Rosalía herself portrays many of our human tend-
encies (pp. 64-65).

Marianela

The fullest discussion of this novel is Ernesto Krebs,
Marianela y Doña Barbara: ensayo de comparación (Bahía
Blanca: Cuadernos del Sur, Instituto de Humanidades, Uni-
versidad Nacional del Sur, 1967, 177pp.), pp. 11-111. This
portion of the book has the following sections: Personajes,
Rasgos quijotescos, Rasgos picarescos, La belleza, Encomio
de Florentina, Caridad, Cátedra, Pedagogía, Formas de
tratamiento para la Nela, Comparación con los animales,
Rasgos personales, La fantasía, Realidad-Irrealidad, Paisaje,
Tiempo, Dios, El suicidio, Lo que no debió decirse.

On p. 9 Krebs writes that "La anotación de temas y
cuestiones de Marianela nos muestra un entrecruzamiento que
trataremos de deslindar hasta donde nos sea posible para
comprender cómo se implican y relacionan unos con otros."
He notes that "tratamos de mostrar el carácter que nos parece deliberadamente negativo de Marianela, analizando una
serie de aspectos de fondo y de composición que compramos
luego con otros, también de fondo y de composición, de
composición, de la novela Doña Bárbara, que nos parece de
tan notorio y también deliberado carácter positivo" (p. 10).

His conclusions are found on pp. 174-177, the last
paragraph reading: "Así, mientras Marianela, con rasgos
de honda tradición española, se desespañoliza con un propósito docente de valor universal, Doña Bárbara, con propósito
semejante, revela lo entrañable de América con la hondura y
amplitud que alcanza a dar al conflicto en la llanura venezolana donde una raza buena ama, sufre y espera ... por esto
mismo, la alta jeraquía de lo universal" (p. 177).

Walter T. Pattison, "The creation of Marianela," in
Galdós and the Creative Process (Minneapolis: University
of Minnesota Press, 1954), pp. 114-36, is the fullest and

best account of not only the sources of this novel but how
Galdós used them in writing the novel. It has the following
subdivisions: Philosophic symbolism, Galdós' contacts with
positivism, Philosophy in Marianela and Wilhelm Meister,
The idyllic element, Humanitarianism and Hugo, Details from
The Wandering Jew, The fusion of the elements.

Joaquín Casalduero discusses the influence of Auguste
Comte and Taine on Marianela in his "Auguste Comte y Marianela," Smith College Studies in Modern Languages, 21
(1939), 10-25, and "Marianela y De l'intelligence de Taine,"
PMLA, 50 (1935), 929-31. These essays appear in Casalduero's Vida y obra de Galdós (1961), pp. 193-95 and 196-213.

Louise S. Blanco, "Origin and history of the plot of
Marianela," Hispania, 48 (1965), 463-67, finds the origin of
the novel's plot in Charles Nodier's "Les aveugles de Cho-
manouny" as published in his Contes de la Veillée. She
notes that other suggested sources have been Victor Hugo's
L'homme qui rit and Les misérables, and Sue's Le juif
errant.

Peter A. Bly, "Egotism and charity in Marianela,"
Anales galdosianos, 7 (1972) 49-66, reviews briefly the
interpretations of this novel and then notes that he will indicate "another possible interpretation which takes into account the significance of references to charity and examples
of selfishness. By examining the manner in which Galdós
depicts his characters and settings, I hope to show how he
sees the overpowering force of egotism in 19th century society,
gives a certain unity to his novel and anticipates a theme
hitherto considered to be limited to the later 'spiritual' novels
of the 'serie contemporánea'" (p. 49). On p. 64, he writes:
"Yet it seems to me that Galdós succeeds in making a serious
study of the ravaging effects of self-interests in 19th century
society. Marianela is a novel about the absence of charity in
society. He discerns two types of egotism: the immoral
materialistic drive which dominates a person's character and
is clearly reprehensible, and the perfectly understandable
weakness of selfcentredness which we all have...."

Rodolfo Cardona, "Marianela: su trayectoria de la
novela al teatro," Homenaje a Casalduero (Madrid, Gredos,
1972), pp. 109-114, reproduces two letters from Ramón del
Valle-Incán, dated Aug. 5, 1904 and Oct. 30, 1906, which
allow us "documentar fácilmente la existencia del proyecto
de dramatizar Marianela que concibió Galdós en 1904" (p. 111).

Cardona reproduces for the first time "un documento interesante" (p. 110), which turns out to be an outline of a proposal, in Galdós' own handwriting, for the dramatization of Marianela. Cardona comments that "Al leer el esquema a veces
llega a parecernos que Galdós lo que tenía en mente era un
libreto operático, puesto que alude a "monólogos," "tríos" y
"coros" (p. 114).

Julio Casares, "Marianela, de Pérez Galdós," Crítica
efímera, II (Madrid: Espasa-Calpe, 1944), 31-44, discusses
both the novel (pp. 31-38) and its adaptation for the stage by
the Alvarez Quintero brothers. As little has been written on
the adaptation, it can be noted that Casares states that "El
lenguaje, cuando no es fiel transcripción de la novela, está
hábilmente zurcido con frases de la misma, y según el más
puro estilo galdosiano" (p. 42). He also writes that "Para
resumir mi opinión, pues me faltaría espacio para exponerla
detenidamente, diré que tal vez procediendo con más desemba-
razo, y ateniéndose únicamente al carácter de Marianela y a
las líneas generales del asunto, podría haberse logrado una
adaptación más teatral que la representada; pero también
creo de justicia declarar que los Quinteros, con las manos
atadas por un respeto escrupuloso, y decididos a oscurecer
modestamente su propia personalidad, han dado cima a una
empresa dificilísima, y se han hecho acreedores al aplauso
del público y al beneplácito de la crítica" (pp. 42-43).

Victor Castro, "Perspectiva de Marianela," Atenea,
72 (1943), 141-44, finds that "Marianela es de esas novelas
cuyo fondo el autor domina a su manera, con un lujo de re-
servas espirituales y con una concepción cabal del espíritu,
en cuanto a personajes se refiere. No sabemos hasta qué
punto la extraordinaria asimilación de Galdós o del Madrid de
aquellos años haya influído en esta obra tan matizada, tan
excelentemente variada en sus caracteres fundamentales. En
ella está lo cáustico y mordaz de un Quevedo. Lo sentimental
de un Lope. Y tiene el colorido paternal de Goya o Velásquez"
(p. 144).

C. A. Jones, "Galdós' Marianela and the approach to
reality," Modern Language Review, 56 (1961), 515-19, re-
jects the interpretation of this novel as found in Casalduero
and Eoff. Jones believes that "Reading Marianela alongside
the other novels of the period, one arrives at the conclusion
that Galdós is suggesting that if opposing reality or trying to
reconcile it with one's ideals leads to disaster, on the other
hand the success which accompanies the heedless acceptance

of reality is a relative and superficial success which takes
no account of the deeper needs and qualities of humanity....
The lesson of Marianela, that in dealing with reality it is
no better to embrace it unthinkingly than it is to fight it, is
one which has permanent value for the understanding of
Galdós' work" (p. 519).

José Manuel Camacho Padilla, "Censo de los personajes que intervienen en la obra Marianela de Don Benito Pérez
Galdós," Boletín de la Academia de Ciencias, Bellas Letras
y Nobles Artes de Córdoba, 13 (1934), 5-15, is an attempt to
produce a description or a descriptive listing of the characters of this novel. According to the article's author, "La
cédula debe hacerse procurando que complete, de la manera
más amplia posible la personalidad del personaje retratado;
y así deberán anotarse las cualidades físicas, el vestido, la
condición social y las cualidades morales es decir, todo
cuanto contribuya a fijar bien el carácter. En todos ellos se
procurará buscar la relación más o menos directa que guarda
con el protagonista de la obra" (p. 8). He finds three types
of characters in Galdós' novels: "unos episódicos, que casi
no intervienen en la acción y no vienen a servir más que de
puntos de referencia; suelen aclarar algún punto a completar
una escena o un carácter..." (p. 8), "personajes secundarios"
and "personajes principales."

Mario E. Ruiz, "El idealismo platónico en Marianela
de Galdós," Hispania, 53 (1970), 870-880, notes that "El
presente estudio tiene por objeto formular la hipótesis, a
través de una comparación de varios paralelísmos metafóri-
cos, de la posible influencia del idealismo platónico en la
realidad galdosiana" (p. 870). Besides an introductory section, this article is divided into: Metáforas relacionadas a
la filosofía platónica and Los tres estados del alma humana.

Miau

Robert J. Weber, The Miau manuscript of Benito
Pérez Galdós: a critical study (Berkeley and Los Angeles:
University of California Publications in Modern Philology, 72,
1964), v + 155pp., is the first attempt to be made of a
thorough study of a Galdós manuscript in an attempt to understand the author's creative processes. Weber states that his
"study is based primarily upon the two manuscript versions
of Miau, dated December 26, 1887, and February 2, 1888,
by Galdós himself, together with the changes in proof; I have

traced the various stages of composition in order to learn
as much as possible about Galdós' creative process. In a
way, this study complements Pattison's book [i. e., Benito
Pérez Galdós and the creative process]; whereas Pattison
moved from outside the novel to within, I have worked from
within the manuscript and then outward. My emphasis is
upon novelistic technique, the ways in which Galdós developed
structure and theme, and the effects of the various textual
changes upon theme and structure. Each of the two versions
is examined in detail: text, structure, theme, and changes
within each version as well as the changes between versions.
Changes in proof are discussed briefly in the last part of the
study" (p. iii). He also notes on the same page that "Berkowitz makes several statements concerning the absence of cor-
rections in Galdós' manuscripts, but, as will be shown in
this study, little of which he claims for the manuscripts in
general is applicable to the Miau manuscript."

        Claire Szoke, Hispanófila, no. 26 (1966), 63-64, states
that "The major weakness of this study is the critic's analysis
of Villaamil." Szoke says that it "offers valuable insights into Galdós' creative process and his use of irony. Although we
question the complete validity of his thematic interpretation,
and his basic approach and frequently perceptive details are
an important addition to the field of Galdosian criticism"
(p. 64).

        Miau, edición, estudio preliminar y bibliografía por
Ricardo Gullón (Madrid: Revista de Occidente, 1957), 677pp.,
is an important scholarly edition of this novel. The introduction, pp. 11-302, is divided into Los supuestos de la creación,
Los ámbitos oscuros, Los Personajes anormales, Lenguaje y
técnica, and a study of this novel. Gustavo Correa, Revista
hispánica moderna, 25 (1959), 102-03, states of the whole
volume that it is "un esfuerzo positivo en la valoración de
Galdós desde un punto de vista estrictamente literario. Queda
por explorar aún lo que todo este mundo representa dentro de
una visión del universo y de la vida" (p. 103). José Blanco
Amor, Sur, no. 265 (1960), 60-68; reprinted in his Encuentros
y desencuentros: ensayos literarios (Buenos Aires, Losada,
1968), pp. 68-81, entitles his review "Miau como justificación de la modernidad de Galdós." His review has the following sections: 1. Apasionado retrato. Villaamil Y José
K ... 3. Por qué Galdós no es un novelista moderno.

        Miau, edición, prólogo y notas de Robert J. Weber
(Barcelona, Labor, 1973), 464pp. (Textos hispánicos mo-

dernos, 25), is an extraordinarily useful edition of this novel.
The introduction, pp. 7-55, deals in some detail with the
novel and the differences in the manuscript versions. The
Appendix, pp. 413-464, is entitled "Miau, redacción alpha
(primera versión del manuscrito)."

Gregorio Torres Nebrera, La Estafeta literaria, no.
524 (Sept. 15, 1973), 1466-1467, provides an interesting review of this section. He notes that "Weber ... publica en
Apéndice lo que él llama Redacción Alpha (primera version
del manuscrito), escrito entre el 26 de diciembre de 1887
y el 4 de febrero de 1888, comprendiendo los seis primeros
capítulos de la novela. No cabe duda del interés que este
texto tiene para el estudio intrinseco de la novela y del 'novelar' galdosiano" (p. 1467). He also states, "Precisamente,
también apoyándose en las tres versiones del párrafo primero conservada, y cotejando en otros textos narrativos anteriores del novelista, Weber expone, en un apartado muy
logrado e inédito en la historia crítica sobre esta novela, lo
que pudo ser la génesis novelesca de Villaamil como personaje central de una epopeya con sordina, cuyo héroe es un
cesante de la Administración que sigue el camino de su
degradación interior (¿o tal vez salvación?) en un medio
degradado" (p. 1467).

A. G. Paradissis, "Una influencia balzaciana en España: Les employés" considerada como una de las fuentes
literarias de Miau de Benito Pérez Galdós," Bulletin hispanique, 74 (1972), 444-452, was provided with the following
abstract: "Este artículo estudia la conexión entre Les
employés de Balzac y Miau de Benito Pérez Galdós. Se
analizan las semejanzas y diferencias entre los temas, los
personajes ficticios y las tramas de las dos obras. De los
temas principales, la mayoria son comunes o tienen semejanzas significativas. En algunos casos la diferencia no es
más que una variación de enfoque. La obra de Balzac es
una inmensa sátira de la corrupción social contemporánea,
la de Pérez Galdós analiza el problema humano total. Muchos
de los personajes presentados por ambos autores se parecen.
Hay semejanzas aun en las intrigas de las dos obras y tenemos que admitir que en el caso de la novela Miau la influencia balzaciana es clara."

Gustavo Correa, "La crucifixión de Villaamil en la
novela Miau," El simbolismo religioso..., pp. 118-34,
shows that "La figura de Villaamil en la novela Miau incorpora, por consiguiente, el simbolismo de la pasión a su vida

personal en diversos módulos de experiencia religiosa. Al
sentirse denigrado por sus semejantes frente a su sentido
misional de reformas administrativas y económicas, acepta
el baldón infamante que le ha sido impuesto como un destino
personal que le asemeja a Cristo, en virtud de su vida de
principios y de su doctrina de moralidad administrativa y de
reformas. Pronto se rebela, sin embargo, ante lo que él
considera una falta de lógica en la ordenación de los destinos
individuales y el mote infamante lo convierte en un desafío
contra el mismo Dios. En los momentos de duda agónica
cree oír la voz de la voluntad divina, a través de las visiones
de su nieto, y concluya que también el debe morir como
Cristo, pues así lo ha decretado el Padre Eterno. La deci-
sión, sin embargo, implica un fondo de locura al hacer del
acto pecaminoso de rebeldía contra Dios (suicidio), la máxima
aceptación de la final voluntad divina" (pp. 133-34).

Gerald Gillespie, "Miau: hacia una definición de sensibilidad en Galdós," Cuadernos hispanoamericanos, nos. 250-
252 (1970-71), 415-429, notes that "Estas notas han intentado
sugerir que Galdós poseyó un poderoso sentido estético,
acerca del cual la crítica ha estado indecisa por causa de la
insistencia acerca del 'contenido,' con sus connotaciones
ideológicas. Pero como muchos investigadores han docu-
mentado, Galdós no fue solamente un 'secretario-narrador'
que anotaba inmediatemente lo que observaba en el transcurrir
de la escena humana, sino también una mente creadora, imbui-
da de la pasión por comprender el sentido de la ficción en sí
misma ... Ha llegado el tiempo, sin embargo, en que el
estructuralismo o la teoría de la gestalt pueden aumentar
provechosamente nuestra comprensión. Cuando el problema alcance, desde esta nueva perspectiva, el grado de completa realización en la correspondencia 'narración' y 'metáfora,' Miau se contará entre las mejoras creaciones de
Galdós" (pp. 428-29).

Alexander A. Parker, "Villaamil--tragic victim or
comic failure?" Anales galdosianos, 4 (1969), 13-23, states
that "The modern tendency to interpret Miau as being more
a criticism of its main character than a condemnation of a
politico-social 'system' conflicts with the way I first read
the novel some thirty years ago and still read it. This paper
will therefore be an attempt to justify an 'old-fashioned' approach" (p. 13). Parker takes special exception to what Eoff
wrote concerning this novel in his The novels of Pérez
Galdós and to Weber's interpretation of the novel as found in
his The Miau manuscript of Benito Pérez Galdós. He finds

Miau's importance in Galdós' development "is that it is transitional between the phase in which interest centres on the different ways in which social pressures crush individual happiness, with the weaker members of society being driven to the wall in the disharmonies created in human relationships by social conflicts, and the phase in which Galdós becomes preoccupied with the question of individual liberty against the hampering and enslaving force of the economic ideals and sanctions which dominate human society" (pp. 15-16). This article is best read with ready reference both to the text of Miau and the works of Eoff and Weber.

Herbert Ramsden, "The question of responsibility in Galdós' Miau," Anales galdosianos, 6 (1971), 63-78, notes that "One's interpretation of the novel and of what it reveals of Galdós as a moralist and as a novelist depends largely on the position one takes on this basic question of responsibility" (p. 83).

Ramsden disagrees at almost all points with Weber concerning Villaamil's character. He believes that "It is circumstances that break Villaamil, and these circumstances, I repeat, are caused by nothing that, by normal ethical standards, can be called a fault in the old man himself. The basic responsibility lies with the administrative system" (p. 77).

A.G. Paradissis, "La mezcla satírica de características humanas y animales en Miau de Benito Pérez Galdós," Thesaurus, 26 (1971), 133-142, discusses the fact that "la palabra Miau y las letras MIAU tienen varios significados satíricos, políticos y religiosas en la novela de Pérez Galdós" (p. 134). He desires to "analizar el uso ... de la mezcla satírica de características humanas y animales" (p. 134). He feels that Los animales pintados por sí mismos "parece ser la fuente literaria del uso satírico por Pérez Galdós del simbolismo animal" (p. 141).

Theodore A. Sackett, "The meaning of Miau," Anales galdosianos, 4 (1969), 25-38, feels that his study "differs fundamentally from the others in its critical approach; none of the cited examinations based its conclusions on an analysis of the dynamic relationship between the protagonist and all of the other personages, and none considers the symbolism and structure in terms of that relationship" (p. 37). It is Sackett's contention that "A meaningful interpretation of Miau must be based on an understanding of Galdós' careful delineation of the protagonist, Ramón Villaamil. If all the motives of his

comportment are not examined it will not be possible to as-
sess with accuracy the implications of his acts. Furthermore, Villaamil's story cannot be comprehended unless it
is analyzed in dynamic interaction with other elements of the
novel, especially point of view, symbolism, and the secondary personages" (p. 25).

His concluding paragraph follows: "Like Cervantes'
masperpiece before it, Miau is constructed with a conscious
process of ambiguity, irony, shifting levels of appearances
and reality, and above all, with a sense of comedy. Several
generations passed before readers and critics realized that
Don Quijote de la Mancha was in fact a tragicomedy; the
complexity of intention encompassed in Galdós' novel Miau
has not been easily comprehended either" (p. 37).

On p. 37 Sackett summarizes the most important previous criticisms of the novel and shows how these differ
from his own.

Antonio Sánchez Barbudo, "Vulgaridad y genio de
Galdós: el estilo y la técnica de Miau," Archivum, 7 (1957),
48-75 (reprinted as "El estilo y la técnica de Galdós" in
Estudios sobre Galdós, Unamuno y Machado [Madrid: Guadarrama, 1968], 2nd ed., pp. 21-45), presents some general
remarks concerning his style and technique with special emphasis on Miau, which he considers to be one of the best of
Galdós' novels. He discusses the so-called "vulgaridad" that
many critics have thought they have found in Galdós' works.
He finds that "Hay, pues, en formas diversas y por razones
varias vulgaridad en la prosa de Galdós, como creo se habrá
visto con los ejemplos citados. Una vulgaridad que, por
otra parte, casi siempre resulta completamente eficaz;
aunque no es ni mucho menos seguro que sea siempre tan
sólo para lograr efectividad, viveza en sus personajes y en
las situaciones que describe, por lo que él emplea ese estilo vulgar" (p. 42). He finds that Galdós' style reflects his
timidity and his shyness. In the last paragraph he notes
that "El crea al imaginar lo real, al ahondar en lo real y
formar para el lector, con sus hallazgos, un mundo que
parece conocido, vulgar, pero que no hubiéramos conocido
sin él; un mundo y unos personajes más transparentes que
los que pudieran contemplar nuestros ojos" (p. 45).

Geraldine M. Scanlon and R.O. Jones, "Miau: prelude to a reassessment," Anales galdosianos, 6 (1971), 53-
62, note that, "In contesting Weber's interpretation of the

novel and his view of the central character we have no wish
to present Villaamil as enjoying an angelic immunity from
human weakness. In the novels of this period Galdós does
not present us with characters who are wholly black or wholly
white but with complex individuals who, like their counter-
parts in real life, are both good and bad. All we intend to
show is that Villaamil is a victim of the state rather than of
his own weaknesses; that it is principally the system and not
the individual that Galdós is criticizing" (p. 54).

They note that "Galdós' main concern as a novelist
was with social relationships and not with individual psychology.
In Miau he describes how unjust government contaminates pri-
vate life, and can create the conditions for the destruction of
social order" (p. 61).

In Anales galdosianos, 6 (1971), 50-51, the editors
published "More on Miau," in which they briefly discuss the
various views on this novel held by Ricardo Gullón, R.J.
Weber, R. Cardona, Geoffrey Ribbans, Theodore Sackett and
A.A. Parker.

Gerald Gillespie, "Miau in translation," Anales galdosianos, 4 (1969), 119-121, is a rather critical review of J.M.
Cohen's English translation of this novel, even though he does
call it "a commendable accomplishment" and finds that it
"fills a pressing need" (p. 121). He states that "Cohen has
undertaken certain arbitrary and ill-advised changes" and
notes that "Whereas Galdós' prose is rich in shifts of tone
and form, Cohen's tends to lack analogous distinctions and to
sound all virtually alike" (p. 119). He comments further on
the translation's style.

The French translation of Miau by Juan Marey (Paris:
Les Editions Français Reúnis, 1968), 412pp., has a brief
preface by Manuel Tuñon de Lara, pp. 7-17.

Edward R. Mulvihill and Robert Sánchez have edited
this novel (New York: Oxford University Press, 1970),
xxiii + 339pp. The introduction is too brief to be called
noteworthy. The editors have divided their text into five
parts. Each of these five parts contains discussion questions.
There are also sections entitled Modes of narration, Point of
view, The art of characterization, The world of the novel and
Plot, form, and structure. These teaching aids and suggestions make this one of the better text editions of a novel by
Galdós.

Misericordia

José Fradejas Lebrero, "Para las fuentes de Galdós,"
Revista de literatura, 4 (1953), 319-44, shows Galdós' indebtedness to Francisco Cutanda's Doña Francisca, el portento
de la caridad (1969). The plots of both books are outlined;
part three is a discussion of the similarities and differences
between the two novels under the following headings: La ruina
y sus consecuencias, Nombres, Carácter, El reparto del pan:
Ingratitud, La herencia, El amor, Los hijos and El lenguaje.
The study's conclusions are found on pp. 339-44.

José Schraibman, "Las citas bíblicas en Misericordia
de Galdós," Cuadernos hispanoamericanos, nos. 250-252
(1970-71), 490-504, has an introduction and then a discussion
of the various biblical references found in the novel. The
author notes that "Galdós utiliza la Biblia extensamente al
escribir Misericordia, ya sea citando palabra por palabra o
cambiando ligeramente las citas para moldearlas al lenguaje
del personaje y crear un lazo de humor con el lector. Todas
estas referencias, pues, así las directas como las indirectas,
ayudan a expresar temas importantes de la obra y a enrique-
cer su contendio" (p. 490).

Rupert C. Allen, "Pobreza y neurosis en Misericordia,
de Pérez Galdós," Hispanófila, no. 33 (1968), 35-47, discusses first the views of Chamberlin and Correa concerning
this novel. He analyzes "las principales características
neuróticas observadas por Galdós" (p. 38) in the following
characters: Frasquito Ponte, Obdulia, Antonio, Doña Paca,
Don Carlos, Almudena, Benina and Juliana. The author
states that "Según nuestro punto de vista interpretativo, pues,
el tema central de Misericordia no es el de la pobreza urbana propiamente dicha, sino más bien de la dinámica de la
pobreza urbana--una situación desesperada que, en el fondo,
va quitando poco a poco la libertad moral de la víctima.
Estas gentas carecen de libre albedrío porque se encuentran
dominadas por las fuerzas del inconsciente" (p. 46).

Theodore S. Beardsley, Jr., "The life and passion of
Christ in Galdós' Misericordia," Homenaje a Sherman H.
Eoff, pp. 39-58, states that "From Miau to Misericordia there
is a growing preoccupation with these 'simple fundamentals of
Christianity,' that is to say a growing preoccupation with the
example of Christ himself rather than with abstract or formal-
ized Christianity as an institution" (p. 40). He notes that "In
this novel, the fusion of elements from the life and Passion

of Christ with what seem to be completely natural elements
within Benina's milieu is so well achieved that many readers
seem unaware of any parallel at all" (p. 41). On p. 42, he
writes that "Galdós' method of establishing parallels between
Christ and Benina is correspondingly subtle. His technique
might well be described as subliminal."

Donald W. Bleznick and Mario E. Ruiz, "La Benina
misericordiosa: conciliación entre la filosofía y la fe,"
Cuadernos hispanoamericanos, nos. 250-252 (1970-71), 472-
489, compares don Buenaventura, a character in Gloria,
with Benina in these words: "A diferencia de don Buenaventura, que actúa 'por el respeto a las creencias generales,'
Benina, no conformándose con la conducta moral de su sociedad, busca la moralidad auténtica del cristianismo primordial,
La filosofía y la fe se encarnan en las dos fuerzas conflicti-
vas pero complementarias de Benina: su espíritu prometeico
y su espíritu jobiano" (p. 473).

Besides a brief introduction, pp. 472-474, the article has
three sections: El espíritu prometeico de Benina, El espíritu
joviano de Benina and La conciliación entre la filosofía y la fe.

José Schraibman, "El ecumenismo de Galdós," Hispania, 53 (1970), 881-886, "focuses primarily upon the novel
Misericordia and its protagonist Benina--who is very important not only for an understanding of this particular novel but
also for comprehending the essence of Galdós' own personal
concept of religion. After a review of the preceding novels,
[he] shows Benina to be the ecumenical culmination of the
religious figure in the later novelas contemporáneas, giving
us also more light and new angles for a fuller understanding
of this character and consequently a deeper appreciation of
Galdós' didactic message in Misercordia" (Chamberlin in
Hispania, 53 [1970], 824).

Pablo Cabañas comments in Hispanic Review, 39
(1971), 473-74, on the statement by Edwin B. Place, Hispanic Review, 37 (1969), 519-524, that "One finds it difficult,
however, to accept this unsupported statement that Misericordia represents a parody of Romanticism!" (p. 473).

Joaquín Casaludero, "Significado y forma de Misericordia," PMLA, 59 (1944), 1104-10, has the following parts:
Argumento, El mundo de Misericordia, Galdós y la generación del 98, Materia y espíritu, fluctuación del hombre and
El tiempo cronológico y el psicológico; el epílogo.

Vernon A. Chamberlin, "The significance of the name
Almudena in Galdós' Misericordia," Hispania, 47 (1964),
491-96, is an investigation and commentary upon this character's name. He finds that "with customary Galdosian irony,
the word, when investigated, turns out to be more Spanish
than Arabic and is, in its present form, completely Madrilenian.... Since 1085, citizens of Madrid have honored the
Virgin as their patroness under the name Nuestra Señora de
la Almudena" (p. 491). He concludes: "Thus Galdós' Almudena, is, in many ways, clearly a connotatively symbolic
character, participating in an allegorical novel (Misericordia)
vis-à-vis a clearly allegorical protagonist, Beniana (from
'Benigna')" (p. 494).

Gustavo Correa, "La santificación por la caridad en
Misericordia," in El simbolismo religioso..., pp. 195-215,
is divided into an introduction, El camino de la mendicidad,
Almudena y la mujer de promisión and Sueño y creación. On
p. 195 Correa writes: "Si Nazarín es la definición del ser
religioso en un plan consciente de perfeccionamiento espiritual, Misericordia es la realización espontánea y auténtica de
la criatura perfecta por el camino de la cridad. El personaje principal de la novela constituye, además, el anverso de
la figura de Torquemada, quien impúdicamente trata de
comprar el cielo con limosnas calculadas." The first section elaborates upon the point that "En la concepción galdosiana de la persona humana, la mendicidad puede tener varios sentidos" (p. 197) and that in this novel "tenemos una
visión objetiva y casi documentada de un sector de la miseria de Madrid" (p. 199). The second section shows that "La
trayectoria amorosa de Almudena es, por consiguiente, la
emoción religiosamente sentida de llegar a poseer la más
alta perfección espiritual" (pp. 210-11). The third section
notes "Característica de Misericordia es la ordenación del
mundo dentro de un esquema armónico de la caridad universal en el interior de la conciencia religiosa" (p. 211).

Marcel Crespil, "La fe religiosa de Almudena en
Misericordia," Romance Notes, 13 (1972), 463-467, feels
that "El moro Almudena es un carácter cuya presentación
muestra algunas inconsistencias curiosas y cuyo desarrollo
revela contradicciones muy significativas en cuanto a sus
creencias religiosas" (p. 463). Crespil attempts to determine
if Almudena is Jewish, Muslim or a Berber. His last paragraph follows: "Es posible que la presentación de Almudena
por parte de Galdós represente un esfuerzo de imitar la
opinión pública en cuanto a las razas semíticas. La gente

española, a una distancia de casi cuatro siglos de contacto directo con moros y judíos, guardaba todavía una idea errada de las formas de la creencia religiosa de los semitas, confundiéndolas por considerarlas todas falsas y paganas. Por eso Almudena, a pesar de las contradicciones evidentes en la obra, parece muy auténtico examinado desde el punto de vista español del siglo diecinueve" (p. 467).

Robert Kirsner, "La ironía del bien en Misericordia," Actas del tercer congreso internacional de hispanistas (México, El Colegio de México, 1970), pp. 495-499, denies that this novel is "un ejemplo de caridad humana, una consagración a la virtud" (p. 495). He writes that "La visión del bien es un estado de tensión irónica, entre y dentro de lo serio y lo absurdo, se mantiene en toda la obra. Tenemos un juego dinámico entre la virtud y el vicio, la verdad y la mentira y entre lo inventado y lo real" (p. 497). On p. 499 he notes that "Sin quitarle a Benina la posibilidad de heroísmo que tiene todo personaje novelístico, se puede ver esta obra de Galdós en perspectiva de comedia humana. Se ha puesto en escena lo que es por fuera una representación de las hazañas de una santa mujer. La fachada vale en si, pero también sirve para encubrir la estructura estilística; La visión inmanente nos proporciona otra realidad. Cuando se corre la contina moral, se discierne el proceso creativo del artista. Se puede ver entonces al titiritero sonriéndose mientras que juega con sus muñecos para ilusionar al público."

Denah Lida, "De Almudena y su lenguaje," Nueva revista de filología hispánica, 15 (1961), 297-308, states that "El novelista se ha aplicado intensamente a hacer vivir a Almudena a través de su extraño lenguaje, ya haciéndonoslo oír directamente, ya en eficacísimas fusiones con el del narrador" (p. 297).

Of value also is the "Introduction" by McKendree Petty, vii-xii, and "A note on Misericordia" by Angel del Río, xii-xxii, which precede their edition of Misericordia, edited for college students (New York: Holt, Rinehart and Winston, c1946).

Robert Ricard, "Sur le personnage d'Almudena dans Misericordia," Bulletin hispanique, 61 (1959), 12-25 (reprinted in Galdós et ses romans, pp. 51-62), is a provocative analysis of the ambiguities found in Galdós' portrayal of Almudena. He suggests that "Peutêtre, à la lumière du personnage de Misericordia, voudrait-il mieux parler d'un

théisme que retient, dans un syncrétisme plus sentimental
que dogmatique, les éléments communs aux trois grandes
religions venues d'Orient" (p. 25). "Peut être aussi le grand
romancier a-t-il voulu évoquer les temps lointains de l'histoire espagnole où ces trois religions coexistaient sur le sol de
la patrie comme elles coexistent en la personne d'Almudena,
Juif, Musulman et baptisé" (ibid.).

Angel del Río, "Aspectos del pensamiento moral del
Galdós," Cuadernos americanos, 12, 6 (1943), 147-68, contains three parts: Hacia una revision necesaria, Lo moral
y lo psicológico en algunas Novelas contemporáneas and Moral
y religion en Misericordia. Del Río states that "La concepción ideológica de la novela está encuadrada, como veremos
más adelante, en una serie de ideas religiosas y sociales que
preocupan al pensamiento europeo a fines del siglo XIX, pero
en su arranque directores fundamentalmente española" (p. 158).
On p. 168 he writes: "supo unir Galdós su vigoroso realismo
con un profundo sentido moral y religioso de la vida y con su
humorismo de superior calidad artística, que es, en último
termino, lo que garantiza su permanencia."

José Enrique Rodó's "Una novela de Galdós" can best
be found in his Obras completas, compilación y prólogo por
Alberto José Vaccaro (Buenos Aires: Ediciones Antonio Za-
mara, 1948), pp. 727-34. Rodó calls this novel "el poema
prosaico de la escasez y la miseria; de la miseria, en sus
manifestaciones, moral y materialmente, más despiadades y
más duras...." (p. 720). He analyzes the characters and
has special praise for Galdós' "admirable creación de Nina"
(p. 734).

Carlos Rovetta, "El naturalismo de Galdós: Misericordia," Nosotros, series 2, no. 77 (1942), 203-09, is a
discussion of the naturalistic elements of the novel. He
stresses among other things the reproduction of the language
of those about whom Galdós is writing and notes that his
naturalism is not as extreme as that found, for example, in
Zola.

Robert H. Russell, "The Christ figure in Misericordia,"
Anales galdosianos, 2 (1967), 103-30, is an analysis of the
character of Benina. Russell states that "The real key to
Misericordia's successful artistic elaboration is the ironic
fact that Benina does not ever know that she is a Christ figure; the world is so constructed that his idea never occurs
to her...." (p. 103). He finds that "The changing relation-

ship of the figura evangélica to society in Galdós' three
novels dealing with the Christ figure is also symptomatic of
the trajectory they represent" (p. 129). He compares
Nazarín, Halma and Benina and his concluding paragraph is:
"Nazarín and Halma give up the world in seeking themselves,
and the world defeats them. Benina has given up herself to
the world, seeking nothing, but the world cannot overcome
her" (p. 130).

    Teresa Silva Tena has contributed a brief discussion
of the novel to Doña Perfecta [y] Misericordia (Mexico:
Porrúa, 1968 [Sepan Cuantos, no. 107]), pp. xiii-xviii.

    J. E. Varey, "Charity in Misericordia," in Galdós
studies, pp. 164-194 shows that "In this novel, Galdós presents charity from many angles. He shows us charity in
terms of social realities, and in terms of the microcosm of
the society of the beggars. He looks at the New Testament
virtues, and as in Nazarín and Halma, sets the lessons of
the New Testament against the background of the class situation and of the social evils of nineteenth-century Madrid.
Misercordia here differs from the two preceding novels, in
that the Christian virtues are suggested directly--by reference,
for instance, to the parable of the Good Samaritan--and are
not seen reflected in the deforming mirror of the novels and
works of Tolstoy. Galdós further recalls the parable of the
Widow's Mite, teaching us that terrestrial values are relative, whilst spiritual values are eternal. And he shows us
how charity can enable man to survive, and to overcome,
the despairs and frustrations engendered by modern society"
(pp. 192-193).

    On p. 194, he writes that "The novel which began as
though it were to be another L'Assommoir, ends as an irra-
tional statement of faith in the positive good to which the
human being can attain." On this same page, he states that
"Man can escape from his surroundings; he is not inevitably
conditioned by his heredity and his environment, nor by any
other external force. And true charity, pure charity, will
enable man to face all adversities. Charity is more than the
giving of alms, the unthinking scattering of a handful of coins,
the calculated bribery of Saint Peter: charity is a state of
mind, a way of life which enables the human being to escape
from his own troubles because it allows him to escape into
the troubles of others."

    María Zambrano has been interested in the interpreta-

tion of this novel for three decades. She is the author of
"Misericordia," Hora de España, no. 21 (1938), 29-52, which
has been reprinted in La España de Galdós (Madrid: Taurus,
1959), pp. 87-114, and as the introduction to Misericordia
(Mexico: Editorial Orion, 1964), i-xxviii. She discusses in
detail the various characters, their philosophy and what they
symbolize. La España de Galdós has 115 pages and most of
it deals with this novel. She has also published a discussion
of Nina's character in "Nina o la Misericordia," Insula, no.
151 (1959), 1.

Misericordia. Con un prefacio del autor escrito especialmente para esta edición (Paris: etc., Thomas Nelson and
Sons [1913]), pp. 5-9, "es un verdadero prólogo en que
Galdós presenta Misericordia y explica entre otras cosas elementos de la novela y de sus personajes" (Shoemaker, Los
prólogos de Galdós, p. 35). The text of Galdós' "prefacio"
to his novel can best be found in Shoemaker, Los prólogos
de Galdós, pp. 108-10.

A Brazilian study of this novel is found in Sylvio Julio,
"Pérez Galdós num romance," Estudos hispanoamericanos
(Rio de Janeiro: Libreria Espanhola, 1924), pp. 101-12.

Pierre Guenoun has written an interesting preface to
his French translation of this novel, pp. 7-12 of Miséricorde
(Paris: Les Editeurs Français Réunis, c1964). Pages 8-10
discuss the earlier translation into French of this novel which
was produced with Galdós' assistance. The translation was
the work of Maurice Bixio and ran first as a serial in Le
temps; it then appeared in Paris (Hachette, 1900, vi, 316pp.)
with a preface by the great French Hispanist Morel-Fatio.
Guenoun finds much to criticize in this early translation.
The translator views the novel as "l'allégorie d'une Espagne
déchirée que se réconcilie dans le roman des gueux. Galdós
y décrit une novelle fois la bourgeoisie de Madrid, un Madrid
auquel il a laissé son nom est qu'on appelle communement
galdosiano, un Madrid qui es en train de disparaître et dont
il ne reste plus que quelques lambeaux accrochés à des dé-
cors. La réussite de Galdós est d'avoir fixé, comme il le
souhaitait, les traits de l'Espagne de son temps. Ce grand
imaginatif, que se voulait réaliste, a même fait plus que de
fixer des traits: il leur a donné la sensibilité" (p. 13).

Misericordia (play). Alfredo Mañas Navascues has
produced a theatrical version of this Galdós novel. It was
published in Madrid by Escelier in 1972 as Colección Teatro
721 with 86 pages.

While the compiler knows of no reviews of the printed version based on this novel, two reviews have reached his attention concerning the play itself. They are: Angel Fernández-Santos, Insula, nos. 308-309 (julio-agosto 1972), 27, and Enrique Climent, Reseña, no. 56 (junio 1972), 28-29.

Fernández-Santos finds Misericordia "un ejercicio literario expertísimo ... un auténtico muestrario de recursos dramatúrgicos, de ingenio coloquial y de sentido de la escena. En rigor, se trata de un verdadero trabajo de autoría teatral ... trabajo muy personal suyo [que] sin embargo deja a salvo en su singularidad la singularidad galdosiana, como consecuencia de su carácter profundamente fiel a la materia prima...."

Climent discusses briefly some reasons for the revival of interest in Galdós and compares the characters of the novel with those of the dramatic version performed in Madrid in 1972.

Nazarín and Halma

These two novels are often discussed together by the critics. Much additional data on them will be found in the section devoted to religion in the works of Galdós. This section dealing with these two novels is divided into two parts: 1) several recent important studies concerning the two novels, and 2) a note of the important criticism of Buñuel's movie version of Nazarín (1958).

Walter T. Pattison, "Verdaguer y Nazarín," Cuadernos hispanoamericanos, nos. 250-252 (1970-1971), 537-546, writes: "De lo que acabamos de citar es evidente que existían ciertas relaciones, no muy íntimas, entre el novelista y el poeta y que las semejanzas entre Verdaguer y Nazarín eran notables. Queda saber si, en efecto, Galdós conocía el caso Verdaguer cuando escribía sus dos novelas" (p. 538). He notes that "De lo que quedo dicho inferimos que hay una fuerte posibilidad de influencias verdaguerianas en la concepción de las dos novelas de Galdós" (p. 454).

Gustavo Correa discusses these novels in his El simbolismo religioso.... Chapter X is "La definición del ser religioso en Nazarín," pp. 166-78, and chapter XI is "La fundación ideal de la Condesa de Halma," pp. 180-94. The chapter on Nazarín contains an introduction and two sections: La biografía externa and La biografía interna. He notes that "En la evolución de la novela galdosiana, la

figura de Nazarín representa la reafirmación del ente religioso como manera de ser del hombre en este mundo" (p.
166). This same paragraph states that "Nazarín da plena
expresión al sentir trascendente con su doctrina de la anula-
ción del ser, la imitación del ser, la imitación de Jesucristo
y la práctica efusiva del amor al prójimo. Veamos en qué
forma la biografía novelística perfila los rasgos de este
personalidad característica" (p. 166).

The chapter on Halma contains an introduction and
three sections: El amor y la regeneración del ser, La fundación utópica de Halma and La santidad como cordura. Correa
finds that "La novela se desarrolla, así, en dos planos bien
definidos que corresponden a las dos figuras de Nazarín y
Halma, cuya mutua interrelación decide el destino personal de
esta última" (p. 180). He states that "Lo característico de
la novela Halma es, por consiguiente, la integración del amor
humano dentro del amor divino" (p. 182).

The second volume (1967) of Anales galdosianos contains the following articles which are of interest for the study
of Nazarín: Frank P. Bowman, "On the definition of Jesus
in modern fiction," pp. 53-66; Ciriaco Morón Arroyo, Nazarín y Halma: sentido y unidad," pp. 67-81; Alexander A.
Parker, "Nazarín, or the Passion of Our Lord Jesus Christ
according to Galdós," pp. 83-101. Also in this issue, pp.
157-64 of Vera Colin, "A note on Tolstoy and Galdós," show
Tolstoy's influence on this novel and on Halma.

Bowman discusses narrative literature produced between 1780 and 1940 in which Christ or a Christ figure is a
leading character. In addition to an introduction, this article
has the following subdivisions: The literary "imitation" of
Christ; Teacher of love, tormented prophet, or revolutionary;
The types of narrative imitation, the rhetoric of narrative
imitations of Jesus; and The meanings of Jesus in modern
narrative. His concluding sentences (p. 66) are: "I hope
my methodology does explain why Galdós should place a Jesus
figure in Spain...; why he introduces the long conversation
with Belmonte as a means of didactically expressing such
themes as that of the 'socialist Jesus'; and why his novel
ends as it does, partly because of the necessary contamination
of sources in Nazarín, partly because the willing march toward meaningful and victorious suffering or death is the major
constant of the myth of Jesus in the age in which he wrote.
I also hope I have suggested how he sought and achieved both
verisimilitude and a certain high seriousness by making of his

hero a figure of Jesus." Besides the Bible, Bowman suggests Don Quijote and the works of Al-Hallaj as sources.

According to Morón Arroyo, "propongo la tesis siguiente: Nazarín y Halma están íntimamente conexas y son una novelación de los dos primeros tomos de la Historia de lo origines del cristianismo de Renan: Vida de Jesus y Los apóstoles" (p. 67). He also states that "La primera pregunta la plantea Nazarín como protagonista: ¿Es una personalidad equilibrada? No se presenta a veces orgulloso, otras demasiado inocente, otras inactivo e indisciplinado? Hasta qué punto ha logrado Galdós un 'alter Christus' más o menos digno? Estas preguntas nos fuerzan a acercarnos al Evangelio para catalogar los rasgos esenciales de Nuestro Señor Jesucristo y compararlos con el psicograma de Nazarín" (p. 67). His discussion of Jesucristo en el Evangelio has the following divisions: 1) Ideal evangélico de vida, 2) Testimonio y orgullo, 3) Santa ira, 4) Misterio, casi tragedia. His discussion of Nazarín protagonista has almost the same divisions. The third section of this article is entitled Jesucristo, mimo; the fifth deals with Galdós and Renan.

Parker notes the influence of Tolstoy, Cervantes and the Bible upon this novel. He quotes a passage from a letter by Angel Ganivet that is "a protest against crude materialism and against the selfishness of the rich, rather than a religious awakening" (p. 85). He does not feel that the novel "is a failure because of its excessive symbolism" (p. 87), but feels that "it is a powerful and moving presentation of the anguish of existence in the world of men's own creating--a world in which the goodness, charity and compassion to which men are called are racked and broken by the brutal selfishness and callous cynicism that they in fact embrace" (pp. 90-91). Pages 96-99 are a discussion of Halma. Parker states that "By comparison with its predecessor the climax is a descent into bathos" (p. 98).

Julian Palley, "Nazarín y El idiota," Insula, no. 258 (1968), 3, is a comparison and discussion of these two novels, especially of the characters of Nazarín and Prince Myshkin. He finds that "Cuando se lanza Galdós a una dirección nueva, como en Nazarín, no puede mantener los matices, la sutileza y la profundidad de su mejor obra. Si concluimos diciendo que Nazarín, es más bien para afirmar la grandeza de Dostoyevsky que para disminuir el acierto indudable de Galdós."

Critics in the United States have paid little attention
to the movie version of Nazarín, which won a "gran premio
internacional" at the Cannes Film Festival. Vernon A.
Chamberlin, Hispania, 42 (1959), 620-21, had high praise
for the film. He notes that "Movie goers will find the ending
decidedly, but not ineffectively changed" (p. 620).

Reviews in journals and newspapers of a general nature
are found in the Christian Century, 75 (Nov. 6, 1968), 1410,
by Marion Armstrong; Nation, 207 (July 8, 1968), 28-29, by
Robert Hatch; Commonweal, 88 (July 26, 1968), 505-06, by
Philip T. Hartung; and New York Times, June 21, 1968,
p. 48, by Renata Adler.

Film Culture, no. 21 (Summer, 1960), 60-62, publishes
a review by the well-known Mexican novelist Octavio Paz, and
Film Quarterly, 13, no. 3 (Spring, 1960), 30-31, publishes
one by Gavin Lambert.

Paz finds that "Nazarín follows ... in the great tradition of mad Spaniards, originated by Cervantes. His madness
consists of taking seriously great ideas and big words, and
trying to live accordingly. Mad is he who refuses to admit
that reality is real but not an atrocious caricature of true reality; Nazarín sees a helpless image of 'the fallen people' behind the monstrous features of Andara and Ujo; and behind
the erotic frenzy of Beatriz--the echo of divine love" (p. 61).

Lambert summarizes the film's plot, discusses the
character, and notes that Buñuel once said "that his aim in
making films was to convince people that they don't live in
the best of all possible worlds" (p. 30). His knowledge of
Pérez Galdós is slight, for he writes: "I haven't read the
original, but suspect--since it was one of Galdós' last works,
written after a nervous breakdown which resulted in religious
conversion--that Buñuel has turned it inside out, just as a
few episodes in the film (notably the healing of the sick child)
seem to turn the New Testament inside out. In any case,
the result has all the impact of an absolute masterpiece,
a work of beautiful, explosive force and strangeness"
(p. 31).

The English script translated from the French as
found in L'avant scène du cinéma can be found in The Ex-
terminating Angel, Nazarín and Los Olvidados: Three films
by Luis Buñuel, translated by Nicholas Fry (London, Lorrimer Publishing, 1972), pp. 117-205. The screen credits
are found on pp. 114-115. An English translation of the

French article by J. Francisco Aranda in Cahiers du cinéma
appears as "The passion according to Buñuel," pp. 107-113.

The French have produced the most and the best criticism of this Buñuel film. The French bibliography of the
film is more or less as follows: Ado Kyrou, Luis Buñuel
(Paris: Seghers, 1962, [Cinéma d'aujourd'hui 4]); Michel
Estève, "Nazarín et Le journal d'un curé de campagne: La
passion refusée et aceptée," Etudes cinématographiques, no.
10-11 (1961), 217-34; Gérard Gozlan, "Les lettres du généri-
que sont en forme de croix (Nazarín)," Positif, no. 42
(novembre, 1961), 31-51; J.-P. Torok., "La passion de Nazarín,"
Positif, no. 38; (mars, 1961), 61-64; Henry Magnan, "Nazarín ou Luis Buñuel et la fidelité," Combat, May 11, 1959,
p. 2; Pierre Marcabru, "Nazarín ou l'ambiguité," Combat,
Dec. 2, 1960, p. 8; Jean de Baroncelli, "Nazarín de Luis
Buñuel," Le monde, Dec. 3, 1960, p. 12; André S. Labarthe,
"Un désespoir actif," Cahiers du cinéma, Jan., 1961, pp. 46-
49; Jean Domarchi, "Eros contre le Christ," Arts, no. 799
(Dec. 7, 1960), p. 7; Louis Soler, Clarté, journal des étu-
diants communistes, in no. 32 (1960?); Jean-Louis Tallenay,
Radio-Cinéma-Télévision, in no. 488 (May, 1959); *Gilbert
Salachas, in Télé-Ciné, Oct., 1959; *Father Avril, in Télé-
rama, no. 570 (Dec., 1960); Georges Sadoul, "Un nouveau
Don Quichotte," Les lettres françaises, dec. 8, 1960, p. 10;
Max Aub, "Galdós et Nazarín," Les lettres françaises, Dec.
15, 1960, p. 7, and J. F. Aranda, "La passion selon Buñuel,"
Cahiers du cinéma, 16 (1959), 27-32.

Kyrou calls this film, "une des oevures les plus complexes de toute sa carrière" (p. 56). He also states that
"On a assez disséqué ce film ... pour qu'il ne soit pas nécessaire d'expliquer encore l'évidence: Buñuel n'est plus
anti-clérical, il est athée, il a décovert le calme, il
emprunte dorénavant les chemins de la révolte essentielle,
il mine les bases même et non plus les seuls épiphénomènes
de la société très sante et très bourgeoise qui nous opprime"
(p. 57). A French translation of a portion of the script of
this movie appears in this volume, pp. 155-61. Selections
from the film's scenario have also appeared as "Nazarín:
un film de Luis Buñuel, prix international Cannes 1959,"
Radio-Cinéma, Télévision, nos. 491-96 (1960).

The film aroused much controversy in the French
press and Kyrou notes that "On a beaucoup parlé de ce film,
on en a dit surtout beaucoup de bêtises et les sempiternels
fossoyeurs se sont empressés d'enterrer Buñuel sous des
louanges dont il n'avait que faire" (p. 56).

Estève's article appears in an issue devoted to "La
passion du Christ comme thème cinématographique." The
author compares the film version of the Galdós novel with
that of the novel by Bernanos. He compares the novel to the
movie version, and finds that Buñuel has been unfaithful to the
novel, whereas Bresson, the director of the Journal d'un
curé de campagne, has remained faithful to Bernanos. He
finds that "Le spectateur de Nazarín a l'étrange impression
d'assister à un récit didactique; devant ses yeux, Buñuel
presente une expérience imaginaire idéale (comment réagirait
la société face au comportement d'un chrétien authentique?)
où le héros n'a acucun contact direct avec la transcendance
divine; conçu comme un hypothétique concept, Dieu n'est pas
celui qui semble avoir abandonné son serviteur, mas celui
qui ne l'a jamais aimé au point de vouloir communiquer"
(p. 234). Estève has carefully studied both the novel and the
film.

Torok writes that "Buñuel ne s'interesse dans le mythe
chrétien qu'à ses incidences morales, et étudie le cas d'un
homme en proie à la morale chrétienne" (p. 61). For this
reviewer "Nazarín est un personnage sublime parce que Dieu
n'existe pas. Paraphrase: un homme qui aime à la folie
une femme irréelle est un personnage beaucoup plus intéressant que le héros sans surprise d'un amour partagé. La
vie, les actes et les paroles de Nazarín sont absurdes parce
que ne tenant à rien, et pour cette raison étrangement fasci-
nants. Qu'est-ce que le christianisme pour Buñuel, sinon un
aspect de la folie?" (p. 62).

The article by Gozlan is an extraordinary piece of
movie criticism. Pages 46-51 contain an elaborate collection
of footnotes in which the author produces a running commentary on remarks made by other French critics on this movie.
Gozlan discusses the movie's symbolism and its ideology. It
is of interest to note that "De toutes façons, l'essentiel du
film est dans sa substance, non dans sa conclusion. Nazarín
est une machine de guerre qui attaque la religion catholique
au profit d'un humanisme anticlérical et athée, qui, dans le
contexte de plusieurs scènes du film et de l'oeuvre entière de
Buñuel, passe nécessairement par le stade de la Révolution
prolétarienne et travailleuse. Je ne veux pas dire que ce
soit obligatoirement formulé ainsi dans l'esprit de Buñuel. Je
veux dire que la révolte bunéélienne suppose et envisage des
conflits d'ordre révolutionaire et pas des conflits d'ordre religieux. C'est pourquoi cette révolte est féconde. Luis Buñuel restera, c'est clair, comme l'un des plus lucides et

passionnés chroniqueurs de la décomposition implacable de
notre société bourgeoise, que cette décomposition soit intel-
lectuelle, morale, sentimentale, sexuelle, artisque ou politique" (p. 45).

Magnan calls the film an "oeuvre sincèrement irreli-
gieuse, voluntairement démystificatrice."

Pierre Marcabru finds that Nazarín "est le contraire
d'un film chrétien, tout mysticisme en est absent ... ce
n'est past un film que va audelà des formes sensibles, un
film d' apprehension et d'intuition c'est essentiellement,
profondément un film matérialiste. Et c'est un très
beau et tres noble film dans l'affirmation de ce matérialisme. "

Jean de Baroncelli states that "Tout Buñuel est là,
présent, avec sa cruauté, sa violence, son goût du sacrilège
(la prostituée regardant dans son délire une image pieuse et
decouvrant un Christ déformé par un horrible rictus), mais
aussi avec sa douceur, sa tendresse, cette pure et dure
amité qu'il porte aux 'autres.'"

Labarthe's remarks for the most part are a discussion of Buñuel as an artist. He finds the film to be "une
oeuvre paisible et claire. Car ce qui rend Nazarín ambigu,
ce n'est pas l'opacité de sa représentation, mais au contraire
sa transparence. Son itinéraise est une lente el douloureuse
prise de conscience, une lutte où s'affrontent en lui sa
fonction et sa concience (p. 48) ... Nazarín, on le voit, ne
peut se définir par l'affirmation brutale d'une morale,
puisqu'il montre au contraire l'impossibilité provisoire d'une
morale veritablement humaine" (p. 49).

Domarchi's comments are of interest because of his
discussion of Buñuel's atheism as shown in the film version
based on the Galdós novel. He notes that "Un athée espagnol
ne peut pas ignorer la présence de la Croix. Il est contraint
au blasphème et la seule façon efficace de blasphémer c'est
de chanter de manière provocante les joies de l'amour physique." He finds that the movie "est donc le combat de l'amour
et de la religion." He states that "Buñuel est fasciné par le
catholicisme car en tant que'artiste il ne peut pas être insen-
sible à son sens du cérémonial de la fête." Domarchi claims
that "Nazarín n'est ni catholique ni athée, il est un épisode
d'un nouveau combat avec l'Ange que Buñuel n'a pas fini de
livrer."

The article by Aranda has the following sections: Introductory remarks, Un match Buñuel-Figueroa, Nazarín ou l' "antichurro," Le Christ pile et face, Don Quichotte et ses deux Sanchos, and Les bourgeois et l'ananas. The article is illustrated with four photographs. The title promises much more than is delivered.

Soler's "Dieu est mort en exile" is of interest for several reasons. He presents us with an opinion by a French communist on Galdós, Buñuel and Nazarín. He writes: "Voilà donc ce que Galdós, à la veille du XXème siècle, oppose à un matérialisme à courte vue, à un capitalisme encore peu hypocrite. Mais cet homme qui a eu un grand-père secrétaire de l'inquisition, un oncle prêtre ... n'a pas eu a souffrir personnellement de l'infâme ni de la Grande Muette, ce qui explique en partie le réformisme délirant de Nazarín. Il n'aura pas de mal à se réfugier momentanément dans un spiritualisme à la russe, à se laisser porter par les fictions qui croient dépasser les réalitiés." Soler speaks of "l'originalité généreuse de Buñuel au cours de son travail d'adaptation, malgré une apparente fidélité à Galdós." Comparing the novel by Galdós with the film version by Buñuel, he finds that "le roman de Galdós a subi une heureuse condensation dans le scénario" and that in the film version "Chaque personnage est aussi plus proche de nous: Nazarín, le doux Nazarín, a perdu cette débilité un peu romantique qu'il gardait encore chez Galdós: il est aussi plus humain dans sa perfection, moins facilement exemplaire, même avant le fin du film." Soler states that "Dans Nazarín, il ne propose pas un système humaniste. Dans son domaine, il ne tombe pas dans le travers naivement didactique de Galdós. Au fond, il aborde par l'intermédiarie de la religion, et avec plus de succès encore, le même aspect que dans Cela s'appelle l'aurore l'état de notre société ne laisse espérer qu'une solution venue de l'amour et de l'amitié."

Tallenay's brief comments note that "Nazarín est la plus pure illustration d'un christianisme vécu." He feels that never before in the history of the movies have the three virtues--poverty, chastity and obedience--been so well portrayed on the screen. He writes that "grâce au génie de Buñuel les scènes qui illustrent la pratique de ces vertus son simples, naturelles et vraies, sans ressemebler jamais à un sermon, sans que jamais soit en rien diminuée la valeur humaine de set homme ... qui vit intensément sous nos yeux 'dans le monde comme n'en étant pas.'"

Aub's comments deal more with Galdós in general than with the movie. He finds that "Buñuel a respecté très consciencieusement le roman qui lui avait été donné et on ne peut que s'étonner de constater que la plupart des critiques aient cru que le thème avait été imaginé par lui." He finds that moving the setting of the movie from Spain to Mexico "n'a rien ajouté ni rien retranché."

Sadoul's remarks are of interest for his discussion of Nazarín and Don Quijote.

Raymond Durgnat, Luis Buñuel ([London], Studio Vista, [1967]), pp. 109-113, is entitled "The acts of an apostle." This chapter is illustrated with four photographs from the movie. Durgnat makes no mention of Galdós' novel. He finds that "The film's magic arises from the interpenetration of fault and force, of hypocrisy and purity on all the characters" (p. 111). He elaborates for most of p. 112 on the topic that "From a variety of Christian viewpoints it can be argued that the film is not anti-Christian at all."

Though Buñuel is considered to be Spain's greatest movie producer, he has produced many of his most important films outside of Spain. In comparison with the dozen or more important reviews of the movie version of Nazarín found in the French newspapers and journals, little of this nature seems readily available in regard to Spanish newspapers and journals. Manuel Rabanal Taylor, "Nazarín: Galdós visto por Buñuel," Insula, no. 163 (junio de 1960), 14, is the only such study of importance that I have found. This reviewer attempts to describe briefly the economic state of affairs in Spain at the end of the 19th century when the novel was written. He compares Nazarín's character as depicted in the novel and in Buñuel's film version. The article is of particular importance for showing that Buñuel includes "secuencias y variantes que no figuran en la novela de Galdós." The reviewer notes that more social protest appears in the film than in the novel and he elaborates upon these differences. There is also an evaluation of this film as a work of art.

Lo prohibido

The most important of the recent studies on this novel are: Vernon A. Chamberlin, "Galdós' chromatic symbolism

key in Lo prohibido," Hispanic Review, 32 (1964), 109-17;
Sherman Eoff, "A Galdosian version of picaresque psychology,"
Modern Language Forum, 38 (1953), 1-12; Robert Ricard,
"De los nombres de Cristo a Lo prohibido," Les langues neo-
latines, no. 160 (1962), 36-39, reprinted with important addi-
tions in Aspects de Galdós (Paris: Presses Universitaires
de France, 1963), pp. 94-104; "Un roman de Galdós: Lo pro-
hibidio. Remarques et suggestions," Les langues neo-latines,
no. 155 (1960), 3-15, reprinted in Galdós et ses romans,
pp. 75-88; "Nouvelles remarques sur Lo prohibido de Galdós,"
Bulletin hispanique, 69 (1967), 389-406; Gustavo Correa, "La
expulsión del paraíso en Lo prohibido," in El simbolismo religioso..., pp. 80-95; and Arthur Terry, "Lo prohibido: unreliable narrator and untruthful narrative," Galdós studies,
pp. 62-89.

Chamberlin shows in a discussion of each of the following colors that red symbolizes inmoralidad matrimonial,
adulterio, belenes; blue, inmoralidad política y administrativa, ilegalidad, arbitrariedad, cohechos; yellow, inmoralidad
pecuniaria, usura, disipación; green, inmoralidad física,
embriaguez; and purple, inmoralidad religiosa, descreimiento.
There is a section on polichromatic symbolism and occasional
references to the use of color in other Galdosian novels.

Eoff's article has as its thesis that "there is a strong
possibility that he [i.e., Galdós] thought seriously of the
basic attitude toward life incorporated in Alemán's novel
[i.e., Guzmán de Alfarache], as seen especially with respect
to Spanish society." He also states that "The central personage of Lo prohibido, without being an outright pícaro,
possesses the essentials of the picaresque attitude, as this
is exemplified in Guzmán de Alfarache" (p. 2). Eoff finds
that the two novels resemble each other in their "view of
personality and its relation to environment, not in the narration of events" (p. 3). The personality and psychology of
Guzmán de Alfarache and José María Buenos de Guzmán are
compared and contrasted, pp. 5-7. Eoff feels that this
"novel should be regarded as anti-naturalistic in its thought
content, rather than naturalistic" (p. 11) and that this literary
genre has been revived by Galdós "as a study in psychology
and morality" (p. 12).

Ricard's "De los nombres de Cristo a Lo prohibido"
finds that "Le titre du roman de Galdós Lo prohibido attire
l'attention parce qu'il est exceptionnel de voir l'auteur re-
courir ainsi à une notion abstraite pour désigner un de ses

récits" (p. 99). He feels that Galdós drew his title from the
second book of Fray Luis de León's De los nombres de
Christo.

Ricard's "Un roman de Galdós..." notes that the critics
have paid relatively little attention to this novel, yet he feels
that "L'oeuvre cependant n'est pas négligeable et elle tire un
interêt particulier du fait que c'est peut-être le roman le plus
gratuit de Galdós, celui où il s'est le moins engagé, un récit à l'état presque pur. Loin d'être spectateur ou temoin
comme il arrive si souvent ailleurs, le romancier, dissimule
dernière la personnage qui raconte ses souvenirs, se montre
aussi peu que possible. Ce trait ne facilite assurement pas
l'interprétation, mais, s'il nous interdit pas non plus de
chercher à mettre en incite à la prudence et à la reserve,
il ne nous lumiére quelques aspects de ce roman un peu mé-
connu" (p. 75). Ricard notes that "Un des traits distinctifs
de Lo prohibido, c'est donc qu'il est écrit à la précision
chronologique est donc une des qualités les plus spécifiques
de Lo prohibido" (p. 80). After discussing the fact that
Galdós is not a blind disciple of Taine, Comte or Zola, Ricard states that "Le naturalisme doctrinal, qu'on trouve
implicite dans son oeuvre romanesque, est celui que j'ai
indiqué tout à l'heure à propos de Camila. C'est une vision
du monde, de l'homme et de la vie qui donne la primauté
à la nature sans aucune référence à un être transcendant et
à un absolu" (p. 88).

"Nouvelles remarques..." examines the "structure
du récit, réapparition des personnages et peinture d'une société, évocation des faits d'actualité, importance des vévro-
ses, rapports avec les autres romans, continuité et cohérence dans les détails que aboutissent à donner l'illusion de
la réalité" (from the abstract).

Correa's study has an introduction which places this
novel along with La desheredada, El doctor Centeno, Tormento and La de Bringas in Galdós' so-called naturalist phase.
The characteristics of this group of novels are noted and a
plot summary then provided. There then follow "La fruta
prohibidia y el demonio tentador," "La pareja primaria y la
concepción del paraíso" and "Nabucodonosor y la expulsión
del paraíso." Correa's final paragraph (p. 95) neatly summarizes his arguments: "La novela Lo prohibido encarna,
por consiguiente, la historia bíblica de la expulsión del Paraíso en la persona de José María Bueno de Guzmán, cuya
debilidad física constitucional y sus fallas morales lo

sumieron en el abismo del mal, haciendolo actuar al mismo
tiempo como demonio tentador y víctima que se deleita en la
fruta prohibida.   Al dar rienda suelta a su pasión mórbida
se convirtió en ente constitutivo de maldad que atentaba contra
la institución de la familia y la inocencia paradisíaca de la
pareja primria y natural.   La fortaleza moral de los esposos
Miquis y su mutua lealtad inconmovible, permiten revirir el
concepto de un paraíso terrenal perpetuado en el reino del
amor.   Por el contrario, el demonio tentador es no solamente expulsado de este paraíso, sino que es condenado a
sufrir el castigo degradante a que fue sometido Nabucodonosor también en la historia bíblica."

Arthur Terry first reviews some of the previous critics of the novel.   He finds that "The richness of Lo prohibido
comes from the ways in which the suggestion of a basic
scheme is overlaid and complicated in the interests of truthfulness, a fact which is brought out clearly by Galdós' use
of first-person narrative" (p. 65).   Terry analyzes the character of José María and the role that he plays in the novel.
He writes: "Once it has been shown that a particular narrator is unreliable, we must ask 'to what extent'?   If we
apply this question to José María Bueno, we find that the
answer is extremely complex: that it implies nothing less
than the total effect of the novel.   One guiding principle,
however, stands out: if for the greater part of the novel
José María is an unreliable narrator, by the time we reach
the closing chapters he has become rather less so, though
he still falls short of total reliability" (p. 67).   He discusses
the "two driving forces of José María's existence, money
and sex" (p. 74).   Terry feels that "What makes Lo prohibido a masterpiece is not the observation of society or the
dissection of character, but the steady revelation of values
which are in constant danger of being falsified by the narrator
himself.   This narrator, unreliable and unprincipled as he is,
is the essential instrument in Galdós' imaginative achievement" (p. 89).

La razón de la sin razón

Eduardo Gómez de Baquero, "La razón de la sin
razón," Novelas y novelistas (Madrid: Calleja, 1918),
pp. 108-12, devotes half of his discussion to the novela
dialogada.   Very little criticism has appeared concerning
this novel.

Realidad

The most important studies on this novel are: Shirley
Russell Fite, "The literary origins of Realidad by Benito Pé-
rez Galdós" (Ph.D. dissertation, University of Minnesota,
1958, 234 leaves; Dissertation Abstracts, 19 [1959], 2088);
Joaquín Casalduero, "Ana Karenina y Realidad," Bulletin
hispanique, 39 (1937), 375-96, reprinted in his Estudios de
literatura española (Madrid: Gredos, 1962), pp. 121-46;
Benito Pérez Galdós (1973), pp. 209-230; Ricardo Gullón,
"Una novela psicológica," Insula, no. 82 (oct., 1952), 4; and
Gonzalo Sobejano, "Forma literaria y sensibilidad social en
La incógnita y Realidad de Galdós," Revista hispánica mo-
derna, 30 (1964), 89-107.

Fite shows the influence of Tolstoy, Bourget and Ibsen
on this novel. The author suggests that the Fuencarral murder trial "provided Galdós with the germinating idea for the
novel" and states that "The character of Orozco is shown to
be an example of the krausista lay saint" (p. 208).

Casalduero states that "sería prudente revisar la
doctrina de Portnoff, pues no sólo podemos hallar que es
incorrecta, sino que impide captar la contextura del cosmos
galdosiano, la gravedad de lo cual no se escapará a nadie"
(p. 122-23). He analyzes the plot and characters found in
both novels and denies any Tolstoian influence. On p. 146,
he writes: "Galdós en Realidad trata tres problemas distintos:
a) insuficiencia de la razón y de la observación para captar
el mundo; b) la España tradicional en lucha con el Tiempo
se ve vencida y obligada a desaparecer si no quiere terminar
en la ignominia; c) la nueva conciencia, el hombre nuevo."

Gullón's article is a commentary on both La incógnita
and Realidad. He states that these two novels "no son primera y segunda parte de una novela, sino dos aspectos de la
misma y, en cierto modo, dos novelas que tienen idéntico
asunto, personajes, tipos y lugares, diferenciándose en cuanto
a la técnica expositiva." Besides elaborating on this point,
he points out the importance of dreams in both novels.

Sobejano finds that "La incógnita (1889), Realidad
novela en cinco jornadas (1889), y Realidad drama en cinco
actos (1892) son tres formas literarias distintas de una misma
materia argumental" (p. 89). He notes that "El tema principal de las consideraciones que siguen es otro valor de las

obras aludidas, que ... merece un análisis más detenido:
la correspondencia entre las formas literarias aplicadas por
Galdós al tratamiento de aquel solo y mismo asunto y las
modalidades de su sensibilidad al interpretar el contenido
social en ese asunto entrañada ... Con estas tres versiones
de un mismo asunto, Galdós verifica una súbita revolución
en su tecnica cuyo sentido importa esclarecer" (pp. 89-90).

Robert H. Russell, "La óptica del novelista en La
incógnita y Realidad," Filología, 10 (1965), 179-85, is a study
of the two novels that the author suggests "nos dan la idea de
que Galdós va utilizando los dos relatos para decirnos entre
otras cosas que las novelas espitolares son imprecisas y
vagas y las dialogadas exactas y visibles" (p. 179). Russell
further states, "No se trata, pues, de hacer un contraste
puramente formal y mecánico de las dos obras. Hay que
buscar los íntimos lazos de unión, hay que solucionar el
problema de las perspectivas con algo más unitivo que una
simple declaración de la preferencia de Galdós, que indubable-
mente si inclinaba por el procedimiento dialogado" (p. 180).
The article is concerned with "el problema de la visibilidad
de los personajes y de los hechos" (p. 180). Russell's concluding sentence notes that "En La incógnita y Realidad Galdós
nos da esta lección de arte de novelar: observar la vida es
tan inseguro y accidentado como vivirla, pero la novela tiene
que crear la ilusión de estarla viviendo" (p. 185).

La sombra

        Rodolfo Cardona, "Introducción a La sombra," trans-
lated by Antonio Martínez Herrarte from Cardona's W. W.
Norton edition of this novel, Benito Pérez Galdós (1973),
pp. 247-255, presents a variety of interesting ideas concerning this early Galdós novel. Cardona writes that "El propósito de esta introducción no es hacer un análisis completo de
la novela para mostrar, paso a paso, que es posible explicar,
desde una perspectiva psicoanalítica, todos los sucesos del
relato de Anselmo, sino simplemente señalar que tal posibilidad existe" (p. 252). He notes that he anticipated Freud
in many respects and states that "Cuando observamos el uso
que Galdós hace de lo 'fantástico' en La sombra nos damos
cuenta de que las fantasías que presenta no son sino proyec-
ciones de la forma de ser de sus personajes, muchos de
ellos anormales" (p. 254). He notes that Galdós uses "lo
'fantástico' para sondear en el carácter y la conducta de los
seres humanos. Como tal, esta novela es probablemente

una de las primeras en toda Europa que presenta el 'historial'
completo de un psicópata con el proposito de explicar sus
autoengaños, logrando así una novela notablemente 'freudiana'
mucho antes de que Freud hubiera comenzado sus investigaciones" (p. 249).

E. Chamorro's prologue to La sombra (Madrid: Miguel Castellote, 1972), pp. 7-9 (Colección de Bolsillo basico,
15), is too short to be really useful.

Andrés Amorós, "La sombra: realidad e imaginacion,"
Cuadernos hispanoamericanos, nos. 250-252 (1970-71), 523-
536, is an analysis of the plot, characters and style of this
novel. The critic finds that he himself feels that the fact
that "El sueño--la imaginación--se ha instalado en medio de
la realidad" "parece más interesante de toda la novela"
(p. 533). His concluding paragraph states that "Resulta interesante hallar, al comienzo de la carrera de Galdos, en su
período más 'realista,' una obra como ésta, en la que hallamos rasgos que suelen ser tenidos por característicos del
último período. Esa es la coherencia personal y estilística
de toda la obra de Galdós. Y ése es el tipo de 'realismo'
tan poco unilateral, que le caracteriza" (p. 536).

Rafael Bosch, "La sombra y la psicopatología de
Galdós," Anales galdosianos, 6 (1971), 21-42, writes that
"lo que nos importa ante todo hacer constar es que desde
ésta su segunda novela ha adoptado Galdós posiciones importantes y originales en cuestiones psicopatológicas, y debemos discutir si estas posiciones son freudianas o anti-freu-
dianas" (p. 21).

An editorial note, "La sombra: dos interpretaciones,"
Anales galdosianos, 6 (1971), 3, notes that this article presents "con gran detalle y erudición, todo el trasfondo científico implícito en esta obra primeriza que, lejos de apuntar
hacia lo freudiano, como algunos habian propuesto, parece
más explorar las vías que la fisiología y la neuropatía de
su tiempo le proporcionaron a traves de ciertos tratados y
textos que, como el autor demuestra, estuvieron al alcance
de Galdós."

Carlos Rovetta, "La sombra, novela primigenia de
Galdós," Nosotros, series 2, 23 (1943), 180-86, feels that
this novel has been unjustly ignored and neglected. He notes
its scarcity and states that it was first published in 1870 in
the Revista de España. It was then reprinted "en folletines

de diversos periódicos" (p. 182). This article is of value
as being one of the first written on this novel. He finds in
this early novel many of the characteristics that are considered now to be typically Galdosian.

Harriet S. Turner, "Rhetoric in La sombra: the
author and his story," Anales galdosianos, 6 (1971), 5-19,
notes that this novel "deserves attention and respect ...
because of the novelistic techniques Galdós used to develop within
his story a difficult question of moral responsibility. Even in its
rudimentary form La sombra anticipates in both manner and matter the artistry characteristic of later masterpieces" (p. 5).

She analyzes Cardona's view of this novel as expressed
in his introduction to La sombra. On p. 6, the author writes
that "A discussion of La sombra from the point of view of
rhetoric focuses upon the effects certain novelistic elements
produce and whether such effects are appropriate to the novel.
In this essay I am primarily concerned with the problem of
how Galdós, as an author present in his own novel, handles
his relationship to Don Anselmo so that, upon arousing and
guiding certain sympathetic reactions, he induces the reader
not only to recognize but to accept the message ultimately
embodied in the facts of the story."

This novel has been the inspiration of León Felipe's
drama, "La manzana: fabula o juego poético y simbólico de
hombres y mujeres contando en español" which can be found
in at least three places: La manzana: (poema cinematográfi-
co) (México: Tezontle, 1951), 125pp.: Cuadernos americanos, 12 (1954), 221-93; and pp. 425-521 of his Obras completas (Buenos Aires: Losada, 1963). He acknowledges the
source for this work in these words: "Yo he recogido, además, para componer este poema dos episodios que casi se
han disuelto ya en el juego poético de los simbolos, de un
cuento de D. Benito Pérez Galdós llamado La sombra...."
(p. 424 of his Obras completas).

Tormento

Alfredo Rodríguez, "Sobre el contenido y el uso líri-
cos en Tormento," Romance Notes, 8 (1967), 204-06, is an
analysis of "el papel que desempeñan en Tormento los trozos
de calidad poética que se han señalado" (p. 206). He differs
with various critics and believes that "Galdós no carece ni

de sensibilidad ni de conocimientos poéticos" (p. 206). This article has been reprinted in his Aspectos de la novela de Galdós, pp. 145-50.

Rodríguez, "Otras perspectivas sobre Tormento," Aspectos de la novela de Galdós, pp. 66-81, is to a great extent a reply to R. Ricard, "Place et signification de Tormento entre El doctor Centeno et La de Bringas," Aspects de Galdós, pp. 44-60, and F. Durand, "Two problems in Galdós' Tormento," Modern Language Notes, 89 (1964), 524-25.

His two final paragraphs are: "Difícil será que haya otra novela de Galdós que ofrezca, como Tormento, un número tan alzado y un repertorio tan variado y completo de recursos estilísticos (lingüístico-retórico-poéticos) dirigidos a destacar e intensificar el tono y el timbre de una complejísima elaboración paródica. Y éstos tan artística y diestramente incorporados al texto literario, por lo general, que enriquecen--con sus múltiples apartados irónicos--la lectura de la obra que estudiamos.

"En conclusión, creemos haber rastreado, en todos los aspectos novelísticos indicados al comenzar este análisis, la amplia vena de un perspectivismo irónico muy afin al cervantino. En todo caso, de lo que apenas puede caber duda, tras el estudio que precede, es de la riqueza estética de la creación galdosiana en Tormento" (p. 81).

Ricard finds that El doctor Centeno and Tormento are connected in regard to form and content. "On peut se demander si l'epilogue dialogué du premier n'a pas engendré le prologue dialogué du second. Ce détail de structure montre une fois de plus comment les romans de Galdós s'emboitent les uns dans les autres. En tout cas, le procédé permet de relier le plus récent de ces deux romans au plus ancien, dans cet espirt cyclique et synthétique qui est une des marques fondamentales de la création galdosienne" (p. 45). He states that "Les pages finales de El doctor Centeno annoncent en effet Tormento sur deux points" (p. 45). He finds that La de Bringas is "un prolongement ou même une suite" (p. 49) to Tormento. He finds these two novels to be good examples of Galdós' "l'humour noir" (p. 52). Their themes are those of regeneration and return to nature and to truth (p. 53). He notes that Tormento is the last novel in which Felipe Centeno appears (pp. 56-59).

Durand's first paragraph shows the scope of the problems to be dealt with in his article. It states that "An examination of the form of Tormento with a view toward assessment of Galdós's choice and handling of subject matter reveals two problem areas, either of which may seem to be superfluous to the main action and unnecessary to the movement of the novel--two possibly gratuitous ingredients, as it were. One of these is the author's social criticism and the question of its function in the main action; the other is the function of Ido del Sagrario's novel as it develops within Galdós's work. Do these merely represent, in the one case, the author's extra-novelistic interests and, in the other, a well-handled but non-essential device to vary the presentation without any deeper relationship to form and action? Although these questions bear on different aspects of the novel, they are related in their pertinence to the matter of form and, more broadly to the total effect of the novel" (p. 513).

Eamon Rodgers, "The appearance-reality contrast in Galdós' Tormento," Forum for Modern Language Studies, 6 (1970), 382-398, intends "to concentrate primarily on the various types of contrast between appearance and reality in the novel. I have selected this aspect because it seems to me to be the principal unifying element in the book, and also to provide a key to the understanding of a whole body of work which must surely rank as one of the major contributions to European realist fiction" (p. 382). In his last paragraph he writes: "What makes Tormento a masterpiece is the lucidity of its insight into the moral quality of everyday life, in which the more undramatic forms of evil are less easily recognized as such.... In its maturity of vision, moral seriousness and formal brilliance, Tormento must surely rank not only as one of the best and most representative of the novelas contemporaneas, but also as a major contribution to the literary imitation of life" (p. 398).

Germán Gullón, "Tres narradores en busca de un lector," Anales galdosianos, 5 (1972), 75-80, has the following sections: Tormento, perteneciente a un ciclo, Estructura de la obra, Función de la estructura y sentido de la distancia and El lector y la ironía galdosiana.

The Torquemada series

Critics would appear to study Torquemada en la hoguera (1889), Torquemada en la cruz (1893), Torquemada en

el purgatorio (1894) and Torquemada y San Pedro (1895) as
a unit, and the novels are so considered here.

Gilbert Graves Smith, "The Torquemada novels of Pérez Galdós: a structural and thematic analysis," (Ph.D. dissertation, Brown University, 1971, 232 leaves; Dissertation
Abstracts International, 32 [1972], 5245A), is the fullest treatment yet of these four novels. Smith states: "This analysis
of the novels proposes that Galdós wrote Hoguera somewhat
prematurely, without any definite plans for continuing the
history of the usurer, and that when he did return to Torquemada, he made every effort to create a unified series
of the four novels through an examination of the structural
and thematic development of the three later novels. This
study shows that the continuation of the series is based
on an elaboration of the events and characterization of
Hoguera."

Smith finds that "Because of the unusual manner in
which Galdós composed the series, writing the first novel
without definite plans for the last three, the Torquemada series is in some ways the most revealing single body of material in all of Galdós work. The way in which he expanded the
short novel into a series indicated more about his concept of
the novel as a literary form than any other single novel that
he produced."

Francisco Ayala, "Los narradores en las novelas de
Torquemada," Cuadernos hispanoamericanos, nos. 250-252
(1970-71), 374-381, reprinted in Homenaje a Casalduero
(Madrid, Gredos, 1972), pp. 63-69, and in his Los ensayos
(Madrid, Aguilar, 1972), pp. 990-1001, uses the Torquemada
series for "el estudio del proceso por virtud del cual el orbe
artístico cervantino se transmuta en un orbe artístico galdosiano. Debería mostrar ese estudio, mediante el rastreo de
las huellas, cómo, a partir de la más externa, superficial y
obvia imitación, que a veces resulta incluso inocentona y
tosca, llega a descubrir y utilizar Galdós los más sutiles
secretos de la refinadísima técnica desplegada en la elaboración de El Quijote, con una apropiación fecunda de recursos
que, en manos de Cervantes, su inventor, sirvieron a inten-
ciones muy distintas, como correspondientas a tan distinta
realidad histórica" (pp. 63-64).

His concluding paragraph is: "Esa gran pluralidad
de perspectivas que, según hemos comprobado, usa Galdós
en su narración tiene por objeto proyectar sobre su asunto

puntos de vista diversos, enriqueciendo poderosamente la
ilusión de realidad, y muestra cuán fecundos han sido los
frutos de la lección cervantina en la obra de su madurez de
novelista" (p. 69).

T. Folley, "Clothes and the man: an aspect of Benito
Pérez Galdós' method of literary characterization," Bulletin
of Hispanic Studies, 49 (1972), 30-39, notes that "There are
numerous references to clothes in Galdós' novels, both as a
means of characterization through description of external appearances and as a social phenomenon of the historical period
in which the author lived" (p. 30). Folley's purpose is the
analysis of Galdós' "various references to the clothes worn
by the usurer, Francisco Torquemada" (p. 30).

Peter G. Earle, "Torquemada: hombre-masa," Anales
galdosianos, 2 (1967), 29-43, writes that "Será mi intento, al
seguir en algún detalle la evolución de Torquemada desde su
sencillez usurera hasta su enmarañamiento social, señalar
algunos fundamentales del hombre-masa orteguiano: la subver-
sión de los valores, el derecho de la vulgaridad, la fe in el
especialismo, el triunfo del mediocre (Torquemada) sobre el
selecto (Rafael del Aguila) ... El personaje Torquemada
también es concepto; el concepto hombre-masa ('señorito sa-
tisfecho,' 'novísimo bárbaro,' 'niño mimado' de la sociedad)
también es personaje. Finalmente, notaremos, al comentar
el desarrollo novelístico de Torquemada, la paradoja de una
transformación circunstancial (el usurero primitivo converti-
do en un hombre representativo del siglo XIX) al lado de un
absoluto estancamiento espiritual" (p. 29). Besides the introduction, it has the following parts: 1) Hacia una teoría
de la mediocridad, 2) El Torquemada constante: el primitivo,
3) El Torquemada variable: el civilizado, and 4) El Torquemada colectivo, y el derecho a la vulgaridad.

Otis H. Green, "Blanco-Fombona, Pérez Galdós, and
Leopoldo Alas," Hispanic Review, 10 (1942), 47-52, shows
that obvious analogies exist between Blanco-Fombona's El
hombre de oro and Pérez Galdós' Torquemada series.

H.B. Hall, "Torquemada: the man and his language,"
Galdós studies, pp. 136-163, feels that this series "is the
work most central to his concerns as a novelist, the most
coherent expression, in almost pure linear form, of his vision of nineteenth century man and society. Stated in the
crudest terms, Torquemada is the capitalist class, his life,
the rise of that class and the transformation it effects in

society. This somewhat obvious symbolism, together with the touches of caricature and the burlesque tone in which Galdós so frequently indulges, may lead the reader to underestimate the complexity and the humanity of this comic figure" (p. 136-137). This article is especially interesting for its study of Torquemada's "linguistic evolution" (p. 145) and for its comments on "the evolution of the hero in the last three of the novels [which] may help us to see more clearly the nature of this relationship between the man and his manner" (p. 148).

Anales galdosianos, 6 (1971) contains two articles of interest for the study of the Torquemada series. They are Charles A. McBride, "Religion in the Spanish novel," pp. 125-129, a review of Brian J. Dendle's The Spanish Novel of Religious Thesis, 1876-1936, and Nicholas G. Round, "Time and Torquemada: three notes on Galdosian chronology," pp. 79-97.

McBride comments that "Particularly the first and last novels in the Torquemada series show us a protagonist who does not conform to the conception of character drawn along simplistic, dogmatic lines" (p. 127). Pages 127-128 of the article offers other insights into the characterization of Don Francisco Torquemada.

The Round article has four sections: "I. Naturalistic time; the overall biography" takes issue with Ricard's "chronology of Don Francisco Torquemada's life as recorded in the various Galdós novels in which he appears" (p. 79). On p. 84, Round presents his own chronological scheme for the biography of Torquemada. "II. Subjective time and artistic distance: Torquemada en la hoguera" states that "Adjustment of the time dimension here has two functions: to serve as an index of the character's emotional state, and to act as a control on the reader's point of view. This is a delicate operation, one which, if clumsily done, could quickly wreck any impression of realism. Galdós has carried it off with entire success; yet it seems very unlikely that his deployment of the time-scheme in Torquemada en la hoguera was the result of deliberate and conscious planning" (p. 88). "III. Disrupted time and flawed morality: Torquemada en la cruz" notes that in this novel "a flawed time-scheme becomes the image of a flawed moral world, as well as the initial vehicle of information as to what is wrong with it. But the departures from temporal realism, while they may cast doubt on the moral valuations which the story so far has taken more or less

for granted, are not so obstrusive as to destroy the illusion
that it is a story of real events" (p. 96). "IV. Conclusion"
is a brief summary of time in the Torquemada series. He
states: "Yet the present study has perhaps demonstrated
with some precision how Galdós' realism works in a field
where what matters is the nature of his fictional imagination
rather than his conscious intentions" (p. 96).

Arthur L. Owen, "The Torquemada of Galdós," Hispania, 7 (1924), 165-70, is an analysis of the character of
Torquemada. The author believes that "Galdós' miser deserves to live among the great misers of fiction. In Torquemada the two parallel passions of stinginess and greed are
carefully and clearly differentiated, but Galdós has not made
of him either a caricature, like Molière's Harpagon, or a
monster, like the Père Grandet of Balzac ... Torquemada,
on the other hand, is a human being after all, with some
claims upon our sympathies. He has other emotions than
that of avarice. He hopes, fears, suffers, even loves.
Herein lies the strength of Galdós' characterization--that he
has created a figure of flesh and blood, not an idealized
abstraction" (p. 170).

Robert Ricard, "L'usurier Torquemada: histoire et
vicissitudes d'un personnage," Aspects de Galdós, pp. 61-
85, is an analysis of the character of Torquemada as seen
in this group of novels. Ricard finds that "Quand on étudie
avec soin la carrière de Torquemada à travers les romans
où il figure d'une façon ou d'une autre, on aboutit à la conclusion qu'il est impossible d'en tirer une biographie à la
chronologie cohérente" (p. 83). On p. 85, he writes: "En
revanche, à defaut de cohérence chronologique parfaite, la
cohérence psychologique et, partant, la cohérence esthetique
du personnage sont totales, et les deux choses se tiennent:
sous ce rapport, l'examen le plus attentif ne peut déceler
aucune faiblesse."

A. Sanchez Barbudo, "Torquemada y la muerte," in
Estudios sobre Galdós, Unamuno y Machado, 2nd ed., (Madrid: Guadarrama, 1968), pp. 47-61, is a study of the character of Torquemada as seen in four novels and of his attitude
toward death, a theme that the author finds predominates in
the first and fourth volumes of this series. This essay also
is found in Anales galdosianos, 2 (1967), 45-52.

J.E. Varey, "Torquemada and 'la lógica'," Studies
in modern Spanish literature and art presented to Helen F.

Grant, edited by Nigel Glendinning (London, Tamesis Books, 1972), 207-21, studies "Torquemada's attitude to what he habitually calls la lógica, as it is disclosed during the four works dedicated to him" (p. 207).

F. Vézinet, "Un avare espagnol," Les maîtres du roman espagnol contemporain (Paris: Hachette, 1907), pp. 70-97, is an extremely interesting analysis of Torquemada's character and a comparison of him with Molière's Harpagon and Balzac's Père Grandet. Pages 92-97 are a comparison of the three characters. Vézinet finds that Torquemada "comparé à ses frères français, il ne manque ni d'allure ni d'originalité" (p. 92). He finds that "Harpagon et Grandet ont plus de relief parce qu'ils sont d'un seul bloc; mais Torquemada enferme plus de verité parce qu'il est plus complexe" (p. 97). His last paragraph states that "Molière et Balzac ont peint chacun un colosse, une manière de Titan, d'une carrure exceptionnelle; Galdós a peint un homme."

Thelma Louise Houston Hamilton, "Torquemada's cross: a translation of Benito Pérez Galdós's Torquemada en la cruz," (Ph.D. dissertation, University of Denver, 1973), 378 leaves; abstracted in Dissertation Abstracts International, 34 (1973), 3396-3397A, states that Torquemada's cross challenges "attention in its contrast of the uncouth miser with the noble Aguila ladies. A continuous plot and a symbolic trajectory unify the series, and the symbolism suggested by the titles also capsulizes the major events" (p. 3396A). The abstract's last paragraph makes the following comments concerning the translation itself: "Rendering the precise quality of the many different voices that find expression in Torquemada's Cross posed one of the major problems of the translation that appears here. Consistently allowing the tone to reveal social backgrounds and psychological states challenged ingenuity. Whatever phrases or sentences could be treated 'literally' were transferred to English in this fashion; but where constructions had little similarity to English, substitutions and compensations became obligatory, in order to convey in English to a contemporary audience the spirit and significance that the language of Galdós's Torquemada en la cruz had for his generation" (p. 3397A).

Robert Kirsner, "Pérez Galdós' vision of Spain in Torquemada en la hoguera," Bulletin of Hispanic Studies, 27 (1950), 229-35, is an analysis of Torquemada's character and reaction to the death of his son. Torquemada "is seen as an integral being whose reality is irreducible to social

symbols" (p. 229). Kirsner concludes with these remarks:
"As he re-creates Spain in this novel, Pérez Galdós presents
us with characters who experience all aspects of their Spanish
environment as their own personal attributes. The bond that
links them to their environment is one of sympathy. They
do not logically decide to conform with social customs; instead, they express their attachment to these customs by making them part of their own lives. Consequently, the reader
re-creates Spanish customs with the same intensity with which
he re-creates all characteristics of the literary process"
(p. 235).

Rudolf Köhler, "B. Pérez Galdós' Novelle: Torquemada en la hoguera," Germanisch-Romanische Monatsschrift,
19 (1969), 277-91, is an extremely detailed study of the novel's
structure and use of irony.

Matías Montes Huidobro, "Benito Pérez Galdós: lo
prosaico como recurso estilístico," XIX: Superficie y fondo
del estilo (University of North Carolina, Department of Romance Languages, 1971), pp. 37-51 (Estudios de Hispanófila,
17), is a lengthy stylistic analysis of Torquemada en la hoguera.

Pierre L. Ullman, "The exordium of Torquemada en
la hoguera," Modern Language Notes, 80 (1965), 258-60, suggests that the volume's "introductory paragraph is closely
akin to the proem of a romance de ciego" (p. 258), through
he feels that "This is indeed a moot hypothesis, and I cannot
seriously propose this concept qua nomenclature. Nevertheless, it may help us to understand the relation of the pre-
amble to the whole" (p. 259), if one were to attempt to understand this novel as "an historia de ciego novelada." A few
remarks are made concerning the style and literary processes
involved in this novel.

B. J. Zeidner Bäuml, "The mundane demon: the
bourgeois grotesque in Galdós' Torquemada en la hoguera,"
Symposium, 24 (1970), 158-65, finds that this novel "ex-
amplifies this transmutation of the prerealistic to a thoroughly realistic bourgeois grotesque in a particularly succinct
manner. A partial acceptance of the above definitions of the
grotesque will facilitate an analysis of Galdós' technique of
stylistic and structural integration of this essentially pre-
and anti-realistic phenomenon into his novelistic realism:
posited that the grotesque is capable of existing only in the
immediate juxtaposition of fear-generating evil and the

ludicrous in a given situation or individual, the text can be analyzed in order to clarify the nature and validity of the bourgeois grotesque as a concept" (pp. 158-59).

Rafael Bosch, "La influencia de Echegaray sobre Torquemada en el purgatorio de Galdós," Revista de estudios hispánicos, 1 (1967), 243-253, shows that "La novela Torquemada en el purgatorio, como parte de una tetralogía, tiene ciertos elementos de fondo que corresponden a la continuidad con las otras tres partes y a la finalidad general de la obra. Pero el mundo del argumento y su problematicidad está constituido sobre todo por elementos paralelos a los de El gran Galecto, si bien, claro está, Galdós no imita, no se confina a desarrollar la idea de otro, sino que da al tema nuevas dimensiones que son suyas propias" (p. 246).

Victor Pérez Petit, "El 'Torquemada,' de Pérez Galdós," Obras completas (Montevideo, 1942), pp. 13-33, uses the publication of Torquemada y San Pedro as the occasion to make remarks concerning Galdós as "un finísimo humorista" (pp. 16-19) and to analyze Torquemada's character as seen in this series of novels. The reviewer finds that Torquemada is the "encarnación de la avaricia" (p. 19). He compares Torquemada with other great literary misers and finds him not to be a type, but "un verdadero tipo humano" (p. 29).

Robert J. Weber, "Galdós' preliminary sketches for Torquemada y San Pedro," Bulletin of Hispanic Studies, 44 (1967), 16-27, states that "The purpose of this brief study is to examine three character sketches, almost medical case histories, which Galdós prepared prior to writing the last novel in his Torquemada series, Torquemada y San Pedro. Also, I hope to shed some light on Galdós' creative process and his views concerning the relationship between medicine and literature. The three sketches or outlines, which deal respectively with Valentín, Fidela, and Torquemada himself are presently located in the Casa-museo de Pérez Galdós...." (p. 16).

The sketches are compared to the corresponding portions of the published novel.

The article supports the belief that "to assure himself of the medical accuracy of their sicknesses, Galdós apparently prepared a 'case history' for each of the three and gave them to his close friend Dr. Manuel Tolosa Latour, to review

before Galdós himself incorporated the sicknesses into the
fabric of his novel" (p. 27).

Tristana

Until the release of the Buñuel film based on this
Galdós novel, critics had almost completely ignored Tristana.
Many of the film critics compared the movie version with the
novel and it is for this reason that these notes study in some
detail the movie reviews.

The most valuable studies on the novel are: Francisco
Fernández Villegas, "Tristana, novela...," La España moderna, 38 (1892), 198-199; Leon Livingstone, "The law of nature and women's liberation in Tristana," Anales galdosianos,
7 (1972), 93-100; Marina Mayoral, "Tristana: ¿una feminista
galdosiana?" Insula, nos. 320-321 (julio-agosto, 1973), 28;
Emilio Miró, "Tristana o la imposibilidad de ser," Cuadernos
hispanoamericanos, nos. 250-252 (1970-71), 505-522; Suzanne
Raphael's preface, pp. 13-26, to her Spanish-French bilingual
edition of Tristana (Paris, Aubier-Flammarion, 1972), 375pp.;
and Gonzalo Sobejano, "Galdós y el vocabulario de los amantes," Anales galdosianos, 1 (1966), 85-100.

Fernández Villegas finds that "El carácter de la protagonista está bien estudiado" (p. 199). He finds the novel
inferior to the drama version of Realidad and notes that in
this novel, "particularmente en las últimas páginas [existe]
cierto desfallecimiento y asi como el deseo de acabar pronto
y de cualquier manera, cosas ambas que borran el recuerdo
de las muchas bellezas que en este libro se contienen"
(p. 199).

Livingstone discusses the difference between Buñuel's
film version and Galdós novel Tristana, "a distance which
is roughly equivalent to the difference in temperament between
Galdós and Buñuel" (p. 93). The last paragraph is of particular interest.. Livingstone writes: "And so with all human
actions and social institutions: when they are natural, they
contribute to unity among men; but when they are unnatural
obsessions, mania, fanaticisms, they pit man against man.
This law extends to the complete range of human activity....
And especially to feminine emancipation. Women's liberation
is admirable when it seeks to restore women to a position
of dignity comparable to that of men, for in thus enhancing
their individuality they are equilibrating the relationship be-

tween the sexes, and that makes for a more natural union, one of social cohesion, of basic harmony. Galdos' support of this aspect of the question is fully evident in Tristana in his advocacy of a broader education for women that will equip them for a more adequate role in life and for an improved economic status that will free them from a virtual social slavery, progressive tenets that for a nineteenth century Spaniard are quite visionary and prophetic. But once again Galdós applies his rule of the law of Nature to show that even a virtue, carried beyond reasonable limits, becomes a vice. Feminine liberty does not extend to an inversion of the relations between the sexes with the creation of male women, nor does it condone the flouting of social conventions which serve to unite. Extra-marital relations, as exemplified in Tristana, tend ultimately to separate; marriage, when it is not a forced union but the wedding of comparable and compatible (but different) equals, serves to bind and thus constitutes a positive force in the onward movement of society" (p. 99).

Mayoral notes that "Con Tristana, Galdós nos presenta el problema de una mujer 'de ideas,' de una mujer que ama su independencia y su libertad ante todo, immersa en la sociedad española de fines del diecinueve." The author discusses the relationship between Tristana and Horacio. She writes that "Creo que no me equivoco al afirmar que Galdós piensa que una mujer como Tristiana tiene que fracasar o, mejor dicho, frustrarse." She discusses the ideas of Emilio Miró and Carmen Bravo Villasante concerning the character of Tristana.

The preface by Raphael is of interest for its discussion of the characters of Lope and Tristana. She discusses the influence of Cervantes, pp. 14-15. Her notes, pp. 367-375, are helpful, especially in their identification of place and proper names.

Miró presents a chapter by chapter discussion of the development of both the characters and the plot. He is interested in showing the influence of Cervantes on Galdós as shown in this novel, and in discussing Galdós' portrayal of women and of Tristana in particular. Miró shows a knowledge of what has been written concerning women and their psychology in recent years and quotes such feminists as Simone de Beauvoir and Betty Friedan.

He writes: "Galdós ha escrito una novela muy cruel. Parece que se ha burlado sangrientamente de su criatura, que se ha complacido en abatirla, en humillarla Derrotada

como el loco cervantino. Pero la creación galdosiana, como
la de Cervantes, como la de todos los auténticos grandes
creadores, está hecha con sabiduría. Y en esta se encierran
amor, dolor y rabia como principales ingredientes. Yo veo
en Tristana no solo la condena de la quimera, que causa desolación, como dirá el poeta, la burla de un mal entendido
feminismo, sino tambien, y en primer lugar, el firme alega-
to, disfrazado de ironía, suavizada con humor, en favor de
la auténtica libertad que proporciona el que uno puede ser
quien debe ser, quien podrá ser si la cultura hubiera abierto
verdaderos caminos; si los hombres y las mujeres no se
movieran torpemente en la oscuridad, entre jadeos o alaridos,
siervos de sus instintos o sus fantasías, entregados al juego
--unos por ambición, otros por ignorancia--de vencedores y
vencidos, de dominadores y dominados, de verdugos y vícti-
mas" (p. 621).

Sobejano states that "No es Tristana de las mejores
novelas de Galdós, pero dos aspectos al menos hay en ella
que la hacen interesante: uno, aquella disolvencia de la ilusión vital en términos de olvido y de abandono a la servi-
dumbre de lo cotidiano...; otro, el vivaz y condensado re-
flejo de la relación amorosa entre hombre y mujer en su
modo privado de hablarse. Los cápitulos XIV a XXI de
Tristana constituyen un ejercicio de penetración en la realidad del lenguaje amoroso no llevado hasta ese límite por
ningún novelista español del siglo XIX ni por Galdós mismo
en otra de sus novelas.... El objeto del presente comentario es poner de relieve las características de ese vocabulario de los amantes en Tristana y comprender su function en
el arte dialogal de Galdós...." (pp. 85-86). The first half
of this article has sections on Marianela, La desheredada,
Lo prohibido, Fortunata y Jacinta and Realidad. "El lenguaje
de los protagonista de Tristana (1892) puede definirse como
un intento de evitación del uso normal con arreglo a estas
tendencias: aniñamiento, popularismo, comicidad, invención,
extranjerismo, literarizacion" (p. 96). This is one of the
most exciting of the linguistic-stylistic studies that exist on
Galdós' works.

Tristana (film directed by Luis Buñuel). The film
script is available in the following editions and translations:

Tristana con textos de Arnau Olivar y Enric Ripoll-
Freixes, (Barcelona, Am Yá, 1971), pp. 22-133 (Colección
Voz Imagen, 24);

Tristana: a film by Luis Buñuel, translated by Nicholas Fry (London, Lorrimer Publishing, 1971), pp. 15-144 (Modern Film Scripts, 27);

L'Avant-scène, no. 100 (Jan. 1971) contains the following material on Tristana: screen credits, p. 7; André Cornand, "Le chemin de la liberté," p. 8; "Biofilmographie: Luis Buñuel," p. 9; Catherine Deneuve, "En travaillant avec Buñuel," p. 10, and "Découpage et dialogues in extense," pp. 13-53; and "Tristana ... et la presse," p. 54. This issue is illustrated with several pages of stills from the film.

Besides the script, the Spanish edition contains the following items of interest: "La Tristana de Don Lope" by Arnau Olivar, pp. 7-15; "Trabajando con Luis Buñuel" by Catherine Deneuve, pp. 17-19; "Ficha tecnicoartistica," p. 137; "Reparto," pp. 139-140; "Biofilmografía de Luis Buñuel" por Enric Ripoll-Freixes, pp. 141-160; and "Tristana y la prensa," pp. 161-169. This volume contains 34 photographs from the film.

The English version of the script contains the following: "A note on this edition," p. 4; "Introduction" by J. Francisco Aranda, pp. 5-11, has the following sections: "How the script was born," "The adaptation," "The filming" and "The final film"; "Credits" and "Cast," pp. 12-13. It also reproduces stills from the movie.

Freddy Buache, Luis Buñuel (Lausanne, La Cité 1970) contains a discussion of Nazarín, pp. 89-97, and of Tristana, pp. 176-183. Screen credits are given of Nazarín on p. 191 and of Tristana on p. 194. Reviews of the two films are found on pp. 198-199 and p. 201.

This bibliographer has been interested in the reactions of critics to the film versions of Galdós' novels and here wishes to deal with some of the more important reviews of Buñuel's Tristana.

Among the reviews in Spanish of this movie are: Francisco Ayala, "La creación del personaje en Galdós: Tristana," La nación (Buenos Aires), March 28, 1971, 3rd section, pp. 1-2; María Rosa Alonso, "Cine y literature: Tristana," Insula, no. 282 (mayo 1970), 15; Julio Pérez Perucha, "El cine español durante 1970," Insula, no. 291 (feb.

1971), 15; Julio Pérez Perucha, Urogallo, no. 2 (1970), 100-
103; César Santos Fontenla, Nuestro cine, no. 96 (abril
1970), 59-64; Angel A. Pérez Gómez, Reseña de literatura,
arte y espectáculos, no. 35 (mayo 1970), 298-302; Manuel
Villegas López, Revista de Occidente, no. 89 (agosto 1970),
231-236; Pedro Altares, "Bunuel ¿ante el pasado efímero?"
Cuadernos para el diálogo, no. 79 (abril, 1970), 47; and
Miguel Bilbatúa, "Tristana," Cuadernos para el diálogo, no.
79 (abril, 1970), 48. Most of the Spanish commentators
compare in some detail the novel and the film.

Ayala finds that in this novel "se destaca de un modo
muy particular este encuadramiento de nuevas criaturas ima-
ginarias en el marco de la tradición literaria, suscitando en
nosotros algunas reflexiones sobre su alcance y consecuencias"
(p. 2). He also writes that "...la novela--a la que en el
fondo le es bastante ajena la película en ella inspirada--mi
lectura última me ha descubierto en esta obra, no por cierto
una de las mejores de su autor, el intento deliberado--más
deliberado y sistemático que en ninguna obra--de superponer
a los materiales de la existencia cotidiana que trata de representar según el modelo realista un revestimiento de literatura
lo bastante fuerte como para imprimirle forma y prestarle
caracter" (p. 2). He mentions the influence of Cervantes on
this novel and discusses the character of don Lope de Sosa.

Alonso finds that "Buñuel ha hecho una hermosa peli-
cula; ha construido una Tristana tal vez menos nueva que la
de don Benito, que la Tristana de 1892, pero ha hecho una
lograda criatura que pasa, de una manera lenta, de la
frialdad al hielo; lo que el azar y la desventura han hecho
con ella." She quotes from the contemporary reviews of the
novel by Clarín and Pardo Bazán. She finds that don Lope
of the movie is much like that of the novel; whereas Buñuel
has made Tristana "una creación personal."

Pérez Perucha in Insula finds the film a masterpiece
and one of the best of a handful of Spanish films ever made.
For this reviewer, "Tristana es un clásico en el más noble
sentido del término. En él se da una madurez de pensamiento y estilo sorprendentes. Buñuel ha despojado a su film de
ornamentos, elementos accesorios y estridencias. Tristana
es un film casi subterráneo, equilibrado y armonioso, pero
por ello pierde causticidad o valor provocativo. La acción
progresa con gran economia de medios, los diversos elementos en juego revelan un notable poder de sintesis, y un
estilo suave, un conjunto de relaciones pausadas y metódicas

nos subyuga. Este estilo melancólico consigue contrastar vivamente la serenidad de la realización y la violencia de la anécdota, evidenciando así contradicciones detonantes en sus personajes y situaciones injustas."

This reviewer also emphasizes that "Tristana es un testimonio reflexivo sobre la violencia."

Pérez Gómez' criticism is worth reading not only for its comments upon Buñuel as a master of the cinéma, but for its critical comments that compare Galdós and Buñuel. He writes: "Al referirnos a don Lope como protagonista es preciso aclarar la inversión de papeles que Buñuel ha introducido con respecto a la novela de Pérez Galdós. En el relato galdosiano prima la figura de Tristana sobre la de don Lope; no así en la película ... La Tristana galdosiana es una mujer 'no hecha para las cosas pequeñas' como cocinar o cuidar de la casa, que intenta por todos los medios a su alcance salirse de una situación de inferioridad mediante la dedicación a una profesión liberal y vivir independientemente. Incluso el amor por el pintor con la negativa respecto hacia el matrimonio es un ataque a esta institución, entendida como opresora de la mujer y esterilizante para lo que no sea casa, lecho e hijos. Tristana es una mujer que un día despierta de un letargo y se da cuenta que es persona y quiere hacer valer sus derechos. Pero la enfermedad y la inconstancia de Horacio, el pintor, le impiden conseguir sus propósitos y debe resignarse" (pp. 299-300). The critic next shows that "Buñuel, en cambio, ha prescindido por completo del feminismo y ha encarrilado el peso de la acción sobre don Lope. Tristana es el sujeto pasivo de las contradicciones de este viejo liberal, su víctima más directa...."

He notes that the movie contains "el exhibicionismo sexual (aspecto ajeno por completo a Galdós)" and that "Buñuel ha ido más lejos que Galdós. Mientras éste se contenta con hacer entrever su escepticismo ante la vida matrimonial de la 'extrana pareja,' Buñuel hace morir a Lope a manos de Tristana" (p. 300).

Perucha writes that "Uno de los valores fundamentales del film Tristana es la caracterización de los personajes principales que hacen progresar la acción y a los que vamos conociendo mediante sus actos, de una ejemplar claridad expositiva" (p. 101). On the whole the review is a discussion of Buñuel and his film techniques.

Villegas López writes that "La Tristana de Galdós es
la realidad naturalista, con su ideología dentro" (p. 232). He
claims that "...Buñuel alcanza en esta película el máximo
objetivo del artista creador: la suprema depuración" (p. 232).
He compares this film with others directed by Buñuel. He
comments on the portrayal of Tristana's character and the use
of humor in the movie. His last paragraph shows the high
esteem in which the film is held by him: "Bajo su estructura
rectilínea y su forma clásica, en su alto punto de sencillez
inverosímil, es una película de una riqueza inabarcable,
increíble. Una de las más grandes obras maestras del cinema, un arquetipo cristalizador de un siempre posible y
esperado cine español" (p. 236).

The article by Santos Fontenla deals more with Buñuel
and his greatness as a movie director than it does with his
use of the Galdós novel. Santos Fontenla writes that "A
partir de la obra galdosiana Buñuel construye, respetando
muchos de sus esquemas, una obra absolutamente nueva y
personal, expresión de sus propias preocupaciones...."
(p. 60). He also compares the characters found in the novel
with those depicted in the movie based on or adapted from
the novel.

Miguel Bilbatúa's last paragraph follows: "En este
análisis de nuestro inmediato pasado, Buñuel aparece como
un frío diseccionador de la burguesía liberal española, de su
fracaso histórico. La ironía que recorce la película no va
solamente dirigida contra sus personajes, va dirigida también
contra el espectador, contra esa burguesia--heredera de la
que él retrata e igualmente incapaz--que asiste a la proyec-
ción creyendo encontrarse con un Buñuel domesticado, servi-
dor del sistema."

Altares comments on Buñuel's present-day popularity in
Spain. He writes of Galdós: "El redescubrimiento de Galdós
para el cine español significativo. Son envolturas 'à jour'
para un contenido viejo, un contenido que tiene ya moho en
las estanterías y en los museos. Galdós fue, sin duda, un
escritor burgués importante, pero es también uno de los
principales culpables de la tendencia, tan actual, a 'literatu-
rizar' la vida y la historia, de buscar la inspiración en la
literatura como sustitutivo de la realidad, siempre más
frágil, más movediza, menos fosilizada. Galdós es una pe-
ligrosa fuente de inspiración que Buñuel sorteó esplendida-
mente en Nazarín, pero que, sin embargo, aherrojado dentro
de los habituales esquemas y exigencias de una producción

'a escala internacional,' no ha sorteado en 'Tristana,' que
queda como una recreación, hermosamente inútil, del anterior mundo de Galdós, del mundo anterior del Buñuel."

     José Manuel Alonso Ibarrola devotes pp. 653-655 of
his article in Cuadernos hispanoamericanos, nos. 250-252
(1970-71), to a discussion of reactions of certain Spanish
publications to this film.

     Reviews in publications of the United States have not
been as uniformly flattering. Nor have the critics been able
to make a meaningful comparison between the novel and the
film. The following are some of the English reviews of the
film: Richard Schickel, Life 69, 19 (Nov. 6, 1970), 11;
Stefan Kanfer, Time, 96, 13 (Sept. 28, 1970), 74; Alex
Keneas, Newsweek, 76 (Oct. 12, 1970), 112, 114; Vincent
Canby, "Bravo Buñuel!" New York Times, Sept. 27, 1970,
section 2, pp. 1, 3; Penelope Gilliatt, The New Yorker, 46,
32 (Sept. 26, 1970), 123-124; Andrew Sarris, "Films in
Focus," Village Voice, 15, 40 (Oct. 1, 1970), 53, and 14,
42 (Oct. 15, 1970), 55; Roger Ebert, "Tristana: another
look into Buñuel's mind," Chicago Sun-Times, April 26, 1971,
p. 56; Robert Giard, Film Heritage, 7, 2 (1971-72), 1-9;
David I. Grossvogel, "Buñuel's obsessed camera: Tristana
dismembered," Diacritics, 2, 1 (Spring, 1972), 51-56; Marion
Armstrong, Christian Century, 88 (March 3, 1971), 301-2;
and J. Mellen, Film Quarterly, 24 (1970-71), 52-5.

     Schickel calls this one of Buñuel's "finest, most deli-
cately controlled studies of the perversity of human nature."

     Kanfer notes that it was shown at the New York Film
Festival and calls it "a coda of inexhaustible power and
sophistication. Like the world reflected in a convex mirror,
every element is in this masterwork--but somehow trans-
figured and amplified."

     Keneas' comments are extremely favorable and he
notes that "the story is an updated adaptation from a novel
by Benito Pérez Galdós" (p. 112).

     Canby's remarks are both a review of the film and of
Buñuel's career as a movie director. He finds the film "reasonable and humanistic and only ambiguous to the extent that
since we care about both Don Lope, the foolish old seducer,
and Tristana, the victim triumphant, we are ultimately torn
by an open-ended sorrow" (p. 3).

He also notes that "it is often extremely funny, bluntly fast-pace and very, very beautiful in an almost casual, untidy way" (p. 3).

Gilliatt finds this "one of the most Spanish of all his pictures, and the work of a master at the height of his powers" (p. 123). She calls it a "brilliant film" (p. 124) and feels that "Only Buñuel could have made this picture" (p. 124).

Sarris does not seem quite to know what to make of the film. The first article is chiefly in praise of Catherine Deneuve. On the whole, these two discussions are hardly worth noting except that one would expect a higher level of criticism from this weekly.

Mellen states that "Throughout the film Buñuel comments on the psychological effects of social dependence" (p. 52). The reviewer finds that "Tristana reflects as well Buñuel's preoccupation with the decay of Spain" (pp. 53-54). According to her, "Don Lope stands for the impotence and historical amnesia of Spain" (p. 54). The review's last paragraph follows: "The circular structure of the imagery, the rapid repetition of the images of Tristana's life until we return to the first sequence of the film, reflects the hopelessness Buñuel feels, both toward Spain and toward its victims. Buñuel has relentlessly and brilliantly exposed the destruction of the individual by a corrupt, hypocritical moral code which makes no pretense of improving a society in which class animosities are deepening and brutality is growing" (p. 55).

Ebert states that this movie "is a haunting study of a human relationship in which the power changes hands. Power over human lives is a lifelong theme of Buñuel, that most sado-masoschistic of directors, and Tristana is his most explicit study of the subject. Not his best, but his most explicit." Though he finds the movie disgusting, he admires it because "Buñuel is in control of every shot and every scene, and he is having at our subconscious like a surgeon."

Grossvogel's article can be divided into three parts. Pages 51-53 are a discussion of the Galdós novel with emphasis on character analysis; pp. 53-54 deal with some of Grossvogel's ideas concerning Buñuel as a film maker, while pp. 54-56 discuss Tristana, the film. He shows how the characterization, especially of Tristana and Don Lope, differ in the two media. "The motion-picture and the book are different primarily because they are the work of different men. But do the different media in which each expresses himself not contribute to their differences? Buñuel, who is not dependent on literary sources for his shooting scripts, has twice turned to Galdós and, in the case of Tristana, to a little known work: the dissimilarity between Galdós and Buñuel would seem to be the alteration of an initial similarity. The same idea may interest both men originally, but 'ideas' are primarily of concern to Galdós; Buñuel, whatever the 'idea,' begins with an image" (p. 55).

Armstrong states, "Irony, irony. It is of course Don Lopez (Fernando Rey) who is Tristana's real protagonist" (p. 301), and more than half of the review develops this theme.

Giard's is probably the longest discussion yet of this film in English. It is an extensive analysis of the characters of Don Lope and Tristana, with not a mention of Galdós. He makes the following comment on Buñuel: "Buñuel is uncompromising in style and content. He makes no concession to fashion or titillation. The details of the films are so consistent with the whole as to seem inevitable and necessary. The film unravels with lightning speed and precision. The technique is exact and self-effacing. Never once does it attract attention to itself; always it is subservient to the total vision. Formally the film is as ineluctable as the progression of its characters. So appropos [sic] is every move Buñuel makes--only so much and no more--that the result smacks precariously of the obvious. Only a master would risk some of the rueful self-parody in which Buñuel indulged in his portrait of the free-thinking Don Lope" (p. 9).

Most of Cahiers du cinema, no. 223 (août-septembre 1970), is devoted to critical studies on Tristana. The following articles deal with this film: Pascal Bonitzer, "Le cure de la guillotine," pp. 5-7; Jacques Aumont, "Le plaisir et le jeu," pp. 7-10; Sylvie Pierre, "Les deux colonnes" (suite), pp. 10-12; Jean-Pierre Oudart, "Jeux de mots, jeux de maître," pp. 13-17; "'Tristana,' notes sur dossier de presse" compiled by Pierre Baudry, pp. 24-27; and Ricardo Muñoz Suay, "Buñuel et Galdós vus d'Espagne," p. 28.

Muñoz Suay discusses the differences between the novel and the film. He writes that "De ce roman, Buñuel n'a gardé qu'un fil conducteur ténu, enrobé de casusticite. Tout d'abord, au lieu de situer l'action, comme le roman, dans un quartier populaire de Madrid, il la place dans une

ville de province aussi caractéristique que Tolède...." He
compares in some detail the differences in the characters
between the novel and the film and states that "seuls les
noms sont conservés." Of all the characters, he finds Tristana the most changed, for in the film she is "un caractère
plus violent, plus dramatisé, plus rempli de complexes, de
haine et d'expériences oniriques."

Pierre Baudry summarizes and comments upon the
following reviews of this film published in the French press:
Louis Chauvet in Le figaro, Henry Chapier in Combat, Guy
Teisseire in L'Aurore of May 6, 1970, Michel Mardore in
Nouvel observateur of May 11, 1970 (he commented also on
this film in the same newspaper on May 18 and June 8),
François Nourissier in L'Express, Claude Mauriac in Le figaro littéraire, Jean-Louis Bory in Le nouvel observateur,
and Jacques de More in Le nouveau cinémonde.

Pierre's article discusses the numerous scenes which
deal with food in the film. Almost twenty scenes are summarized "parce qu'une lecture littérale et pour ainsi dire
statistique du film nous y oblige: la fréquence et la précision
des notations alimentaires ne pouvant pas manquer ici de
sauter aux yeux" (p. 11). The reviewer comments briefly on
(1) nourritures de riche / nourritures de pauvre, (2) Qui
nourrit qui? and (3) Nourritures partagées / Nourritures re-
fusées. She also notes that "Le système de manipulations
signifiantes qui lie entre elles les notations alimentaires dans
Tristana fonctionne essentiellement, comme nous avons essayé
de le montrer, dans le sens d'une inscription des personnages
et de la fiction dans le champ du social et du sexuel. En
particulier ce système contribue à y installer la différence de
Tristana: sa dépendance / indépendance" (p. 12).

Oudart comments on this film, with no mention of
Galdós, in a very complicated and dense fashion which defies
summarization. Thus point 9 of the 11 numbered points of
the article states that "Ce film érotique se donne ainsi à lire
comme une fiction théologique et blasphématoire de la même
manière que les films d'Eisenstein apparaissent surdeterminés
par les figures de la Trinité: ce qu'ils signifient ne s'articule
que d'un déjà écrit qu'ils réinvestissent non sans en subir
consciemment ou inconsciemment les effets" (p. 16). On the
same page, it is stated that "Le travail très conscient de
Buñuel consiste à chercher à en tirer le maximum d'effets de
perversion, le plus petit commun dénominateur du choix de
chaque proposition étant sa possibilité de signifier, dans un

contexte différent, ceci et cela, tout le film se produssant
en fait comme un gigantesque jeu de mots auquel il serait
certainement vain de chercher une autre cause que la
recherche, par le cinéaste, de tous les doubles sens qu'il
pouvait en tirer."

Aumont's article is written in critical terms that
mean little to me, perhaps because of my ignorance of both
the movie and of the film as a fine art. The first sentence
of this article is enough to show its style: "Survenant à ce
moment et de cette façon Tristana ne d'abord être saisi
(accepté) que dans la perspective de son intégration à une
oeuvre: être reconnu unanimement comme la condensation
(l'épuration) du film bunueliantype. C'est-à-dire comme
une sorte de modèle réduit, représentant assez parfait de
tout un cinéma plus explicitement (et, dans le cas particulier, plus franchement) que tout autre s'articulant sur le
symbolique" (p. 7).

One of the key sentences of Bonitzer's article is:
"Que l'inceste et la castration constituent les paragrammes
principaux du film, c'est trop évident pour que j'y insiste.
En revanche, la logique qui les inscrit est moins apparente"
(p. 5).

Tristana is reviewed by Pascal Kané, Cahiers du
cinéma, no. 225 (nov.-dec. 1970), 58, 60. It is written in
an almost incomprehensible jargon. The last paragraph is
typical of the review as a whole: "C'est en dévoyant de la
sorte l'inscription du signifiant, c'est-à-dire en substituant
à une liaison verticale signifiant-signifié un système hori-
zontal reliant des signifiants entre eux (Chaine dont le phallus
est l'origine absente et dont chacun des maillons se donne
comme son tenant-lieu) qu'un film comme Tristana produit sa
transgression véritable: le signifiant comme imposture avé-
rée, le refus de signe comme modèle de clôture et de pléni-
tude" (p. 60).

Robert Benayoun, "Trois tempéraments à leur parfaite
extrémité (Antonioni, Buñuel, Kazan)," Postif, no. 117 (juin
1970), 8, 10-13, asks "Alors, pourquoi tant d'articles embau-
més, tant de faux départs, tant d'attaques à vide pour analyser
un film aussi limpide, aussi déchiffrable que Tristana?" (p. 8).
He states that "le vieillissement devient le ressort primordial"
(p. 12). He finds that "...Tristana possède un mélange de
tendresse goguenarde et d'élégance calme, de sérénité et de
frénésie que l'on ne trouve nulle part ailleurs chez Buñuel.

Le rêve se limite à un plan obsessionnel pour Tristana,
et qui nous rappelle que Buñuel est lui-même la proie de
songes récurrents: celui-ci est rigoureusement absent chez
Perez Galdos, comme sont absents les pois chiches, la jambe
artificielle, et bien d'autres touches inimitables de Don Luis.
Rien n'est pour autant absent des éléments moteurs habituels,
et il serait un peu précipité de conclure, comme le sousentend
Claude Mauriac, que Buñuel, fatigué par l'âge, renonce comme
Don Lope au blasphème et à la révolte" (p. 13).

Max Tessier reviews Tristana in Cinéma 70, no. 147
(juin 1970), 126-27, 130. Tessier develops the theme that
Tristana "est la critique reiteree, acharnée, mais tranquille,
de la bourgeoisie" (p. 127). He also notes that "Il y a, dans
le film, une progression parallèle et inversement proportion-
nelle des épreuves de Tristana et de son assurance personnelle,
qui grandit à mesure qu'elle devient plus belle; plus elle est
en butte à l'adversité de son destin, et plus elle devient arro-
gante et superbe" (p. 127). He concludes with these words:
"...Tristana est d'une admirable pureté, inaltérable comme
les pierres de Tolède. Buñuel, auteur español, a réveillé sa
véritable Espagne ensevelie sous un fatras d'hypocrisie 'libérale.' Qu'il lui plaise d'y retourner" (p. 130).

Jean-Elie Fovez' review in Telecine, no. 162 (mai-
juin 1970), 22-23, provides data on the screen credits and
brief excerpts from the reviews by Michel Mardore in Le
nouvel observateur, Louis Marcorelles in Le monde, Henri
Rabine in La croix, Francois Nourissier in L'Express and
Michel Duran in Le canard enchainé. It has two sections:
Les deux instincts majeurs and Le meurtre du père. On the
whole these notes emphasize the study of the characters of
Lope and Tristana and of what they symbolize. "Dramati-
quement, le film reste attachant; malgré les outrances du
scénario aucune scène ne fait rire a contrario; ici, on re-
connait le très grand talent de Buñuel, la fluidité nuancée de
sa narration: il escamote aussi bien l'amour physique que
l'opération chirurgicale; mais il multiplie les détails qui sug-
gèrent les deux instincts majeurs (selon Freud): la libido et
l'agressivité, la luxure et le sadisme" (p. 22).

According to Raymond Lefevre, La revue du cinéma:
image et son, no. 240 (juin-juil 1970), 128-129, this film
"est le drame de la vieillesse qui croit encore vivre des
sentiments qu'on sait être le privilège de la jeunesse. La
viellesse comme handicap ... Est-ce à dire que la vieillesse
est vulnérable en face des valeurs rétrogrades? Le propos

est important, et le film de Buñuel nos invite à une profonde
réflexion" (p. 129).   Comments are also made on the character of Tristana and Lope.

Arnau Olivar's "Luis Buñuel vu d'Espagne, " Jeune
cinéma, no. 49 (sept.-oct. 1970), 27-30, is translated from
Questions de vida cristiana, no. 52 (June 1970).   Olivar states
that "Si on veut porter un jugement sur Tristana de Luis Buñuel, son second film tourné en Espagne (après Viridiana), il
faut tenir compte de trois éléments: ce qui se réfère à l'attitude personnelle de Luis Buñuel, ce qui manifeste son évolution comme auteur, et l'oeuvre filmique considérée en soi.
Il importe que ces éléments étroitement liés entre eux et
interdépendants ne nous lassent pas oublier que l'essentiel
est le résultat obtenu: le film en tant qu'objet vivant de
notre temps--quelle que soit l'orientation qu'il prend au sein
de la creation artistique et ce qu'il exprime d'une culture
vivante" (p. 27).

He notes that "Tristana es un film extrêmement
intéressant; Buñuel a réalisé un film profondément castillan.
A ce niveau le film 'opère' pleinement, avec au naturel aussi
séduisant que difficile à atteindre.   Aucun autre film ne fait
'vivre' si intensivement certaines rues, certains coins,
certains intérieurs de la province castillane que la reconsti-
tution tolédane de Tristana.   Cela constitute la réussite el
l'apport majeurs du film de Buñuel" (p. 28).

Jean Collet's review of Tristana in Etudes, 333 (juillet
1970), 78-80, discusses the movie, its plot and its characters.
He makes numerous remarks concerning this movie and its
place in Buñuel's overall production.   Its last paragraph follows: "L'extrême dépouillement de ce film est à la mesure
de sa richesse mythique.   Jamais Buñuel n'avait exprimé
avec cette force et la simplicité d'une fable, la cassure ra-
dicale qui le hante.   Jamais il n'avait suivi avec une amertune
aussi poignante les ravages d'un idéalisme qui déchire ce qu'il
n'a pas su réconcilier" (p. 80).

SPECIAL TOPICS

The Novelas contemporáneas españolas have been the subject of numerous articles, books and dissertations. This section attempts to discuss some of these which deal with such topics as Galdós' views on education, religion, politics, women, children, etc.

Abnormal Characters

John Iwanik, "A Study of the Abnormal Characters in the Novels of Benito Pérez Galdós" (Ph. D. dissertation, Cornell University, 1949), iii + 210 leaves, contains an introduction, conclusion, bibliography and seven chapters: I. National problems and the realistic writing of Galdós; II. Types of characters in the realistic novels of Galdós; III. The abnormals: borderline; IV. The abnormals: psychoneurotic; V. The abnormals: psychotic; VI. The abnormals: feeble-minded; VII. Sources and influences. The introduction notes that "The aim of the present dissertation is to show the nature and extent of Galdós' abnormal characterizations from the point of view of the novelist's well-known preoccupation with national problems. In pursuing this aim, the writer of this thesis has in a sense broadened his subject by not only examining the psychological data that were uncovered, but also by trying to determine what significance they might have in the literary production of Galdós. In analyzing the various abnormalities depicted in Galdós' work, therefore, he has at the time looked for an explanation of Galdós' purpose. In seeking out Galdós' motives, he has had to study the ideas, attitudes, and personal convictions of Galdós which explain in large part the novelist's tendency to portray abnormalities in his works" (1. ii-iii).

America

The most important study on this subject is Angel del Río, "Notas sobre el tema de América en Galdós," Nueva revista de filología hispánica, 15 (1961), 279-96 (reprinted

in his Estudios galdosianos, [New York: Las Américas Publishing Co., 1969], pp. 119-39). On p. 280 the author states
that "Ordenamos la materia en tres secciones: 1. América
como parte de la realidad social española: personajes que
han estado en ella, relaciones de familia, etc.; 2. América
como una realidad nueva, patria de un hombre dignificado por
el trabajo, el self-made man, y como un mundo donde aún le
es posible al europeo fracasado rehacer su vida; 3. América
como parte integrante del complejo hispánico, cuyo sentido y
realidad en el pasado y en el por venir obsesionan a Galdós
en los últimos años.

"Corresponden, como se verá a las tres etapas fundamentales en la evolución del arte galdosiano senaladas por
Casalduero: la naturalista, la de confrontación de materia y
espíritu y la extratemporal."

Art and Society

Federico Sopeña Ibáñez, Arte y sociedad en Galdós
(Madrid: Gredos, 1970), pp. 179 [Campo abierto 28]), has
the following chapters whose titles show the general scope
of the work: Galdós, artista; Galdós, creador; La lucha
contra la retórica; Galdós, crítico de Arte; La imagen artística en la prosa de Galdós; El Arte en las formas y maneras
de amar: la ópera; La sensibilidad artística del rico; La
sensibilidad artística de los nuevos ricos; El Arte, signo de
intimidad y de ostentación en la clase media; La sensibilidad
artística de la mujer; La sensibilidad artística del varón;
La influencia de lo popular; Un escolio significative: la
zarzuela; El múltiple "signo" del arte religioso and Angel
Guerra, novela-síntesis. The volume has a prólogo and an
índice de nombres citados.

Blind and Handicapped Characters

Vernon Chamberlin, "The Blind and Other Physically
Handicapped Characters in the Novels of Benito Pérez Galdós"
(Ph. D. dissertation, University of Kansas, 1953), xv + 294
leaves, is the fullest discussion of its subject yet written.
This dissertation has a preface. The seven chapters are:
I. Introduction. The physically handicapped as a perennial
concern of literature; II. The physically handicapped and his
sociological environment in nineteenth century Spain; III. The
blind characters in Galdós' novels; IV. Progressive blindness

(and near blindness) in three Galdosian characters and in the life of the author; V. The lame; VI. Miscellaneous handicaps and deformities; VII. Conclusions; VIII. Appendices; IX. Bibliography. "The aim of this study is to provide answers to the [following] questions: Was there something in the life of Galdós himself that caused him to have a premonition of his own loss of sight? Did he unconsciously reflect a fear of blindness throughout his novelistic production by creating so many blind characters? Or were there other reasons why Galdós alone, of all the modern Spanish novelists, chose to include so many sightless individuals in his works? These questions imply others: What, in fact, are these blind characters of Galdós like? What seems to be their literary and artistic functions? And what similarities do they bear to the blindness of their author?" (ℓ. vii).

The outline of the conclusions (see ℓ. v) shows that Galdós was a realistic and humanitarian observer and that his documentation was sociologically accurate. He was the one major writer concerned with Madrid. Four types of physically handicapped characters are discussed and described. The focus of Galdosian interest belies any abnormal interest or fear of blindness. Galdós was unaware of the onset of his own affliction. Galdós is compared with certain of his blind characters. His illness is noted as well as his compensations.

Characters

Edward Dale Appleton Randolph, "Pérez Galdós and the European novel, 1867-1887. A study of Galdosian characters and their European contemporaries" (Ph.D. dissertation, Tulane, 1965, 307 leaves; Dissertation Abstracts, 27 [1966], 484), states that "By relating Galdós to his contemporaries it has been demonstrated that all five of these novelists [i.e. Dostoyevsky, Eliot, Daudet, Fogazzaro and Galdós] are not national, but are European on the basis of their characterizations." Randolph also states that "his novels of this period can be thought of as contemporary European novels of character, original and individualistic to some extent, but definitely reflecting the common problems and aspirations of the European novelist as seen in his fictional characters of the period 1867-1887."

Francisco Ayala, "Galdós entre el lector y los personajes," Anales galdosianos, 5 (1970), 5-13, deals with "el asunto de la relación entre autor, personaje y lector" based on his reading of Tristana, El amigo Manso and Misericordia.

Peter G. Earle, "La interdependencia de los personajes galdosianos," Cuadernos hispanoamericanos, nos. 250-52 (1970-1971), 117-134, has the following parts: introduction, Los espacios simbólicos, El fondo histórico, El Amigo Manso, Fortunata y Jacinta and Misericordia. Earle elaborates on the theme that "El ambiente galdosiano no es más ni menos que la compleja relación, o interdependencia, de los personajes y ésta, sin duda, es la mejor clave para comprender el arte de novelar de Galdos" (p. 117).

Joaquín Gimeno Casalduero, "La caracterizacion plastica del personaje en la obra de Perez Galdos: del tipo al individuo," Anales galdosianos, 7 (1972), 19-25, develops the theme that "Se pueden señalar tres grados de precision en esta comparación caracterizadora: 1) se compara al personaje con los de la pintura o la escultura de un país, de una época o de una escuela; 2) se le compara con los de un pintor o de un escultor determinado; 3) se le compara con los personajes de un cuadro o con una figura escultórica conocida" (p. 20).

Children and Adolescents

Almost nothing appears to have been published concerning children in Galdós' works. One can mention Carmen Lira, "Los niños de Pérez Galdós," Repertorio americano, 6 (1923), 225-26, 292-95, which deals with Marianela and El doctor Conteno, and her "Los niños de Pérez Galdós: Nell y Dolly," ibid., 27 (1933), 212-14, which may be useful for the study of El abuelo. This same journal has published R. Brenes Mesén, "Nell," (1930), 71.

The thesis by Edgardo Henry Ríos, "El adolescente en la novela de Galdós" (Universidad de Chile, 1951), 110 leaves, is a study of the 33 adolescents "más o menos definidos" (leaf 78) found in the novels of Galdós. This thesis has an introduction, chapters on the "Characterización del adolescente" and "Principales adolescentes galdosianos." His "Conclusiones" is a section with the following subdivisions: Número de adolescentes, Edades, El sentimiento del amor, Los intereses estéticas, La profesión, La política, Espíritu aventurero, La fantasía, Precosidad intelectual, Retratos, Cambios de carácter, El matrimonio, Estampas de la vida

del hombre. He notes that "Sus adolescentes no son en
ningún momento estáticos, sino que se desarrollan a medida
que la obra adelanta, y van sufriendo los cambios psicologi-
cos de cada edad" (leaf 79).

In the United States, there exists the unpublished doctoral dissertation by Edna H. Cobb, "Children in the novels
of Benito Pérez Galdós" (Kansas, 1952), 430 leaves in 2
volumes. Cobb states: "In their varying degrees of importance, this study attempt to deal with all the children mentioned by Galdós in his novelas de la primera época and las
novelas contemporáneas" (ℓ. 12). On ℓ. 15, she writes that
"One of Galdós' primary interests was in education. He believed in it for people of every age. Children and education
presents a survey of all the aspects of the Galdós treatment
of primary education." On this same page she notes that
"the children have been studied by sex to see what variations
in treatment may have been accorded them by Galdós." The
concluding chapter, "Birth and death of children," shows that
"Galdós gives far more importance to death as might be expected since the life and death of a personality is of greater
meaning to readers and other characters alike than the ar-
rival of a baby which has great meaning for others but little
for the newborn one himself" (ℓ. 19). For Cobb, "The pre-
vailing tone of the Galdós treatment of children seems a re-
spectful blend of affectionate interest and scientific curiosity.
He was their champion because he saw their need and developed their novelistic personalities because he was interested
in them as individuals" (ℓ. 20).

Color Symbolism

Vernon A. Chamberlin, "Galdós' use of yellow in
character delineation," PMLA, 79 (1964), 158-63, is a discussion of the symbolism involved in the color yellow in such
novels as La Fontana de Oro, Doña Perfecta, Gloria, Nazarín, Torquemada en la hoguera, etc. Among his conclusions
is that "Galdós used yellow as a conscious, effective facet of
his characterization technique throughout the major part of
his long literary career" (p. 162). He notes that "Yellow,
whenever symbolic values are implied, is for Galdós a consistently negative, opprobrious color" (p. 162), and that because yellow is used not only for avaricious characters, but
also for religious fanatics "it can be seen that the creative
originality of Galdós lies not in his choice of color but must
rather be sought in the adaptation of it to his own particular
value system and style of writing" (p. 163).

Concept of Life as Dynamic Process

Sherman H. Eoff, The novels of Pérez Galdós: the concept of life as dynamic process (St. Louis, Washington University Studies, 1954, 178pp.) has an introduction, chronological list of novels, notes, index and the following eight chapters: I. The narrative plan; II. Personality formation: importance of environment; III. Complexity of personality: adjustment and change; IV. The psychological structure; V. The social process; VI. The moral perspective; VII. The philosophic perspective; VIII. The personality of Galdós.

Eoff writes, p. 4: "In brief, the object of this study is to learn what the novelist's narrative plan is, how he visualizes personality and merges it with plot development, and what, on the basis of this investigation, his perspective of life is. This is another way of saying that the goal is to define Galdós' stature as a novelist by examining the design that he follows as he molds his conception of the individual-social relationship into novelistic form."

Creative Processes

Walter T. Pattison, Benito Pérez Galdós and the Creative Process (Minneapolis: University of Minnesota Press, 1954), 146pp., is one of the most widely reviewed of the recent books on the novelist. It has an Introduction, Formative period: foreign influences, The genesis of Gloria, The creation of Marianela, Conclusion and Index. The chapters on Gloria and Marianela are dealt with in the sections of this volume that treat these two novels. Pattison states that "Many elements of these novels do not depend upon creative imagination but can be traced back to real-life people or places or again to literary sources; many ideas which we might at first believe original with Galdós find frequent expression in the magazines he read. So by a detailed study of what Galdós was reading and observing before composing these particular novels, I hope to reduce in size, but not eliminate, the central core of mystery which must always defy the efforts of the scholar" (pp. 3-4). The first chapter discusses the many foreign authors that Galdós read and had in his library. The scholarship of the volumes is shown by its more than five hundred footnotes.

Doctors and Medicine

The following books and articles would seem to be the

most important that deal with Galdós' use of doctors, medicine,
illness and death in his works: E. Amat and C. Leal, "Dos
observaciones de síndrome de Sanchis Banus--reacciones pa-
ranoides de los ciegos dentro de la obra literaria de Benito
Pérez Galdós," Medicina española, no. 326 (1966), 347-358;
E. Amat and C. Leal, "Muerte y enfermedad en los personajes galdosianos," Asclepis, 17 (1965), 181-206; Fernando
Bravo Moreno, Síntomas de la patología mental que se hallan
en las obras literarias de D. Benito Pérez Galdós: discurso
leído en la Sesión inaugural del curso de 1922-1923 en la
Sociedad de psiquiatría y neurología, 54pp.; J. Cortezo-
Collantes, "Benito Pérez Galdós y la medicina," Semana
médica española, 2 (1945), 759-61, and El siglo médico, 114
(1946), 126-128, 163-164, 202-205, 237-241, 286-287, 319-
320, 382-383, 416-422, 491-493, 577-582, 695-698, 722-724
and 814-816; Luis S. Granjel, "Personajes médicos de
Galdós," Cuadernos hispanoamericanos, nos. 250-252 (1970-
1), 656-663; Luis S. Granjel, "El médico galdosiano," Archivo ibero-americano de historia de la medicina y antropología
médica, 6 (1954), 163-176; reprinted in his Baroja y otras
figuras del '98 (Madrid, Guadarrama, 1960), pp. 247-272;
José María López Piñero, "La medicina y la enfermedad en
la España de Galdós," Cuadernos hispanoamericanos, nos.
250-252 (1970-1971), 664-677; Walter Rubin, "Galdós y la
medicina," Atlántida, 8 (1970), 68-80; and Jack Raymond
Willey, "The médico as a literary personage in the works
of Benito Pérez Galdós" (Ph.D. dissertation, University of
Illinois, 1969, 209 leaves; Dissertation Abstracts International, 30 [Feb. 1970], 3482A).

   The first article by Amat and Leal studies "un cuadro
delirante en un ciego" as found in Cánovas and Misericordia.
The passages of medical interest are quoted and an evaluation is made of Galdós as a describer of physical conditions;
they note "la meticulosidad y perfecta descripción del comienzo de la enfermedad que padece Tito" (p. 351). The
authors find that "Galdós describe de modo magistral dos
reacciones delirantes de los ciegos en dos de sus criaturas
literarias" (p. 357). They find the clinical descriptions
better in Cánovas than in Misericordia and pose the question
that they leave unanswered: "¿Es Galdós, ciego, un de-
scriptor, sobre todo en Cánovas de sus propias e íntimas
vivencias?" (p. 357).

   Bravo Moreno's published speech would appear to be
the earliest discussion of Galdós' treatment of mental illness

("patología mental"). His purpose is to provide data on "los síntomas elementales de la patología mental" (p. 1). His emphasis is on the novelas contemporáneas, "metodizando su examen con arreglo a las sencillas nociones de la patología mental, pues estimo que de esta suerte coopero a la divulgación de esta ciencia; objetomás propia de estas solenidades que lo fuera la exposición de un tema doctrinal y bizantino que, por lo general, es lo que se usa en tales casos" (p. 2).

The following is an outline of this speech: Introducción, pp. 1-2, Episodios nacionales, pp. 2-5; Novelas, pp. 5-7; Degeneración, pp. 7-11; Degenerados: anomalías de la inteligencia en los degenerados, pp. 11-15; Anomalías del sentido moral y del carácter en los degenerados, pp. 15-20 (a study of the character of Doña Perfecta); Se impone un ligero bosquejo para distinguir las pasiones de la locura moral, pp. 21-27, which discusses Pasiones, Locura moral and Disimulación; Torquemada and La avaricia como enfermedad mental, pp. 27-33; Anomalías de la emoción y de la voluntad en los degenerados, pp. 24-28, is of special value for its comments on Lo prohibido; Miedos morbosos, pp. 39-42; Vejez o demencia, pp. 42-46; Medicina legal, pp. 46-47; Signos psiquiatricos, pp. 48-51, deal with Trastornos en las operaciones intelectuales, Trastornos en las percepciones and Trastornos de la afectividad; Conclusiones, pp. 51-53, is subdivided into Degenerados, Confusión mental, onirismo, Demencia and Locura.

The editor of El siglo médico describes the series by Cortezo-Collantes as an attempt to reproduce and to comment upon what Galdós wrote on medical topics (p. 126). The first article is almost entirely devoted to the reproduction of a "primorosa descripción de la epidemia gripal en Madrid" (p. 126; this article is reprinted from Semana médica española). The author does not provide the source of his quotation. The second and third articles discuss and reproduce "Un enemigo del cólera," written in June 1885. The fourth article reproduces with a brief note "Un duelo científico." The fifth article reproduces with a brief note Galdós' comments on Medidas sanitarias, a play. The sixth reproduces a letter by Galdós of Dec. 1, 1884 which comments on the health of King Alfonso XII and the rumors which existed concerning it. The seventh reproduces and praises the chapter in Tristana which describes an amputation. The eighth deals with a letter of June 19, 1885 which discusses a cholera epidemic. "La

ceguera de Don Benito" is not part of the series; it discusses
Galdós' blindness.   The ninth article is entitled "Herida y
muerte del infante don Enrique."   The tenth, "El mayor
monstruo, el crup," is based on a diphtheria case described
in La familia de León Roch; the eleventh, "El profesor
Brouardel y Jaime Ferrán"; the last, "El caso del Cura
Merino," discusses Galdós' portrayal of Martin Merino as
found in La revolución de julio.

This series is interesting to read.   There are, however, no indications concerning the sources of the texts reproduced.   The articles contain no footnotes.

The first article by Granjel shows that "En los médicos de Galdós se hacen patentes, en suma, los ideales que
alimentaron la vida de quien los creó, que son los profesados
por los convictos y confesos adeptos del naturalismo decimo-
nónico, liberal, teñido de humanitarismo y sostenido con firme
fe en un utópico, perfeccionamiento sin límites de la condición humana" (p. 663).

Granjel writes in the second article: "Dos partes
componen mi ensayo.   En la primera expondré las ideas de
Galdós sobre la Medicina, el modo como pensó de ella y
la enjuició; en la segunda trataré de dibujar el retrato del
médico galdosiano, que vive, con categoría de personaje en
tantas novelas suyas, y que es, lo repito, transunto fiel de
lo que fueron, ante sus coetáneos, los grandes médicos de
entonces, a varios de los cuales trató con intimidad y también
con admirativo respeto nuestro novelista" (p. 249).

López Piñero writes that "Mi propósito ... es ofrecer
una visión de conjunto de la medicina y la enfermedad en la
España de Galdós, pero no sobre la base de los testimonios
contenidos en sus escritos, sino de acuerdo con las investigaciones realizadas sobre fuentes médicas.   Pienso que los
resultados de estas últimas no sólo conciernen a los historiadores de la medicina, y que en este caso pueden tener algún
interés como información complementaria para conocer el
mundo del propio Galdós" (p. 664).

Rubin's article has six parts.   The introduction lists
all doctors, both fictional and real, mentioned in Galdós'
works.   The last paragraph of this section follows: "Son
admirables los cuadros clínicos que aparecen en la obra
galdosiana.   Los desarrollos de las enfermedades están pre-

sentados sin excluir los antecedentes y hereditarios de los enfermos, pero con una terminología que no sólo demuestra un aspecto más de la requeza y elasticidad del lenguaje de Galdós, sino un dominio que desborada la mera brillantez literaria para entrar en el campo de la ciencia. Es evidente que Galdós, en esto, no era solo literato, sino un gran admirador y aficionado de la Medicina. Y quizás, debido a esta admiración, es por lo que eligiera a los médicos para expresar a través de ellos ideales humanos de los más altos de su obra" (p. 70). Part II deals with Teodoro Golfín, a character in Marianela. Part III discusses "El doctor Guillermo Bruno de "El doctor Guillermo Bruno de Amor y ciencia." Part IV deals with "El doctor Moreno Rubio"; part V is "Augusto Miquis"; and VI suggests that a medical career was Galdós' "frustrada vocación" (p. 78). He reprints a portion of the prologue to Tolosa Latour's Ninerías to elaborate on this point (pp. 78-80).

Jack Raymond Willey, "The médico as a literary personage in the works of Benito Pérez Galdós" (Ph.D. dissertation, University of Illinois, 1969, 209 leaves; Dissertation Abstracts International, 30 [Feb 1970], 3482A), "aims to trace this interest in the doctor and his profession throughout the works of Galdós in order to accomplish three goals: first, to present an analysis of the médico as a literary creation, thus revealing the ways and means selected by the author to bring life to his doctors; secondly, to determine from the characteristics with which Galdós endows these men whether or not there exists a tipo médico galdosiano or a multitude of médicos who share certain characteristics; finally, to formulate an idea of the extent of the novelist's medical knowledge and its function in his novelistica" (p. 3482A).

Florencio L. Pérez Bautista, El tema de la enfermedad en la novela realista española (Salamanca, Instituto de historia de la medicina española, 1972), 259pp. (Cuadernos de la historia de la medicina española, Monografías, XXII), contains numerous scattered references to the fiction of Galdós. Besides an introduction, it has the following eleven chapters: La realidad humana y la enfermedad; Patología médica; El tema de la tuberculosis; Afectos epidémicos; La enfermedad mental; Pediatría; Puericultura; Cirugia y traumatología; Saberes especializados; Tocoginecología; Farmacología. Toxicología and Terapéutica general.

Dreams

The finest and most complete treatment of this subject
is Joseph Schraibman, Dreams in the novels of Galdós (New
York: Hispanic Institute in the United States, 1960, 199pp.).
This volume has the following sections: I.   Introduction.
II.   The dream as an element of plot.   III.   Character rein-
forcement in the dream--major characters.   IV.   Character
reinforcement in the dream--minor characters.   V.   The
dream as a vehicle for the expression of the supernatural.
VI.   The use of the descriptive device in the dream.   VII.
Conclusions.   Appendix and Bibliography.

Sherman Eoff, Hispanófila, no. 14 (1962), 51-54,
states that "This is a brief, instructive, well written study
of dreams in Galdós' social novels, with attention to the
incidence and distribution of the dreams, the manner of their
presentation, and, above all, the function that they have in
the novels' structure" (p. 51). This reviewer finds chapter
six to be the most interesting part of the study, "for it
directs our attention to the novelist's artistry and style,
which have never been widely discussed" (p. 53).   Schraibman
is also the author of "Dreams in the novels of Pérez Galdós:
psychological approach," Literature and Psychology, 10
(1960), 91-96.

Schraibman's study was a pioneering one.   Gerald
Gillespie, "Dreams and Galdós," Anales galdosianos, 1
(1966), 107-15, feels that Schraibman's volume is often reduced to a mere catalog of dreams without showing their
importance and meaning in the overall picture of Galdós'
style.   Gillespie argues that "Galdós' vision of humanity
summons forth the shapes and problem of Dream in such a
way that it is inextricably tied with the issue of his style"
(p. 110).   Pages 113-14 should be of special interest to
students of the Torquemada series.

Educational Attitudes

Charles William Steele is the author of "The literary
expression of educational attitudes and ideas in the novels
of Pérez Galdos" (Ph.D. dissertation, Ohio State University,
1957, 257 leaves; Dissertation Abstracts, 18 [1958], 2150);
and "The Krausist educator as depicted by Galdós," Kentucky
Foreign Language Quarterly, 5 (1958), 136-42.

The dissertation considers "Three essential aspects of Galdos' literary treatment of the educational theme ... (1) its evolution, (2) its relationship to plot and characterization, and (3) its effect on language." Steele found that "Five definable phases in the evolution of the educational theme in the novels of Galdós afford the same number of variations in the degree of integration of the educational theme into the total plan of the novels."

The article shows that Galdos presents "in his novels certain characters who resemble the Krausista in various ways, especially as regards their role as educators. Two such Galdosian characters are León Roch and Máximo Manso" (p. 136). These two characters are analyzed in some detail. Steele's last sentence is: "The novelist would seem to be saying--and this does not in any way imply hostility or disparagement--that the Krausist educational program, with reference to its given environment, was unrealistic" (p. 140).

Eros

Luis Alberto Oyarzun, "Eros en las novelas sociales de Pérez Galdós" (Ph. D. dissertation, University of Illinois, 1973), 543 leaves, is a study of "el origen y desarrollo de las implicaciones emocionales, pasionales, sociológicas y morales provocadas por la atracción sexual en los protagonistas de las novelas sociales de Galdós" (p. 1). In the conclusion it is noted that "El estudio detallado ... muestra al eros actuando como el resorte íntimo que mueve a algunos individuos y los hace tomar conciencia de sí mismos y del mundo que los rodea" (p. 518).

The introduction has two parts: Deslinde del tema and Eros en la novelística galdosiana. Part One: Concepción romántica del eros en las noveleas de la primera época, has the following chapters: I. Locura, fantasía y celos en La sombra; II. Historia, política y amor en La fontana de oro y El audaz; III. Eros en las novelas tendenciosas o de tesis: Doña Perfecta, Gloria, Marianela; IV. Transición al realismo: La familia de León Roch. Part Two: Concepción realista del eros en las novelas españolas contemporaneas, has the following chapters: I. El "suicidio" érotico en La desheredada; II. Intermedio idealista: El amigo Manso; III. De Ariel a Calibán: El doctor Centeno, Tormento, La de Bringas; IV. Amor y adulterio: Lo prohibido, Fortunata

y Jacinta, La incognita y Realidad; V. Eros como elemento
incidental en novelas de Galdós: Miau, La serie de Torquemada, El abuelo; VI. Amor y religion: Angel Guerra, Nazarin y Halma, Misericordia; VII. Autonomía y revaloración
de la mujer: Tristana, La loca de la casa, Casandra. Conclusiones and Bibliografía are the last sections of the dissertation.

Eroticism

        Gonzalo Sobejano, "Aburrimiento y erotismo en algunas
novelas de Galdós," Anales galdosianos, 4 (1969), 3-12, desires "llamar la atención sobre un aspecto poco considerado,
según creo, en los estudios que acerca de Galdós conozco:
la relación, muy sintomática de su época, entre el aburrimiento y la aventura erótica" (p. 3). The article is of special interest to students of Lo prohibido and Fortunata y Jacinta. He finds that "el concepto y sentimiento del amor en
la obra de Galdós" has not yet been adequately studied and
that whoever makes this study should not neglect "los aspectos
aquí sólo esbozados: la conexión entre la impotencia para
comprometerse y el aburrimiento, y entre éste y la aventura
erótica o ruleta del adulterio; la actitud condenatoria de
Galdós hacia este proceso erosivo; y el papel que esta con-
sciencia del aburrimiento invasor--del vacío de un mundo
sin Dios--hubo de desempeñar en la forja galdosiana de
ciertos personajes para quienes el más hondo compromiso,
la más elevada forma de redención individual y social, con-
sistía en el ejercicio de la misericordia" (p. 11).

Ethics

        Ruth E. Garwood, "The ethical aspect of human be-
havior as interpreted by Galdós: a study in Spanish social
values" (Ph.D. dissertation, University of Wisconsin, 1935),
171 leaves, contains in addition to an introduction, conclusion and bibliography, four chapters: Philosophical background, The generation of 1868, Ethical principles of Galdós
in reference to society and Ethical principles of Galdós in
reference to religion. She writes on ℓ. 3: "It is the purpose
of this discussion to show that the fundamental thought in the
approach to life in the writings of Galdós is based upon ethical principles, and that these principles are apparent in his
fiction from youth to old age, modified only at times by a
natural intensity or reserve that accompanies advancing years.

Such principles will be treated under the heading of ethics in society and ethics in religion. In the ethical criticism of religion in the writings of Galdós, an effort will be made to show the effect of religion upon the conduct of the individual, and to show whether or not that conduct leads to the betterment of human welfare or to the betterment of society."

The Fantastic

Carlos Clavería has been interested in the study of the fantastic in Galdós' works. His "Sobre la veta fantástica en la obra de Galdós," Atlante, 1 (1953), 78-86, 136-143; and "Galdós y los demonios," Homenaje a J. A. van Praag (Amsterdam: Plus Ultra, 1956), pp. 32-37, deal with this topic. Clavería writes that "Es hora ya de que para comprender la novela galdosiana, juzgada casi siempre unilateralmente como novela realista, se insista en todo eso que constituye su trasfondo: la veta fantástica que da original carácter a la obra de un gran novelist español del siglo XIX" (p. 143). On p. 82, he states that "Hay, sin embargo, también en ella un elemento fantástico que merece especial consideración por su importancia y su constante presencia en la creación literaria galdosiana. Puede hablarse de una veta fantástica que corre a lo largo de toda su obra y que se nos aparece en múltiples formas y en distintos momentos y aspectos. Su complejidad y su riqueza no excluye la posibilidad de que la veamos con criterio unificador, como manifestaciones de una misma tendencia del pensamiento galdosiano, de una fuerza creadora dentro de su obra."

In the second article, Clavería writes that "El interés demonológico de Galdós no queda únicamente reflejado en la composición de Casandra, ni hay sólo demonios en esa novela. Sin ir más lejos, en La razón de la sinrazón, que es de 1915, hay diablos y brujas que intervienen en la vida de los mortales de Ursaria, un simbólico Madrid. Determinar lo que sus nombres y papel significan presentaría problemas nuevos, ofrecería nuevos caminos para esclarecer las relaciones que tuvo Galdós con los demonios" (p. 36)

Guilt

Antonio Román Rigual, "Guilt in selected Novelas contemporáneas of Benito Pérez Galdós" (Ph.D. dissertation, Louisiana State University, 1971, 153 leaves; Dissertation

Abstracts International, 32 [1972], 3962A), states that "The
second chapter ... concentrates on guilt as a motivating
factor in the characters' behavior in eleven novels ... The
third portion ... examines guilt as an incidental happening
in human nature.'...

"...The fourth part is devoted to three novels which
do not describe any kind of guilt experiences 'per se'." The
abstract concludes with this paragraph: "Guilt is perceived
by Pérez Galdós as a beneficial factor, wherein the characters are forced to reflect upon their actions and make positive adjustments in their situations and personalities."

Jew

Sara E. Cohen, "The Jew in the works of Galdós"
(Ph.D. dissertation, State University of New York at Buffalo,
1973), v, 179 leaves, states that "of all these writers it is
Galdós who creates the most comprehensive portrait of the
Jew...." (p. iii). She finds that "A study of the Jew as he
is therein presented yields valuable insights into the social
and moral philosophy of the novelist. It demonstrates particularly how Galdós avails himself of the Jew and his religion in order to criticize the evils of Spanish society and the
shortcomings of the church" (p. iv). The dissertation has a
preface, conclusion and bibliography as well as the following
three chapters: The Jew in Gloria, Almudena and the Jewish
theme in Misericordia and The last appearance of Jewish
characters: Aita Tettauen and Carlos VI, en la Rápita.

José Ido del Sagrario

William H. Shoemaker, "Galdós' literary creativity:
D. José Ido del Sagrario," Hispanic Review, 19 (1951), 204-
37 (reprinted in his Estudios sobre Galdós, pp. 85-122),
examines "the creative genius Galdós displayed in his characters and of the power and integrity or wholeness of that
genius as well as something of its means and modes of expression. The method of the examination consists in part of
the isolation of a personaje, a compilation of the isolated
textual data to form a 'case' record, and an analysis and
an evaluation of the data in the light of other relevant considerations. The personaje chosen for this study is the
minor fictional character D. José Ido del Sagrario, a pathetic and comic schoolmaster, whom Galdós introduced into

eight of his works. The method thus seeks to take advantage
of the 'system' of reappearing characters, a 'system' consciously and intentionally employed for another purpose. The
fruits yielded and the truths drawn for the study of character
creation may then be considered rather as indirect results,
indeed as by-products of the 'system.' Hence these results
are rather betrayed than explicitly offered by the author and,
as such, may be accepted not only at full value, without res-
ervation or suspicion of hidden ulterior motive or meaning,
but as deeply significant revelations of the author's inner
realities, together with their power and vitality--in short,
his genius as a literary creator" (p. 88).

Madrid

        Madrid con un ensayo a manera de prologo por José
Pérez Vidal (Madrid: Afrodisio Aguado, c1957), 253pp.,
could have been much better edited. Pages 9-51 contain an
essay, "Madrileñización de Galdós," while the volume proper
is composed of: I. Primeras impresiones (1865); II. El
mismo Madrid de la juventud recordado cincuenta años
después (1915), Madrid; III. El primer cuento desarrollado
en Madrid (1865). Una industria que vive de la muerte.
(Episodio musical del colera); and IV. Al comeznar la producción novelística (1870). Observaciones sobre la novela
contemporánea en España. Exact bibliographical data on the
various items reprinted are not given. The prologue is more
popular in nature than scholarly. It has the following parts:
Anticipo de Madrid, La llegada a Madrid.--Primeras impresiones, El primer curso, Un curso crítico, Veraneo en Canarias.--"Viaje de impresiones," El año decisivo.

        Other studies on Galdós and the importance of the
Spanish capital in his life and work are: Federico Carlos
Sainz de Robles, El Madrid de Galdós o Galdós, uno de los
"Cuatro grandes," no madrileños, de Madrid (Madrid: Instituto de Estudios Madrileños, 1967), 27pp., and Jose Rodulfo
Boeta, "El Madrid de Galdós," Villa de Madrid, 3 (1962),
20-23. Sainz de Robles' study is a brief account of the accuracy of Galdós' depiction of Madrid. The author writes:
"Don Benito Pérez Galdós fue quien, continuando en cierto
sentido el designio goyesco, convirtió en documentos histórico pletórico de verdad y de calidez, de emocion y de suge-
rencias, un siglo de vida matritense. Aun mas: Galdos fue
para el alma de Madrid del siglo XIX lo que fue para el
cuerpo del mismo Madrid don Ramón de Mesonero Romanos:

el gran notario cuyos testimonios hacen fe en juicio y senta-
rán jurisprudencia" (p. 6).

Boeta states that "Hay algo más que un Madrid de
Galdós. Es toda una dimensión intemporal del vivir--de
un vivir con melodía--la que brota del fabuloso censo galdosiano sobre la capital de España. Madrid--un Madrid importante, acaso el de su cristalización definitiva, el de la
segunda mitad del siglo XIX--se remansa porosamente en la
obra de Galdós par entregarse en síntesis pura, en absoluta
intimidad de existencia, paisaje y sentimiento" (p. 20). The
author finds that Galdós "fue el gran observador y auscultador
de Madrid" (p. 22).

Luis Bello, Ensayos e imaginaciones sobre Madrid
(Madrid: Editorial "Saturnino Calleja [1919]), pp. 95-129,
has the following chapters which deal with Galdós' treatment
of the Spanish capital: XVII, Con el cristal de color de rosa;
XVIII, crepúsculo; XIX, La objectividad de Galdós; XX,
Madrid, 'lugar de la escena'; and XXI, Madrid, protagonista.
Bello uses as his source material references found to Madrid
in Galdós' Episodios nacionales, Novelas contemporáneas,
"Guía espiritual de España. Madrid," and a speech that he
gave to the Madrid Ateneo. He states that "Galdós describe
Madrid tal como es y lo acepta tal como lo ve" (p. 110).

Manuel del Pez

George J. Edberg, "Un estudio de don Manuel del Pez,
una creación literaria galdosiana," Humanitas (Monterrey), 2
(1961), 407-17, notes that "El presente estudio es un análisis
y valoración del genio creador de Benito Pérez Galdós tal
como puede apreciarse en la manera en que trazó y desarro-
lló uno de sus personnages réaparaissants. El próposito de
nuestra investigación es determinar hasta qué punto el novelista español ha tenido percepción de la naturaleza interior
de una creación literaria, suya, cuánto éxito ha alcanzado a
través de su desarrollo y si ha dada una presentación consistente
a dicha creación. El estudio sigue un método de análisis e
investigación, que si fuera aplicado al crecido número de
personajes de la obra galdosiana ... daría como resultado un
cuadro de conjunto del proceso creativo e intelectual del autor. Esta empresa, sin duda alguna, presentaría tamañas
dificultades, pero la feliz realización de tales propósitos
contribuirá en buena parte al futuro entendimiento del arte
literario del gran escritor novecentista" (p. 407). This
character appears in ten novels.

Miser

The most important readily available studies of the miser in Galdós' works are: J. J. Alfieri, "The miser in the novels of Pérez Galdós" (Ph. D. dissertation, State University of Iowa, 1957, 223 leaves; Dissertation Abstracts, 17 [1957], 1079-80), and his "The double image of avarice in Galdós' novels," Hispania, 46 (1963), 722-29. After noting that Galdós "presents these avaricious pairs not only as an example of the upsurge of materialism which, he insists, has begun to spread through late nineteenth-century Spanish society or--the episodios bear this out--as unsavory characters who heighten the suffering of an unsuspecting victim but also as latent cases of folie à deux," he states that "This paper concerns itself with two aspects of these pairs: (1) their tendency on the one hand, to reflect the medieval sin of avarice and, on the other, to fit Marx's definition of the capitalist; and (2) their relation to a pervasive kind of 'gemelismo' in the author's works" (p. 722). The dissertation shows that "The miser is the key to Galdós' preoccupation with the materialism of the Spain he knew."

Money

Romeo Rolando Hinojosa-Smith, "Money in the Novels of Galdós" (Ph. D. dissertation, University of Illinois, 1969, 493 leaves; Dissertation Abstracts, 30 [1970], 3009-10A), "attempts to show the function of money in Galdós' novels by focusing itself on the works themselves in a minutely detailed linear textual analysis in a chronological novel-by-novel examination" (p. 3009). The dissertation "also disclosed that money served, in many instances, to forward or to anticipate the plot; as a means of aiding in the description and the development of a character, and as a useful object in establishing the setting. The three elements, plot, characterization, and setting, were usually intertwined in such a way that the occurrence of money in any one element was not completely isolated from the other two in the development of the novels" (p. 3010).

Nature

Gustavo Correa, "La presencia de la naturaleza en las novelas de Pérez Galdós," Thesaurus, 18 (1963), 646-65, believes that "Una de las características fundamentales

de la novelística galdosiana es, sin duda, la presencia afirma-
tiva de la naturaleza, la cual se manifiesta en diversidad de
matices y funciones, tanto en lo que se relaciona con el mundo
de la realidad ambiente, como en el plano de la acción y de
la personalidad individual" (p. 646). The article has the following parts: Norma, diversidad y magisterio, La naturaleza
como madre, El hombre natural, Vida y razón, naturaleza y
sociedad, Autonomia y dualidad. Correa states that "La naturaleza se revela en Galdós, por consiguiente, como una de
las constantes de su novelística y constituye fundamentalmente
el suelo nutricio en donde el hombre hunde sus raíces"
(p. 664).

Nuns

Walter Rubin, "Las monjas en la obra de Galdós,"
Atlantida, nos. 53 (septiembre-octubre 1971), 604-25, writes,
"Más de cincuenta son las monjas y novicias que aparecen,
extensa pinaceteca de interesantísimos tipos de mujeres,
todas diferentes en caracteres y apariencias; no son religiosas ni estereotipadas ni de fórmulas, sino que representan
fielmente todo la gama de virtudes y defectos humanos tal
como se ve en la vida misma" (p. 604).

This is an interesting study that discusses the role of
nuns in Galdós' works. Rubin notes that "Su actitud no es
una crítica en contra del clero sino en contra del mal clero,
de lo falso con apariencia de religiosidad" (p. 625).

Positivism

Gerald Gillespie, "Galdós and positivism," in Galdós
... Mary Washington College, pp. 109-20, is one of the few
treatments of its subject. References are made to Gloria,
El amigo Manso, La sombra and Marianela. It is a pity
that this paper does not elaborate on the interesting idea that
Galdós is "one of the first major Impressionist writers, a
master of psychological existence" (p. 118). Gillespie writes
that "Though he never lost his trust in the ultimate rightness
of natural law, Galdós never allowed himself to grow smug
about the meaning of the existence of such law. With a sure
instinct, he chose the pathway of irony. It was not a matter
of compromising between certainty and doubt, so far as con-
fidence in fundamentals went; rather, it was a matter of
artistic integrity.... While Positivism gave Galdós a working

model and reinforced his youthful courage to investigate the
behavior of his fellow men, he eventually discovered the in-
congruity of any mere model and the puzzling complexity of
'life'" (p. 120).

Poverty

The fullest discussion of this problem is by Robert
Marion Fedorchek, "The theme of poverty in the Novelas
españolas contemporáneas of Pérez Galdós" (Ph. D. dissertation, University of Connecticut, 1966, 156 leaves; Dissertation Abstracts, 27 [1967], 3450-51A). "Galdós explores the
many kinds of poverty, understands its evil and its good, its
close ties with charity, and its multiple effects on man."
Fedorchek's "The Ideal of Christian Poverty in Galdós' Novels," Romance Notes, 11 (1969), 76-81, considers "two figures who willingly adopt poverty to live a life of charity:
Leré (Angel Guerra) and Nazarín" (p. 76). "Leré and Nazarín who make open declarations about poverty as a way of
life and reject all material possessions, are divinely inspired
and their commitment is total. They see in the adoption of
poverty an efficacious means of serving God" (p. 81).

Javier Martínez Palacio, "Miseria y parodia galdosiana de la restauración," Insula, no. 291 (Feb. 1971), 4-5,
contains interesting comments on La de Bringas, Misericordia
and several other novels He finds La de Bringas to be "una
de sus novelas menos leídas pero más transcendentales desde
el punto de vista literario como del histórico. En La de
Bringas se ejemplifica el proceso de una sociedad que marcha
al desastre con la más alegre de las inconsciencias" (p. 4).
He believes that "Galdós, novelista eminentemente imaginativo, no quiso acudir al recurso del testimonio directo ni convertir a sus personajes en simples portavoces de sus ideas;
prefirió la parodia y la caricatura, recursos que habia
practicado antes y a los que volvería después, siempre con
éxito" (p. 4). He also finds that "Ricardo Gullón ha sido el
primero en destacar de modo admirable el papel que juega
el tema del lujo en esta novela." In this regard one should
examine the Gullón edition of this novel published by Prentice-
Hall in 1967.

Psychology

Sherman Eoff, "The formative period of Galdós'

social-psychological perspective," Romanic Review, 41 (1950),
33-41, states that "He becomes in effect a literary social
psychologist, and his basic strength as a novelist lies in his
psychological portrayal of character in close relation to the
social medium in which it grows. This is an important line
of development which should be distinguished in the novelist's
early works" (p. 33). The article is a valuable discussion
of several of Galdós' works, books and articles, produced
before 1872. Eoff states: "Like most of his contemporary
novels, they combine the objective of social depiction with
that of studious character portrayal. This was an ideal perhaps only vaguely felt in the novelist's youthful aversion to
the novela por entregas but which crystallized into a definite
procedure: the development of a plot in which the psychology
of personality takes precedence over narrative events, and
which at the same time receives its essential substance from
sociological background" (41).

Arnold M. Penuel, "Galdós, Freud and humanistic
psychology," Hispania, 55 (1972), 65-75, desires "to illuminate some of the factors contributing to the universality of
don Benito's characters. My method is to examine two representative characters against the background of Freudian
psychoanalysis and humanistic psychology" (p. 65). The two
characters studied are Daniel Malavella in La loca de la casa and Benina in Misericordia.

L.B. Walton, "La psicología anormal en la obra de
Galdós," Boletín del Instituto español, no 4 (Feb. 1948),
10-13, states that "Fué, en efecto, Galdós el primer propug-
nador en España de unas concepciones psicologicas que hoy
en dia ya van para viejas, pero que en la época de Galdós
fueron profundamente revolucionarias" (p. 10). "En sus obras,
llamémoslas monda y lirondamente, psicoanalíticas, Galdós
sobresale en la descripción de estados de animo patológicos
y se entusiasma por las reconditeces psicológicos casi, por
asi decirlo, profesionalmente, demostrando dotes de refinado
observador, que pasan más allá de los limites del mero afi-
cionadeo, especialmente por lo que atañe a los términos
técnicos" (p. 11). He notes briefly the abnormal psychology
found in La fontana de oro, Fortunata y Jacinta, La desheredada, La familia de León Roch. However, the article is
especially valuable for its discussion of Angel Guerra, which
he believes could serve as "un libro de texto admirable para
ciertos clínicas psiquiátricas" (p. 12). He concludes with the
thought that "Galdós ... estuvo, en efecto, muy de vanguardia
en relación con las ideas psicológicas de su época" (p. 13).

Pueblo

Peter Bernard Goldman, "Galdós' Pueblo: a social and religious history of the urban lower classes in Madrid, 1885-1898" (Ph.D. dissertation, Harvard University, 1971), 308 leaves, has two main sections: The Social role of the Church and The Urban lower classes in Spain: Madrid, 1885-98. There are also an introduction, conclusions, a list of abbreviations and a classified bibliography. To a great extent this dissertation is less a critical study of Galdós than a history of the Spanish society of the period. Goldman argues "that a knowledge of life among the lower classes in end-century Madrid is so vital to a knowledge of Galdós and his novels" (1. 276).

Religion

The question of Galdós' religious views continues to be discussed on many different levels. A balanced view of the subject based on a careful reading of Galdosian texts would seem to be John Devlin, Spanish clericalism: a study in modern alienation (New York: Las Américas Publishing Co., 1966), pp. 81-95. This section has the following parts: "Pérez Galdós and Liberalism," "The important anti-clerical novels: Gloria, Doña Perfecta, La familia de León Roch," "Other novels and dramatic works" and "Some evaluations." Devlin is the author of the article on Galdós in The New Catholic Encyclopedia (New York: McGraw-Hill, 1967), 11: 122-123.

T[homas] L[awrence] C[ummerford] Dawson, "Religion and anticlericalism in the novels of Benito Pérez Galdós" (Ph.D. dissertation, University of Toronto, 1957), 609 leaves, has as its "purpose ... to trace the development of the attitude towards religion of Benito Pérez Galdós throughout all of his novels" (1.1). This would appear to be the fullest treatment yet written concerning this topic.

José Bergamin's "El pensamiento religioso de Galdós," De una España peregrina (Madrid, Al-Borak, 1972), pp. 57-76, is divided into four parts: Mundo y trasmundo galdosiano, El ateismo práctico de los españoles, La realidad novelesca and Las camarillas y el duende. The same volume contains his "Hablar de Galdós," pp. 35-56. Bergamin discusses some of the views of Azorín, Menéndez y Pelayo and Antonio Maura concerning Galdós and some of his works.

Bergamin's reputation as a critic has been quite high; otherwise his work on Galdós would hardly seem worth mentioning.

Josette Blanquat, "Galdós et la France en 1901," Revue de littérature comparée, 42 (1968), 321-45, states in its
abstract that "Galdós est à la tête de la campagne anticléri-
cale, en Espagne ... Nous avons essayé d'éclairer l'anticléricalisme de Galdós, les raisons qui le motivèrent au cours
de sa vie, les nuances que le distinguent de l'anticléricalisme
français. Son éloge de la piété mariale nous rappelle que le
positivisme qui se développe en Amérique du Sud et en
Espagne grâce aux publications des frères Lagarrigue, à
partir de 1884, vante l'utopie de la Vierge Mère et répand
les idées due Catéchisme positiviste et du Système de politique positive que les disciples français d'Auguste Comte ont
préféré ignorer. Ce fait contribue à expliquer l'évolution
des romans naturalistes de Galdós, si différents de ceux de
Zola."

Though Rafael García y García de Castro, Los intelectuales" y la iglesia (Madrid: Fax [1934]), praises Galdós
for his patriotism as shown in the first series of the Episodios nacionales, his "Galdós y Núñez de Arce," pp. 85-101,
is, on the whole, an attack on what he considers Galdós'
anti-clerical attitude.

Eugene Savaiano, "An historical justification of the
anticlericalism of Galdós and Alas," University Studies, 27,
1 (Feb. 1952), 1-14 (The Municipal University of Wichita
Bulletin), states that "In their novels, Alas and Galdós adhere
to the nineteenth century's liberal and progressive ideals and
view Spain's clerical problems in the same general perspective. In this respect, two important comparisons can be
made: (1) of the undesirable qualities which each attributes
to his clergymen; (2) of the similarity in characterizations
and situations presented" (p. 4).

F. Vézinet, "L'Espagne et le cléricalisme," Les
maitres du roman espagnol contemporain (Paris: Hachette,
1907), pp. 43-69, is a discussion of Galdós' anticlericalism
as seen portrayed in Doña Perfecta, Electra and Mariucha.

Robert Ricard, "La 'segunda conversión' en las novelas de Galdós," Revista de Occidente, no. 10 (1964), 114-18,
notes that "En todo caso, el análisis descubre aquí un fenómeno muy conocido de todos los que se interesan en la vida
espiritual, pero que no parece haber sido señalado en sus

obras; el de la 'segunda conversion'" (p. 114). His emphasis on this problem is centered on Nazarín and Halma.

Eduardo Gómez de Baquero, "El problema religioso en dos novelas de Galdós: Torquemada y San Pedro y Nazarín," Novelas y novelistas (Madrid: Calleja, 1918), pp. 58-75, is a discussion of religion as found in these two novels. Concerning Torquemada y San Pedro, Andrenio writes: "El drama interior que se desarrolla en el alma de Torquemada está muy bien descrito. Hay allí observación psicológica muy perspicaz y muy honda. Aquel fuerte apego a la vida y a las cosas temporales, aquella idea de ganar el cielo como se asegura en el mundo una renta vitalicia por medio do ut des de los contratos, son rasgos muy propios del espíritu positivo de Torquemada, que no le libra son embargo, de un vago temor el infierno" (p. 67). He finds Nazarín "una de las obras más originales de Pérez Galdós y de las mejor concebidas y ejecutadas" (p. 69). According to the author the problem of the two novels is the same "¡pero es tan diverso su desarrollo dramatico! En la primera de estas obras vemos el aspecto vulgar de la cuestión religiosa: la recompensa o el castigo individual en la vida futura; en la segunda pasamos a la región de los espíritus elegidos, de los que podrían llamarse, usando la frase de Schopenhauer, Los vencedores del mundo. El problema se agranda y se transforma. Le han tocado con su varita mágica las dos grandes hadas de todos los tiempos, el ideal y el amor que aquí se presenta en su forma más pura y desinteresada: la caridad" (p. 68).

An early full-length treatment is *Stephen Scatori, La idea religiosa en la obra de Galdós (Toulouse-Paris: E. Privet, 1927), 135pp.

Of extreme interest is Gustavo Correa, El simbolismo religioso en las novelas de Pérez Galdós (Madrid: Gredos, 1962), 278pp. It is a fundamental work on its subject. It has an introduction, a conclusion and twelve chapters on individual novels and their religious symbols. Each of these twelve chapters is briefly discussed under the individual novel. This volume examines "las características de la conciencia religiosa en que se halla immerso el mundo galdosiano y sus particulares relaciones con la creación artística" (p. 34).

Galdós' religious views are portrayed in his descriptions of the clergy and of Christian virtues in his novels.

Sister Evangela Vanacore, "The characterization and
literary function of the priest in the novels of Pérez Galdós"
(Ph.D. dissertation, Yale University, 1968, 370 leaves; Dissertation Abstracts, 29 [1968], 917A), is the fullest treatment
of the subject. The author notes that "this study examines
in detail both the ideological content and the artistic methodology in the characterization and literary function of the
clerical figures, since the selection and the manner of expression commit the author to some kind and degree of interpretation." She further states "that the priest is of singular artistic importance within the literary framework of Galdós novelistic plan as well as within his religious consciousness."

Robert Hilton Russell, "The figura evangélica in three
novels of Pérez Galdós: Nazarín, Halma, and Misericordia"
(Ph.D. dissertation, Harvard University, 1963), 215 leaves,
is the fullest discussion of the figura evangélica motif. Chapter I, "Definition and isolation," is followed by three chapters
on each of the novels dealt with; Chapter V, "The trajectory,"
is followed by a postscript entitled "The achievement of
Galdós" and a bibliography.

Two dissertations discuss charity. They are: Gilberto
Paolini, "An aspect of spiritualistic naturalism in the novels
of Benito Pérez Galdós: Charity" (Ph.D. dissertation, University of Minnesota, 1965, 351 leaves; Dissertation Abstracts,
27 [1967], 1832-A) (published under the same title, New York,
Las Américas Publishing Co., 1969, 155pp.--our quotations
are to the dissertation); and Arnold McCoy Penuel, "Charity
in the novels of Galdós" (Ph.D. dissertation, University of
Illinois, 1968, 179 leaves; Dissertation Abstracts, 29 [1969],
2721-22A; an abridged version of this dissertation with the
same title was published in Athens, Ga., University of Geor-
gia Press, 1972, 130pp.).

Paolini feels that "To be able to establish that Galdós
recognizes the existence of this charitable embryo in each
person is tantamount to destroying the hypothesis that certain
of his novels belong to French naturalism. We studied
Galdós' novelistic production from La fontana de oro to
Misericordia to ascertain how Galdós deals with charity."
He concludes his abstract with these sentences: "For the
purpose of clarification and of reference, we prefaced our
study of Galdós' works with four preliminary chapters. Because of Galdós' Catholic background, one should expect his
position toward Charity to be influenced by Catholicism;
therefore, we have included the Catholic view on the subject.

Furthermore, we know that Galdós kept well abreast of philosophical, religious, and literary developments in Europe. Of
the contemporary writers whose works he knew, we included
chapters on the evolutionist philosopher Herbert Spencer, the
English novelist Charles Dickens, and the Russian novelist
Leo Tolstoy because all three were concerned with charity.
Our study was not intended to show any influences, but rather
to present similarities and dissimilarities among the four
writers."

Paolini's "The benefactor in the novels of Galdós,"
Revista de estudios hispánicos, 2 (1968), 241-49, is probably
derived from the dissertation. The article is a study of
"charity in its theological, philosophical, economical-political
and sociological aspect[s]" in the works of Galdós. He concludes: "we have observed the presence of a common denom-
inator in all the novels in the form of charitable persons who
embody the two component elements of charity: benevolence
and beneficience. Real charity knows no boundary, and it
is a unifying force which the author illustrated beautifully
with the episode of mistaken identity of Guillermina Pacheco
and Benina. Galdós has introduced this paradox in order to
dramatize better what he wanted to indicate throughout his
work: that is, charitable persons can belong to any level
of society--their origin is not limited to nobles, to the rich,
to the poor, to men, or to women. Charity is a leveling
force with a sanctifying resultant" (p. 249).

Penuel writes: "In this study charity or nonsexual
love in Galdós' thirty-one social novels, i.e. Novelas de la
primera época and Novelas españolas contemporáneas, was
analyzed with two overall purposes. First, charity was examined from the ideological standpoint to reveal the degree
of consistency in the psychological, sociological, ethical,
and religious principles underlying the novelist's treatment
of the theme. Secondly, the novels were analyzed to determine the literary functions served by charity. Galdós was
found to use charity to aid in characterization, establishing
the tome, advancing the plot, and providing the setting"
(p. 2721A) He concludes the abstract with "The numerous
occasions in which Galdós was revealed to use a single instance of charity for multiple purposes without sacrificing
meaning made it clear that he possesses a greater stylistic
economy than most of his critics have indicated" (p. 2722A).

John Albert Pettit, "Las ideas morales en las Novelas españolas contemporáreas de Galdós" (Ph.D. dissertation,

University of Illinois, 1955, 275 leaves; Dissertation Abstracts,
15 [1955], 827), is "Una investigación de las ideas morales
expresadas por Galdós en sus obras puede dar una idea clara
de su intención idealista de utilizar la novela para despertar la
conciencia nacional y para señalar al pueblo español la necesidad de emplear buenos principios morales para lograr el
mejoramiento social de la patria." This dissertation covers
the novels published between 1881-89.

Students of the Torquemada series, La fontana de oro,
Angel Guerra, Fortunata y Jacinta, Doña Perfecta and La
familia de León Roch will find Nazario García, "Religious
equivocation in the novels of Benito Pérez Galdós" (Ph.D.
dissertation, University of Pittsburgh, 1972, 163 leaves; dissertation Abstracts International, 33 [1973], 6908-6909A) of
interest.

García writes: "Galdós' literary world is a very
wide one, and all aspects of religion are represented in the
sum total of the large galaxy of characters that he created.
This study, however, deals with only a small segment of
what can be called religious activity. In so doing, we concentrate on representative cases concerned with the way
Galdós treats a negative aspect of religion, one which we
have chosen to call religious equivocation. It is my contention, and the thesis of this dissertation, that many characters
who call religion to their aid are either consciously equivocal
or unconsciously mistaken. The purpose of this study, then,
is to advance the examination of the manner in which Galdós
deals with the role of religious equivocation, through the
analysis of religious crises experienced by some of his characters" (p. 6908A).

Satanism

Gustavo Correa, "El diaboloismo en las novelas de
Pérez Galdós," Bulletin hispanique, 65 (1963), 284-96, states
that "Podemos distinguir varios tipos fundamentales en la
metamorfosis de Satán en las novelas de Galdós: 1) el diablo
de la magia, de los encantamientos y de las ciencias ocultas,
2) el diablo de las coordenadas culturales, 3) el diablo luci-
ferino de los blasfemos, rebeldes y endemoniados, 4) el
diablo de la lujuria y de la seducción paradisíaca, 5) el
diablo de la mentira y de la sinrazón" (p 284).

Science

Francis M. Kercheville, "Galdós and the scientific approach," in Castilian Catalysts (issued by the author, c1967), pp. 59-75, shows briefly the author's knowledge and use of science in his fiction. Kercheville believes that "The scientific attitude and documentary approach in Pérez Galdós accounts for much of his attention to minute detail, even to the point, at times, of overemphasis. On the other hand, this same attitude undoubtedly contributes much to the liberal and tolerant treatment usually found in his works" (p. 75). This same volume contains "Protest and tolerance in Pérez Galdós: a preliminary survey of Spanish liberal thought," pp. 37-56.

Setting

Richard Allen Curry, "The creation of setting in the novels of Benito Pérez Galdós: Doña Perfecta and Misericordia (Ph.D. dissertation, University of Washington, 1971, 427 leaves; Dissertation Abstracts, 32 [1972], 6421A), states that "The specific topic is the heretofore unstudied area of background creation and this element's contributions to diverse scenic effects, characterization, themes, the socio-historical plane of reality and implied world view." He finds that "Together the two compositions indicate that as Galdós wrote he was clearly aware of form and structure as it relates to setting. An exploration of these fictive backgrounds aids immeasurably in the elucidation of themes and the comprehension of the characters."

Social Pathology

William T. Belt, "Social pathology in the novels of Galdós" (Ph.D. dissertation, Kansas, 1954), 308 leaves, is a study of "the unreasoning love of money, the unrestrained passion for luxury and pleasure, and the unhealthy preoccupation and ostentation and a higher rank in society" (ℓ. 22). The last paragraph of his "Introduction" follows: "In addition to examining these social ills and the effect on the lives of those who fell prey to them, this study will also attempt to substantiate the factuality of these problems which are presented in Galdosian society with observations of other writers

of both the nineteenth and twentieth centuries.   A study will
also be made of the role that Galdós assigns to these three
problems in the novels, and careful attention will be given
to the attitude that Galdós displays toward these subjects and
to any variation in this attitude during the course of his
lengthy novelistic career" (ℓ. 25).

Society

Pilar Fause Sevilla, La sociedad española del siglo
xix en la obra de Pérez Galdós (Valencia: Imprenta Nacher,
1972), 348pp. (Estudios galdosianos), won in 1957 the Premio
"Antonio de Nebrija." The author states that "Mi trabajo
pretende hacer el estudio sereno de la sociedad española decimonónica, que con bastante objectividad nos proporcionó
uno de sus hombres más ilustres" (p. 8). The table of contents shows its scope: I. La vocación histórica de Galdós.
II. Fuentes históricas. III. El rigor histórico en la obra
galdosiana. IV. La historia de la sociedad española del
siglo xix. V. La aristocracia española decimonónica. VI.
Burguesia y clase media. VII. La obra del agitador. VIII.
La burguesia española. IX-X. La clases medias. XI-XII.
El proletariado. XIII. El estamento religioso. Apendices:
Epistolario Pereda-Galdós, Epistolario Galdós-Narciso Oller,
Epistolario del Archivo particular de don Benito.

Considering the fact that the author is identified on
the title page as "del cuerpo facultativo de archivos y biblio-
tecas," the two-part bibliography has no scholarly pretensions
whatsoever. The author shows no knowledge of either French
or English. Material in these languages is mangled almost
beyond belief.

The text itself would seem to be a useful introduction
to the study of Spanish society as seen in Galdós' works.

Antoni Jutglar, "Sociedad e historia en la obra de
Galdós," Cuadernos hispanoamericanos, nos. 250-252 (1970-
1971), 242-55, has an introduction and the following sections:
Entre los Episodios nacionales y Fortunata y Jacinta (1873-
1887), Entre Angel Guerra y Misericordia (1890-1897), Del
"desastre" de 1898 a la "crisis" de 1909 and El declinar de
una viad y una obra. His theme is "la captación constante
de la realidad social de su época y su sensibilidad profunda
y seria por el pasado histórico más próximo a la España
decimonónica, en que vivía" (p. 244). On p. 254, he states

that "he tratado solamente de trazar ... la realidad de la
labor de tipo histórico y sociológico efectuada por Galdós a
lo largo de su obra."

Spain

Robert Kirsner, "The role of Spain in Representative
Novels of Galdós" (Ph. D. dissertation, Princeton University,
1949, 184 leaves; Dissertation Abstracts, 15 [1955], 416),
"proposes to study the literary significance of Spain in the
representative novels of Galdós, namely La Fontana de oro,
El Audaz, Doña Perfecta, El amigo Manso, Fortunata y Jacinta, Torquemada en la hoguera and Misericordia. Since
in the novels of Galdós Spain appears as a literary creation,
the treatment accorded to Spain is studied in relation to the
treatment accorded to the literary persons. The novelistic
technique of Galdós, then, is a significant factor in determin-
ing his literary approach to Spain" (p. 416).

Suicide

Robert Ricard, "En marge de Galdós: 'Révolution des
allumettes' et clichés romanesques," Bulletin hispanique, 72
(1970), 148-51, has been provided with the following abstract
by the editors: "Los suicidios provocados por la ingestión
voluntaria de fósforos que aparecen en las novelas españolas
y portuguesas del siglo xix con la consecuencia natural de la
invención de estos fósforos a la que el escritor costumbrista
Antonio Flores (1821-1865) concede un lugar importante en
sus comentarios." Several references are made to Galdosian
characters who considered this method of suicide.

Toledo

Gregorio Marañón, "Galdós en Toledo," Elogio y
nostalgia de Toledo (Madrid: Espasa-Calpe, 1958), pp. 151-
77, states that "Rasgo esencial de lo que Galdós fue, en su
vida íntima y en su vida de escritor, era este amor a Toledo, que siempre le acompañaba en sus andanzas y viajes"
(p. 176). This chapter discusses Galdós' friends from this
city and his accurate knowledge and affection for this city.
This chapter originally appeared in La nación (Buenos Aires),
July 25, Aug. 22 and Sept. 5, 1937 Vol. IV of Marañón's
Obras completas (Madrid: Espasa-Calpe, 1968), pp. 349-
53, reproduces the article of July 25, 1937.

Tragic Import

Joaquin Santalo, The tragic import in the novels of
Pérez Galdós (Madrid: Playor, 1973), 176pp. (Colección
Scholar), states: "Concerning itself primarily with indicating,
analyzing, and evaluating the many aspects of the tragic essence in his novels, this investigation will direct its attention
toward establishing their significance as motivating and uniting
powers in Galdós fiction" (p. 9). The table of contents indicates the scope of the volume. There is an introduction, a
list of references and the following chapters: I. Tragic perspective: Galdós and his contemporaries: Triumphant and
tragic endings, Novelistic and artistic theories, Galdós and
Dickens and Galdós' affinity to other tragic contemporaries;
II. Tragic characterization: Main personages: Personal
problems against a social background, The religious question,
Psychological problems, Physiological problems; III. Tragic
characterization: secondary personages; IV. Plot, ideologies
and symbolism; V. The Central tragic themes. Fantasy ver-
sus reality, Alienation, The quest for money and its conflicts,
Unrequited love, The religious themes, Ethical themes; VI.
Tragic version; VII. Conclusions.

Train as Symbol

Joaquín Casalduero, "El tren como símbolo: el
progreso, la clase social, la cibernética en Galdós," Anales
galdosianos, 5 (1972), 15-22, discusses the train as a symbol found in several novels.

Women

The fullest treatment of women in Galdos' novels is
Marie-Claire Petit, Les personnages féminins dans les
romans de Benito Pérez Galdós (Paris: Société d'édition
"Les belles lettres," 1972) (Bibliothèque de la Faculte des
lettres de Lyon 31), 506pp. The main divisions of the work
are the following: Introduction. First part: Genèse des
personnages feminins. Chapter 1. Nombre et genèse des
personnages féminins. Chapter 2. Personnages féminins et
sociéte. Chapter 3. La dynamique des personnages féminins. Chapter 4. Les groupes de personnages féminins.
Conclusion. Second part: Etude psychologique des personnages feminins. Chapter 1. Les personnages féminins en
face de la société: hérédite et forme d'esprit. Chapter 2.
Personnages féminins et imagination. Chapter 3. L'amour

chez les personnages féminins. Chapter 4. La religion et
ses déguisements. Third part: Le monde symbolique des
personnages féminins. Chapter 1. Occupations et plaisirs.
Chapter 2. Eléments et instruments de la beauté. Chapter
3. La ville et la maison. Chapter 4. La maladie et la
mort. Conclusion. Bibliography and an appendix that shows
the number of masculine and feminine characters per novel
(excluding those in the Episodios nacionales). There is an
elaborate and useful index.

Petit writes: "De la genèse des personnages féminins
au symbolisme du monde familier dont ils sont inséparables,
sans oublier l'étude attentive de leur psychologie, cet ouvrage
s'efforce donc de comprendre et de démontrer pourquoi
Galdós les a voulus si nombreux, et comment il les a si
souvent créés inoubliables" (p. 12).

She also comments: "Par leur présence constante,
leur richesse psychologique et leur signification toujours révé-
latrice d'un aspect important de l'oeuvre, les personnages
féminins lui donnent donc une coloration très particulière, En
effet, l'univers de Galdós est commandé par la femme, du
moins en ce qui concerne les Novelas de la primera época et
les Novelas contemporáneas où la première place revient à
la famille ou à la vie futile de la capitale. Par un phénomène
inverse les Episodios, consacrés le plus souvent au récit
d'événements historiques ou politiques, appartiennent aux
hommes et les femmes y ont peut de relief. Il semble que
l'inspiration de Galdós se soit divisée et qu'il ait confié aux
romans proprement dits le fruit de contacts intimes, d'observations passionnées qui, sous l'impassibilité voulue du chroni-
queur naturaliste, donnent aux personnage féminins la vie
intense qui les anime" (p. 10).

Shirley Ann Orsag, "Galdós' presentation of women in
the light of naturalism" (Ph. D. dissertation, University of
Pittsburgh, 1971, 167 leaves; Dissertation Abstracts International, 32 [1972], 5195-96A), is based on Marianela, La-
desheredada, Tormento, Lo prohibido and Fortunata y Jacinta. Orsag states that Galdós "in the novels written between 1871 and 1890, adopted a naturalistic approach based
on the qualitative analysis of empirical data and that keeping
with this objective attitude of the natural scientist, he modified his art as directed by the discovery of new data." She
finds that in this period "he appears to have set out systematically to investigate the behavior of women from the point
of causality. The manner of his investigation, his goals and

resulting system were all linked with literary naturalism.
The image of woman that emerged from the combination of
his use of positive criteria and personal creativity violates
neither the scientific principles of the nineteenth century nor
one's ideal interpretation of the meaning of life."

The fullest treatment of this subject in English is
Elizabeth T. Scott, "Women in the novels of Benito Pérez
Galdós" (Ph.D. dissertation, University of New Mexico,
1951), 223 leaves. This study has an introduction and bibliography as well as the following main divisions: Religious
fanatics, Spenders, Amigas, Regulators, Interesting women:
unclassified, Forerunners of independence, Benina and Conclusion. She writes that her purpose is "to analyze the most
important or the most interesting women which were created
by Pérez Galdós and to show that the character analysis in
which the author was so successful is the result of observation and documentation as well as of intuition and understand"
(ℓ. 8). The concluding paragraph of her introduction follows:
"To ensure some sort of order, it is necessary to divide
these women into general classes or types. So complex are
they and so far-reaching are the psychological ramifications
of their characters, however, that many fit into more than
one category and many have only a tenuous relationship with
those with whom they have been grouped. Thus, the divisions
must be considered as a convenience, not as an attempt to
show any basic similarity" (ℓℓ. 8-9).

Rafael Altamira, "La mujer en las novelas de Pérez
Galdós," Hispania (Barcelona), no. 11 (30 julio de 1899),
116-18, and Atenea, 72 (1943), 145-59, along with María
Zambrano, "La mujer en la España de Galdós," Revista
cubana, 17 (1943), 74-97, are important studies on the subject of Galdós and his treatment of women.

Altamira states that "Galdós es, efectivamente, ante
todo, un creador de caracteres; y en la serie innumerable
y rica que ofrecen sus novelas, quizá no hay otros--si se
exceptúan los de curas--más completos y de mayor alteza
artística que los caracteres de mujer. Esta condición de
la literatura galdosiana, es de los más relevantes, porque,
no obstante el extraordinario desarrollo que la novela ha
alcanzado en nuestros días, apenas si se pueden citar unos
cuantos tipos femeninos, que sean fruto de verdadera penetración psicológica, o que traspasen los linderos de las más
externas, incoloras y futiles manifestaciones del alma femenina" (p. 116). He then analyzes several important

feminine characters created by Galdós.   In Atenea he finds
Galdós' three greatest feminine characters to be Camila of
Lo prohibido, Fortunata of Fortunata y Jacinta and Augusta
in Realidad.   About half of this article deals with the Episodios nacionales.

      Zambrano claims that "Galdós es el primer escritor
español que introduce valientemente las mujeres en su mundo.
Las mujeres, múltiples y diversas, las mujeres reales y
distintas, 'ontológicamente' iguales al varón. Y esa es la
novedad, esa la deslumbrante conquista. Existe como el
hombre, tienen el mismo género de realidad ontológica; es
lo decisivo" (p. 81).   The author discusses the character of
several of Galdós' feminine figures.

LINGUISTIC STUDIES

While many studies exist on Galdós' style, few linguistic studies of his works exist.

The fullest published discussion of Galdós' vocabulary is that of Manuel C. Lassaletta, Aportaciones al estudio del lenguaje coloquial galdosiano (Premio Rivadeneyra de la Real Academia Española) (Madrid, Insula, 1974), 288pp. The volume has an introduction that discusses Galdós' use of colloquial language and his methodology. The three chapters: Sustantivos y locuciones nominales, Adjetivos y locuciones adjetivales, and Verbos y locuciones verbales, are followed by a Conclusion, brief bibliography, an alphabetical word index and a general index.

This study is based on Fortunata y Jacinta, Miau, Torquemada en la hoguera and Tristana.

The inside cover states that "El objetivo del autor es mostrar el medio de que se servía Galdós para devolver al lenguaje literario el aliento vital de la palabra hablada. Es sabido cómo el lenguaje galdosiano es el producto de una paciente y amorosa atención al habla espontánea del pueblo español. De aquí el rico tesoro de coloquialismos que hallamos en las novelas de don Benito y el tono directo, expresivo, plástico, coloreado y lleno de inmediatez que nos gana cuando las leemos.

"En su detenido estudio examina el autor centenares de vocablos y locuciones coloquiales usados por Galdós en las citadas novelas, distribuyéndolos y organizándolos metódicamente de acuerdo a su función sintáctica y psicológica. Su conclusión es que una parte esencial del valor de la novela galdosiana se debe precisamente al arte con que supo Galdós llevar a ella el lenguaje coloquial de los espanoles de su siglo, gracias al cual consigue una atmósfera de familiar intimidad que logra meter de lleno al lector en el ambiente de la ficción.

"El examen del lenguaje coloquial que usa Galdós nos

muestra, además, que la inmensa mayoría de sus expresiones gozan todavía de vigencia."

The same source notes that "Galdos no solo ha puesto
en boca de sus personajes el lenguaje que realmente habrían
usado de existir como personas de carne y hueso, sino que
él mismo, al hablar como autor, usa una lengua de una riqueza extraordinaria en giros populares y expresiones coloquiales."

On p. 16 he writes: "El criterio seguido para selec-
cionar los elementos a los que he atribuido el carácter de
lenguaje coloquial ha sido el propio y personal del autor de
este trabajo, guiado, eso sí, por una cuidadosa atención a
los matices del lenguaje, pero independientemente en última
instancia y, desde luego, expuesto a posibles malas interpretaciones y sujeto a las limitaciones del tiempo, lugar y
ambiente en que me ha tocado vivir. La distancia que se-
para mi época de la de Galdós, sin embargo, no me parece
tan grande, dada la lentitud de la evolución lingüística,
como para que mi sentido de la lengua no pueda aplicarse
al del período galdosiano y obtener resultados útiles, aunque
el lector será el encargado de juzgarlo."

On pp. 16-17 Lassaleta states: "Una vez decidido el
criterio a seguir para escoger los elementos integrantes
del lenguaje coloquial se presenta el problema de distribuirlos
y organizarlos metódicamente de acuerdo a su función sintáctica y psicológica. Lo primero que salta a la vista al
revisar el material lingüístico reunido es la presencia de
dos grupos diversos por su aspecto formal: los vocablos y
las locuciones. Es decir, expresiones integradas por una
sola palabra o por más de una. En vez de trazar una
línea divisoria entre los dos grupos, puesto que ambos
integran con igual derecho el lenguaje coloquial y desempeñan idénticos efectos estilísticos, he creído conveniente
presentarlos conjuntamente y clasificarlos siguiendo el
mismo método."

Graciela Andrade Alfieri and J.J. Alfieri, "El
lenguaje familiar de Galdós y de sus contemporáneos,"
Hispanófila, no. 26 (1966), 17-25, state that "Nuestro propósito en este artículo es comparar el lenguaje familiar
de Galdós con el de otros novelistas de su época, y para
hacerlo escogemos novelas de Alarcón, Clarín, Pardo Bazán, Valera y varias de Galdós" (pp. 17-18). The comparison shows that Galdós' use of "lenguaje familiar" was

much greater than of the other writers. The authors conclude that "Para Galdós el lenguaje familiar, considerado por
él como poético, desempeña la función de comunicar realidad y humanidad a lo descrito" (p. 25). The same authors
conclude in "El lenguaje familiar de Pérez Galdós," Hispanofila, no. 22 (1964), 27-73, that "La característica predomi-
nante del lenguaje familiar de Galdós es el tono humorístico.
Según nuestra estadística, las dos terceras partes de las
expresiones familiares encontradas son humorísticas, y si al
tomarlas aisladamente o desde el punto de vista del personaje
que las dice no lo parecen, lo son por el efecto que en el
lector y por el propósito que impulsó al autor a intercalarlas
en sus obras" (Hispanófila, no. 26: 17-18). This article has
an "Apéndice de expresiones familiares de Fortunata y Jacinta, con el número de veces que aparecen en la novela,"
pp. 38-73. Unfortunately, this list gives neither the meaning
of the word or expression nor the reference to the text should
a further context be desired.

S. G. Armistead, "The Canarian background of Pérez
Galdós' echar los tiempos," Romance Philology, 7 (1953-54),
190-92, concludes that the expression "is, then, an essentially
Canarian idiom, a recollection of the author's youth, which he
has adapted and interpolated into the speech of his Madrilenian characters in Fortunata y Jacinta" (p. 192).

Sebastián de la Nuez Caballero, "Introducción al vocabulario canario-galdosiano (los guanchismos)," Anuario de
estudios atlanticos, 12 (1966), 317-36, is a brief comment on
Galdós' Colección de voces y frases canarias. The author
notes that "queremos ... a hacer un breve análisis de las
palabras que aparecen en este vocabulario y que, con toda
probabilidad--según testimonios histórico-lingüísticos y pruebas que aducen los investigadores--, pertenecen al lenguaje
de los primitivos pobladores de Canarias, y que han llegado,
en uso corriente, hasta la época de Galdós y la nuestra"
(p. 319). The author suggests that "otra interesante problema, que tampoco aquí vamos a tocar, pero de indudable
interés para el estudio filólogico de la obra de Galdós, es
ver hasta qué limites el léxico, la morfología y la sintaxis
de su habla nativa se refleja en su obra" (p. 319). Thirty
items are discussed in the "catálogo de guanchismos" (pp.
323-334). It is of interest to note that the author feels that
"un estudio detenido de sus obras nos darían muchas sorpre-
sas en el terreno semántico, morfológico y sintáctico de su
léxico y de la estructura de sus frases y giros peculiares"
(p. 322).

On p. 322 of this article, the author mentions a study by María Rosa Alonso, "'La dije,' 'le vi' de los canarios," Pulso del tiempo (Universidad de la Laguna, Tenerife, 1953), pp. 55-57, in which she notes that Galdós "siguiendo el habla madrileña usa incorrectamente el acusativo 'la' para indicar el dativo, aduce que alguna vez deja escapar su canarismo y usa el dativo etimológico le para el femenino en algún caso como éste: 'Infame--le dije--, tú no eres hija mía' (Zaragoza: Ed. Hernando, 1928, pág. 160)."

Rolf Obrich, Syntaktisch-stilistiche Studien über Benito Pérez Galdós (Hamburg: Paul Evert, 1937), xiv + 155pp., is described by Hinterhäuser as "el primer intento importante de investigar la sintaxis del novelista" (p. 12).

Yelmo began to publish José Polo's discussion of Galdós' colloquial speech in its issue no. 9 (1972-1973). Polo's series is entitled "El español familiar y zonas afines: ensayo bibliográfico." As of early 1974, this series continued to deal with Galdós' speech.

A portion of José Polo, "El español familiar y zonas afines: ensayo bibliográfico," published as a serial in Yelmo, deals with the colloquial speech of Galdós as seen in his fiction.

Polo writes that "...queremos expresar dos cosas: 1) Las ideas lingüísticas de Galdós como ciudadano, como hombre culto, como persona que tiene que vérselas--y mucho con el lenguaje, con su lucha diaria: observación del habla real y transmutación literaria; 2) las ideas lingüísticas tal como aparecen reflejadas en los personajes de Galdós" (Yelmo, no. 9:48).

No. 9 (diciembre 1972-enero 1973), 48-54, has the following parts: Introducción, Ideas de Galdós en materia no lingüística, Ambiente y lenguaje en Galdós (vistos por Sainz de Robles), Observaciones de Galdós sobre el lenguaje; no. 10 (febrero-marzo 1973), 46-50, discusses Afasia, Lenguaje infantil, Lenguas en contacto and Distopía; no. 11 (abril-mayo 1973), 50-54, discusses Diafasia/Diastratía and Personas y caracterización lingüística (idiolectos); no. 12 (junio-julio 1973), 50-53 deals with Personas y caracterización lingüísticos (idiolectos), De la burocracia a la retórica; no. 13 (agosto-septiembre 1973), 48-51, is divided into Etimología popular ("culta" e "inculta") and De la etimología popular a otros fenómenos; no. 14 (octubre-noviembre 1973), 51-53 deals

with El pueblo (estrato inculto y "económicamente débil");
no. 15 (diciembre 1973-enero 1974) is devoted to Niveles
socio-lingüísticos y estilos (del pueblo a la aristocracia; del
estilo familiar al formal), and no. 16 (febrero-marzo 1974),
51-63, has four parts: Gramática normativa (en sentido
lato), Lo coloquial (tal como se definió en 692), "Lenguajes"
diversos (cf. 1, afasia, en Yelmo/10) and Final sobre Galdós.
Polo hopes that this collection of articles will appear in book
form.

Frederick Courtney Tarr, "Prepositional complementary clauses in Spanish with special reference to the works
of Pérez Galdós," Revue hispanique, 56 (1922), 5-264, is
divided into two parts. The first part is entitled "The prepositional complementary clause in the novels of Benito Pérez
Galdós," pp 19-102. On p. 16, Tarr states that "all the
examples of prepositional complementary clauses that occur
in twelve of the novels of Pérez Galdós have been collected....
Part II will be devoted to the presentation of material which
it is hoped will throw some light upon the historical background of the modern Spanish usage."

Robert Ricard, "Trois mots du vocabulaire de Galdós:
cebolla, araña et barbero," Annali, Sezione romanza, Istituto
Universitario Orientale, 5 (1963), 173-75, is a brief note concerning these three words found in Lo prohibido. The article
shows how Galdós uses these words with a meaning different
from that given in the Academy Diccionario.

V. A. Smith and J. E. Varey, "'Esperpento': some
early usages in the novels of Galdós," Galdós studies, pp.
195-204, find that Galdós used esperpento in the first part
of La desheredada (1881). The word occurs in La de Bringas
(1884), the second part of Lo prohibido (1885) and in Torquemada en la hoguera (1889). The earliest previous recorded
use of this word is that found in Juan Valera's "Pequeñeces.
Currita Albornoz, al padre Luis Coloma" (1891). The authors
discuss two other uses of the word in Galdós works and note
that "Galdós's use of the term is not incompatible with these
definitions" (p. 201), i.e., a term applied to a "persona fea,
extravagante y de aspecto ridículo" (p. 201). They note
that the word's etymology is still uncertain.

STYLISTIC STUDIES

The majority of stylistic studies on Galdós are on individual works rather than his over-all production. The material listed below would seem to be the best of the stylistic studies that deal as a whole with the Novelas contemporáneas españolas.

Arte pictórico

J. J. Alfieri, "El arte pictórico en las novelas de Galdós," Anales galdosianos, 3 (1968), 79-85, states that "Hay a través de la obra de Galdós un evocar continuo del arte pictórico, sea en forma de alusiones a cuadros famosos, sea en su técnica de 'retratar' a los personajes o de darles una base iconográfica. Galdós muchas veces pinta a sus criaturas adoptando el punto de vista del retratista o del caricaturista y para realzar características físicas y morales de ellas las compara con retratos de pintores conocidos" (p. 79). Alfieri feels that "La fusión pictórica del pasado con el presente nos ayuda a entender el aspecto temporal en la obra de Galdós" (p. 85).

Caricatures

M. Baquero Goyanes, "Las caricaturas literarias de Galdós," Boletín de la Biblioteca de Menéndez Pelayo, 36 (1960), 331-62, explains why "Galdós, en novelas de textura e intención realistas, incluye descripciones tan hiperbólicas y caricaturescas que inciden en lo irreal y que sirven para acentuar el vaivén y fusión que en toda la obra galdosiana suele darse, entre lo mágico-alegórico y lo documental-realista, entre el sueño alucinante y la observación cotidiana" (p. 331).

Costumbrismo

Verena McCririck, "Costumbrismo in the novels of

Pérez Galdós" (M.A. thesis, Birmingham University, 1949),
105 leaves plus 1 of bibliography, has the following contents:
I. Introduction: "Costumbrismo in Spanish literature. II.
The provincial novels: Doña Perfecta, Gloria, Marianela.
III. Two historical novels dealing with life in Madrid: La
fontana de oro and El Audaz. IV. A novel of transition:
La familia de León Roch. V. Two masterpieces presenting
life in Madrid: La desheredada [and] Fortunata y Jacinta.
VI. Conclusion: Galdós as a "costumbrista."

Mrs. Vera Colin of London has kindly provided the
abstract that follows of this thesis.

Verena McCririck writes that although Spanish writers
have been conscious exponents of "costumbrismo" throughout
many centuries, it was during the nineteenth century that
this genre came into vogue first in journalism and later in
novels. Fernán Caballero was especially significant for the
purpose of this study because she represents the "costumbrista" and novelist combined. Pedro Antonio de Alarcón,
Pereda and Pardo Bazán were also brilliant "costumbristas."
The aim of this thesis is to illustrate the extent of "costumbrismo" in Galdós' novels, noting that Galdós did not produce
regional novels in the conventional sense of the term, although Madrid is the setting of almost all of his works. His
interest in humanity transcended mere local interest, and the
"costumbrismo" of his novels portrays not only the society of
Madrid but of all Spain.

"Costumbrismo" in Doña Perfecta and Gloria: these
novels of predominantly religious and political interest, dealing with life in the provinces, offer comparatively little material for discussion. Galdós succeeds in revealing the mentality of the provincial Spaniard, rather than describing the
more visible aspects of surroundings and life. Marianela
scarcely merits mention because it not only lacks the minutely detailed "costumbrismo" of the Madrid novels, but is un-
concerned with those problems which are peculiarly Spanish.

"Costumbrismo" in La fontana de oro and El Audaz
serves as a vivid and realistic background for the unraveling
of the rather diffuse plots of both novels. The first chapters
of La fontana de oro could well stand apart as complete
"cuadros de costumbres" and they form the main part of its
"costumbrismo" content. The realistic pictures of Madrid
and life in Madrid also form a part of "costumbrismo" in this
novel. El Audaz, like La fontana de oro, is important for

the purpose of this study, because both novels reveal Galdós' interest in lower classes and his intimate knowledge of Madrid.

La familia de León Roch stands half-way between the "Novelas de la Primera Epoca" and the "Novelas Contemporáneas." It is a novel of transition; a religious problem is still its main concern, but the Madrilenian society of Galdós' own time serves as a realistic background to it. The function of "costumbrismo" in this work is to give a detailed picture of the Restoration society (the old decadent aristocracy of birth and the new wealthy bourgeois aristocracy) and an idea of the general affairs in Spain of that time.

La desheredada: the novel gives a panorama of life in Madrid; every class is depicted, every type of district described. Galdós' genius as a "costumbrista" is most evident in the descriptions of the lower classes, of humble districts and of the speech and mode of existence of the very poor.

Fortunata y Jacinta: there is no limit to the extent or scope of "costumbrismo" in this novel, although in the last volume "costumbrismo" has ceded almost entirely to the narration of absorbing events.

In Verena McCririck's opinion Galdós' masterpieces are those in which he is most truly a "costumbrista."

Humor.

Michael Nimetz, Humor in Galdós: a study of the Novelas contemporáneas (New Haven: Yale University Press, 1968), is the fullest study of this phase of Galdós' works. Besides acknowledgments, conclusions, bibliography and index, it contains six chapters: Realism and humor, Satire, Irony, Metaphor, Caricature and type and The humor of familiarity. The first paragraph of his "Conclusion" states that it has been his plan "to examine the humor of the Novelas contemporáneas in relation to realism. We have seen how irony and satire are implicit in the novel, the realistic genre par excellence. We have also seen how metaphor, caricature, and type prevail in, though are by no means limited to, the works of certain nineteenth century novelists known as romantic realists. Finally, in the last chapter, I have tried to describe a kind of humor born of low-key realism, dependent on colloquial speech and familial relationship. Of these various kinds of realism and their accompanying forms of humor, the last is undoubtedly the most typical of Galdós. Familiarity is the stock-in-trade of the Novelas contemporáneas" (p. 209).

Frank Durand, Modern Language Notes, 84 (1969), 361-62, notes that this book "is the first to undertake a comprehensive and methodical study of this aspect [i.e., "an ironic viewpoint ranging from the composition of scenes, situations, and plots to characterization and style"] of the Novelas españolas contemporáneas" (p. 361). He finds that "The greatest asset of this study is the perceptive and intelligent panoramic view of these novels. The examples used for purposes of illustration and analysis are well-chosen and representative and demonstrate the author's critical judgment and thoroughness" (p. 361). His chief criticism is that "the organization of the book relies too heavily on critical labels which tend to get in the way of the author's interest in presenting the scope of Galdós' humor and realism" (p. 362).

Gerald Gillespie, "Galdós and the humoristic tradition," Anales galdosianos, 4 (1969), 99-111, deals with Herman Meyer, "The poetics of quotation in the European novel," pp. 100-03, and Michael Nimetz, Humor in Galdós..., pp. 104-11. Gillespie has almost nothing but praise for the volume by Nimetz and feels "that no more productive an approach could have been taken to Galdós' Novelas contemporáneas, since the approach goes right to the heart of his greatness as a writer and man. Galdós emerges for what he is: a worthy link in a strong and powerful tradition, which he renewed with a spaciousness unequaled in his own nation in modern times. Second, that Nimetz, as a critic, is unusually gifted--if not by temperament, perhaps by sheer will-- to recognize and convey these qualities of Galdós" (p. 111).

H.B. Hall, Bulletin of Hispanic Studies, 49 (1972) 410-12, feels that "the subject is a fundamental one for an understanding of Galdós, and the book has some good things to say about it" (p. 411). He also states that "More important, he has enough human sympathy to be able to deepen our awareness of this quality in his author. He is helpful both in the discussion of general topics (there is much good sense, for instance, in the chapter on 'Irony') and in the analysis of aspects of particular novels...." (p. 411). Yet he goes on to declare on the same page, "All of which makes one regret the fact that his chosen method of approach prevents him from exercising his skill and sensitivity in a sustained exploration of any of the novels as a complete work of art."

D. Lida reviews the Nimetz volume in the Hispanic Review, 39 (1971), 112-15. He calls it "sound, serious and fairly thorough, if not exhaustive" (p. 112). His last paragraph follows: "Individual differences notwithstanding, this book is one of the most important contributions made recently to Galdós studies in as much as it is a perceptive and systematic inquiry into a largely unexplored, yet vital, area. It will have to be the point of departure for any future study of humor in Galdós" (p. 115).

J. E. Varey, Modern Language Review, 65 (1970), 924-25, objects more to the volume's structure, "which does not allow whole works to be analyzed in any satisfactory way" (p. 924), than to anything else. However, he praises the study and states that "We are greatly indebted to Professor Nimetz for an adult and perceptive analysis of an important epic" (p. 925). He finds also that "It sparks off critical reactions in the reader and illuminates in a more lasting fashion whole aspects of Galdós's technique" (p. 925).

Ironic Reprise

Monroe Z. Hafter, "Ironic Reprise in Galdós' Novels," PMLA, 76 (1961), 233-39, has the following sections: Introduction, I. La fontana de oro and the early novels; II. El amigo Manso and the transition; III. Fortunata y Jacinta. Hafter states that "The present essay focuses on Galdós' developing skill with internal repetitions from La fontana de oro (publ. 1870), through the rich complexities of the novels written between 1887-1889, to their almost stylized simplicity in El abuelo (1897). Always related to Cervantine irony, the variety of verbal echoes, the mirroring of one character in another, the unconscious illumination each may offer the other, underscore the increasingly intimate wedding of form and matter with which Galdós came to unfold his narratives" (p. 233).

La muletilla

Vernon A. Chamberlin, "The Muletilla: an important facet of Galdós characterization technique," Hispanic Review, 29 (1961), 296-309, defines muletilla as "speech tag." He deals with the following questions: 1) Can any further amplification of alleged Dickensian influence be effected? 2) During what periods of his novelistic career did Galdos use the muletilla as a part of his characterization technique? 3) What

types of personajes are involved? 4) What are some of the
more important features and artistic functions of these mule-
tillas?" (p. 297).

Naturalism

Walter T. Pattison, "Galdós and Naturalism," in
Galdós ... Mary Washington College, pp. 95-107, is an excellent brief summary of the "elements of the naturalistic
doctrine" that Galdós accepted (p. 103) and those that he
"adopted only to a limited extent." Pattison notes that "as
the years pass, the spiritual factor is to become constantly
more prominent in Don Benito's works" (p. 106). He concludes with the remark that "The adoption of naturalism and
the subsequent discovery of the importance of the spirit are
factors which raise him to a rank reached by him alone"
(p. 107).

Nomenclature in Characterization

Wendolyn Yvonne Bell, "Galdós' use of nomenclature
in characterization" (Ph.D. dissertation, State University of
Iowa, 1964, 264 leaves; Dissertation Abstracts, 25 [1965],
5272), is devoted to a study of the Novelas contemporáneas
españoles. "Basically, the novels are treated chronologically in order to discover those techniques which remain constant as well as any changes which may be involved." The
author notes that "An important facet of Galdós' creative art
is his rather complicated system of nomenclature. All names
do not have symbolic value, but with few exceptions those of
major characters do cloak a hidden meaning. Not only are
the majority of the characters assigned very meaningful
names, many are also further identified by equally expressive nicknames and epithets." Appendix A is an index of
names treated; Appendix B is an index of nicknames discussed.

Novela dialogada

Willa Sack Elton, "La novela dialogada de Benito
Pérez Galdós" (Ph.D. dissertation, City University of New
York, 1972, 587 leaves; Dissertation Abstracts International,
32 (1972), 6971A), states that "El presente estudio se propone precisar esta motivación en términos generales, y más
específicamente intenta llegar a precisar una teoría literaria

de la novela dialogada específicamente galdosiana" (1. 2).
There is an introduction, a conclusion and a bibliography as
well as the following six chapters: La loca de la casa,
Cassandra, El abuelo, Realidad, La razón de la sinrazón
and Novelas no dialogadas y sus adaptaciones teatrales.

Novelistic Theory and Technique

Gustavo Correa, "Pérez Galdós y su concepción de
novelar," Thesaurus, 19 (1964), 99-105, summarizes Galdós'
theories concerning the novel as found in his "Observaciones
sobre la novela contemporánea en España" (1870) and in his
speech made upon his becoming a member of the Real Academia Español (1897).

John P. Netherton, "The Novelas españolas contemporáneas of Pérez Galdós: a study of method" (Ph.D. dissertation, University of Chicago, 1951), 425 leaves, is, according
to Robert J. Weber (The Miau manuscript of Benito Pérez
Galdós, p. 4), "probably the best single work on Galdós novelistic technique." Netherton's dissertation has an introduction,
conclusion, bibliography as well as the following seven chapters: The structure of the social novel; Background: the
settings in time; Background: the physical settings; Characterization: the description of physical appearance; Characterization: psychological analysis; The forms and functions
of dialogue; Composition: the narrative units in sequence.
"The sector here examined is his technique in the writing of
fiction" found in the nineteen Novelas españolas contemporáneas written between 1881 and 1897 (1. 4). The dissertation
concentrates on the subject of method. "Such concentration
is based on a pragmatic separation of form and content, and
an emphasis of formal consideration. It is a distinction between what the novelist expresses and how he expresses it"
(11. 5-6). This dissertation is a study of "the elements of
novelistic technique."

Theodore Alan Sackett, "The crisis in the novels of
Benito Pérez Galdós" (Ph.D. dissertation, University of
Arizona, 1966, 380 leaves; Dissertation Abstracts, 27 [1966],
1384A), states that "...a study has been made of the crisis
of 1881 ... the period when the writer initiated the definitive
method of his novelistic art. In order to determine the success of the crisis, the nature of Galdós' mature novel, and
the importance of his artistic creation to the modern Spanish
novel, three areas have been examined: the problem of

classifying the non-historical novels, the definition of the
goals and characteristics of the writer's mature works, and
their relation to the fiction of later literary generations."

Jose Antonio Torres Morales, "Galdós y sus ideas
sobre la novela," Rio Piedras, no. 2 (March 1973), 71-82,
summarizes his article as follows: "Cualidad de observación, sinceridad en el arte narrativo; verdad de los hechos;
sentimiento para comprender lo observado y trasladarlo
transustenciado a las páginas de la novela; pintura fiel de la
vida, "representando cosas y personas, caracteres y lugares
como Dios los ha hecho', como afirmaba Galdós a propósito
del naturalismo; por ese camino se hallan las virtudes espe-
cíficas del novelista en busca del acierto literario. En última instancia, Galdós resume en dos las cualidades que hacen
el novelista: saber 'sentir y observar'" (p. 82).

Realism

Francisco Ayala, "Pérez Galdós: sobre el realismo
en literatura," Los ensayos (Madrid: Aguilar, 1972), pp.
958-90, has the following sections: El concepto de realismo
literario, El naturalismo de Galdós, El realismo español
tradicional, El concepto galdosiano de realismo, Realismo y
experiencias de signo negativo, Realismo y experiencia social,
La aniquilación quevedesca, Contraste de Galdós con Quevedo,
Realismo y costumbrismo, La "naturalidad" del lenguaje,
Visión de la realidad en Galdós: su novelística. This essay, with fewer sections and with a different title, was previously published in La Torre, no. 26 (1959), 91-121, and
in Ayala's Experiencia e invención (Madrid: Taurus, 1961),
pp. 171-203.

Peggy Muñoz Simonds, "Benito Pérez Galdós, roman-
tic-realist: a study in comparative literature," Mexican
Quarterly Review, 4, 1 (1971) 69-77, 79-80, 82, 84-85,
discusses "the novels of the Spanish author ... as a mani-
festation of romanticism and Neo-Platonism in the latter
half of the nineteenth century when the movement had entered
what Jacques Barzun has termed its second phase, realism"
(p. 69). Besides a brief introduction, the article is divided
into "Influence of Balzac" and "Anti-romantic aspects."

Jeremy T. Medina, "Galdós and the concept of literary
realism" (Ph.D. dissertation, University of Pennsylvania,
1970, 523 leaves; Dissertation Abstracts International, 31

[1970], 2928A), has for its "purpose ... to investigate, define and illustrate to what extent the novels of Pérez Galdós
are actually 'realistic' in relation to the findings of a preliminary analysis of the norms of nineteenth century literary
realism. The initial chapters consist of remarks concerning
the abstract theory of realism itself, Realism as a literary
movement, and realism in Spain, followed by a detailed examination of Galdós' methodology with respect to subject
matter, character, treatment, theme, objectivity, style and
'Galdós' relation to other Realists, respectively."

Judith Kay Engler, "A structural definition of Galdosian realism" (Ph. D. dissertation, University of Texas,
1972), 274 leaves, "attempts to define the nature of realism
as a literary style in the novelas contemporáneas of the nineteenth century Spanish novelist...." She notes that "The
introductory chapter begins with an historical survey of critical commentary on the nature of Galdós' realism.... The
second chapter treats the problem of point of view.... The
third chapter examines the problem of distance.... The
fourth treats the problem of the 'unreliable' narrator in
Galdós' novels, and thus examines some of the questions
basic to the relationship between the narrator and the reader.
It examines some of the ways in which the narrator profoundly affects the reader's perception of the novelistic
world."

She "concludes that the concept of reality basic to
Galdós' novels is inherent in some kind of relationship between external phenomena and perceiving consciousness, and
that the concept is created and defined aesthetically in the
relationship between the narrator and the world of the novel.
That is the formula of art which constitutes Galdosian realism. "

Gustavo Correa, Realidad, ficción y símbolo en las
novelas de Pérez Galdos: ensayo de estética realista (Bogo-
tá: Instituto Caro y Cuervo, 1967), 294pp., states that "En
el presente libro trataremos de fijar los principios directores
del arte galdosiano, con el fin de contribuir a formular con
mayor precisión lo que podemos denominar una estética de su
realismo literario. Si bien, los postulados teóricos que el
autor enunció sucintamente en diversas ocasiones tienen una
importancia manifiesta en la determinación de su concepción
del novelar, éstos no son lo suficientemente aclaratorios
para poder adquirir, a través de ellos una idea precisa e
integradora de su arte. Por tal razón, analizaremos

sistemáticamente la actitud que el novelista asumió frente
al problema de la realidad en sí, y la manera como se pro-
puso proyectarla en una construcción artística que fuese, al
mismo tiempo, una reproducción exacta del mundo observado,
y un mundo específico de ficción. Al mismo tiempo, exami-
naremos la preocupación fundamental del autor por incorporar
a su mundo creado el tema del arte y el de la naturaleza de
la realidad en sí. Además, veremos de qué forma las
estructuras simbolicas que imprimen un sentido de orienta-
ción a la realidad son, a su vez, reveladoras de una particular visión del mundo por parte del autor" (p. 12).

The main divisions of this work are: Introducción.
II. La concepción del novelar. III. La realidad como
problema. IV. La invasión de la realidad. V. El mundo
de la realidad frente al mundo de ficción. VI. La realidad
como ficción. VII. Dos héroes de ficción (i. e. Máximo
Manso in El amigo Manso and José María Bueno de Guzmán
in Lo prohibido). VIII. La dimensión histórica de la realidad. IX. La interpretación de la realidad. X. El proceso
de espiritualización. XI. La creación de la realidad.
XIII. La presencia de la naturaleza. XIV. El simbolismo
mítico. XV. El simbolismo religioso and XVI. Conclusion.

Rodolfo Cardona, "Galdós and realism," in Galdós...,
Mary Washington College, pp. 71-94, proposes "to offer yet
new perspectives on this subject convinced, as I am, that
there can be final definition of Galdós' realism, something
which, in my estimation, is further proof of his greatness
as a novelist" (p. 71). Cardona finds that Galdós swayed
between reality defined as "that which inheres in external
phenomena; and that which exists in some kind of relation
between external phenomena and perceiving consciousness"
(p 72). Cardona states that "No one has succeeded better
than Galdós in incorporating into his novels the historical
events of the present, and of the immediate past they apply
to the present" (p. 81). Interesting remarks are made about
Balzac and Galdós and the many different definitions of the
term realism. Pages 91-94 provide the scholarly documentation for this most interestingly written discussion of this
topic.

Eamonn Joseph Rodgers, "Galdós' art of realism:
character and society in four novels" (Ph.D. dissertation,
The Queen's University of Belfast, 1970), 299 leaves, relates
some of the work of Pérez Galdós to the theory and history
of European realism. The dissertation has six chapters:

Galdós and the realist novel in Spain, Drama and didacticism: La familia de León Roch, New directions: La desheredada, Realism and myth: El amigo Manso, Romanticism and romance: Tormento and Galdós, art or realism. Mrs. Vera Colin has kindly supplied the data that the following annotation is based on.

Dr. Rodgers examines in these novels Galdós' success or otherwise in portraying character and society in a truthful manner, and in establishing a convincing relationship between them. The author suggests that the realist novel reflects the bourgeois and mercantilist way of life. On the other hand the romantic's emphasis on individual personality constitutes an important factor in the development of realism. The intellectual climate in Spain in the 19th century was highly unfavorable to the liberal and pluralistic outlook which is generally associated with the rise of realist fiction. The period of the realistic novel in Spain coincides with a comparative, albeit very limited, widening of the intellectual horizons. In Dr. Rodgers' opinion Galdós' brand of realism arose largely from his consciousness that middle-class morality was little more than a facade, that Spain's economic prosperity rested on very precarious foundations and that the parliamentary system, sustained as it was by the polite fiction of the turno pacífico, was a grotesque charade.

Dr. Rodgers considers the novel La familia de León Roch as the most interesting of Galdós' early group of novels (Doña Perfecta, Gloria, Marianela), not only because it is very representative of Galdós youthful didactic manner, but, more significantly, because it exemplifies, in a very instructive way, certain tensions between the novelist's growing instinct for realism and his self-consciously moralistic attitude. It is undeniable that La familia de León Roch marks a considerable advance on Galdós' earlier novels because its treatment of society is more comprehensive. The presentation of Pepa is, in the author's view, the most realistic element in La familia de León Roch: it is she who is freest from the didactic and dramatic limitations of the work as a whole and who therefore comes closest to achieving fully "novelistic" stature. This is so even though her characterization contains strong traces of the romance Galdós claimed to be repudiating. Her story is therefore interesting for the additional reason that it illustrates what Galdós could achieve when he left his theoretical assumptions behind him. Galdós' deep sympathy with Pepa's feelings foreshadows the way in which he will in due course outgrow his early puritanism.

According to the author La desheredada belongs with
Fortunata y Jacinta rather than with Doña Perfecta, however
imperfectly Galdós assimilated the new insights of Naturalism.
One notices immediately how much more space is given in
La desheredada to money matters. The author mentions that
La desheredada lacks compassion due to Galdós' moralistic
standpoint. Galdós' treatment of the lower strata of society,
in short, is not so much compassionate as moralistic. On
the other hand, it would be unfair to ignore the extent to
which Galdós' canvas has been broadened in La desheredada.
The growth of compassion in Galdós' writing enables him to
reap the full benefit of the central innovation of La desheredada, its attack on romance.

The salient feature of El amigo Manso is that for the
first time in his novels about contemporary society Galdós
does not speak to the reader directly in his own voice. El
amigo Manso is a novel of middle-class life. It seems certain that more of Galdós' deeply felt personal experience
went into the making of El amigo Manso than into any previous novel. Máximo is the first of Galdós' characters to
be seen wholly from the inside. El amigo Manso initiates
Galdós' mature style. In El amigo Manso and subsequent
novels, however, Galdós' commitment to moral values is
expressed through an attitude which is at once deeply sympathetic to the world he creates and sufficiently detached to
enable him to see this world steadily as a whole. The
central moral point of the novel, the narrator's growth toward awareness of his own limitations and towards acceptance
of the weaknesses of others, is balanced by a clear view of
the shallowness and triviality of the morals of society.

"One of Galdós' principal achievements in El amigo
Manso is thus to offer a steady view of the selfishness and
folly of humanity in general, while at the same time uphold-
ing through his presentation of Máximo's painful re-education,
the value of tolerance and compassion towards the weaknesses
of individuals. It hardly needs to be emphasised that this
readiness to take life as it is is the principal feature of El
amigo Manso."

Dr. Rodgers observes that social realism and psychological realism complement each other. He considers that
El amigo Manso takes its place among the masterpieces of
European realism. He is also convinced that Máximo's end
is directly brought about by his failure to come to terms
with the non-rational half of man's nature, to accept that
body and soul, instinct and intellect are inseparable.

He concludes: "...it is appropriate to end our discussion of the emergence and consolidation of Galdós' art of realism with Tormento, because this novel really marks the point at which his mature style becomes finally established. This is why an examination of the group of novels we have analysed is particularly interesting and fruitful: they chart Galdós' progress from his youthful literary endeavours to full artistic maturity. Galdós' position in the European realist tradition is thus highly individual, if not unique. Professor Frye is undoubtedly right, in general terms, when he claims that romanticism is difficult to adapt to the novel, because the novel demands an attitude of empirical observation. But I would suggest that we must regard Galdós as an exception to this pattern. Though his development away from romance towards a more sober and empirical realism parallels, to a greater or lesser extent, that of other major realists like Balzac, Flaubert and Zola, his ultimate personal achievement is to enhance his empirical observation of character and society by suggesting transcendental realities. It is this above all which not only makes his best novels masterpieces in their own right, but makes his work as a whole a major contribution to the literary imitation of life."

Romanticism

Alejandro Casona, "Galdós y el romanticismo," Cursos y conferencias, 24 (1943), 99-111, states that he wishes to deal with the question: "cuáles son las características del romanticismo que se conservan vigentes en la obra del maestro; y sobre todo, cómo esos fermentos idealistas van adquiriendo a través de él nueva personalidad y un tratamiento de maduración hasta incorporarse a la nueva tendencia realista" (p. 100).

Scène à faire

Gloria Manala y Mendoza Fry, "Dramatic structure in the novels of Pérez Galdós: his use of the scène à faire" (Ph.D. dissertation, University of Washington, 1965, 233 leaves; Dissertation Abstracts, 26 [1966], 4657), attempts to apply certain of the critical theories of Archer, Lubbock and Malcolm Brown to Doña Perfecta, Fortunata y Jacinta, Realidad, Angel Guerra and Torquemada en el Purgatorio. She finds that "The scène à faire in Galdós' novels is much more than a unit of narrative structure, or a device to engender and sustain interest. It illustrates in dramatic terms

the most important and profound aspects of Galdós' thought
and philosophy, and his stand on those problems that were of
deepest significance to him and the society of his time"
(p. 4657).

Sistema dialogal

Roberto G. Sánchez, " 'El sistema dialogal' en algunas
novelas de Galdós," Cuadernos hispanoamericanos, no. 235
(julio 1969), 155-67, notes "su hábil manejo del diálogo"
(p. 155). This article attempts to show what Galdós meant
by his term "sistema dialogal." Sánchez states that his purpose is "Examinar estos ejemplos temprano del fenómeno e
indagar en el sentido que esta predilección pueda tener es el
propósito de este trabajo. Toda referencia a 'diálogo,'
'forma dialogada' o 'escena dialogada' se hará pensando en
la forma del 'sistema dialogal,' según se ha explicado" (p.
156). References are made chiefly to La desheredada, El
doctor Centeno and La de Bringas.

Symbolism

Gustavo Correa, "El simbolismo mítico en las novelas
de Pérez Galdós," Thesaurus, 18 (1963), 428-44, has the following subdivisions: Actitudes frente a la mitología clásica,
Reencarnaciones mitológicas, Creaciones míticas. The author
concludes that "A través de este análisis hemos podido examinar la manera como el autor utilizó el pasado mitológico
de la tradición clásica y en qué forma creó símbolos arquetí-
picos de particular significado. La densidad de este simbolismo contribuye a definir la dimensión artística y semántica
en algunas de sus novelas" (p. 444).

El tópico

Joaquín Gimeno Casalduero, "El tópico en la obra de
Pérez Galdós," Boletín informativo del Seminario de Derecho
Político, nos. 8-9 (enero-abril 1956), 35-52, notes that "el
tópico es algo que en la obra de Galdós aparece con frecuencia y que aparece, nosotros al menos lo creemos así, por
algo. Galdós lo usa, y al mismo tiempo persigue, al usarlo,
un fin claro y concreto" (p. 35). He shows the precision
that Galdós uses to delineate his characters and states that
"No creo que haya dificultad en admitir el uso del tópico

como ocasionado por este afán de verosimilitud ... El tópico
serà uno de tantos elementos a travès de los cuales intente
Galdos aprehender la exactitud del mundo circundante" (p. 36).
The article's purpose is "indicar, primeramente, las que
creemos fuentes--para Galdós--de estos tópicos, y más tarde,
teniendo en cuenta estas fuentes, agrupar nuestro corto material en diversos sectores, los cuales ponen de relieve dos
o tres de las posturas de las maneras de actuar más características del XIX" (p. 37). Pages 42-46 are entitled "La
política, según el tópico galdosiano"; pp. 46-52, "La sociedad,
según el tópico galdosiano."

José Schraibman, "Galdós y el estilo de la vejez,"
Homenaje a Rodríguez-Moñino (Madrid: Castalia, 1967),
2:165-75, disputes the idea that "en sus últimos años de vida
literaria sufrió Galdós un grave decaimiento en sus poderes
creadores" (p. 165) and studies in detail the style of Galdós'
El caballero encantado (1909) and La razón de la sinrazón
(1905). "La verdad es que tanto en los últimos episodios
como en las últimas novelas de Galdós hay verdaderas páginas de antología...." (p. 166). "Galdós en su vejez parece
haber levantado vuelo hacia lo fantástico-mitológico..." (p. 167).

"EPISODIOS NACIONALES"

Three book-length general studies of the Episodios
nacionales were published in the 1960's and render earlier
lengthy studies on these novels obsolete. They are: Hans
Hinterhaüser, Die Episodios Nacionales von Benito Pérez
Galdós (Hamburg: Kommissionsverlag: Cram, De Gruyter,
1961), 199pp., translated by José Escobar as Los "Episodios
nacionales" de Benito Pérez Galdós (Madrid: Gredos [1963]),
398pp.; Antonio Regalado García, Benito Pérez Galdós y la
novela histórica 1868-1912 (Madrid: Insula, 1966), 586pp.;
and Alfred Rodríguez, An introduction to the "Episodios nacionales" of Galdós (New York: Las Américas Publishing
Co., 1967), 222pp.

The volume by Hinterhaüser contains the following
parts: Introducción: Situación de los estudios galdosianos.
I. La génesis de los Episodios nacionales. II. Los Episodios nacionales como historia. III. Los Episodios nacionales
como medio de educación política. IV. Los Episodios nacionales como novela, Conclusion, Bibliografía and Indice de
nombres propios. The introduction is an interesting and useful, though somewhat opinionated, survey of previous writings
on the Episodios nacionales. While regretting, for example,
that the dissertations written under Shoemaker at Kansas have
remained unpublished, he then remarks: "Pero, por otra
parte, si como es de suponer, sus autores son los mismos
que firman los artículos galdosianos que regularmente apare-
can en la revista Hispania, entonces no hay por qué lamentar
desmasiado que dichas tesis sean inaccesibles" (p. 14).

The first sentence of his final paragraph follows:
"Espero que todo que una cosa haya quedado clara: los
Episodios nacionales son una obra literaria mucho más esencial de lo que hasta se había querido reconocer; más exacta-
mente: a pesar de que en la concepción fundamental del
autor predomine un juicio crítico-histórico determinado y una
doctrina política, no cabe duda de que pueden aspirar al
rango de obra de arte" (p. 371).

Stephen Gilman's review of this volume was published

in Romanische Forsuchungen, 75 (1963), 434-46. Pages 434-
38 argue the "Hinterhaüser's calculated decision to treat the
two groups of Episodios as a single entity effectively prohibits
a search for this kind of internal comprehension. The mortal
risk of a book so defined is inability to deal with the evolution
of Galdós' thought and creativity as a developing whole" (p.
437). Yet, he calls it an "invaluable contribution to Galdosian studies" despite this "single and grave flaw" (p. 434).
He notes that "The book offers such an abundance of accurate
observations and lucid insights as to make difficult their ex-
hibition within the limits of a review" (p. 439). The general
theme of certain sections is discussed. Gilman feels that the
book offers "a remarkably sensitive critical presentation of
Galdós as an artist of fiction...." (p. 443). He finds that
the author's "analysis of the way Galdós helps his reader
sense the passage of time--biological and historical--through
reappearing and changing characters is both new and instructive. Another intensely interesting subsection is that dedicated
to the increasingly important and complex feminine inhabitants
of the Episodios" (pp. 444-45). He ends his review with this
sentence: "Hinterhaüser's perceptive presentation of the simultaneous opposition and collaboration of the internal and external forms of the Episodios is not the least of his contributions to Galdosian studies" (p. 446). This review, full of
penetrating comments should be thoroughly examined by all
interested in the theory and development of the Episodios nacionales.

The third volume (1968) of Anales galdosianos contains
Joseph Schraibman and Alfredo Rodríguez, "H. Hinterhaüser's
re-examination of the Episodios nacionales," pp. 169-77, and
R. Cardona, "Apostillas a los Episodios Nacionales de B. P. G.
de Hinterhaüser," pp. 119-42.

The review calls this volume "the most serious study
devoted to the Episodios" (p. 169). It finds that Hinterhaüser
"has left few stones unturned in analyzing the genesis of
Galdós' historical novels, in tracing their sources, in discussing their political content and in appraising them as works
of art" (p. 169). In regard to chapter one, they feel that it
"does not underscore a central factor in Galdós' conception
of the present in terms of its dynamic 'becoming' from the
immediate past" (p. 169). Hinterhaüser's statement that
"Galdós utilizaba generalmente para cada episodio una obra
histórica como fuente principal" "is too broad a generaliza-
tion given the scarcity of source studies" (p. 170). The re-
viewers discuss a few of their differences with the author in

regard to philosophical criteria that underlie Galdós' approach
to history. They feel that Hinterhaüser "occasionally tends
to overuse Galdós political biography, too often seeing the
Episodios as a direct growth of the novelist's shifting political
moods--a misleading procedure in dealing with a historically
motivated realist writer" (p. 173). This review and that of
Gilman should be given careful study, both for the volume's
strong points and weaknesses. Schraibman and Rodríguez
in their review emphasize some of the few points on which
they differ with Hinterhaüser. They also praise him for the
novelty of his approach to certain areas of study of these
novels.

Cardona feels that the Spanish translation of this volume should have been postponed until Hinterhaüser had time
to explore the Casa Museo Pérez Galdós. He writes that
"Un examen ... hubiese, por un lado, alterado en parte los
dos primeros capítulos de su estudio ... y por otro, con-
firmando muchisimas cosas que Hinterhaüser intuyo fina-
mente y que constituyen las más significativos contribuciones
de su estudio" (p. 119). The material of use in the Casa
Museo can be divided into "las fuentes librescas," "la correspondencia mantenida por Galdós con personas que le su-
ministraban datos importantes...." (p. 119). This study is
full of suggestive ideas concerning various historical works
that were probably used by Galdós in writing the Episodios.
Cardona notes, for example, the degree to which many of
the books were marked by Galdós.

Angel Antón, "Galdós, historiador y novelista," Die
Neüeren Sprachen, n.s. 11 (1962), 455-61, is an interesting
review of the German edition of this volume.

It must be recognized that few volumes about Galdós
have aroused greater interest in scholarly journals than has
this volume by Hinterhaüser. The student interested in the
Episodios nacionales would do well to begin his critical reading with this volume, then study the most important of the
reviews and then go on to the works of Rodríguez, Regalado
García and others who have written on these novels.

Regalado García states that his purpose is "rescatar
a Galdós de una estricta crítica literaria, necesariamente
incompleta; de la dictada por los apasionamientos ideológicos
y patrióticos en pro o en contra del autor, inadmisibles por
vicio de origen; y de las tendencias del liberalismo humani-
tario, que hasta nuestros días ha sido la nota dominante en

una apreciación, sin lugar para el disentimiento, de las novelas de Galdós. He tratado de ver al autor como fue en la
realidad, de situarlo en las circunstancias que lo rodearon y
lo influyeron, y de apreciar su obra literaria, y en especial
sus novelas históricas, libre de apasionamientos, tradiciones
críticas y doctrinarismos ... La perspectiva histórica que se
refleja en este estudio se la debo en gran parte a la lectura
de Dilthey, de Collingwood y, sobre todo, de Ortega y Gasset,
en cuya extensa obra hay un genial método histórico que los
críticos literarios no han empezado aún a utilizar" (pp. 17-
18).

There are chapters on each of the five series of the
Episodios nacionales as well as a chapter on their origins
and the tradition of the historical novel, a chapter on the
Novelas contemporáneas. Pages 519-38 consist of an epilogue,
while pp. 541-81 are devoted to one of the longest readily
available bibliographies up to that of Sackett. As Sackett intentionally omitted studies on the Episodios nacionales, this
unannotated bibliography can serve in some respects as a supplement to Sackett's volume.

Raymond Carr, "A new view of Galdós," Anales galdosianos, 3 (1968), 185-89, is a review of this volume and is
of special interest since it is the work of a well-known British
historian. Carr states that "Its attempt to connect Galdós'
own views of the historical process with those current in nineteenth century Europe is challenging" (p. 189). He says that
"Antonio Regalado's thesis is simple: Galdós was a compromising bourgeois not a liberal crusader. He feared the
masses, underestimated the significance of workers' move-
ments, and usually avoided 'real' social issues. His anticlericalism was a mask to hide his reluctance to tackle the
most fundamental issues in Spanish politics. To a large extent he was a hypocrite and a fake; he has what Prof. Regalado calls a 'cant mentality' (p. 74)" (p. 185). Carr then
continues: "These propositions have two implications. One
concerns the nature of Spanish political life from the mid-
century up to the death of Galdós. The other concerns the
nature of the novelist's craft and, above all, what can be expected from him in terms of his own experience, independent
of his political position or his views on what would, in the
jargon of our time, he called 'structural change'" (p. 185).

Regalado Garcia's volume is reviewed and discussed
at some length by Paul Olson, "Galdós and history," Modern
Language Notes, 85 (1970), 274-79. Olson takes exception

to Regalado's "concept of the realist novel itself and his in-
sistence on judging the work on Galdós in terms of a fixed
political and social ethic, rather than with a more consistently historical and literary perspective" (p. 278). His concluding sentence states that "Those who disagree with Regalado's
premises and conclusions must still be grateful to him for re-
quiring us to re-examine our own assumptions concerning the
novel and its relation to history, and they can only regard his
work as one of the most original and provocátive studies of
Galdós which have yet appeared" (p. 279).

Peter B. Goldman, "Historical perspective and political
bias: comments on recent Galdós criticism," Anales galdosianos, 6 (1971), 113-124, summarizes his extensive differences with Regalado in these three paragraphs: "The question
of Galdós' historical perspective, that of his ability to 'see'
historical events as they really were and to appraise their
importance accurately, is fundamental. Regalado would have
us see in Galdós a sloppy intellect whose inability to discern
historical fact renders him insidiously middle class and reactionary. Galdós would then be an agent of the status quo
because he is blind to the facts that a) a deep social problem
threatens the country, and b) the social problem is exacer-
bated by the violent forces of revolution which are mustered
and well-organized, waiting for the right moment to precipi-
tate an uprising of the pueblo.

"My own reading and analysis of Galdós' writings during the thirty years between 1868-1898 shows me that Galdós
had adequate 'vision.' He was aware of the existence of the
social ills besetting the masses. A typical liberal, he chose
to search for solutions to the social questions within the
framework of existing institutions and therefore knowingly
supported the status quo. Nor was he blind to a possible
revolt of the masses--insofar as such a circumstance simply
did not exist in late nineteenth-century Spain.

"In accusing him of lack of cognizance of the social
problems, Professor Regalado merely misreads Galdós. But
in bringing him to task for failing to appreciate a revolutionary situation, Regalado is misreading history and then con-
demning Galdós and those of his critics who will not accept
what is an historically untenable position. It is therefore
important that Professor Regalado be answered" (pp. 113-14).

Rodríguez gives the fullest discussion of these novels
in English. He states that his "focus on the Episodios na-

cionales as a homogeneous segment of Galdos' literary production offers a simple division into two parts. The first,
consisting of two chapters, will consider questions pertinent
to the work as a whole, matters of generic classification,
genesis, and historical approach. The second, which consists of three chapters, deals critically with each of the five
series of the Episodios nacionales, and stresses literary
development and technique" (p. 8).

He notes that "The Episodios nacionales have drawn
relatively scant attention from modern critics" who tend "to
relegate Galdós' historical novel to a literary limbo" (p. 7).
This volume contains an introduction, a conclusion, an appendix: "Galdós on Spain and Spaniards," a list of works
consulted and an index.

Madeleine de Gogorza Fletcher reviews this volume
in Anales galdosianos, 3 (1968), 179-83, and finds that except for "the focus on history, Rodríguez' book is a careful
study of the Episodios" (p. 182). His "best observations
are those dealing with plot development and characterization,
while the historical symbolism of the characters is less clearly envisaged" (p. 182). She writes that "The book contains
only one element which, to my way of thinking, blurs its
focus. This is the treatment of the relationship of literary
style to historical content in the chapter 'History in the
Episodios nacionales'" (p. 179). She does not agree with his
central point "that there is no change in Galdós' approach to
history over the course of the forty years in which Galdós
wrote the Episodios and that the stylistic differences visible
in the Episodios nacionales do not reflect any such change"
(p. 179). She differs with Rodríguez on a variety of matters
concerning the nature of historical writing.

Pedro Ortiz Armengol, Aviraneta y diez mas ...
(Madrid, Editorial Prensa Española, 1970), 214pp., "constituye un estudio sobre un grupo de figuras tratadas en los
Episodios nacionales y en las Memorias de un hombre de
accion, acerca de las cuales se aportan en este libro cientos
de documentos inéditos ... que confirman, rectifican, aclaran
o complican los que conocieron Galdós y Baroja pero que, en
todo caso, dan una nueva dimensión de estos personajes"
(book jacket). The contents follow: Prólogo sobre los Episodios nacionales y las Memorias de un hombre de acción.
Papeles nuevos sobre los Avinareta. El traidor don Saturnino Gomez Albuin, "el manco." Van Halen, con la espada y
el folleto. Jorge Bessiere, aventurero, cinico y versatil,
Don Fermin Leguia, vecino de Vera del Bidasoa. Gabriel

Arrambide, ex fraile y espia. Jose Manuel Regato, el malva-
do absoluto. Una vida desaprovechada: la de don Cecilio de
Corpas. Moreno Guerra, oscura pelea. Purgatorío de Ro-
mero Alpuente, Olozaga, politico de cuerpo entero. Notas
bibliograficas.

The prologue contains some especially useful ideas
that compare Pérez Galdós and Baroja and the Episodios nacionales and Memorias de un hombre de acción.

FIRST SERIES. Two book-length volumes deal with
the first series of the Episodios nacionales. They are:
Pedro Rojas Ferrer, Valoración histórica de los Episodios
nacionales de B. Pérez Galdós ([Cartagena]: Baladre, 1965,
418pp.), and Ward H. Dennis, Pérez Galdós: a study in
characterization. Episodios nacionales: first series (Madrid,
1968, 141pp.), which was based on a Columbia University
doctoral dissertation entitled "Characterization in the first
series of the Episodios nacionales of Benito Pérez
Galdós," (1965, 178 leaves; Dissertation Abstracts, 26
[1966], 4655).

The volume by Rojas Ferrer contains a prologue,
twenty chapters, the last being the "Conclusiones," and a
bibliography. The chapter titles will show the volume's
scope: I. Supuestos básicos para una valoración histórica,
II. Literatura e historia. III. Galdós historiador, IV. Los
Episodios nacionales. Historia del siglo XIX español, V.
Mesonero Romanos testigo y fuente de mayor excepción,
VI. Estudio comparativo de Galdós con historiadores y co-
rrientes en su época en Europa. VII. Episodio primero.
Trafalgar, VIII. Precedentes reflejados en el episodio,
IX. El Estado mayor de la escuadra combinada, X. Combate
naval de Trafalgar. XI. La Corte de Carlos IV. XII. El
19 de marzo y el 2 de mayo, XIII. Bailén. XIV. Napoleón
en Chamartin, XV. Zaragoza, XVI. Gerona. XVII. Cádiz,
XVIII. Juan Martín, el empecinado, XIX. La batalla de los
Arapiles.

His general conclusions as found on p. 391 are:
"(1) Los Episodios nacionales contienen Historia auténtica,
que puede ser distinguida perfectamente por el especialista,
de ambientes y personaje imaginados. (2) La forma literaria
de exposición responde a una inquietud de la época y no afecta
a cuestiones de contenido. (3) Las fuentes utilizadas para
los Episodios son auténticas. (4) Constituyen fuente de investigación complementaria para la Historia española del
XIX. (5) Son un ameno instrumento de divulgación histórica.

(6) Galdós es historiador y de una emplia formación histórica.
(7) Dentro de la historiografía, B.P. Galdós se le debe considerar encuadrado en la "Escuela del Lirismo subjetivo" y de un modo personal entre Michelet y Ranque." Passages from Galdós' works are compared with numerous works of history to show their authenticity. This volume was originally a doctoral dissertation from the University of Murcia.

The Dennis study has the following parts: I. Antecedents in the historical novel. II. Novelistic characters. III. Pueblo. IV. Historical characters. V. Conclusion. Bibliography and Index of characters studied. It would seem that the studies on the Episodios nacionales by Rodríguez, Regalado García and Rojas Ferrer all appeared too late to be of use to Dennis, as they are unmentioned in both the text and the bibliography. His bibliography lacks numerous contemporary reviews of this series as well as much of the criticism that exists on these novels.

Dennis is interested primarily in the characters found in these novels, and thus his approach is not the same as the other volumes on the Episodios nacionales. To a certain extent, this study complements the other book-length studies; on the other hand, it seems a little short to do full justice to its subject. According to the abstract the first chapter studies "some of the antecedents to the Episodios in the historical novel. The second chapter contains a lengthy analysis of the protagonist Gabriel Araceli, including his weaknesses as a character. The third chapter is a study of the pueblo as a composite character which acts as the hero of the series.... Chapter four deals with the fifteen extremely significant historical characters who take part in the action of the novels."

L. Louis-Lande, "Le roman patriotique en Espagne," Revue des deux mondes, troisième periode, 14 (1876), 934-45, is an early French critical study on these novels. He finds that Galdós has been influenced by Erckmann-Chatrian as well as by the picaresque novels of the Golden Age. He notes that Galdós' fiction "n'a pas assez de la vraisemblance" (p. 937). He states that the novels do nothing "à dissiper les préventions plus ou moins injustes des Espagnols contre la France" (p. 939). His views of history are lopsided and completely in favor of the Spanish. Louis-Lande provides also an evaluation of Galdós' style which on the whole he praises, yet he is also able to damn it by declaring that "On sent la précipitation, l'absence d'effort sérieux, le contentement trop facile de soi-même" (p. 944).

D[iego] B[arros] A[rana]'s review of the first series
in Revista chilena, 4 (1876), 307-08, notes the influence of
Erckmann-Chatrian and states that "Los hechos verdaderos
sirven de base principal de la naracción; pero el autor los
adorna con heroes i con incidentes novelescos que sirven para
mantener el interés i avivar la curiosidad" (p. 307).   The
reader will find both "entretenimiento e instrucción" (p. 308).
He finds that "estas últimas [novelas] revelan un escritor de
talento que suele abusar de su fecunda facilidad" (ibid.).

Carlos Vázquez Arjona, "Introducción al estudio de la
primera serie de los Episodios nacionales de Pérez Galdós,"
PMLA, 48 (1933), 895-907, states the "Tratamos de hacer
ver en esta introducción el rumbo que sigue el pensamiento
galdosiano, bien cuando ensalza a los héroes y heroínas de
la patria, o cuando nos descubre los orígenes de la decadencia, o bien cuando impugna a los traidores o nos revela
las intrigas del enemigo" (p. 895).

Palmira Arnáiz Amigo, "Particularidades del habla
popular en la primera serie de los Episodios nacionales de
don Benito Pérez Galdós," Acta politécnica mexicana, 9, 44
(1968), 135-144, discusses briefly the following: "1.   Lengua
popular transcrita casi 'ad literam' y en la que el novelista
ha tenido en cuenta, especialmente, la clase social a que
pertenece el hablante y su personalidad.   2.   Locuciones.
3.   Influencia del lenguaje popular en el modo de expresarse
de los aristócratas.   4.   Influencia del lenguaje popular en la
prensa de la época.   5.   Barbarismos.   6.   Lengua popular,
pura invención artística de Galdós: nombres, apodos; personi-
ficaciones; metáforas.   7.   Decoro artístico.   8.   Conclusiones."

Nigel Glendinning, "Psychology and politics in the first
series of the Episodios nacionales," in Galdós studies, pp. 36-
61.   The author writes: "Appealing, then, through form and
subject matter to a wide public, Galdós could create in the
first series of Episodios a more influential depiction of the
inter-relationship between personality and politics than he had
achieved in La fontana de oro and El audaz.   If the whole
series constitutes a view of the forces which could unite or
disunite Spain in the past, it also perhaps shows how individuals contributed to the making or marring of that union.   It
remains to be seen how far individual Episodios support such
an interpretation" (p. 44).

He also states that "...the tensions also reflect the

psychological, moral and political preoccupations of the novelist, and are used by him to describe in dramatic terms the
problems of human society in general and Spanish society in
particular" (p. 44).

Galdós believes "in the inter-relationship of psychology
and politics"; thus "it is easy to see how the novel could become a natural form in which to depict social tension and
political crisis" (pp. 60-61).

José Agustín Balseiro, "Anticlericalismo y religiosidad
en Benito Pérez Galdós (desde los primeros Episodios nacionales)," La torre, no. 67 (1970), 63-83, states that Galdós'
opposition was to "los sacerdotes que olvidaron su ministerio
para cultivar la intromisión en la conciencia y en el hogar
ajenos hasta perturbarlos" (p. 63). Those who accuse him of
being antireligious have not read him with care. He writes:
"No era menos, ni menos ahincada, la frecuencia con que,
en las novelas de su primera época--1870-1879--con las dos
excepciones de La sombra y de Marianela, escribiría Galdós
contra los fanáticos y los curas malhechores. Sin embargo,
no ha solido señalarse suficientemente, mediante las distin-
ciones imprescindibles de justicia, que no pocos Episodios
nacionales eran contemporáneos de aquellas mismas novelas.
Y el análisis, cuidadoso y deliberado, de esas narraciones
evidencia no sólo el espíritu religioso de Galdos; de añadi-
dura, demonstrará, generalmente, la creación de seres
compasivas y cristianos al servicio de su Iglesia y con amor
al semejante" (p. 64).

Galdós' religious views as found in the first series of
the Episodios nacionales are analyzed. Balseiro finds no
reason to consider him an antireligious author and notes that
at his deathbed, there remained a crucifix.

Ricardo Gullón, "'Los Episodios' la primera serie,"
Philological Quarterly, 51 (1972), 292-312, reprinted in Benito
Pérez Galdós (1973), 379-402, is an extremely complex study
of the first series of these novels from strictly the viewpoint
of literary criticism. He desires to deal with a problem
such as why these novels were received not as novels but as
history. He wants to "contrarrestar una inclinación creciente
a utilizar la obra galdosiana como documento, tendencia que
produjo grave desproporcion entre los estudios sociológicos e
históricos dedicados a los Episodios y los de crítica literaria"
(p. 390). He discusses the role of Gabriel Araceli, who appears in nine of the ten volumes. He feels that "La interpo-

sición del narrador (de los diferentes tipos de narrador)
entre la materia novelada y el lector, sirve para eliminar
de la novela al autor.   La eliminación está bien calculada,
pues así la invención parece conseguida por el narrador,
quien a diferencia del autor, es ya ente de ficción, tejido de
la misma fibra y viviente en el mismo espacio que las
restantes figuras novelescas" (p. 387).   This article provides
many worthwhile insights into Galdós' techniques as a novelist.

Walter T. Pattison, "The prehistory of the Episodios
nacionales," Hispania, 53 (1970), 857-63, notes that "The
purpose of this article is to examine Galdós' statements concerning the lack of previous plan for the Episodios nacionales
in the light of objective evidence which tends to show that
he had in fact contemplated and planned the first series of
these novels well in advance of their writing" (p. 857).

His last paragraph states that "It is obviously impossible to say exactly what gave Galdós the initial incentive to
novelize history.   Our concern here is when he began to
formulate this idea.   Despite his avowals that he had no plan
--and by this we feel that he meant a specific, detailed out-
line--we must conclude that the notion of a historical series
had already germinated as early as the article on 'Carlos
Dickens' in 1868.   The early novels, La fontana de oro and
El audaz, showed him that he could succeed as a historical
novelist, and the reviews of the former urged him to do what
he had been contemplating for some time--to write an integrated series of novels setting forth systematically the
history of the early nineteenth century" (p. 862).

GUERRA DE LA INDEPENDENCIA EXTRACTADA
PARA USO DE LOS NINOS.   Alberto Navarro González, "Una
obra olvidada de Galdós," La Estafeta literaria, no. 524
(Sept. 15, 1973), 4-7, has three parts: Adaptaciones de los
Episodios nacionales, Descripción y analisis del libro and
Posibles motivos de su publicación.   The author has studied
two different editions of Guerra de la Independencia, extractada para uso de los niños.   One probably was published
in late 1908 or early 1909; the other appeared in late 1916
or 1917.   Navarro González notes that "El principal interés,
pues, que este libro ofrece a los estudiosos de Galdós acaso
radique en averiguar qué es y por qué motivos lo que quiso
decir o callar Galdós al nuevo público infantil de lo escrito
por él antes en la citada serie de sus Episodios nacionales"
(p. 5).   His concluding paragraph follows: "Yo creo, sin

embargo, que si para el logro de sus citados propósitos pe-
dagógicos y patrióticos escogió de entre toda su producción
literaria la primera serie de sus Episodios nacionales fue por
ver en su más popular obra famosa y vivos ejemplos de
patriotismo generoso, y por creer que el espectáculo de vi-
riles contiendas entre formidables contrarios siempre ar-
rastró el interés de chicos y grandes" (p. 7).

SECOND SERIES. Brian J. Dendle, "The first Cordero: Elia and the Episodios nacionales," Anales galdosianos,
7 (1972), 103-05 presents data to support the belief that
"Galdós' debt to Elia is too specific to be based on the unconscious recollection of an earlier reading...." (p. 105).
Dendle compares Cordero as characterized in Fernán Caballero's novel, Elia, with Primitivo Cordero and Benigno Cordero
found in the second series of the Episodios nacionales.

Javier Herrero, "La 'ominosa decada' en los Episodios
nacionales," Anales galdosianos, 7 (1972), 107-115, notes that
"Tres episodios: El terror de 1824, Un voluntario realista
y Los apostólicos se ocupan del período de nuestra historia
decimonónica conocido bajo el nombre de la 'ominosa década,
es decir, el período del triunfo pleno de absolutismo, de la
máxima expansión de ese furor reaccionario que ocupa un
lugar tan importante en la creación novelesca del Galdós
joven.... (p. 107). He also writes the "Uniendo, pues, las
dos direcciones aquí señaladas, el tema y la técnica literaria,
voy a intentar penetrar en esa pintura del espíritu apostólico
mediante un análisis de las imágenes objetivas utilizadas en
estos tres episodios" (p. 108).

THIRD SERIES. E. Gomez de Baquero, "Cronica
literaria," La España moderna, 145 (1907), 144-51, finds
that in the third series "no se observa el menor síntoma de
decadencia ni de fatiga. El interés novelesco, la hábil combinación de lo histórico y lo fingido, la expresiva pintura de
los personajes y los acontecimientos del período en que coloca
la acción el novelista, se conservan por lo general en la nueva serie a la misma altura que en las dos anteriores. El
estilo me parece más depurado y más acabados ciertos pormenores de ejecucion en descripciones, diálogos y retratos de
personajes de novela. En cambio, acaso hay en los primeros
Episodios mayor aliento épico, más nervio, mas energís"
(p. 144).

Ephrem Vincent, "Lettre espagnoles," Mercure de
France, 37 (1901), 244-49, speaks of the fact that this series

deals with "Environ cinquante années de passions politiques
assimilées sans fatigue au cours d'un récit endiablée" (p.
244). He states that "L'enseignement que Galdós tire de
tout cela est vraiment lumineux: a côté du saynète tragique
et parfois burlesque, il a su trouver des leçons de pitié et
de réconfortants exemples d'humanité" (p. 249).

W. Miller, "The novels of Perez Galdos," The Gentle-
man's Magazine, 291 (Sept. 1, 1901), 217-28, (reprinted in
Living Age, 231 [1901], 509-17) is an evaluation of the first
three series of the Episodios nacionales. The first two
pages deal with Electra and the Episodios nacionales. Miller
writes: "To those who desire to gain some acquaintance
with the romantic episodes which made up so much of Spanish
life in the first half of the last century, no better guide can
be recommended than this popular novelist and dramatist"
(p. 219).

David Renwick Kerr, "Military subject matter in
Galdós: this being a study of the literary treatment of military matters by the Spanish author Benito Pérez Galdós in
ten of his historical novels. Known as the Tercera serie,
Episodios nacionales" (Ph.D. dissertation, George Washington University, 1958), 330 leaves, states that his purpose is
"to examine, in respect of the military content of their texts,
the ten novels..., in order to see how Galdós has treated
that content, how he has worked it into the artistic ensemble
of each novel. The expression 'military matters' of my title
is used liberally, and in this study extends to all military
materials, military matter, affairs, personnel, aspects--in
short textual matter that as raw material has any military
color and meaning" (ℓ. 4). He states that the dissertation
deals with the following questions: "1. What is the nature
of the military subject matter found in the Third series...?
2. In bulk, how much such matter is there? How is it
distributed? and why? 3. What methods and techniques has
the author employed in treating it? 4. Is the literary treatment of this material sufficient and effective, and valid as
viewed from a military standpoint? 5. In what ways has the
style of Galdós been affected by the extensive inclusion of
military material? 6. What, if anything, has the author
achieved by his use of this material in the Third Series?
Has he a message?" (ℓℓ. 7-8). Kerr finds that these novels
"are valid and realistic historical fiction, with an authentic
military component which is vital to his enlightened message
to his countrymen: Stop fighting one another!" (ℓ. 330).

FOURTH SERIES. E. Gómez de Baquero, "Los Episodios nacionales de Pérez Galdos," Cultura española 8 (1907),
979-88, is an evaluation of this set after the concluding volume of the fourth series had appeared. This article has an
introduction and the following sections: Galdós y Erckmann
Chatrian, El asunto historico, Valor historico. --Como trata
la historia Galdos, Los Episodios desde el punto de vista
literario, el estilo y la composición, Personajes y acciones,
El tono y el espíritu de los Episodios. --Mérito relativo de
las series. --Consideración final.

FIFTH SERIES. Miguel Enguídanos, "Mariclío, musa
galdosiana," Papeles de Son Armadanas, no. 63 (junio 1961),
235-49; Benito Pérez Galdós (1973) 427-36, is a discussion
of the final series of the Episodios nacionales. He describes
this series with these words: "Es esta serie la expressión
del pesimismo profundo a que llega su autor después de su
largo viaje por la historia española del siglo XIX. Emana
de ella el intenso olor de la experiencia creadora de primera
clase. Es, también, el legado de su autor a la posteridad
política española: una especie de criptograma en el que aún
se pueden leer respuestas válidas para las angustias del presente" (p. 235). He also states that "La musa inspiradora
de Galdós no es la fría, formal, y académica, Clío, sino
la humana y callejera Mariclío...." (p. 239).

AITA TETTAUEN. Robert Ricard, "Note sur la
genèse de l'Aita Tettauen de Galdós," Bulletin hispanique,
37 (1935), 473-77, declares that Alarcón's Diario de un testigo de la guerra de Africa is not the only source for Galdós'
novel. This article discusses in detail Ricardo Ruiz Orsatti's
"Aita Tettauen," La Gaceta de Africa (Tetuán), enero de
1935, pp. 103-04. Ruiz Orsatti states that he translated for
Galdós' use the Kitab el-istiqusa of El Nasiry. Portions of
Galdós' letters to Ruiz Orsatti are reproduced.

Vera Colin, "Tolstoy and Galdós' Santiuste: their
ideology on war and their spiritual conversion," Hispania,
53 (1970), 836-41, shows that "J. Santiuste's character, as
it is presented in Aita Tettauen, reflects in some of its aspects an influence by Tolstoy" (p. 836). Her concluding
paragraph states that "It is plausible that having been strong-
ly impressed by Tolstoy's Souvenirs de Sébastopol and having
learned about Tolstoy's religious philosophy through Ma religion, Galdós conceived the idea of introducing into the purely
Spanish character of Santiuste some traits of Sebastopol's

protagonist and imbuing him with the most striking ideas of Ma religion" (p. 841).

Tomas García Figueras, "Don Benito Pérez Galdos y su Aita Tettauen," in Recuerdos centenarios de una guerra romantica. La guerra de Africa de nuestros abuelos (1859-60), (Madrid: Consejo Superior de Investigaciones Científicas, 1961), pp. 89-92, notes Galdós' visit to Spanish Morocco in October 1904. This brief comment on Aita Tettauen reproduces a letter that Galdós wrote to Ruiz Orsatti and emphasizes the assistance that this Spanish student of African culture gave to Galdos.

AMADEO I. Jose Francés, "El último libro de Galdos," Por esos mundos, 22 (1922), 157-61, begins his comments on this volume with a general discussion of the Episodios Nacionales as history. He notes the political figures in the novel and its historical basis and declares that "Tito es un admirable acierto simbólico" (p. 161). In regard to style, Frances finds that "hay cuadros de un gracioso desenfado"; he also declares the "Hay tambien páginas frías, impasibles como esos espejos que se olvidan quitar en algunas casas mortuorias" (p. 161).

BAILEN. M. Vázquez Arjona, "Un episodio nacional de Galdós, Bailén (cotejo histórico)," Bulletin of Spanish Studies, 9 (1932), 116-23, says that "No es nuestro objeto, necesariamente, tratar de hallar las fuentes en que se inspirara Galdós en lo tocante a la parte histórica de su obra, aunque en muchas ocasiones creamos haber dado con ellas, sino más bien tratar de hacer notar si la parte histórica del Episodio coincide o no con lo que sobre los mismos asuntos cuenta la Historia" (p. 117).

LA BATALLA DE LOS ARAPILES. Antonio Gómez Galán, "Wellington y los Episodios nacionales de Galdós," Arbor, nos. 285-86 (1969), 37-49, has an introduction and the following sections: Lo histórico y los Episodios, Wellington en los Episodios, La batalla de los Arapiles, El general en jefe and La batalla. It is an interesting discussion of how Galdós portrays Wellington in this episodio nacional.

CADIZ. J. Sarrailh, "Quelques sources du Cádiz de Galdós," Bulletin hispanique, 23 (1924), 33-48, finds that Galdós used secondary rather than primary sources for this novel. The author wishes "indiquer ceux qu'il a consultés pour écrire son Cádiz et examiner de quelle manière il a utilisé l'oeuvre de ses prédécesseurs" (p. 33). He finds that Galdós used Adolfo de Castro's Cádiz en la guerra de la Independencia (1862) and Count Toreno's Historia del levantamiento, guerra y revolución de España (1862). He used these dry historical accounts to assist his imagination. "Il anime leurs phrases froides en tirant des dialogues pleins de vie. Un détail lui suggère un merveilleux dévoloppement lyrique. D'un récit incolore il fait un drame qui passionne. Ainsi s'explique le pouvoir magique des Episodes où la fiction se mêle si parfaitement à l'histoire que l'on ne sait plus 'ce qui est vrai et ce qui ne l'est pas'." (p. 48).

LA CAMPAÑA DEL MAESTRAZGO. E. Gómez de Baquero, "Crónica literaria," La España moderna, 132 (1899), 128-34, finds that this novel is "una de las obras mejor concebidas y mejor planeadas de Galdós, singularmente por el acierto con que ha sabido compendiar en algunas situaciones y escenas culminantes, lo característico de los hechos que describe, y cuya larga y minuciosa narración, además de haberle llevado fuera de los límites de la novela histórica, no daría acaso al lector una representación tan viva y apropiada del asunto como los cuadros trazados por el novelista" (p. 132). He describes D. Beltrán de Urdaneta as "una figura tolstoiana" (p. 133).

Ephrem Vincent, "Lettres espagnoles," Mercure de France, 32 (1899), 841, is a brief note on this volume.

CANOVAS. Ricardo Gullón, "La historia como materia novelable," Anales galdosianos, 5 (1970), 23-37, reprinted in Benito Pérez Galdós (1973), 403-26, has the following sections: La última serie, El narrador, La novela del "cómo se...," La musa: criatura, creadora y creación, La materia-historia, Espacio y tiempo and estructura.

CARLOS VI EN LA RAPITA. E. Gómez de Baquero, "Crónica literaria," La España moderna, 201 (1905), 172-79, finds that Galdós offers in this novel and Aita Tettauen an "aspecto bilateral de la historia" (p. 173). He finds that the pages "de más vivo colorido son las que pintan a los moros y judíos de Marruecos" (p. 174). "Concediendo poco a la historia, Galdós ha concentrado el interés de su novela en la creación de un tipo y en el interés dramático de una aventura amorosa" (p. 187).

Robert Ricard, "Pour un cinquaintenaire: Structure et inspiration de Carlos VI en la Rápita (1905)," Bulletin

hispanique, 57 (1955), 70-83, is the fullest published discussion of this episodio which "ne figure pas parmi les plus
connus ni parmi les meilleurs des Episodios nacionales. Mais
Galdós a un tel talent de narrateur et une telle maîtresse de
son métier que, même dans ses oeuvres manquées, il est
instructif et presque passionnant d'étudier la manière dont il
procède et dont il travaille" (p. 70). He complains that the
volume is composed of two very different elements and that
this peculiar structure is unfortunate regardless of its cause.
The novel's structure is discussed in some detail.   Pages
76-79 discuss the influence of Don Quijote on this novel,
while pp. 79-81 deal with this novel and Alarcón's Diario
de un testigo de la guerra de Africa.   Pages 81-83 discuss the language of the Moroccan Jews of Sephardic
origins.   He makes a few pertinent comments in this regard on Misericordia's Almudena.

LA CORTE DE CARLOS IV.   Paul Patrick Rogers,
"Galdós and Tamayo's letter-substitution device," Romanic
Review, 45 (1954), 115-20, states that Galdós "appropriated
Tamayo's strategem for the culminating point of the action
is one of his most entertaining episodios....   And the case
under consideration is an excellent example of the way in
which he made appropriated material his own.   He cannot be
accused of plagiarizing Tamayo here any more than he can
be charged with plagiarizing elsewhere the facts of history.
He simply 'took' the device because he needed it fitted into
his story.   Galdós was fully aware that every reader of his
day would know whence it came" (p. 117).

Pablo Cabañas, "Comella visto por Galdós," Revista
de literatura, 29 (1966), 91-99, is a study of Galdós' portrayal of the Catalan dramatist Comella as seen in the Episodios nacionales, especially La corte de Carlos IV and
Napoleón, en Chamartin.

DE OÑATE A LA GRANJA.   Ephrem Vincent, "Lettres espagnoles," Mercure de France, 29 (1899), 835-37, is
a brief comment on this work.

EL 19 DE MARZO Y EL 2 DE MAYO.   Carlos
Vázquez Arjona, "Un episodio nacional de Benito Pérez
Galdós: El 19 de marzo y el 2 de mayo (cotejo histórico),"
Bulletin hispanique, 33 (1931), 116-39, notes "la fidelidad
con que sigue Benito Pérez Galdós a la Historia....   Sin
embargo no vaya a creerse por ello que Galdós no hace más

que copiar, antes, al contrario, échase de ver su genio en la tan acertada y original combinación que ha hecho de la verdad histórica y la verdad del arte literario" (p. 116). Vásquez Arjona quotes a passage from the novel and then a passage from a history concerning the period so that "el lector ... podrá forma su propio juicio respecto de la exactitud o inexactitud histórica del relato galdosiano" (p. 116).

LOS DUENDES DE LA CAMARILLA. For a most unfavorable contemporary review see José María Aicardo. Razón y fe, 7 (1903), 272-73. This work, according to the reviewer, contains "Ni un dato histórico nuevo, ni una relacion desconocida. En una palabra, no puede agradar este folletín sino al que busca ávido en la lectura lo que huele a podrido, lo que subleva sus pasiones antirreligiosas y sensuales...." (p. 273).

F. Navarro y Ledesma reviews this novel in La Lectura, año 3, 2, no. 5 (1903), 89-93. He finds that Dominiciana is a "personaje de los mas cuidados y perfectos que de la pluma de Galdós hayan salido" (p. 90). He notes that Galdós' "incomparable maestría se muestra tanto como en el arte de comunicar interés a cuanto escribe, en el divino acierto de la sobriedad compositiva, de no sobrar ni faltar, de aliar la verdad histórica, es decir, la verdad más semejante a la mentira, con la verdad humana, que debe ser la substancia de la novela" (pp. 89-90). He discusses briefly the symbolic nature of some of the novel's characters.

ESPAÑA SIN REY. E. Gómez de Baquero, "Cronica literaria," La España moderna, 234 (1908), 157-61, has the following parts: La psicología de los personajes, La verosimilitud en literatura, Los retratos históricos, and Alusiones a sucesos públicos. This article also deals with Prim.

ESPAÑA TRAGICA. E. Gómez de Baquero, "Crónica literaria," La España, moderna, 245 (1909), 170-77, begins his comments on this novel with a few general comments on the Episodios nacionales. He notes that this novel "sólo contiene un mínimum de novela, la suficiente apenas para mantener ligados, por la intervención de algunos personajes comunes, los varios incidentes históricos que forman el asunto de esta obra. España tragica es una novela que se compone de unas cuantas escenas históricas, relacionadas entre sí por un ligero armazon novelesco. Es una novela compuesta de descripciones y episodios, en que la modestia

de la acción principal no distrae ciertamente la atención del
lector de esas escenas salientes. Tiene España trágica más
de historia poética y novelada que de novela" (p. 172).

     Brian J. Dendle, "Galdós and the death of Prim,"
Anales galdosianos, 4 (1969), 63-71, states that "Prim's
death and the circumstances surrounding the crime are described by Galdós in España trágica (1909), a novel of unusual interest for in it Galdós relates incidents which took
place during his own youth in Madrid" (p. 63). Dendle
finds that "the broad outlines of Galdós' earlier mythological
vision of the mysteries surrounding Prim's death remain un-
changed in España trágica, no such fidelity can be observed
in Galdós' treatment of individual historical figures. When
considering the possible identities of the murderers of Prim,
Galdós revises in large part the opinions which he had expressed in the 1870's. To reflect his changed ideological
position, he distorts, and at times suppresses, the testimony
of historical sources; to fit historical events to the literary
ends of the novel, evidence against individuals and dynastic
or political groups is presented in a deliberately ambiguous
manner. The purpose of this paper will be to illuminate
certain aspects of Galdós' interpretation of Spanish history in
the later episodios by an examination of Galdós' treatment
of three historical figures whose names were mentioned in
connection with Prim's death--Pauly Angulo, the Duke of
Montpensier, and Ruiz Zorrilla" (pp. 63-64).

     LA ESTAFETA ROMANTICA. G. Le Gentil, "Re-
marques sur le style de la Estafeta romántica," Bulletin
hispanique, 13 (1911), 205-27, states that "On peut ramener
les faits que nous avons observés à quatre tendances principales: l'abréviation, la simplification, le renforcement, la
dissymétrie" (p. 207). These are discussed in pp. 207-26.
He concludes with several interesting remarks. "Il serait
particulièrement intéressant, au surplus, d'examiner l'adaptation du langage aux différents milieux sociaux... Ce n'est
pas trop s'aventurer néanmoins que d'affirmer que M. Pérez
Galdós est avant tout préoccupé de la vraisemblance it du
naturel. Le dédain qu'il semble affecter pour certaines
formes compliquées de 'l'écriture artiste,' pourrait bien venir d'une conception définie de l'art, des moyens d'expression qui conviennent au réalisme, des resources du castillian
et des effets qu'on est en droit de lui demander sans aller
contre le génie même de la langue" (p. 227).

     E. Gómez de Baquero, "Crónica literaria," La

España moderna, 132 (1899), 134-36, is a brief note on this novel. Gómez de Baquero finds that Galdós points out "muchas observaciones atinadas y sagaces de psicología feminina" (p. 136).

Ephrem Vincent, "Lettres espagnoles," Mercure de France, 32 (1899), 841-42, speaks of the volume's "si large dose de philosophie" which is mixed with "la plus merveilleuse imagination."

GERONA. Rafael Alberti, "Un episodio nacional: Gerona," Cursos y conferencias, 24 (1943), 13-24; reprinted in Benito Pérez Galdós, pp. 367-78, notes the impact of Galdós' Episodios nacionales on the Republican side of the Spanish Civil War. He notes that "algunos de estos episodios, reeditados por el Gobierno español en miles de ejemplares durante aquellos años de lucha, fueron recibidos al lado del fusil de nuestros soldados con ansia...." (p. 16). He has nothing but high praise for the Episodios nacionales, which he calls "historia verdadera, pero de tal modo mezclada a la vida, metida en los tuétanos de ella, que todo fluye tan bien armonizado, tan magistralmente entramado, que el total es un soberbio edificio, un raro y claro monumento de proporciones perfectas" (p. 19). He finds in the novel both romantic and realist elements: "A través de dos planos fundidos lleva Galdós hasta el final el torrente de vida y heroismo de este gran episodio. Romántico y realista. Imaginación y verdad. Romántico, si dijimos, en lo que se refiere a la atmósfera, --al aire de aventura, de amor en medio de la guerra, de sacrificio, de locura tocando lo poético--que envuelve las peripecias y trances porque pasan los personajes--trances no tan artificiosos, tan arreglados, hay que aclarar, como conviene en otros episodios para enhebrarlos con el siguiente--; y realismo, preciso, hasta frío si se quiere en lo que respecta a la verdad del suceso" (p. 18). This article by a great Spanish poet who lived through the siege of Madrid was originally the text of a speech given in Buenos Aires.

JUAN MARTIN EL EMPECINADO. Gabriel H. Lovett, "Some observations on Galdós' Juan Martín el empecinado," Modern Language Notes, 84 (1969), 196-207, feels that the novel's importance "is due to Galdós' felicitous rendering in fictionalized form what was easily the most essential historical aspect of the war against Napoleon and to his ability to give epic grandeur to this aspect through a truly heroic figure" (p. 196). Lovett states that "what was most

characteristic of the struggle against French invasion was
Spanish guerilla warfare, and that is what Galdós forcefully
portrays in Juan Martín el empecinado" (p. 196). The novelist "had to consider the problem of integrating epic elements with novelistic form" and "he also had to reconcile
his ambivalent attitude toward guerrilla warfare with the ne-
cessity of portraying this side of the war in an epic light"
(pp. 196-97). This is one of the few important commentaries
on this novel. The critic discusses the various guerrilla
personalities portrayed in the novel as well as the novel's style.
The few flaws in the volume are pointed out on pp. 206-07.
His concluding sentence notes that in this novel "Galdós has
once more successfully integrated epic elements with novelistic form." (p. 207).

Gabriel H. Lovett, "Two views of guerrilla warfare:
Galdós' Juan Martín el empecinado and Baroja's El escuadron
del Brigante," Revista de estudios hispánicos, 6 (1972), 335-
44, notes that both of these novels deal with the same period
of Spanish history. Lovett finds that "It is particularly interesting to see how these two novelists dealt with what was
easily the most important aspect of Spain's War of Independence against Napoleon, the guerrilla war" (p. 335). He feels
that "Galdós does not give as penetrating a vision of guerrilla
warfare, but where he is superior to Baroja is in the presentation of a heroic figure, whose epic stature is achieved
through conflict with disruptive elements represented by the
two sinister figures of Albuín and Trijueque" (p. 344).

LA DE LOS TRISTES DESTINOS. William H. Shoemaker, "Galdós La de los tristes destinos and its Shake-
spearean connections," Modern Language Notes, 71 (1956),
114-19 (reprinted in Shoemaker's Estudios sobre Galdós,
pp. 139-44), shows that Galdós did not get "Adiós, mujer de
York, la de los tristes destinos" from Richard III, IV, iv,
114, but that it is a variant of the quotation from this play
found in a speech which was delivered in 1865 by Antonio
Aparisi y Guijarro. Shoemaker suggests that Aparisi probably is translating from Guizot's French translation of this
play. His last paragraph is an excellent discussion of the
author's historical thinking and of his novelistic method. He
notes that "the influence of Shakespeare on Galdós still remains to be published" (pp. 115-16).

Antonio Urrello, "Isabel II y su reinado en una novela
de Valle-Inclán y un episodio galdosiano," Hispanofíla, no.
46 (1972), 17-33, has the following sections: La historia,

La "Intrahistoria," Lo novelesco y el material histórico,
Presentacion del personaje historico, Angulo de visión de las
voces narradores. This article compares and contrasts the
treatment of this period of Spanish history as found in La de
los tristes destinos and Valle-Inclán's La corte de los mi-
lagros.

LUCHANA. Ephrem Vincent in Mercure de France,
série moderne, 31 (1899), 853-54, reviews this volume in a
flattering way. He feels that the last chapters can be compared to the Russian retreat as described in Tolstoy's War
and Peace (p. 854). With great enthusiasm he concludes his
review with "heureux le peuple qui possède de tels roman-
ciers!"

MENDIZABAL. Eduardo Gomez de Baquero, "Mendizabal," La España moderna, 121 (enero 1899), 171-74, finds
that "hay en Mendizábal y en su época materia historica y
materia novelable sobradas para inspirar a un escritor ex-
perto como Galdós en la evocacion de tipos, costumbres y
acontecimientos pasados" (pp. 171-72). The reviewer notes
that in this novel "predomina lo novelesco sobre lo histórico"
(p. 172). He declares that "no es en realidad una novela
completa, sino un fragmento de novela en que ha quedado por
escribir el desenlace" (p. 173).

Ephrem Vincent, "Lettres espagnoles," Mercure de
France, 29 (1899), 272-73, is a brief comment on this work.

NARVAEZ. F. Navarro y Ledesma reviews this nov-
el in La Lectura, 3 (1902), 468-73. He states that the artist
and critic find the first 100 pages of the book "mas importantes y mas sugestivas" (p. 471). However, he finds that
"son mucho más interesantes las doscientas treinta páginas
siguientes, todas ellas novela con mucho de teatro, franca,
apartosa, alegre, inundada de luz, pero (dicho sea en honor
de Galdós) de luz tan cruda que permite distinguir el colorete
y las pelucas de los actores y acorta las distancias que nos
separaban de ellos y nos los hace ver su verdadero tamaño,
por ese fenómeno de óptica en virtud del cual diez kilómetros
al sol de Andaulucía parecen mucho menos que cinco kilo-
metros a la luz de Inglaterra" (p. 471).

PRIM. E. Gómez de Baquero, "Crónica literaria,"
La España moderna, 216 (1906), 154-65, is chiefly an analysis of the character of Prim and of the volume's plot with
additional remarks concerning España sin Rey.

Robert Ricard, "Mito, sueño, historia y realidad en
Prim," Cuadernos hispanoamericanos, nos. 250-52 (1970-71),
340-55, writes that "Prim me parece ejemplar simplemente
porque es precisamente un ejemplo casi perfecto de ciertos
rasgos fundamentales y de ciertos 'constantes' de las obras
galdosianas: influencia de Cervantes y más especialmente
del Quijote, problema de la historia, primacía de la naturaleza, problema de la realidad (p. 342). These various
points are discussed in detail.

LA REVOLUCION DE JULIO. F. Navarro y Ledesma
reviews this novel in La Lectura, año 3, I, no. 4 (1903),
495-99. He states the "El maestro Galdós siempre tuvo ojos
de médico: ahora, con la práctica y el ejercicio, con tanto
revolver en la clínica humana, los tiene más finos y pe-
netrantes que nunca. Lo mas sutil y menudo en los casos de
la Historia pública, extensión y a veces encanallamiento de la
privada, no se le escapa" (p. 496). Comments are made
concerning the political activities of the period covered by
the novelists and concerning some of the characters. The
reviewer finds that "el estado de la nación se refleja
en los diálogos entre le protagonista, y su mujer....
(p. 497).

Eduardo Gómez de Baquero, "Crónica literaria: La
Revolucion de julio...," La España moderna, 135 (mayo
1904), 162-71, finds in this novel a "espíritu de gran mode-
ración, la serena indulgencia filosófica con que Galdós juzga
(pues juicios implícitos hay en la novela) a los hombres y
cosas de aquel período al sacarlos a escena. Más libertad
tiene sin duda en este punto la novela histórica que la historia" (p. 163). Most of this review deals with the political
history of the period this novel covers (1852-54). He finds
certain portions of the novel to be somewhat revolutionary
both in its discussion of history and its treatment of the
actions of some of its characters.

TRAFALGAR. Jack Gordon Bruton, "Galdós visto
por un inglés y los ingleses vistos por Galdós," Revista
de la Indias, no. 53 (mayo 1943), 279-83, feels that "el genio
de Galdós fué un genio puramente masculino, que solamente
rara vez supo describir acertadamente a una mujer" (p. 280).
Bruton finds that Miss Fly is a "Buen ejemplo de esta falta
de comprensión" and that her character depicts "un conjunto
de todas las características más superficiales del turista
inglés" (p. 281). He feels that she is used by Galdós as a
" 'dea ex machina' para sacar a Araceli de sus apuros, y es
igualmente inverosímil. En eso consiste la explicación y la

justificación de Miss Fly" (p. 281).   He notes that in this
novel "Galdós muestra una profunda admiración por Inglaterra
y los ingleses" (p. 281).

VERGARA.   Eduardo Gómez de Baquero, "Crónica
literaria: Vergara...," La España moderna, 135 (marzo
1900), 123-30, notes that Episodios nacionales "han contri-
buído a popularizar el conocimento de nuestra historia contemporánea" (p. 123).   Pages 123-26 are a general discussion as to the importance of this novelistic genre.   Among
his concluding remarks are such statements as "En general,
el autor hay aprovechado con habilidad los datos de la historia, así en la parte principal de la acción.... (p. 129).
"Pudo, quizás, sacar mayor partido de algunos incidentes
dramáticos que ofrece aquel período, pero hay que tener en
cuenta los límites naturales de un libro de esta clase, dentro
del plan de los Episodios" (p. 130).

UN VOLUNTARIO REALISTA.   Paul Rogers, "A
Galdosian parallel for part of Guzmán's El águila y la
serpiente," Hispanic Review, 18 (1950), 66-68, suggests that
Martin Luis Guzmán may "have had this incident from Un
voluntario realista fresh in mind, and thus could easily have
been inspired by it to create a fictional chapter set in the
framework of the Mexican civil war" (p. 68).   The episode
in Guzmán's novel is that of the method used by an unnamed
general to raise 30,000 pesos.

ZARAGOZA.   Most of the studies concerning this novel deal with its sources.   One can mention Marcel Bataillon,
"Les sources historiques de Zaragoza," Bulletin hispanique,
22 (1921), 129-41, and two articles by Alfredo Rodríguez,
both published in Aspectos de la novela de Galdós, "Shakespeare, Galdós y Zaragoza," pp. 15-34, and "El uso de los
clásicos en Zaragoza," pp. 131-36, which is a translation
of "Galdós' use of the classics in Zaragoza," Modern Language Notes, 79 (1964), 211-13.

Bataillon finds that Galdós has used the following important sources: Count Toreno's Historia del levantamiento
..., Agustín Alcaide Ibieca, Historia de los sitios que pu-
sieron a Zaragoza ... (1830).   He also feels that Galdós
may have known of La jota aragonesa, a play by Antonio
Hurtado and Gaspar Nuñez de Arce.   He insists, as do almost all students of the Episodios nacionales, that this novel
is based on a thorough knowledge of the period's history and
that Galdós read and used the standard histories of the period
available to him.

It is the contention of Rodríguez that "Toda la trama de Zaragoza se halla relacionada, de un modo u otro, con el teatro de Shakespeare" (p. 20). He also writes, "La transformación de temas tan identificados con el dramaturgo inglés --siempre la suficiente para que éstos hayan pasado desapercibidos--constituye un asunto de verdadero interés, y su estudio permite perfilar, aunque esquemáticamente, algo de la técnica de Galdós al reelaborar materiales literarios" (p. 26). He mentions in particular Romeo and Juliet and The merchant of Venice.

The second article by Rodríguez shows how "mediante el empleo de un solo verso de Horacio, y de solo un par de versos de Vergilio, Galdós consigue afectuar, con gran atino estético, un importante y deslumbrador contraste" (p. 133). He believes that this is the first novel "en que elementos de procedencia clasica aparecen extensamente y con función artística" (p. 135).

Three critical articles of importance are Stephen Gilman, "Realism and the epic in Galdós' Zaragoza," Estudios hispanicos (Wellesley, Mass., 1952), pp. 171-92; Elba M. Larrea, "Épica y novela en Zaragoza," Revista hispánica moderna, 30 (1964), 261-70; and Ricardo Navas-Ruiz, "Zaragoza: problemas de estructura," Hispania, 55 (1972), 247-55.

Gilman, who can speak of Doña Perfecta's "novelistic failure" (p. 172), feels that "Zaragoza is a novelistic success because Galdós in the process of writing it realized intuitively the close generic relationship of two apparently dissimilar varieties of narration, 'epic' and 'realistic'" (p. 172). He finds "The values of Zaragoza at once admit the esteem and transcend the estimation of the novelist; like those of epic poetry, they are, in the altitude of their human significance inherent" (p. 175). Gilman feels that this novel "stands apart from the other novels of the first series, indeed, apart from the whole of Galdós' work, as his one best 'realistic' novel" (p. 175). Gilman's discussion of style, plot and characters and his arguments in favor of an 'epic' classification of the novel should be of interest to readers of this novel in particular and to others interested in Galdós and his novelistic technique.

Larrea concludes with this paragraph: "es una novela histórica en la que el sentido del heroísmo tiene caracteres épicos revelados en ese darlo todo, hacienda y vida, en ese existir intrepido y glorioso donde todo aparece deslucido, sin importancia, frente a los valores, a los ideales que se sostienen con la ilusión, con la fuga de lo real cuando todo está perdido, cuando ya no queda sino desolación y ruinas, muerte, hambre y harapos bañados en sangre enlodada. Su sentido religioso, la extracción y características de la actuación de sus personajes, la posición del autor frente a los hechos, su selección su presentación, dan a este episodio una estructura básicamente novelesca" (p. 270).

Navas-Ruiz feels that an answer must be given to such questions as "¿es Zaragoza un poema épico? ¿O es más bien una novela histórica ocupada en el análisis y juicio de una realidad que por acaso resulta aquí épica?" (p. 247). The interpretation of the volume will depend as to what literary genre the critic places it in. Navas-Ruiz develops in his article that "el mensaje que Pérez Galdós ha plasmado en una sólida y coherente estructura novelesca: no a la guerra como tal guerra; no a la usurpación y al imperialismo; no al viejo espíritu tradicional que resucitaba con todas sus lacras pasadas; sí al amor de la vida; sí al progreso y a la burguesía mercantilista; si a la dignidad y la soberanía nacionales" (p. 254).

José García Mercadal, "Galdós, Aragon y la ópera 'Zaragoza,'" Cuadernos hispanoamericanos, nos. 250-52 (1970-71), 727-36, first discusses the novel Zaragoza and its importance, then notes that Galdós celebrated the centennial of the event portrayed in the novel composed "en prosa rítmica la letra de una ópera basada en su libro...." (p. 730). The opera was first performed on Oct. 5, 1908 in Zaragoza with Galdós and representatives of the Madrid press on hand. The article summarizes the opera's plot and the reactions of the critics; the leading actors are named as well as some of the more important members of the audience. The author interviewed Galdós several days after the performance and the last two pages discuss his memories of his meeting with Galdós.

ZUMALACARREGUI. Two French articles are recommended for this novel. They are: Ephrem Vincent, "Lettres espagnoles," Mercure de France, 27 (1898), 305-07; and G. Boussagol, "Sources et composition du Zumalacarregui de B. Pérez Galdós'" Bulletin hispanique, 26 (1924), 241-64.

Boussagol's discussion is an analysis of Galdos' use of J.A. Zaratiegui's Vida y hechos de Zumalacárregui....

(1845). He states that "Je crois pourtant pouvoir affirmer
que Galdós n'a pas emprunté seulement à Zaratiegui les faits,
la substance historique, mais aussi l'expression, dans ce
qu'elle a de strictement personnel" (p. 243). Pages 256-64
discuss several other sources which Boussagnol considers to
be less important.

Vincent suggests that Galdós has been stimulated by
the works of Erckmann-Chatrian, though he doubts if Galdós
imitated him. He finds the dominant idea of the novel to be
"L'antinomie qui existe entre les lois relatives et temporaires
et l'idéal immuable d'éternelle justice...." (p. 307).

E. Gómez de Baquero, "Crónica literaria," La España
moderna, 115 (1898), 172-82, finds that this is not one of the
best of the Episodios. Had it been the work of some other
novelist, it might have been considered a triumph; "Pero como el autor de Realidad vale y puede mucho, a mucho
también está obligado" (p. 181). Pages 172-77 are a general
discussion of the first two series of the Episodios nacionales.
The novel's chief defect is "el escaso interés de la acción
novelesca"; the reviewer finds that in this novel "la parte
histórica ahoga la parte novelesco" (p. 180).

C. Silva Vildósola, "Zumalacárregui. La nueva serie
de Episodios nacionales de Pérez Galdós," La Revista de
Chile, 3, 4 (August 15, 1899), 113-17, is a discussion of the
period's history and of the book's characters. The reviewer
mentions Galdós' "arte frío i sereno que le es peculiar"
(p. 114) as well as his "fuerza del dibujo de los carácteres
i al drama íntimo de las conciencias que es lo mejor en todas
sus novelas" (ibid.).

Juan Bautista Avalle-Arce, "Zumalacarregui," Cuadernos hispanoamericanos, nos. 250-252 (1970-71), 356-373,
notes that this is an "ensayo de interpretación de Zumalacarregui" (p. 372). He notes that the Christ figure appears in
several Galdosian novels, "Pero no es ése el tema de Zumalacárregui, sino el del Santo Guerrero, presentado con un
simbolismo heterogéneo pero adecuado" (p. 373). This essay
is of value for its discussion of the novel's sources and its
position in the Episodios nacionales; for its comparison of the
historical and fictional character of Zumalacarregui and its
discussion of the novel's style.

The following studies, which have been arranged in
alphabetical order, for the most part, deal with the Episodios

nacionales as a literary genre and with Galdós as a historian.

Rafael Altamira, "Galdós y la historia de España," Psicología y literatura (Barcelona: Imprenta de Henrich, 1905), pp. 192-96, is an analysis of certain phases of Galdós' work as an historian. More than half of this article discusses Narváez. He notes that in this novel "no sólo penetra Galdós resueltamente en la Historia--el retrato de El Espadón es de primer orden, así como las escenas en que se bosqueja, valientemente, el de Isabel II, etcétera, --sino que repite y desarrolla una y otra vez sus ideas históricas. Dos puntos parecen atraerlo principalmente: el valor de lo anecdótico y la consideración del sujeto popular como verdadera raíz de la Historia" (pp. 195-96).

Joaquín Casalduero, "Historia y novela," Cuadernos hispanoamericanos, nos. 250-52 (1970-1971), 135-42, has the following sections: Trayectoria de un conflicto, El escritor y la sociedad, Un nuevo tipo de historia, Orden y revolución, La serie inacabada. Casalduero notes that "Un episodio se compone de elementos--historia y novela--. La parte histórica obedece a lo que Galdós considera como de mayor importancia o más significativo dentro de un cierto período. Aparcela los años alrededor de un hecho, de una figura o de una situación. La Historia le da una pauta que era fácil ver y seguir" (p. 136). Casalduero shows how the two, history and the novel, interact on each other. His next to last paragraph states that "Al abandonar su posición de mero estudioso de la Historia para intervenir en el viviente proceso de los hechos, cambia la relación entre pasado y presente y sustituye los personajes históricos por los mitológicos y a los novelescos les da una transparencia imaginaria, Si en su primera época magnifica la realidad hasta hacerla depositaria de la idea, en su última etapa la idea se encierra en un trazo imaginario e irónico" (p. 142).

Carlos Clavería, "El pensamiento histórico de Galdós," Revista nacional de cultura, no. 121 (marzo-junio 1957), 170-77, is a philosophical discussion of the sources of Galdós' ideas and models for the writing of his historical novels. Clavería notes: "En la creación galdosiana, el gran poder imaginativo del novelista iba con frecuencia a aprovecharse de sus hechos, y a teñirse no sólo de emoción ante la Historia, sino también sus ideas acerca de lo que la Historia representa como médula de la vida humana, y como ciencia y arte de contar la sucesión de los episodios de esa vida" (pp. 170-71).

A. R. de Contreras, "La evolución galdosiana," Razón
y fe, 20 (1908), 82-92, declares that the Episodios nacionales
"nos pone ante los ojos una evolución de las ideas y facultades
de su autor, tanto más digna de notarse, cuanto que la in-
sensible gradación con que han ido desenvolviéndose sus libros,
ha adquirido por ventura al Sr. Galdós gran número de lectores, que no le hubieran seguido, sin duda alguna, si la primera de sus novelas hubiera tenido las tendencias y caracteres de la última. Por esto no nos parece será trabajo inútil
el que tomemos en poner de manifiesto estas diferencias"
(p. 83). Contreras feels that there "se ha verificado una
verdaders evolución específica, y que su cuantitativa obra
señala uno de los mayores triunfos que puede celebrar la
teoría darwinista, por lo menos en el terreno de las artes"
(p. 84). He then compares the religious and moral ideas
found in the first and the last of the Episodios. The article
seems marred by an attempt to be witty, as when he wonders, "si es la mano de las musas ó la musa de la contabi-
lidad quien ha dirigido la obra" (p. 82). It is interesting as
an example of criticism presented by a representative of
religious conservatism.

Jane Hamilton Cory, "Las Guerras carlistas en la
literatura contemporánea," Revista de la Universidad de
Madrid, 3 (1954), 532-33, is an abstract of a doctoral dissertation, which studies the literary treatment of the first
and third Carlist wars in Spain. The dissertation has a
chapter in its first part that "se ha enfocado ... para hacer
resaltar las diferencias y las analogías entre Baroja y Galdós
en su diferente manera de documentar novelescamente este
período histórico...." (p. 533). She also notes that "También
se comparan en lo posible los sentimientos y opiniones de
Baroja con los de Galdós sobre personas e ideas que los dos
han tratado" (ibid.).

Madeleine de Gogorza Fletcher, "Galdós in the light
of Georg Lukács' 'Historical novel,'" Anales galdosianos,
1 (1966), 101-05; and Rafael Bosch, "Galdós y la teoría de
la novela de Lukács," ibid., 2 (1967), 169-84, are two essays
that attempt to apply some of the theories of Lukács concerning the historical novel to the work of Pérez Galdós. Fletcher
writes: "this essay presumes to set forth some of the elements of his critical argument, and to focus them upon
Galdós' Episodios nacionales, always conscious that in discussing these novels separately from the rest one makes an
artificial distinction for the purpose of convenience" (p. 101).
The article by Bosch has an introduction and (1) La Teoría
de la novela, (2) La novela histórica de Lukács y los Epi-

sodios nacionales and (3) Las ideas de Lukács y las novelas realistas de Galdós.

Eduardo Gómez de Baquero, Novelas y novelistas, (Madrid: Galleja, 1918), contains "Los Episodios nacionales de Pérez Galdós," pp. 11-24, and "La serie final de los Episodios," pp. 25-57. The first article contains a brief introduction which treats the importance of the Episodios in Galdós' literary production. This article then has the following subdivisions: Galdós y Erckmann Chatrian, El asunto histórico, Valor histórico. Cómo trata la historia Galdós, Los Episodios desde el punto de vista literario. El estilo y la composición. Personajes y acciones, El tiento y el espíritu de los Episodios. Mérito relativo de las series and Consideración final. The second article is an analysis of España sin rey, España trágica, Amadeo I, La primera república, De Cartago a Sagunto, and Cánovas.

Gaspar Gomez de la Serna "El Episodio nacional como género literario," Clavileño, 3, no. 14 (marzo-abril 1952), 21-32, can be divided into two parts. The first four parts, pp. 21-26, deal with the 19th-century Spanish historical novel before Galdós. Part 5, Galdos creador, has the following sections: Mesonero y Galdós, La proclividad historiadora de Galdós y el alumbramiento del nuevo genero, Lo épico en los Episodios and La historia como suceso, tema de los Episodios. Part 6 is El episodio nacional, género literario.

Eleazar Huerta, "Galdós y la novela histórica," Atenea, 72 (1943), 99-107 has the following sections: La novela histórica española hasta Galdós, La novela histórica galdosiana, Historia y costumbrismo, La técnica novelesca, and La influencia de Galdós.

Vicente Llorens, "Historia y novela en Galdós," Cuadernos hispanoamericanos, nos. 250-252 (1970-71), 73-82, is too short to be a very helpful treatment of its topic. The author notes that "En primer termino, Galdós tiene a su favor un conocimiento poco comun de ese pueblo anónimo cuya vida cotidiana va a incorporar por primera vez a la historia ... En segundo lugar, parte del principio de la identidad sustancial del pueblo español a través del cambio histórico" and "Por último, Galdós cuenta con lo más importante: la naraccion novelesca" (p. 75).

Richard M. Mikulski, "The Carlist Wars in the serial novels of Galdós, Baroja, and Valle-Inclán," (Ph.D. disserta-

tion, University of Kansas, 1956), xiv + 304 leaves, should
be examined by those interested in Galdos' treatment of this
phase of Spanish history.

Alfred Rodríguez, "Unos Don Juanes de Galdós,"
Studies in honor of M. J. Benardete (New York: Las Américas Publishing Co., 1965), pp. 167-76, writes on p. 167:
"Nuestra selección de personajes donjuanescos, que no pretende agotar el rico filón de los Episodios, se ha hecho con
miras al desarrollo que Estos revelan como entes de ficción
y la variedad que ofrecen en cuanto recreaciones del tipo
universal. Los seis seleccionados con este criterio pueden
repartirse, por la indole de su caracterización, en dos categorías generales: 1) la de los Don Juanes de tipo tradicional,
que se desvían poco del modo conocido, 2) la de los Don
Juanes divergentes, de concepción y finalidad peculiares, de
psicopatía pronunciada o de estructura compleja."

Carlos Seco Serrano, "Los Episodios nacionales como
fuente histórica," Cuadernos hispanoamericanos, nos. 250-
252 (1970-1), 256-284, writes that "Pero en todo caso debe
recordarse que éstos--o al menos cada una de sus series--
constituyen un todo indivisible; y que en su conjunto suponen
algo así como una sistematización de las experiencias sociales del siglo xix, en cuanto aún planean, o palpitan como
ingredientes vivos, en el complejo presente desde el que el
autor escribe. De aquí que los Episodios resulten, con
frecuencia, mucho más históricos cuando se apartan o se
olvidan de la reconstrucción del entramado político en que
se teje la historia que pudiéramos llamar convencional
(pp. 257-8). He finds in each of these novels "tres elementos o estratos constitutivos: (a) El esquema de los sucesos políticos, que va condicionando cronológicamente el relato; b) la anécdota novelesca, insoslayablemente pautada por
aquél; c) la pintura del "cuadro social" en que se enmarca
todo el conjunto" (p. 263). He feels that more attention
should be given "la obra de Galdós como fuente histórica"
(p. 258).

Carlos Vásquez Arjona, "Cotejo histórico de cinco
Episodios nacionales de Benito Pérez Galdos," Revue hispanique, 68 (1926), 321-551, has the following parts: Introducción, Trafalgar, La Corte de Carlos IV, Zaragoza, Gerona,
Cádiz, Conclusión, Bibliografía. The author states that
"Nuestro deseo es pues, llegar a saber en virtud de las citas
sacadas de otras fuentes hasta que punto sigue Pérez Galdós
la historia" (p. 321). The first paragraph of his conclusion

is: "Lo primero que habrá notado el lector al leer las páginas
que anteceden es la casi infalibilidad con que don Benito Pérez
Galdós ha interpretado la Historia. Los deslices históricos
cometidos por el novelista en estos cinco Episodios son tan
contados y de importancia tan nimia, que muy bien podemos
pasarlos por alto sin violentar la verdad de los hechos y
decir que estos libros en realidad no son novelas sino verdadera historia" (p. 518).

Vincente Lloréns, "Galdós y la burguesia," Anales
galdosianos, 3 (1968), 51-59, and Clara E. Lida, "Galdós
y los Episodios nacionales: una historia del liberalismo
español," ibid., 61-77, both deal with the ideological basis
of certain of the Episodios nacionales. Lloréns notes "Por
todo ello no es de extrañar que en los últimos Episodios,
redactados a principios del siglo XX, Galdós vuelva sus ojos
a Europa, concretamente a Inglaterra y Francia, donde la
burguesía seguía viviendo al menos dentro de la tradición
liberal a que debió su existencia, y fiel por consiguiente al
principio de la libertad de conciencia, que constituye el
fundamento del anticlericalismo galdosiano" (p. 58). He
notes the changing role of the members of the middle class
in the Episodios.

Lida writes: "Esta es la revolución que defiende
Galdos: la regeneración, que predica conjuntamente con los
sectores más conscientes de la intelectualidad español. A
lo largo de los cuarenta y seis Episodios nacionales que
historian casi el siglo XIX español, Galdós pasa del opti-
mismo patriótico y la fe en las ideas liberales y virtudes
burguesas al desengaño ante la progresiva decadencia de
España. Sin embargo, nunca reniega de su confianza inicial;
al final de su vida continúa fiel a los principios de justicia,
libertad y progreso que defendió y exaltó durante cuarenta
años" (p. 73).

José Schraibman, "Patria y patriotismo en los Episodios Nacionales de Galdós," Boletín del Seminario de Derecho Público, no. 27 (1962), 71-86, deals with "los con-
ceptos de patria y patriotismo que se encuentran en los
Episodios nacionales a medida que Galdós cuenta la historia
de España desde 1805 a 1879" (p. 72). The last half of the
last paragraph states that "El patriotismo de Galdós radica,
pues, en su intento de captar el verdadero ethos español y
esto lo hace mezclando en su paleta literaria el amor por
las ciudades y campos de España; por sus personajes--
buenos y malos, locos y cuerdos, prácticos y soñadores--;

por la lengua castellana cuyos múltiples matices trata de captar fielmente; por su afán de novelizar los hechos históricos para asi divertir y enseñar a la vez; finalmente, por su fe en España y en los españoles, profetizando que han de andar largo trecho antes de salir del cieno y entrar en la vereda del progreso" (p. 86).

CENSUS OF CHARACTERS. Federico Carlos Sáinz de Robles is the compiler of a two-part "Ensayo de un censo de los personajes galdosianos comprendidos en los Episodios nacionales," Obras completas (Madrid: Aguilar, 1951, 3rd ed.) III, pp. 1368-1805, and "Ensayo de un censo de los personajes galdosianos comprendidos en novelas, cuentos y teatro," (Madrid: Aguilar, 1951, 2nd ed.), pp. 1701-2078. This work should be of inestimable value to the student, especially to anyone who desires to study Galdós' characters. For a discussion of these "ensayos" see Shoemaker, Hispanic Review, 12 (1944), 261-64, who concludes his remarks with these words: "If his censos serve no other purpose than as a guide to a more complete understanding of Galdós characters and of the autor de sus días, they will have solidly established their worth" (p. 264).

Of value also is Glenn R. Barr, "A census of the characters of the Episodios nacionales of Benito Pérez Galdós" (Ph.D. dissertation, University of Wisconsin, 1937), 306 leaves.

According to University of Wisconsin, Summaries of Doctoral Dissertations, 2 (1937), 347-48, this census of the characters in the Episodios nacionales "includes their physical, moral and social traits; the province of origin or residence; their age and occupation; the part they play in the various novels; and their relation to the historical events" (p. 347).

GIBRALTAR. Pedro Ortiz Armengol, "Gibraltar, en los 'Episodios nacionales,'" La Estafeta literaria, no. 534 (15 de febrero de 1974), 4-7, studies references to Gibraltar found in the five series of the Episodios nacionales. On p. 7 the author writes that "...no nos hemos propropuesto sino señalar lo que Gibraltar evocaba en la conciencia de los españoles entre 1805 y 1880."

INDEX. Dorothy Helen Geironimus, whose M.A. thesis was on Galdós, is the author of "Indexes to the Episodios nacionales of Pérez Galdós" (Ph.D. dissertation, University of Colorado, 1938), 560 leaves. She writes that "The present study was begun as an attempt to index the actual personages of the nineteenth century who appear or are mentioned, and also the fictitious characters around whom Galdós has woven his story. But it soon became evident that these alone did not give a complete picture either of his purpose or of his method, and the index was expanded to include all references to individuals, even characters from myths and from literature, references which might be confused with people, and finally the numerous animals to which Galdós has given names" (ℓ. 2).

SEPHARDIC TYPES. Vernon A. Chamberlin, "Galdós' Sephardic Types," Symposium, 17 (1963), 85-100, is a discussion of the sixteen Sephardic characters found in Aita Tettauen and Carlos VI en la Rápita. These characters "are the last of Galdós' clearly-definable Jewish characters remaining to be studied" (p. 85). The author desires to answer the following questions: "What then, we may ask, are the basic techniques used by Galdós, working from inanimate sources, for populating such a microcosm? What did Galdós consider the basic requisites for making such types, whose flesh and blood models he never met, seem realistic to his reader? What was essential and what could he omit? In addition, we may even ask how and why some of the characters are more complex and seemingly more genuinely realistic than those found in the Diario of on-the-spot eyewitness Alarcón. Finally, we will surely want to know if Galdós shows the same liberal attitude toward Jews and Judaism when writing to be historically accurate in an episodio as he did when deliberately creating the religiously tendentious Gloria and Misericordia" (p. 86).

THEATRE

Material on Galdós' theatre is not as plentiful as that on his fiction. It is, of course, true that many of his plays are adaptations made from his novels or adaptations produced by his friends. This section provides data on a handful of general studies on his plays, followed by publications on individual plays arranged in alphabetical order.

J. M. Aicardo, De literatura contemporánea (1901-1905) (Madrid, 1905), pp. 316-50, is a bitter attack on Galdós as a dramatist, with adverse comments on Electra, Alma y vida, Mariucha, El abuelo and Bárbara. Aicardo is a Jesuit who judges Galdós on his ideology, with which he is almost in complete disagreement. He writes: "El desvío de Madrid, de España entera el menosprecio de París, era lo que Electra, drama falso, inverosímil, de gastadísimos recursos de diálogo escabroso, de estilo pedregoso y lánguido, había merecido desde su nacer" (p. 319). Because of ideological differences, Aicardo finds nothing in Galdós to praise regardless of the literary genre on which he is commenting. Little would be gained by extensive quotations from these comments, for few other critics have found the Galdosian theater to be as terrible and evil as has Aicardo.

Rafael Altamira, "El teatro de Pérez Galdós," in De historia y arte (Estudios críticos) (Madrid: Victoriano Suárez, 1898), pp. 275-314, is one of the earliest long critical studies published in Spanish. It has the following sections: (1) Introducción, (2) Realidad, (3) Más sobre Realidad, (4) Orozco y Juan Lanas, and (5) La loca de la casa.

Rafael Altamira y Crevea, Arte y realidad (Barcelona: Editorial Cervantes, 1921), pp. 51-77, deals with Galdós. "Galdós y Marianela," pp. 51-56, speaks of the play's theatrical triumph and of the "piedad y el gusto exquisito de los hermanos Alvarez Quintero" (p. 52). "Un drama de Galdós," pp. 61-64, discusses Jacinto Benavente's "arreglo" of El audaz. He finds no reason to believe that the novel has gained in its theatrical representation. He comments briefly on Benavente's ultraconservatism and feels that his views towards this play and its ideology present "un problema de psicología benaventina, que sugiere muchas reflexiones" (p. 64). He suggests that "La condición psicológica del protagonista de El audaz y el drama sentimental e ideológico que en su espíritu se produce, ofrecen grandes dificultades para lograr que en la escena no resulten, más de una vez, ilógicos o desconcertantes los cambios" (p. 62). He finds that "Sin querer, el espectador de El audaz, y el drama sentimental e ideológico que en su espíritu se produce, ofrecen grandes dificultades para lograr que en la escena no resulten, más de una vez, ilógicos o desconcertantes los cambios" (p. 62). He finds that "Sin querer, el espectador de El audaz, no siente arrastrado, en la hora presente, fuera del terreno del arte, y considera la obra en la relación que forzosamente le obligan a tener las circunstancias con el estado actual de nuestro país" (p. 62). "La resurrección teatral de Galdós," pp. 73-77, provides brief remarks on El abuelo, La loca de la casa and Realidad.

Manuel Alvar, "Novela y teatro en Galdós," Prohemio, 1:157-202 (1970), has the following parts: Algo de teoría, Las novelas dialogadas, Doña Perfecta, Los Episodios nacionales, Algunas enseñanzas, Apendice, pp. 187-202. I find the Appendix of great interest. Alvar writes that "...me decido a señalar los resultados que he obtenido al cotejar las siete novelas con sus correspondientes versiones teatrales." (p. 187). The appendix compares the novel and drama versions in great detail. This is one of the few detailed studies that shows how Galdos adapted plays from his novels.

R. Blanco-Fombona, "El puesto de España en el teatro contemporáneo," Motivos y letras de España (Madrid and Buenos Aires: Renacimiento, n.d.), pp. 273-81, is a review of Isaac Goldberg's The Drama of Transition and especially of the section of the volume that deals with Galdós, pp. 279-80, Echegaray and Benavente.

Manuel Bueno, Teatro español contemporáneo, (Madrid: Biblioteca Renacimiento, 1910), pp. 81-107, is a discussion of the following plays: Alma y vida, El abuelo, Mariucha, Bárbara. He comments briefly on the theme and characters of each. Of Alma y vida he wonders if "es posible que haya entrado en la intención de Galdós el demonstrar que la realidad y el ensueño son casi siempre irreconciliables" (p. 84). Of El abuelo, he states that "es la obra escénica más grande que ha producido el Teatro nacional contemporáneo" (p. 91). On p. 101, he declares that "Hay en Mariucha verdades de

una belleza incomparable, bellezas que ya indiqué somera-
mente desde Barcelona. Galdós, como Nietzsche, considera
llegada la hora de la transmutación de los valores morales,
de que sucumban para siempre ciertos prejuicios que aplica-
mos a la vida y que se impongan determinadas ideas que
pugnan con la sensiblería ambiente." Of Bárbara he writes:
"Lo que me encanta, por su extraordinaria belleza, es el
entramado artístico de la tragedia, la poesía violenta y sana
que circula al través de la acción, el humano relieve de los
caracteres y, sobre todo, el ambiente de ingenuo helenismo
que se cierne sobre Bárbara, Oracio, Filemón, Demetrio
Paleólogo y los demás personajes que intervienen en la obra"
(p. 104).

Eduardo Bustillo, Campañas teatrales (crítica dramati-
ca) (Madrid: Tip. Sucesores de Rivadelneyra, 1907), contains the following chapters devoted to the theater of Galdós:
"La loca de la casa," pp. 42-46; "Gerona," pp. 47-50; "La
de San Quintín," pp. 104-17; "Los condenados," pp. 153-58;
"El prólogo de 'Los condenados," pp. 159-64; "Voluntad,"
pp. 180-85; "Doña Perfecta," pp. 222-29. The critic is not
a blind devotee of the dramatist. This is a collection of
contemporary dramatic criticism of the plays as presented on
the stage. The critic is interested in the works as drama;
he discusses such things as plot, staging, characters and the
quality of the acting.

Hal Carney, "The dramatic technique of Benito Pérez
Galdós" (Ph.D. dissertation, University of Nebraska, 1957,
352 leaves; Dissertation Abstracts, 17 [1957], 1081), is a
study of Galdós' 22 dramas with special emphasis on El
abuelo, La loca de la casa and Doña Perfecta. He states
that "The study of three phases of dramatic technique--ac-
tion, characterization and dialogue--has revealed that Galdós'
success varied from play to play, and even within one play.
He was more consistent in the impressive characters he
created, many of which rank with the finest in the novels.
The handling of dramatic action was less uniformly well done.
He frequently allowed the thesis of the work to intrude to
such an extent that it impeded smooth, direct progress towards the climax. The later plays make apparent the play-
wright's skill in writing dramatic dialogue" (p. 1081).

A brief account of Galdós as a dramatist is found in
Frank W. Chandler, Modern continental playwrights (New
York: Harper & Brothers, 1931), pp. 475-81.

Vernon A. Chamberlin, "A Galdósian statement in 1899 concerning dramatic theory," Symposium, 24 (1970), 101-10, reproduces a brief statement by Galdós published in Revista nueva in 1899 and here reprinted for the first time. Chamberlin provides a thorough study of this statement and concludes that it "indicates that at that date Galdós had, at least temporarily, abandoned his Messianic vision of the theater in favor of a theory of drama that was essentially novelistic" (p. 109).

José Deleito y Piñuela, Estampas del Madrid teatral fin de siglo, I. Teatros de declamación: Español, Comedia, Princesa, Novedades, Lara (Madrid: Saturnino Calleja, n.d.) has the following sections devoted to Galdós: Revelación de Galdós como dramaturgo, pp. 170-74; El primer estreno dramático de Galdós [Realidad], pp. 175-80; El estreno de La loca de la casa, pp. 181-85; Estreno de La de San Quintín, pp. 186-91; El teatro de Galdós desde Los condenados hasta Doña Perfecta, pp. 192-97. The author surveys Galdós' dramatic productions through the end of the 19th century. Lack of space does not allow for extensive quotations from these studies. The author takes pains to explain Galdosian innovations in the theater. Thus, in his discussion of Realidad, he writes: "Todo el drama Realidad era un ataque a fondo y una revolución práctica contra el carácter tradicional del teatro español. A la pasión sucedía la idea; a la acción sucedía la idea; a la acción rápida, el proceso gradual de los espíritus. Un nuevo concepto, más humano, cristiano y filosófico del honor conyugal, venía a romper, con audaz ímpetu, el cliché de la moral doméstica triunfante e indiscutible en el proscenio durante tres siglos" (p. 175). He believes that with Realidad Galdós "no solo se alteraba allí la estética teatral, sino que se atacaba fondo, con audaz denuedo, la moral centenaria del mundo de bastidores..., de bastidores afuera, se entiende" (p. 174).

Enrique Díez Canedo, "Galdós y el teatro," Filosofía y letras, 5, no. 10 (1943), 223-35, presents brief remarks on Realidad, El abuelo and Electra; there are also short comments on his "humorismo" and "realismo."

Five of Enrique Díez Canedo's newspaper reviews of performances of Galdós' plays are reprinted in the first volume of his Artículos de crítica teatral: el teatro español de 1914 a 1936 (México: J. Mortiz, [1968]), pp. 84-98. Comments on these performances appear in this bibliography under the title of the individual play.

Isaac Goldberg, The drama of transition (Cincinnati:
Stewart Kidd Co., 1922), pp. 74-92, deals with Galdos'
theatre. Pages 74-80 are general remarks on his life and
on the Episodios nacionales. The rest of this section is
chiefly quotations translated into English from the works of
Manuel Bueno, Ramon Perez de Ayala. El abuelo and Electra
are given the most attention.

Hope K. Goodale, "Pérez Galdós: dramatic critic and
dramatist" (Ph.D. dissertation, Bryn Mawr College, 1965),
236 leaves, is composed of an introduction, twelve chapters,
two appendices and a bibliography. Goodale writes that "By
a study of the reference Galdós makes in his own works to
plays and dramatists of all eras, and then an examination of
his dramas, it is hoped that we may gain insight into his own
theory of the drama and appreciate why he shaped his dramas
as he did" (1. 3). The first six chapters deal with Galdós
and Shakespeare, La Celestina, the Golden Age, the 18th
century, Romanticism and his contemporaries in the drama.
Chapter VII, Galdós and his early plays; VIII, Galdós' theory
of the drama; IX, Dramatic structure and means of expression; X, The subject matter and purpose in Galdós's dramas;
XI, Characterization in Galdós' dramas; and XII, Galdós'
purpose as a dramatist, complete the main body of the dissertation. The first appendix is a "List of Eighteenth-Century
plays mentioned in Galdós' works," while the second appendix
reproduces the text of Ricardo de la Vega, "Revistas cómi-
cas," El Liberal, 5-II-1893.

Jacinto Grau, "El teatro de Galdós," Cursos y conferencias, 24 (1943), 39-55, only deals in part with Galdós'
theater. There are brief comments on Realidad, Los condenados and La incógnita.

Jordé [Constantino Suárez Fernández], Galdós y el
teatro contemporáneo (Las Palmas: Imprenta T.E.M., 1943,
122pp.), is an undocumented study, the following parts of
which deal with Galdós' theater: Aparece Galdós en la escena, pp. 21-25; Realidad, pp. 26-36; La loca de la casa, pp.
37-43; Gerona, pp. 45-47; La de San Quintín, pp. 49-54;
Los condenados, pp. 55-64; Voluntad, pp. 65-66; Doña
Perfecta, pp. 67-70; La fiera, pp. 71-73; Electra, pp. 75-
81; Alma y vida, pp. 83-93; Mariucha, pp. 95-99; El abuelo,
pp. 101-16; Más consideraciones, pp. 117-20. The author
undertakes to evaluate and analyze the characters, plot and
style of Galdós' first eleven plays. He denies the influence
of Ibsen and states that Galdós "es original, tanto en la

concepción y planteamiento de los problemas, cuanto en su
desarrollo y resolución" (p. 118). "Galdós transforma el
teatro español, en su esencia ideológica y en sus formas
arcáicas y rutinarias, presentando problemas fundamentales
españoles y humanos relacionados con la intolerancia y el
fanatismo religioso, el régimen social, la moral, los costumbres, la libertad de espíritu, los principios democráticos,
etc. Colocando el arte por encima de todo, no lo subordina
a la tendencia, ni lo sacrifica a la tesis de la obra por lo
general, salvo el caso de Electra en que hizo flagrantes con-
cesiones a galería" (p. 118). Most critics have found little
influence of the Canary Islands on his works, Jordé states
concerning "el humorismo peculiar de Galdós ... en su
suave ironía y en su ingeniosa malicia, sin aceda acrimonia
nunca queremos descubrir algo de espíritu insular, de substancia de la tierra atlántica y del carácter y manera de ser
y ver las cosas de los canarios" (p. 120).

Ernest Martinenche, "Le théâtre de M. Pérez Galdós,"
Revue des deux mondes, cinquième période, 32 (1906), 815-50,
is one of the earliest French critical studies on his plays.
The author notes that La de San Quintín was almost completely ignored when it was first presented in Paris; however,
when Electra was played in French it was "un succès rapide
et retentissant" (p. 816). Pages 815-26 present a variety
of biographical data (some erroneous, such as his birthdate
of 1855) and comments on Galdós' character and on him as
a novelist. He discusses the plots, theme and characters
of the most important of the thirteen plays that Galdós had
written up to this time. Pages 845-50 summarize his views
of Galdós as a dramatist. This article was translated into
Spanish and published in España moderna, 210 (1906), 118-
58.

The "Introduction" by G. G. Morley to his edition of
Mariucha (New York, D.C. Heath, 1921), vii-xiv, is the
most important of the early English studies on the drama of
Galdós. This study contains a brief biographical study,
"Benito Pérez Galdós as a dramatic writer," with sections
devoted to "the background," "Galdós turns from novel to
drama," "his dramatic technique--his success," "the development of Galdós," "the subject matter of his plays," and "the
position of Galdós as a dramatist." The third section of the
introduction presents a brief comment on each of 21 plays.
His comments include such data as when and where the play
was first presented; the number of performances given; brief
plot summary and a short critical comment.

Gonzalo Sobejano, "Razón y suceso de la dramática galdosiana," Anales galdosianos, 5 (1972), 39-53, writes: "Las consideraciones que siguen acerca de la dramática galdosiana no pretenden ser una apología de ella, sino un ensayo de explicación que coordine las razones por las cuales Galdós escribió tales dramas. Creo que no los compuso así por ser él inhábil dramaturgo, sino por un complejo de razones que le llevaron a moldear conscientemente un tipo de obra dramática característico de la época en que el teatro se hallaba en crisis y buscaba la fecundación del género entonces dominante: la novela. Lo que muchos críticos han juzgado incapacidad de Galdós para pasar de la novela al drama por invencibles hábitos de narrador, fue en él deliberado propósito de regenerar el drama por aproximación a la novela, empresa de la cual es parte complementaria la aproximacion de ésta a aquél" (p. 39).

Walter Starkie, "Galdos and the modern Spanish drama," Bulletin of Spanish Studies, 3 (1925-26), 111-17, discusses Realidad, La loca de la casa, Los condenados, Electra, Doña Perfecta, La fiera, Mariucha, El abuelo, and Bárbara. Starkie seems to find much more to praise in Galdós as a dramatist than do most critics. His concluding sentence is: "It is to Galdós, however, that we must ascribe the foundation of the modern drama in Spain so brilliantly developed by Benavente and the moderns, wherein an attempt is made to express in Spanish garb the ideas of Europe."

Leopoldo Varó and Carlos Caballero, Los saraos de Colombina (Barcelona: Imprenta Artística, 1919), pp. 158-67, provide data on the staging of Galdós' plays. Discussed are: Margarita Xirgu's company's performance of Santa Juana de Castilla; and Pipiola by Quintero, which is compared to Marianela. The authors find that "Santa Juana de Castilla ni quita ni pone hoja en los laureles ganados por don Benito" (p. 162). El amigo Manso, adapted for the stage by Francisco Acebal, "es una acertada labor llevada acabo con todo el respecto que pueda tenerse a un original al cambiarle de condición" (p. 163).

Elizabeth Wallace, "Spanish drama of today," Atlantic Monthly, 102 (Sept., 1908), 357-66, devotes almost half of her article to a discussion of Galdós' plays.

Jacob Warshaw, "Galdós apprenticeship in the drama," Modern Language Notes, 4 (1929), 459-63, is a brief useful study of Galdós as a dramatist and drama critic.

José Yxart, El arte escénico en España (Barcelona),
2 (1894), 309-52, discusses Realidad, La loca de la casa and
La de San Quintín. Concerning La loca de la casa, Yxart
believes "que el drama se alza cien codos por encima de lo
que se escribe y piensa en España. Pérez Galdós conserva
su alta primacia de ser el más profundo pensador de todos
los escritores contemporáneos espanoles y muestra en los
dos primeros actos un arte de maestro delicadísimo. Pero
al lado de esto, o las exigencias del público, o la dificultad
de hallar una forma dramática a la segunda parte de la obra,
dejan ésta interrumpida y como pendiente y sin acabar. La
loca de la casa no es una obra completa" (p. 342). He finds
La de San Quintín inferior to the other two plays that he has
reviewed. "Más cuidadosamente compuesta que una y otra,
peca precisamente por el uso de algunas convenciones teatrales de que estaban exentas y limpias sus dos hermanas, que
siendo más inexpertas, resultan por lo mismo más frescas,
vigorosas y geniales" (p. 248). He also writes that "Es de
notar además en la obra la superioridad del estilo dramático,
sencillo, vivo, sereno, no atormentado ni declamatorio"
(p. 350). Realidad is discussed from the standpoint of its
characters, theme and reactions of the audience and the
critics.

EL ABUELO. Enrique Anderson Imbert, "Un drama
ibseniano de Galdós," Sur, no. 167 (1948), 26-32, states:
"Pero Galdós siguió a Ibsen--directamente o a través de lo
que él mismo llamaba 'ventolera de las modas;' y el objeto
de esta nota es tan sólo mostrar cómo en El abuelo (me
refiero al drama de 1904, no a la novela dialogada de 1897),
Galdós tuvo que pagar las consecuencias de su teoría de los
Ibsen, el claro y el oscuro" (pp. 26-27).

An early French discussion is that of E. Martinenche,
"El abuelo, de M. Pérez Galdós," Revue latine, 4 (1905),
419-28, who presents interesting comments on the transformation of this "novela en cinco jornadas" to a play. He is
pleased that Galdós has undertaken the task of this transformation. According to him, "El abuelo n'a pas beaucoup
perdu et il a beaucoup gagné à se dépouiller de quelques
ornements romanesques pour ne plus se draper que dans sa
cape dramatique" (p. 421).... "La marche de son action
est d'une simplicité plus vive, et la beauté en est plus
émouvante" (ibid.). Martinenche provides a summary of the
play with special emphasis on the characters. He feels that
"jamais M. Galdós ne s'est montré plus souple et plus pro-
fond psychologue" (p. 422). He is especially taken with the

character of D. Pío Coronado (p. 424). He sees no reason
to find any influence of Shakespeare's King Lear and he disagrees with the interpretation of Manuel Bueno in Le temps,
feuilleton du Temps, Aug. 22, 1904, pp. 1-2. He compares
José Echegaray and Galdós, and notes that Galdós "est ...
le plus illustre représentant de l'école qui cherche à faire
pénétrer sur la scène de son pays les idées et les sentiments
de l'Europe d'aujourd'hui et même de demain" (p. 428).

Joaquín Casalduero, "El abuelo, de Galdós," Cuadernos
(Paris), no. 57 (1962), 64-70, besides an introduction, has
the following sections: Cambios entre las dos redacciones de
El abuelo, Los nombres, significativos, "Motivos" en la obra
galdosiana, Prefiguración de personajes, Shakespeare, Ibsen,
Cervantes y Don Quijote, Historia-mitología, Los tres tiempos, El apuntar de la vida y la vejez, La presencia del bien
y del mal, Salvarse y elegir, and Voluntad y corazón. In
regard to a "filación" between El abuelo and King Lear,
Casalduero writes "yo no puedo ver ni sentir" that such
exists (p. 66). He analyzes the various characters and what
he feels they symbolize.

Luis Morote, "El abuelo (drama en cinco acts de D.
Benito Pérez Galdós)," Teatro y novela, 1903-1906 (Madrid:
F. Fé, 1908), pp. 59-75, notes that "alcanzó Galdós con El
abuelo, el triunfo más grande de su vida y demostró a los
que aún lo dudaban ó le negaban, que es autor dramático, el
primero de los autores dramáticos españoles y uno de los
primeros del mundo" (p. 64). This contemporary account
summarizes the plot, discusses the characters and ends with
a two-page comparison of this play and Shakespeare's King
Lear. Morote declares that "El Rey Lear y El abuelo no se
parecen en cuanto á argumento, sino en el concepto total de
la obra, en el espíritu que vivifica los dramas" (p. 75). His
concluding paragraph is: "Galdós ha llegado en El abuelo á
reencarnar Cordelia. ¡Qué mayor alabanza cabe tributarle!
Por su gran drama nuestro Galdós merece figurar al lado de
Shakespeare, junto á la impercedera gloria de Shakespeare
en la región serena de los iguales...." (p. 75).

ALMA Y VIDA. José Maria Aicardo, Razón y fe,
4 (1902), 114-20, 252-57, discusses the symbolism found in
the play as well as immorality. On the whole, this is a
rather violent attack on the play.

E. Gómez de Baquero, "Crónica literaria," La España
moderna, 142 (junio de 1902), 172-83, discusses the prologue

and the symbolism found in the play, as seen by Galdós.
This is a review of the prologue which "es extenso y en él
discurre el famoso novelista y autor dramático sobre varias
y diferentes materias: el simbolismo de Alma y vida, los
defectos y execesos de la crítica teatral en los periódicos, la
falta de protección oficial al teatro, los méritos de los actores que representaron el drama, los cuidados del autor para
ponerlo con toda propiedad en escena, y algún otro que justi-
ficara que añadamos a la enumeración anterior un et cetera"
(p. 172). The reviewer's comments concerning both the value
of prologues by authors who wish to explicate their plays and
the differing views concerning the play's symbolic features
are both interesting and well worth reading.

AMOR Y CIENCIA. E. Gómez de Baquero, "Crónica
literaria," La España moderna, 204 (1905), 167-74, states
that "tratemos de explicarnos el por qué de la impresión
pálida y fria que produce esa obra y que, sin duda, ha expe-
rimentado la mayoría del público al verla representar"
(p. 166). He finds that Amor y ciencia "parece una comedia
que estaba todavia en gestación, que ha salido prematuramente
al mundo y que no ha logrado alcanzar la luz, el colorido y
el hondo relieve de la realidad" (p. 169). He summarizes the
play's plot in detail so as to put into focus his observations
concerning certain scenes. He concludes with these remarks:
"Lo que nos deja fríos, inciertos y vacilantes ante Amor y
ciencia, no obstante las bellezas parciales que la obra contiene, es su débil trabazón, su falta de vida y de intensidad.
Es una comedia cuyos personajes parecen sombras, mario-
netas grandes un poco tristes, en vez de seres animados.
Algo, en suma, del infantilismo de Maeterlinck, con menos
poesia" (pp. 173-174).

ANTON CABALLERO. When Galdós died there was
found among his papers an unfinished play, "Los bandidos,"
later renamed "I masnodieri." The Quintero brothers
adapted this unfinished play and renamed it Antón Caballero
after the leading character. The play was first presented on
Dec. 16, 1921. S. Griswold Morley, "A Posthumous Drama
of Pérez Galdós," Hispania, 6 (1923), 181-84, discusses the
background, style and plot of this play. Morley has nothing
but praise for the skill of the adapters, who "have concealed
their hand, and adapted their genius to that of their friend
and master.... All the stylistic features ring true to him.
The turn of phrase, the words seem lifted bodily from his
known writings.... Only in the skillful conduct of the dialogue, a branch of art in which Galdós was weak, do we

detect the magic touch of the two masters of scene-writing. Interest is sustained throughout, and there are no dull pages" (p. 184).

André Nougué, "Antón Caballero de Benito Pérez Galdós," Cuadernos hispanoamericanos, nos. 250-252 (1970-1), 641-649, discusses this comedy "poco conocida y casi nunca estudiada" (p. 641). Nougué finds that "El problema principal, el más auciante, es en esta comedia el de la justicia y de la sociedad" (p. 642) and that "El amor es otro elemento fundamental en la temática galdosiana de Antón Caballero" (p. 646). His last paragraph follows: "Esta comedia, con ambiente y personajes románticos, encaje bien en la temática teatral galdosiana. Sabe el autor que desde el escenario se puede dirigir con más comodidad y eficacia que en una novela a la muchedumbre para convertirla a sus teorías sociales, religiosas y humanitarias. Por eso expone con ánimo y convicción sus ideas sobre el estado de la justicia en España, sobre los daños del caciquismo, sobre la libertad humana y la religión. Esta comedia plantea, en definitiva, el problema de la necesaria transformación de la sociedad española. El país vive demasiado estancado; hay que renovarlo, hay que cambiar algo. Antón Caballero es una comedia de tema político y de preocupaciones sociales" (p. 649).

BARBARA. Eduardo Gomez de Baquero, "Bárbara," La España moderna, 197 (mayo 1905), 170-80, finds this play "una de las mejores obras escénicas de Galdós, y por una de las más hermosas de nuestro teatro moderno, aunque su belleza no sea llamativa y chillona, sino austera y armoniosa, a estilo clásico" (p. 170). He finds that "La tragicomedia de Galdós se presta a ser examinada desde muchos puntos de vista diferentes. Es una obra en extremo sugestiva, que solicita al pensamiento y le llama con señuelos diferentes. El desarrollo de la acción, el lenguaje que hablan los personajes, la caracterización historica de la época, el pensamiento capital de la obra, el caracter de Horacio y el fin que persigue, ofrecen, sin duda, materia para largas disquisiciones; pero yo voy a hablar muy brevemente de estos puntos, a los cuales añadiré algunas observaciones sobre varias escenas de la obra que, sin ser las principales, me han llamado especialmente la atención" (p. 172).

A French discussion of this play is found in F. Vézinet, "Bárbara," Les maitres du roman espagnol contemporain (Paris: Hachette, 1907), pp. 98-128. He provides a summary of the play's plot and says that "Elle contient

quelques invraisemblances" (p. 106). He writes: "Ces reserves faites, nous n'aurons guère qu'à louer l'auteur. Il
sait animer des personnages, construire un drama, meler
sans extravagance le tragique et le comique" (p. 110). For
Vézinet, "Galdós est un peintre d'âmes, clairvoyant, parfois
subtil, souvent vigoureaux, habil à creer des héros qu'enflam-
ment de grands sentiments, l'amour mystique, la passion de
l'art, le besoin de purification, de rédemption" (p. 124). He
praises Galdós as an "Excellent psychologue, il n'est pas un
moins bon dramaturge" (p. 124).

   CASANDRA. Díez Canedo, "Casandra," in Artículos
de crítica teatral..., pp. 96-98, was first published in La
Voz, April 13, 1936. Canedo compares the play with the
novel and finds that "La obra dramática es más brusca; todo
en ella aparece menos claro, un tanto caprichoso y llevado
a punto de exageración" (p. 97). He notes that in Galdós'
plays "vemos de batirse a las almas nobles con las asechanzas
de la superstición" (p. 98).

   Ramón Pérez de Ayala, "Casandra," Obras completas
III (Madrid: Aguilar, 1966), 27-31 (reprinted in Benito Pérez
Galdós (1973), pp. 439-443), deals briefly with some of the
criticisms made concerning the play. "Lo primero, hay una
rara unanimidad en calificarlo de pesado" (p. 27). "Otro
punto en que hay unanimidad crítica: los herederos de doña
Juana, con la codicia por todo móvil volitivo, son antipáticos.
Doña Juana, contrariamente, es una figura que, equivocada o
no en sus ideas, por su entereza moral, merece nuestra
simpatía" (p. 28). There is a brief discussion of the play's
"problema." He finds that "En suma: los sobrinos de doña
Juana, con todos sus defectos, son la fecundidad social;
doña Juana es la esterilidad social" (p. 31).

   DONA PERFECTA. Almost nothing of a critical nature has appeared concerning the play-version of Doña Perfecta.
Henry Lyonnet, Le théâtre en Espagne (Paris: Ollendorff,
1897), pp. 83-95, provides an early French view of this play.
This critic has his humorous side, and notes that Galdós first
became known for his humorous side. He notes that Galdós
first became known for his Episodios nacionales "où la haine
contre le Français en envahisseur est un peu trop cultivée
systématiquement à chaque page pendant dix volumes ...
N'ayant plus de Français à se mettre sous la dent, Galdos
s'en prend aux moines et aux ultramontains, ce que, en
Espagne, peut passer pour une audace extrême" (p. 84). He
summarizes the plot, discusses the characters and states

that "Et si je me suis arrêté si longuement sur cette oeuvre,
c'est bien pour démontrer qu'elle put être considerée comme
une audace" (p. 94). He finds that in Spain "ce conflit
d'âmes et de consciences est encore mieux compris que chez
nous" (p. 94).

Díez Canedo, "Doña Perfecta," in Artículos de crítica
teatral..., pp. 84-87, is reprinted from El Sol, Oct. 31,
1924, and reprinted in Benito Pérez Galdós (1973), pp. 445-
447. Díez comments that "Al pasar de la novela al teatro,
Doña Perfecta hubo de sufrir, por mano de su autor, grandes
modificaciones, y el teatro perdió mucho de lo que vive en la
novela, quedándose sólo con leves indicaciones, encerradas en
personajes no episodicos, pues en el drama no hay apenas
incidentes, sino secundarios, de suficiente claridad para los
familiarizados con el mundo galdosiano, y nada importunos
para el que se llegue al drama sin conocer la novela. Ganó,
en cambio, el teatro esa gran figura tallada de nuevo y lograda en plena expresión" (p. 86).

ELECTRA. Most of the April 1901 issue of El teatro,
no. 6, pp. 2-16, was devoted to this play. This issue is of
interest because it presents a contemporary view of the play's
reception. Zeda, "Don Benito Pérez Galdós," pp. 2-3, concludes with this thought concerning Galdós' drama: "Sus
obras se proponen principalmente hacernos pensar, lo que no
quita para que nos hagan sentir, y quizás con más intensidad
que los dramas puramente pasionales" (p. 3). Pages 4-15
are an anonymous discussion of the play with numerous illustrations which depict the setting and the actors. Certain
passages of the play are reproduced. Page 16, "Galdós
juzgado por la crítica extranjera," is a half-page of quotations from Luis Jacot, B. de Tannenberg, P. Grandmontagne
and Morel Fatio.

Pío Baroja, "El estreno de Electra," Obras completas,
VII (Madrid, 1949), 741-42, is reprinted in Luis A. Granjel,
Panorama de la generación del 98 (Madrid: Guadarrama,
1959), 398-400.

E. Gómez de Baquero, "Crónica literaria," La España
moderna, 147 (marzo de 1901), 152-61, notes that it has been
difficult to judge this play impartially and he discusses in
general terms the reactions of many of the critics. He denies, after a brief discussion of the supernatural in the play,
that the play need have a symbolic meaning. "No hay necesidad alguna de que las obras literarias encierren alguna

significación esotérica o algún sentido alegórico" (p. 155).
He finds that the problem that runs throughout the play "es
un problema de herencia" (p. 156). He states that "Electra
es la obra dramática de mayores vuelos del teatro de Galdós
y la consagración definitiva de ésta como autor dramático.
La exposición es algo lenta, y se haría pesada si no fuese
por el encanto y gracia del acto tercero...." (p. 160). He
briefly discusses Electra and Pantoja.

Díez Canedo, "Electra," in Artículos de crítica
teatral..., pp. 87-89, originally appeared in El Sol, Sept.
11, 1929; reprinted in Benito Pérez Galdós (1973), pp. 448-
49. He finds that this play "es, sin duda alguna, tipo casi
perfecto del drama popular, por su noble pensamiento y su
alto sentido humano, independientes en absoluto de las circunstancias que determinaron la resonante explosión de su
estreno, allá en 1901" (p. 88).

Jorge Byron, "Electra," Instantáneas de luz y sombra
(Santiago), 2, 55 (April 7, 1901), 10-11, notes the different
types of reactions to the play. The reviewer has little but
praise for this work. It is of interest to see that Electra
was performed in Santiago with no difficulty, but that the
mayor of Valparaíso prohibited the performance of what
Byron calls "una obra perfectamente moral" (p. 11).

Two early French discussions are: Georges Lenor-
mand, "A propos de l'Electra de D. Benito Pérez Galdós,"
Revue hispanique, 8 (1901), 567-73, and Ephrem Vincent,
"Lettres espagnoles," Mercure de France, 37 (1901), 860.

Lenormand provides general remarks concerning anticlericalism in 19th-century Spain as well as a summary of
the plot and a discussion of the play's characters. He finds
that "Galdós a voulu montrer du théâtre ce que la tutelle
ecclésiastique a fait de l'âme espagnole" (p. 569). Vincent
feels that "On a bien exagéré ... la portée révolutionnaire
de cette piece, on n'a pas assez vu sa portée littéraire."

Josette Blanquat, "Au temps d'Electra (documents
galdosiens)," Bulletin hispanique, 68 (1966), 253-308, is
important to the student of Galdós for (1) its study of certain
French newspapers of 1901 and their reactions to the play's
performances, (2) the reprinting of Galdós' "La España de
hoy," and (3) "Une interview de Pérez Galdós," reprinted
from Le siècle of April 25, 1901. This article is of special
value for the study of Galdós' reception in France.

The controversy aroused in Spain and France over the presentation of this play was not long in being discussed in the English-speaking world. Havelock Ellis, "Electra and the progressive movement," The Argosy, 75 (1901), 180-88, reprinted in Living Age, 231 (Oct. 26, 1901), 236-41, states that the play "is the symbol of progress and of revolt against clericalism and Jesuitism...." (p. 237).

The anonymous preface, "Benito Pérez Galdós," The Drama, no. 2 (1911), 3-11, to the first English translation of this play, pp. 12-138, is one of the earliest discussions of Galdós as a dramatist published in English in the United States. The author discusses the threefold classification of the plays as presented by Martinenche in his Revue des deux mondes article.

Ignacio Elizalde, "Azorín y el estreno de Electra de Pérez Galdós," Letras de Deusto, 3, no. 6 (julio-diciembre 1973), 67-79, discusses the reactions of the public and various critics to the performance in 1901 of Electra. The article reproduces Maeztu's "El público desde adentro," pp. 72-74, Azorín's "Ciencia y fe," in Madrid cómico, pp. 74-76, and Maeztu's reply to this article published in the same journal, pp. 76-78. One page is devoted to a comment on E. Merimée's discussion of the play published in the Bulletin hispanique. Brief remarks show the development of Azorin's ideas and opinions concerning Galdós.

E. Inman Fox, "Galdós Electra: a detailed study of its historical significance and the polemic between Martínez Ruiz and Maeztu," Anales galdosianos, 1 (1966), 131-41, states that "The performance of Galdós' play Electra in 1901 is mentioned as a significant event in most of the political and cultural histories of Spain, but, as far as we know, never with sufficient detail to explain the reasons for its impact.... The purpose of this study is to document and interpret the circumstances that surrounded the staging of Electra and in this way establish its importance" (p. 131). The article's main sections are: Historical prelude. The performance of Electra, The case of Adelaide Ubao, Electra and Maeztu and Martínez Ruiz. Fox notes that "Galdós, then, with the performance of Electra became the rallying point for intellectuals, politicians and the masses in their drive for liberalism in the Twentieth Century" (pp. 140-41). The article is especially valuable for its reprinting of material from El país (Jan. 31, 1901) by the two authors, and from Madrid cómico (Feb. 9, 1901, by Azorín; Feb. 16, 1901, by Maeztu).

Sergio Beser, "Un artículo de Maeztu contra Azorín," Bulletin hispanique, 65 (1963), 329-32, discusses the article by Azorín published in Madrid cómico of Feb. 9, 1901. In the issue of this same journal for Feb. 16, 1901, Ramiro de Maeztu published his "Electra y Martínez Ruiz," which is reprinted here. This polemic shows the ideological uncertainties of the two members of the Generation of 1898 and their disagreements.

LA FAMILIA DE LEON ROCH. Luis Morote, "La familia de León Roch (Drama inspirado en la novela de Galdós)," Teatro y novela (Madrid: 1906), pp. 17-37, is a discussion of the dramatized version of this novel by José Jerique. Plot comparisons are made between the novel and the play. The author describes Jerique's reading the dramatized version to a group of individuals, including Galdós, who made comments and suggestions.

GERONA. Francisco P. Villegas, "Impresiones literarias," La España moderna, 51 (marzo de 1893), 199-201, finds that this is "una tentativa poco afortunada hecha por Galdós para convertir en drama uno de sus justamente famosos Episodios nacionales" (p. 199). He states: "Con ser nulo o casi nulo el interés propiamente dramático, lánguida y deshilvanada la acción, excesivamente gárrula la locura de la hija del doctor, impropios de la escena varios episodios de la obra, anti-teatral lo del hambre, poco feliz lo relativo a los amoríos de las petimetras y la escena del cesto, aun tuvo Gerona otros enemigos mayores, sin contar los franceses. Los verdaderos destructores de Gerona fueron los actores que la ejecutaron" (p. 201).

EL HOMBRE FUERTE. Eduardo Lustonó, "El primer drama de Galdós," Nuestro tiempo, 1 (1902), 155-57, publishes act one, scene vi of this play which was written in 1870. This three-act play, though the Teatro del Principe was given a chance to perform it, was never presented on the stage.

UN JOVEN DE PROVECHO. H. Chonon Berkowitz, "Un joven de provecho: an unpublished play by B. Pérez Galdós," PMLA, 50 (1935), 828-98, publishes this Galdos play for the first time, with a brief introduction which discusses the date of the play—before 1868; he describes the manuscript and his editorial method. Berkowitz feels that "For all its shortcomings, however, the comedy remains a highly valuable document for the study of Galdós dramatic career" (p. 898).

LA DE SAN QUINTIN. Francisco F. Villegas, "Impresiones literaries," La España moderna, 62 (febrero de 1894), 124-28, finds that "Tiene, es cierto, escenas admirables, como la última del primer acto y el principio y final del segundo, rasgos hermosos, frases felices; pero tanto en la contextura general del drama, como en el desarrollo de los caracteres, como en la lógica de los acontecimientos, falta esa perfección que da perpetuidad a la obra artística y que es el sello de las grandes producciones" (p. 125). The reviewer feels that if one looked for technical defects, they could be found, but he enjoyed the play so much that he does not wish to dwell on these points. Rather he feels that "hay en la comedia tanta fuerza dramática, tanta cantidad de talento, tanta verdad y tantas bellezas, que, al contemplarlas, todo lo demás se borra" (p. 126).

LA LOCA DE LA CASA. Francisco P. Villegas, "Impresiones literarias," La España moderna, 50 (febrero de 1893), 204-08, finds this an inferior play in comparison with others that Galdós has written despite the fact that this one "abundan los primores, las frases gráficas, los pensamientos atinados y profundos, que los diálogos, aunque excesivamente largos, están bien manejados, que la prosa es limpia y gallarda; pero todas estas perfecciones de detalle no consiguen dar a la obra de Galdós el mérito y grandeza que tienen otras producciones suyas" (p. 208). There are presented discussions of plot, characters and style.

Díez Canedo, "La loca de la casa," in Artículos de crítica teatral ..., pp. 94-95, deals more with the fine quality of the leading actress, Margarita Xirgu, and the other members of the cast than with the play itself. He concludes his brief note with this sentence: "Si aún quedan verdaderos amigos del teatro, no han de perder esta ocasión de ver vivo en escena uno de los más bellos caracteres femeninos de la obra galdosiana" (p. 95). This review was first published in El Sol, Oct. 16, 1932.

Hal Carney, "The two versions of Galdós' La loca de la casa," Hispania, 44 (1961), 438-40, states that "Pérez Galdós' second play, La loca de la casa, has often been mentioned as having been derived from a dialogued novel of the same name" (p. 438). The author finds that "a) neither version bears any of the characteristics of the dialogued novels; (b) the second is the result of cuts made during stage rehearsals; (c) extensive rewriting and major alterations required of the plays based on novels in dialogue form were needless here" (p. 438). These points seem to be well-

proved based on a simultaneous examination of the two
works.

Ramón Pérez de Ayala, "El liberalismo y La loca de
la casa," Obras completas III (Madrid: Aguilar, 1966), 47-
68, is the text of a lecture given on May 2, 1916 in honor of
Galdós.   The first several pages deal with "Las similitudes
y correspondencias entre Cervantes y Galdós...." (p. 47).
He states that he will make "unos cuantos comentarios con-
cretos sobre un solo concepto y una sola obra galdosiana...."
(p. 49).   He finds that this play "se nos muestra destacada
el aspecto económico del liberalismo."   The character and
ideas of Pepet are analyzed and it is noted that he has "sobre
lo malo y lo bueno un criterio liberal" (p. 63).

Angel del Río, "La significación de La loca de la casa," Cuadernos americanos, 21 3 (1945), 237-68, has the following parts: Novela y teatro en Galdós, El problema social:
la armonía de clases, El problema económico: la función
del dinero, El problema del bien y el mal, El sentido activo
del misticismo, Razón, imaginación y sentimiento, El pensamiento conciliador de Galdós, Galdós y Unamuno.

Willa H. Elton, "Sobre el genero de La loca de la casa de Galdós," Cuadernos hispanoamericanos, nos. 250-252
(1970-71), 586-607, is a comparison of the two versions of
La loca de la casa.   The author discusses the two versions
and concludes the article with this paragraph: "La precipi-
tación de la acción, el cambio de carácter de varios personajes menores y la reducción de los pasajes narrativos se
efectúan en gran parte como resultado secundario de la con-
densación general de la obra.   Parece que la motivación
principal de Galdós era cuantitative al llevar La loca de la
casa al proscenio.   Ni en este aspecto, la extensión, se
diferencian bastante para justificar una denominación genérica
distinta para las dos versiones.   O sea, que la segunda
versión es poco más que una corrección de la primera hecha
para facilitar la representación, no para hacerla posible como
era el caso en las adaptaciones de las novelas dialogadas.
De manera que la clasificación de La loca de la casa entre
las novelas contemporáneas no significa que es novela dialogada.   Galdós la denominó comedia.   Y era representable en
la primera versión.   La segunda no resulta obra de distinto
género sino comedia aún más representable que la primera"
(p. 607).

Robert Ricard, "Reflexiones inconexas sobre La loca
de la casa de Galdós," Homenaje a Sherman H. Eoff...,

pp. 221-235, notes that Sáinz de Robles "subraya la semejanza que existe entre el principal personaje masculino, Pepet
Cruz, y el usurero Torquemada...." (p. 221). Sáinz de
Robles "cree ver también una semejanza entre la Victoria de
La loca de la casa y la Leré de Angel Guerra, y otra semejanza entre le mismo Angel Guerra y el enamorado de Victoria, Daniel de Malavella" (p. 222). Ricard discusses these
suggested similarities. Pages 232-234 provide data concerning uses of the expression La loca de la casa in other works
by Galdós. Ricard feels that "El título de La loca de la
casa parece la cristalización final de una idea latente en el
espíritu de Galdós desde muchos años antes" (p. 232).

MARIANELA. La condesa de Pardo Bazán, "La vida
contemporánea," La ilustración artística, no. 1819 (6 nov.,
1916), 714, is a review of the Quintero brothers' adaptation
of this book for the stage. Pardo Bazán would favor the
dramatization of more of Galdós' works and laments the fact
that more of the Spanish theater does not use Spanish history
as its source.

MARIUCHA. Jose Maria Aicardo, Razón y fe, 8 (1904),
544-45, is an attack on the play.

E. Inman Fox, "En torno a Mariucha: Galdós en
1903," Cuadernos hispanoamericanos, nos. 250-252 (1970-
1971), 608-22, is one of the few critical articles devoted to
this play. Fox notes that "mi intención en este breve trabajo
es examinar Mariucha 'exteriormente' a través del asesora-
miento crítico del día y un escrito del mismo Galdós, nunca
que sepamos recopilado, para acabar con un planteamiento
del pensamiento político-social de Galdós en relación con las
realidades históricas de 1903" (p. 609).

Pages 612-15 reproduce the text of a Galdós letter published in El liberal on July 17, 1903. Pages 621-22 present
a list of "Artículos de prensa sobre Mariucha publicados en
1903."

REALIDAD. Emilia Pardo Bazán, "Realidad, drama
de D. Benito Pérez Galdós," Nuevo teatro crítico, no. 16
(abril 1892), 19-69, is the longest of the contemporary reviews of this play. The review has the following parts:
(1) Génesis y nacimiento de la obra, (2) La noche del estreno. La segunda noche. Actitud del público. (3) La crítica
periodística de Realidad, (4) La obra. ¿Puede convertirse
una novela en drama? Condiciones externas de Realidad:

estructura, dimensiones, recursos dramáticos. Condiciones
internas: trascendencia, moralidad. ¿Es Realidad un drama
naturalista ó realista, o trae por otro concepto nuevas formu-
las á la escena? (5) Mise en scène y desempeño de Realidad.

Díez Canedo, "Realidad" in Artículos de crítica
teatral..., pp. 90-94, first appeared in El Sol, Jan. 1, 1931.
The critic discusses the novela dialogada, Realidad, as well
as the drama with the same name. He shows the types of
changes that Galdós made in changing genres. He finds that
in this play "ha de verse el comienzo del nuevo teatro español.... (p. 92). He elaborates on this theme for most of
p. 93. A part of p. 93 and most of 94 are devoted to comments on the quality of the performance.

E. Gómez de Baquero, "Impresiones literarias," La
España moderna, año 4, no. 41 (1892), 193-98, finds that
critics of every description are agreed about "la importancia
excepcional de la obra" (p. 193). Only great artistic works
are capable of arousing great controversy. "El pensamiento
capital que se contiene en Realidad es un pensamiento meta-
físico, base de una doctrina moral, si no la más compatible,
una de las más adecuadas al estado de la sociedad presente.
El amor al bien por el bien mismo...." (p. 195). The religious and philosophical elements of the play are analyzed.
He compares the characters of the play with those of the
novel of the same name and finds that "justo es decir que
algo se han falseado al pasar del libro al escenario" (p. 198).
He praises the dialogue in these words: "me refiero al dialo-
go, siempre preciso, vivo, animado y esmaltado de flores, en
que la conexión se une a la profundidad, y expuesto en un
lenguaje que trae a la memoria el recuerdo de nuestros mejores hablistas" (p. 198).

SANTA JUANA DE CASTILLA. Ramón Perez de
Ayala, "Santa Juana de Castilla," Obras completas III (Madrid: Aguilar, 1966), 69-74, finds that Santa Juana de
Castilla no es propriamente un drama, sino la misma quintae-
scencia dramática; emoción desnuda, purísima, acendrada, en
que se abrazan la emoción singular de cada una de las pasiones, pero ya purgadas de turbulencia y en su máxima serenidad.... Religiosidad y españolismo son los rasgos familiares de ésta, como de todos las obras galdosianas" (p. 73).

SOR SIMONA. Ramon Pérez de Ayala, "Sor Simona,"
Obras completas III (Madrid: Aguilar, 1966), 31-46, has the
following sections: El hecho. Las interpretaciones. La

incompatibilidad.   La seriedad.   Brunilda.   Palas Atenea.
Sor simona.

Vicente Aleixandre, "Evocaciones españolas: Don Benito
Pérez Galdós sobre el escenario," Revista Shell, no. 23
(1957), 19-20, is an account of the author's memories of having seen Galdós' Sor Simona in Madrid in Dec. 1915.

VOLUNTAD. Eduardo Gomez de Baquero, "Cronica
literaria," La España moderna, 85 (enero de 1896), 137-47,
regrets that Galdós has not used the play's plot for a novel.
"Voluntad no ha sido todo lo que podía ser" (pp. 137-38).
He finds it superior to other plays being presented at the
same time.   He states that "La acción de la comedia del Sr.
Galdós, es, por el contrario, un tanto lánguida y anémica,
de una tonalidad neutra, floja en ocasiones, como un cuerpo
sin huesos ni músculos" (p. 138).   He believes that dramatists
are not allowed as much realism as the novelist.   He states
that "La falta de interés de esta comedia depende, a mi
entender, de dos causas: una de ellas está en el mismo desarrollo de su acción: otra, acaso la principal, consiste en
que el asunto se presta poco a las condiciones especiales del
género dramático" (p. 140).   He discusses the characters
and their psychology.   He finds more to criticize than to
praise with this work.

Students interested in the presentation of Galdos' plays
in Mexico should consult Enrique de Olavarria y Ferrari,
Reseña histórica del teatro en Mexico; prólogo de Salvador
Novo, tercera edición ... puesta al día de 1911 a 1961
(Mexico: Porrua, 1961), 5 vols. and index.   The index to
this set reveals 29 references to the dramas of Galdós.

JOURNALISM

Alfonso Cervantes, "Influencias del periodismo en la formación de Benito Pérez Galdos," (Ph. D. dissertation, University of California at Los Angeles, 1972), 337 leaves, is the fullest treatment of Galdós' journalism between 1866-1872. It has the following parts: I. Introducción a la época periódistica de Galdós. II. La colaboración periódistica de Galdós. III. La interpretación de la música en los artículos periódisticos. IV. La crítica de Galdós sobre el teatro español. V. Los ideas de Galdós sobre la novela y el cuadro de costumbres. VI. El anticlericalismo galdosiano en los. VII. La postura politica de Galdós en su juventud. VIII. Conclusiones.

In very recent years more and more of Galdós' contributions to newspapers and periodicals have been collected and published.

LAS CORTES. Leo J. Hoar, Jr., "Politics and poetry: more proof of Galdós' work for Las Cortes," MLN, 88 (1973), 378-97, reproduces in pp. 393-97 a review of El libro de la patria by Ventura Ruiz Aguilera, "exactly as it appeared in the Juan Palomo, including a number of minor orthographic differences from the Las Cortes original." This article is an extraordinarily thorough discussion of Galdós' relationship to the Madrid (1869-70) Las Cortes. The review itself is analyzed. Hoar finds that "The article and the circumstances of its appearance in Las Cortes are a special instance of an important phase in Galdós' creative process..." (p. 392) and that "With this article alone, but more appropriately after an examination of all the 'Crónica parliamentaria,' we are able to judge that it was Galdós' association with Las Cortes which was the basis for his sharpened political skills" (p. 392). Much information of importance is produced concerning this 'diario' and Galdós' contributions to it.

ILLUSTRACION DE MADRID. Crónica de la Quincena by Benito Pérez Galdós, edited with a preliminary study by William H. Shoemaker (Princeton, N. J.: Princeton University Press, 1948), vii + 140pp.; the preface is reprinted in

Shoemaker's Estudios sobre Galdós and pp. 27-72 contain the
texts of nine crónicas that first appeared in the Ilustración
de Madrid from Jan.-May, 1872. No critics have ever written about them nor have they been reproduced before. The
preliminary study, pp. 3-58, has the following parts: I.
Ilustración de Madrid. II. Galdós and the Ilustración. III.
Galdós and the "Crónica de la quincena." Contents and subject matter. Ideas and attitudes. Literary and stylistic matters. Shoemaker points out that much more needs to be done
in regard to the study of Galdós as a journalist. The preliminary study is a valuable additon to our knowledge of this
period of Galdos life.

LA NACION. William H. Shoemaker, "Galdós y La
Nación," Hispanófila, no. 25 (1965), 21-50 (reprinted in his
Estudios sobre Galdós, pp. 224-40, and his "Estudio preliminar," to Los artículos de Galdós en "La nación" [Madrid,
Insula, 1972], pp. 7-20) is divided into two parts. The first
discusses briefly Galdós' contributions to this newspaper and
past knowledge of these contributions. The second part is an
"Indice razonada de los escritos de Benito Pérez Galdós publicados en el diario La Nación de Madrid, 1865-1868."

Laureano Bonet, "Galdós y La Nación: años de
aprendizaje," Insula, no. 322 (septiembre 1973), 5, 13, is
a review of Shoemaker's edition of Galdós' articles in this
newspaper. Bonet writes that "el presente libro viene a ser
un hito fundamental para el diseño definitivo de su prehistoria
creativa" (p. 5). He calls this volume "una modélica labor
erudita" (p. 5).

H. Chonon Berkowitz, "Galdós' literary apprenticeship,"
Hispanic Review, 3 (1935), 1-22, is the first article to produce an analysis of Galdós' non-critical contributions to Madrid's La Nación. Though Shoemaker's study is later and
more thorough, Berkowitz' conclusions--that "Form, style,
content, point of view, spirit, prejudices, convictions--these
in the years of Galdós' apprenticeship foreshadow unmistak-
ably the qualities of his literary art after 1868" (p. 22)--
are of interest.

EL OMNIBUS. "Galdós, colaborador de El ómnibus,"
recopilación, prólogo y notas de José Schraibman, Anuario de
estudios atlánticos, no. 9 (1963), 289-334, can be divided into
two parts. Pages 289-92 are an introduction that discusses
the place of these works in the Galdós canon. The rest of
the article reproduces Galdós' contributions to this journal

published in Las Palmas. Schraibman writes that "Además
del interés que tengan para los que desconozcan el substrato
canario que palpita en la obra galdosiana, son asimismo significativos para los críticos, cuya función es atisbar y exponer
los secretos de la creación...." (p. 290).

LA PRENSA. William H. Shoemaker, Las cartas
desconocidas de Galdós en "La Prensa" de Buenos Aires (Madrid: Ediciones Cultura hispánica, 1973), 541pp., contains
an "Estudio preliminar," pp. 9-34, which notes that "Este
libro trae a los lectores de literatura, y sobre todo a los
galdosiastas, un cuerpo de escritos de don Benito no sólo por
completo desconocidos, sino también cuya mera existencia,
sospechada de algunos, sigue siendo prácticamente ignorada.
Son las cartas todavía no coleccionadas y publicadas que
Galdós envió al 'Señor Director' de La Prensa de Buenos
Aires, con fechas desde el 20 de Diciembre de 1883 hasta el
31 de Marzo de 1894 y salidas en dicho diario en 175 núme-
ros distintos a partir del 17 de Enero de 1884, apareciendo
la última el día 29 de Abril de 1894" (p. 9). The introduction discusses the style and content of the letters. The first
appendix, p. 37, notes that La Prensa published another letter from Galdós in its issue of Nov. 17, 1901. The second
appendix, pp. 39-40, discusses briefly Galdós' relationship
with La Prensa as seen through correspondence in the Casa-
Museo de Galdós in Las Palmas.

William A. Shoemaker, "'Los Pepes' of Galdós in
1868 and 1887. Two stages of his style," Hispania, 53 (1970),
887-898, compares the text of this article which appeared in
Madrid's La Nación, March 22, 1868 and Buenos Aires' La
Prensa, May 4, 1887. Shoemaker writes: "But the text is
not quite the same, and the number of changes made in the
new redaction or adaptation of the original version are so
numerous and of such kinds as to constitute important data for
a study of Galdós' stylistic criteria at the beginning and,
after an interval of two decades, in the middle of his literary
career" (p. 887). A detailed analysis of the two texts is
provided.

Denah Lida, "El crimen de la calle de Fuencarral,"
Homenaje a Casalduero (Madrid: Gredos, 1972), pp. 275-
283, discusses Galdós' dispatches for La Prensa of Buenos
Aires concerning the trial of the individual accused of the
murder of Luciana Borcino of 129 calle de Fuencarral. These
dispatches later brought together in a volume entitled El crimen de la calle de Fuencarral "da testimonio del equilibrio

y honradez con que Pérez Galdós busca la verdad, tanto en
el plano literario como en el social" (p. 283).

REVISTA DE ESPAÑA.   Peter B. Goldman, "Galdós
and the politics of reconciliation, " Anales galdosianos, 4
(1969), 74-87, contains an introductory section plus I. The
opposition; II. The government; and III. The politics of reconciliation.   Galdós joined the staff of the Revista de España
in 1870 and contributing "to the magazine's 'Revista política
interior, ' published a total of fourteen installments in 1871
and 1872" (p. 74).   Goldman states that "Because of their
concentration in a fifteen-month period, these articles have
a great historical pertinence as a contemporary account of the
struggles and eventual failure of the monarchy to establish itself.   Equally important is their utility in defining with greater
accuracy Galdós historicism as well as his attitudes to the
various compelling issues of the day.   The years immediately
following the Revolution of September are also the major epoch
to which Galdós returns in his later novels; the disparities
and contrasts (as well as similarities) between the opinions
of Galdós the reporter writing in 1872, and of Galdós the
novelist writing ten to twenty years later, are therefore particularly valuable.   Hence, an examination of the articles in
the Revista de España is in order, and it is this which I
propose to do following a brief chronological sketch of the
historical background against which they were written" (p. 73).

REVISTA DEL MOVIMIENTO INTELECTUAL DE EU-
ROPA.   Leo J. Hoar, Jr. , Benito Pérez Galdós y La Revista
del movimiento intelectual de Europa.   Madrid, 1865-1867
(Madrid: Insula, 1968), 300pp. , provides the text of forty
articles by Galdós that this journal published; each article is
preceded by a bibliographical note.   Pages 13-74 are an introduction with the following sections: I. Introducción.
II. Revista del movimiento intelectual de Europa.   Madrid,
1865-1867.   III. Galdós y la Revista.   IV. Los artículos de
Galdós para la Revista.

SHORT STORIES AND SHORT FICTION

The fullest treatment of Galdós as a short story writer
is that of Walter Carl Oliver, "The short stories of Benito
Pérez Galdós" (Ph.D. dissertation, University of New Mexico,
1971, 321pp.; Dissertation Abstracts, 31 [1971], 6624A).
Oliver's "purpose" according to the abstract "is to provide
the first thorough and systematic study of Galdós' cuentos, to
discover and describe their nature, to relate them to his total
work and to suggest what they reveal about the artist and his
development. Each story's literary elements are identified
and discussed in terms of their function within the organic
whole. The elements considered are the use of costumbrismo,
dominant orientation, humor, language, literary resonance,
lyricism, point of view, structure and symbolism. Chapter
I reviews the major critics and outlines the general characteristics of Galdós' artistry that are related to the short stories.
Chapter II surveys Galdós' early creative activity and suggests its relationship to the cuentos. Chapters III and IV
treat the first period (1870-1872) stories, which are humorous,
satirical and realistic. Chapter V, studies the second period
(1872-1887) stories, which are lyrical, metaphysical and fantastic. Chapter VI presents an overview of all the cuentos."

AQUEL. Vernon A. Chamberlin, "The Riddle in
Galdós' 'Lost Sketch Aquél,'" Symposium, 15 (1961), 62-66,
is a discussion of a sketch that first appeared in Los españoles de ogaño (Madrid, 1872). It was not reprinted in the
Sáinz de Robles Obras completas. The author deals with the
question: "What facts or speculation can be adduced to help
explain [Aquel's] originality of artistic form?" (p. 62). He
concludes that "In all probability, Galdós, a lifelong Madri-
lenean vago and realistic author par excellence, chose to
create Aquél as he himself had experienced the role--with
the vago as the center of conjecture" (p. 66).

EL ARTICULO DE FONDO. Mariano Baquero Goyanes,
"La 'perspectiva cambiante' en Galdós," Homenaje a Casalduero (Madrid, Gredos, 1972), pp. 71-83, is the most important
stylistic study yet written on this relato corto. The last
paragraph indicates some of the author's conclusions: "Como

quiera que sea, el significado que ese relato, El artículo de
fondo, asume dentro de la total producción narrativa galdosiana, se carga de un cierto énfasis, si vemos en él un humorístico empleo de una técnica que el autor había de repe-
tir luego con no pocas y eficaces variantes. El recurso de
la 'perspectiva cambiante' podrá parecer de poca monta dentro
de esa total producción novelesca; pero considerado a la luz
de ciertas constantes galdosianas, se nos revela como algo
muy ligado a una arraigada convincción del autor: la condición humana es tan frágil, tan mutable, tan inconstante, que
si unas veces merce condena y burla en razón de su misma
versatilidad, en otras parece reclamar esa comprensión e
indulgencia que Galdós siempre estuvo dispuesto a otorgar a
sus admirables criaturas novelescas" (p. 83).

    DOS DE MAYO DE 1808, DOS DE SEPTIEMBRE DE
1870. Leo J. Hoar, Jr., "Dos de mayo de 1808, dos de
septiembre de 1870 por Benito Pérez Galdós, un cuento extra-
viado y el posible prototipo de sus Episodios nacionales,"
Cuadernos hispanoamericanos, nos. 250-252 (1970-71), 312-
339, reproduces on pp. 336-9 the text of this piece identified as a short story which first appeared in Apuntes, May 2,
1896. According to Hoar, it was completed in December
1870. Hoar writes of its importance: "En primer lugar, su
importancia como narración desconocida rebasa el mero valor
arqueológico de un cuento perdido y exhumado, porque al
examinarlo con detenimiento descubrimos que es, en realidad,
un prototipo singular o versión anticipada de ciertos temas,
acción, argumento y personajes, que luego alcanzarán distinto
desarrollo en las novelas y episodios siguientes ... Incluso
en la forma embrionaria que aqui presenta 'Dos de mayo de
1808, dos de septiembre de 1870,' da tambien testimonio, el
mas claro y remoto, de que los Episodios como género inde-
pendiente, pudieron inspirarse directamente en los emocion-
antes sucesos de 1860, que se supone impresionaron mucho
al joven Galdós, y dieron lugar a la reflexion creadora en la
que nace un deseo de inmortalizar a España y su historia.
De igual modo es posible que aquella inspiración surgiese de
cualquier otro hecho, por entero ajeno a España pero suce-
dido en el mismo año en que se acaba este cuento, como es
la guerra franco-prusiana. Todos estos aspectos del relato
y otros relativos a sus génesis e importancia, serán objeto
de examen" (p. 313).

    LA NOVELA EN EL TRANVIA. José Schraibman,
"Variantes de La novela en el tranvía, de Galdós," La Torre,
no. 48 (1964), 149-63, states that it "trata específicamente

de ciertas variantes en La novela en el tranvía publicada por
primera vez en La Ilustración de Madrid (30 noviembre y 15
diciembre 1871), y, especialmente, de dos versiones mas
cortas que el original: la primera en Madrid cómico (8 diciembre 1900) y la segunda, aún más reducido, en Hoja de
Parra (29 julio 1911). A continuación sigue un breve resumen manteniendo la división de Galdós de la versión original
en La Ilustración de Madrid" (pp. 150-51). On p. 154
Schraibman notes the different divisions of different editors
and texts.

Walter Oliver, "Galdós' 'La novela en el tranvía':
fantasy and the art of realistic narration," MLN, 88 (1973),
249-263, is the fullest discussion yet made of this Galdós
short story. He finds that it "is an attempt to deal with the
technical problems involved in using the technique of realistic
fantasy and, therefore, is a direct forerunner of the Novelas
contemporáneas ... it not only criticizes as an essay might
but also achieves a mature, miniature (i.e., short story
model) expression of the author's later realistic fantasy technique" (pp. 250-51). He discusses the story's style, plot,
and the humor found in it. He concludes that it "is not a
juvenile exercise in fantasy but rather a complex, if low-
keyed, attempt to show fantasy's realistic role in human ex-
istence--and, by implication at least, its creative function in
narrative art--through a careful structuring and a meticulous
explanation of the psychological and scientific causes of fantasy. In this sense, it is a 'typical' example of one of
Galdós' most important novelistic techniques" (p. 263).

Robert J. Weber, "Galdós inedita: three short stories,"
Modern Language Notes, 77 (1962), 532-33, deals with "Dos
de mayo de 1808, dos de septiembre de 1870," "El pórtico de
la Gloria," and "Rompecabezas." The last paragraph is a
partial list of journals to which Galdós contributed.

PROLOGUES

Los prologos de Galdos por William H. Shoemaker (Urbana, Ill. and Mexico: University of Illinois Press and Ediciones de Andrea, 1962), 142pp.; (prefactory matter reprinted in Shoemaker's Estudios sobre Galdós, pp. 159-99), is a study of the prologues that Galdós wrote. Galdós wrote thirty-six, and Shoemaker reproduces the texts of 24 which do not appear in Galdós' Obras completas. He also reproduces the texts of "tres escritos de Galdós que pudieran parecer prólogos y no lo son" (p. 129). Shoemaker writes: "En la introducción se hace primero un estudio de conjunto de los prólogos de Galdós en sus aspectos bibliográficos, extrínsecos y circunstanciales, y segundo una presentación de cada uno de los treinta y seis en los mismos sentidos, en orden cronológico...." (p. 6).

CRITICAL WORKS

LITERARY CRITICISM. Benito Perez Galdós, Ensayos de crítica literaria, selección, introducción y notas de Laureano Bonet (Marcelona, Ediciones Península, 1972), 226pp., reproduces ten articles by Galdós.

Pages 7-112 are Bonet's introduction entitled "Galdós, crítico literario," which has the following sections: Un programa artístico, Crítica de los métodos narrativos, Novela y lenguaje popular, La sociedad contemporánea como materia novelable, La novela objetiva, El naturalismo y la crisis del 98 and Los personajes galdosianos y su realidad.

Elena Santos reviews this volume in Prohemio, 4 (abril-septiembre 1973), 258-64. She has high praise for Bonet's introduction as well as for the fact that he has anthologized a portion of Galdós' critical articles.

MUSICAL CRITICISM. José Pérez Vidal, Galdós crítico musical (Madrid and Las Palmas, Biblioteca Atlántica,

1956), 211pp., has a prologue by José Subirá. Its two main
divisions are: El crítico y su ambiente and Dos años de
crítica musical en Madrid and an appendix which lists books
on music found in Galdós' library. The first part is divided
into La formación musical de Galdós and El momento musical
en Madrid. The second part is divided into La ópera, La
zarazuela, La Revista de un muerto and Los conciertos.

MISCELLANEOUS WORKS

As a young writer Galdós wrote a few poems. One
should examine particularly Francisco Rodríguez Batllori,
"Galdós poeta," Punta Europa, no. 92 (1963), 15-20; and José
Schraibman, "Poemas inéditos de Galdós," Revista hispánica
moderna, 39 (1964), 354-72.

The first article is a brief comment on some of
Galdós' early poetry interspersed with a few selections from
it.

Schraibman reproduces "Del tiempo viejo" and "La
Emilianada." The introduction, pp. 354-55, provides brief
bibliographical and critical notes on these two poems.

"Benito Pérez Galdós: 'Una industria que vive de la
muerte,'" estudio preliminar de José Pérez Vidal, Anuario
de estudios atlánticos, no. 2 (1956), 1-35, reproduces the
text of this "episodio musical del cólera," pp. 23-35, that
was published in 1865. The introductory material provides
data on Galdós' life in Madrid during the time that he wrote
this story, his education in Madrid and the historical basis
of the story. Briefly discussed is the influence of Larra,
Hoffman, Mesonero Romanos and Ramón de la Cruz. The
last portion of the introduction is an analysis of the story's
style, which Pérez Vidal finds to be "bastante representativo
de la época en que fue escrito y del punto en que es encontraba la formación y evolución literaria de su autor. Su
asunto y el ambiente en que fue concebido determinarion el
desarrollo de la atmósfera romántico-musical que lo envuelve
y de los elementos sobrenaturales que lo ramatan" (p. 22).

Leo J. Hoar, Jr., "'Mi calle,' another 'lost' article
by Galdós, and a further note on his indebtedness to Mesonero Romanos," Symposium, 24 (1970), 128-47, reproduces the

text of this article from El correo de España. It elaborates
on the influence of Mesonero Romanos on Galdós and "it reveals new or heretofore unknown biographical data about one
of Galdós' early residences in Madrid" (p. 129). The five
pages of notes, 142-47, provide much useful data.

H. Chonon Berkowitz has studied "The youthful writings of Pérez Galdós," Hispanic Review, 1 (1933), 91-121.
He reproduces the texts of "El pollo" and "El teatro nuevo,"
poems, "Un viaje redondo," "El sol" and an outline of Galdós
"Un viaje de impresiones" along with the first two chapters
of this title. The article discusses many of Galdós' early
writings while he was still in Las Palmas.

Comments on Galdós' poetry, his costumbrista articles
published in El ómnibus, and "Un viaje de impresiones" are
found in José Schraibman, "Apuntes sobre temas y lenguaje
en la obra canaria de Galdós," Actas del XI Congreso internacional de lingüística y filología románica (Madrid: Consejo
superior de investigaciones científicas, 1969), pp. 2047-56.
Schraibman writes of these early works that he considers
"esta primera parte de su obra clave para comprender la
posterior, la más madura estilística y literariamente, pues
en este primer Galdós se esbozan ya los tópicos, los motivos, y la preocupación de darles forma de acuerdo con una
concepción lingüística-artística que refleja en él una búsqueda artística que caracteriza su obra entera" (p. 2047). He
notes from 1865 on that Galdós wrote nothing concerning the
Canary Islands. This article is one of the few that deals
with his writings before he moved to Madrid.

CONCLUSION

In view of the fact that the majority of recent critics view Galdós as Spain's second greatest novelist, little would be gained by a detailed discussion of the present state of his reputation. The tremendous number of critical studies, translations of his works into foreign languages, movies based on his work--all attest to the fact that he is still greatly studied and appreciated. He is relevant and does have a message for the present-day world.

Insula, no. 82 (Oct. 15, 1952), 3, presents in "Revisión de Galdós" the answers of Pío Baroja, Camilo José Cela, Carmen Laforet, Vicente Aleixandre, Azorín and Juan Antonio Zunzunegui to the following questions: (1) "¿Qué impresión conserva usted de su primer encuentro con la obra de Galdós?" (2) "¿Cree usted que Galdós ha influído algo en su obra o en la de los escritores de su generación?" (3) "¿Cómo ve usted a Galdós hoy y qué papel cree que ocupa en la historia de nuestra novela?" These views of six outstanding Spanish authors concerning Galdós are of interest.

Galdós ... Mary Washington College, contains three articles of interest. They are: Sherman Eoff, "Motives and values in Galdós, with attention to the Twentieth Century, " pp. 5-17; Joaquín Casalduero, "Galdós está vivo, " pp. 19-25; and José Angeles, "Galdós en perspectiva, " pp. 27-39, reprinted in Revista de estudios hispánicos, 3 (1969), 105-16.

Eoff directs "our attention to some of the sources of reader interest to be found in them" [i.e. the novels of Galdós] (p. 5). He compares Galdós to Baroja and Sánchez Ferlosio, and states that Galdós "focuses attention on people and the psychological behavior that makes individual personality an interesting study" (p. 5). It is of interest to note that Eoff states that "Galdós' hold on the reader's interest and his claim to lasting fame rest on his commitment to life, and his commitment to life expresses itself through his portrayal of people on two planes of observation: the collective assemblage--people as milieu--and individual personality, in which he makes us sharply aware of the most fundamental

psychological motives of the individual human being"
(p. 6).

Casalduero writes and elaborates upon the thought
that "Quizás podría abarcarse el mundo galdosiano en su
esencialidad si captamos su sentido de la historia y de la
naturaleza" (p. 22).

Angeles writes that "Galdós es un clásico. Y clásico
es quien en virtud de inteligencia, de fantasía y de temple
humano, en una palabra, de genio, y por encima de épocas,
modas y estilos, nos hace profundizar en la condición humana. Y en esto, que es, en definitiva, lo que más importa,
pocas aventajan a Galdós. La condición viva y palpitante de
su arte protéico ofrecerá siempre facetas luminosas. Así
son los clásicos y así son los valores siempre actuales de
Galdós" (p. 37).

In regard to Galdós' reputation in the United States,
no Spanish author has been more studied in academic circles.
According to James R. Chatham and Enrique Ruiz-Fornells,
Dissertations in Hispanic Languages and Literature (Lexing-
ton, Ky.: University Press of Kentucky, 1970), fifty-four
dissertations have been written on him between 1876-1966.
The same source cites forty-two dissertations on Cervantes
written during the same time span. Enrique Ruiz-Fornells,
"Ensayo de una bibliografía de las publicaciones hispánicas
en los Estados Unidos II," Español actual, no. 19 (nov.
1967), 33, shows that twenty-four text editions of Galdós works
have been published for the use of students in the universities
of the United States.

Vernon Chamberlin, "Galdós and galdosistas in the
United States: on the fiftieth anniversary of the author's
death," Hispania, 53 (1970), 819-27, writes: "The fact that
this is the first issue of Hispania ever dedicated completely
to one author is indicative of the importance and high esteem
which Galdós enjoys both in the field of Hispanic belles-
lettres and among the members of our own American Association of Teachers of Spanish and Portuguese" (p. 819). He
briefly outlines the history of Galdós studies in the United
States. Pages 822-25 discuss briefly each contributor's article to this issue; pp. 825-27 are notes. This is an excellent note on Galdós' reputation in the United States.

Once again, it should perhaps be emphasized that I

have tried to provide the non-galdosiano, i.e., the novice in Galdós studies, with a guide to what I consider the major studies in the field. I have wished to allow the individual authors cited to provide the annotations by quoting from their introductions or conclusions or both. I realize that to a certain degree all have been removed from their original context. To summarize a volume of three hundred pages in three hundred words is obviously impossible; on the other hand, it is possible often to allow the author to describe his purpose in this number of words and then to provide a personal commentary on his success or lack of it. I realize that there are different schools of criticism and I have made an effort to be fair in discussing individual items; I hope that I have not allowed personal prejudices to appear. The function of the bibliographer is to show what has been done and, indirectly, even to show what needs to be done. If I have emphasized studies in English, French and Spanish, this is because I have greater familiarity with research in these languages.

Much still remains to be done in the field of Galdós studies. There is a crying need for critical and collected editions of his works, a true obras completas that would include everything written by Galdós and which would discuss textual changes. Galdós as a dramatist has been slighted. Certain of the novels have had almost no critical attention devoted to them; I doubt that they are so poor as to deserve such critical neglect. It is perhaps now time to consider another attempt at a full-length biography; that of Berkowitz is now dated by a quarter of a century. Few linguistic studies exist on Galdós; more stylistic studies would fill a need. It is a pity that many of the dissertations on Galdós have not led subsequently to even one article based on the research undertaken for the dissertation. The past two decades in particular have seen a tremendous surge in scholarly studies on the great Spanish author. It would not surprise me in the least if this trend does not continue, for each generation seeks to re-evaluate the great masters of the past.

SUPPLEMENT

In July 1974 there appeared vol. 8 of the Anales galdosianos. I am, therefore, taking the liberty of discussing the contents of this issue as well as a few other books and articles that have reached my attention.

It is worth noting that vol. 8 (1973) of the Anales galdosianos does not contain the usual Galdós bibliography. It is to be hoped that Manuel Hernández Suárez has not decided to discontinue its compilation.

Biographical studies

PIO BAROJA. Julio Caro Baroja, "Confrontación literaria o las relaciones de dos novelistas: Galdós y Baroja," Cuadernos hispanoamericanos, nos. 265-267 (julio-septiembre 1972), 160-168, is a discussion by Baroja's nephew of the way the relationship between the two novelists varied from period to period in their lives.

CONCHA-RUTH MORRELL. A. F. Lambert, "Galdós and Concha-Ruth Morrell," Anales galdosianos, 8 (1973), 33-49, is the first article to discuss in detail Galdós' relationship with Concha-Ruth Morrell. Pages 33-37 reproduce a letter from J. B. Sitges Grifoll to Narcís Oller which "gives information on a woman with whom Galdós apparently had a relationship lasting several years" (p. 33). This letter is discussed in detail and Lambert tests the reliability of its facts. The last paragraph is of special interest and states that

> The main conclusions suggested by the document published here are, then, as follows: the popular image of Galdós as a cloistered celibate is false. Conversely, the cognoscenti's image of him as an inveterate but casual philanderer should also be treated with some scepticism. The document would indicate that his emotional and sexual life was intense and dramatic over long periods of time. One

might consequently expect to find a more directly
personal, even sentimental involvement of the author
in his work, especially in the treatment of sexuality
and adultery than has recently been admitted.
The inhibited exploration of the relationship between
Galdós' life and work is largely the result of a historically understandable desire to portray Galdós
as 'pure inventor' in the limited sense referred to
above and legitimate fear of falling into the trap of
crudely determinist biographical criticism.   It is
also due, of course, to the lack of hard information.
Once again the need for sensitive research into
Galdós' biography is manifest (p. 46).

EMILIA PARDO BAZAN and LORENZA COBIAN.
Walter T. Pattison, "Two women in the life of Galdós,"
Anales galdosianos, 8 (1973), 23-31, defends the authenticity
of three letters written by Pardo Bazán to Galdós and published in Excelsior (Mexico City) on Nov. 14, 1971.   Pattison states that "it is my intention to show that they are authentic and to shed more light on the circumstances which
provoked them" (p. 23).   Pages 23-27 discuss these letters
and the Pardo Bazán-Galdós relationship.   The rest of the
article deals with Lorenza Cobián, the mother of Galdós'
daughter, María.   Pattison declares:

> In his constant friendship for Doña Emilia and his
> affection for, and financial support of Lorenza and
> María, Galdós was a much more admirable and
> responsible man than most of his biographers have
> portrayed him.   His extreme reluctance to talk
> about his personal life allowed myths to grow up
> about his 'pathological' interest in sex.   It is time
> that a more restrained and accurate appraisal of
> his love affairs should prevail (p. 31).

William H. Shoemaker, "¿Cómo era Galdós?" Anales
galdosianos, 8 (1973), 5-21, has, according to Cardona
(p. 3), "dos elementos de importancia: el enfoque del
problema fundamental de la importancia de repasar de nuevo
la vida del novelista, utilizando materiales contemporáneos,
para ver, desde más cerca, cómo era Galdós; y, en segundo
lugar, la reunión de todos estos materiales en un artículo
donde quedan en las notas como indispensable bibliografía
para quien, en adelante, quiera ahondar en el problema. "

CONGRESO INTERNACIONAL GALDOSIANO.   Alfonso

Armas Ayala, "Apendice: 1.er Congreso internacional galdosiano. Las Palmas, Gran Canaria, 29 de agosto a 5 de
septiembre de 1973. Resumen del congreso," Anales galdosianos, 8 (1973), 143-149, provides a list of those who at-
tended the conference, the titles of the 46 ponencias, and
other data of interest concerning this Congress.

Galdós and his Contemporaries

RAMON PEREZ DE AYALA. Monroe Z. Hafter,
"Galdós's influence on Pérez de Ayala," Galdós Studies II,
pp. 13-28, shows that "there is evidence that Galdós's works
provided a matrix in which Ayala's ideas took form and were
nourished" (p. 14).

Novelas españolas contemporaneas

ANGEL GUERRA. Geraldine M. Scanlon, "Religion
and art in Angel Guerra," Anales galdosianos, 8 (1973), 99-
105, notes that several critics have commented on the prominent role of religious art in this novel. Yet the author feels
that "the thematic and structural importance of Galdós' use
of religious art in that novel is such that an attempt to get
it steadily into focus seems to be called for. For although the matter has been touched on often enough there is
no study in which it is given sustained attention in a coherent
fashion" (p. 99). The author hopes "to demonstrate that the
religious-aesthetic experiences are fundamental to the structure of the novel and the characterization of Guerra" (p. 100).

DOÑA PERFECTA. J. B. Hall, "Galdós use of the
Christ-symbol in Doña Perfecta," Anales galdosianos, 8
(1973), 95-98, states that "It is the aim of this brief study
to show that in Doña Perfecta we find a central character,
Pepe Rey, who presents analogies with Christ considerably
more extensive than has generally been supposed" (p. 95).

LA FONTANA DE ORO. Guillermo Araya, "La fonta-
na de oro de Galdós: cien años de lucidez política," Estudios
filológicos (Valdivia, Chile), 8 (1972), 89-104, writes that
"Interesará aquí sólo el contenido político de esta novela"
(p. 89). After an introduction, part one, Ambiente, develops
the theme that "Todo el ambiente de la novela está estructu-
rado políticamente" (p. 91). Part two, Absolutismo y abso-
lutistas, states that "Hay un importante grupo de la fauna

novelesca de La Fontana de Oro que aspira a restablecer la
monarquía absoluta" (p. 92) and this group is discussed.
Part three is entitled Reacción y ultraizquierda and part four
deals with Opinones e intuiciones del narrador.   On p. 90
the author briefly compares the Spain of 1870 as described by
Galdós with the political situation in Chile in the early 1970's.

FORTUNATA Y JACINTA.   John H. Sinnigen, "Individual, class, and society in Fortunata y Jacinta, " Galdós
Studies II, pp. 49-68, states that "As Raymond Carr has
suggested, the Restoration tried to incorporate peacefully all
dissident forces in a futile effort to avoid social revolution.
In this study I shall examine--with particular reference to the
unresolved class conflict--the portrayal in Fortunata y Jacinta
of the hypocrisy of that attempt" (p. 49).   In addition to the
introduction, this article has the following parts: I.   The
bourgeoisie.   II.   The petty bourgeoisie.   and III.   The
pueblo.

GLORIA.   Natalio Plaza and José Quirós, Gloria de
Lantigua: drama en un prólogo y cuatro actos, adaptación
de la novela Gloria de Don Benito Pérez Galdós.   Madrid,
1922 contains "Al lector: por que se escribió Gloria para el
teatro, " pp. 7-13, which provides some interesting remarks
concerning Gloria.   Pages 147-156 provide excerpts from
contemporary drama critics as published in the Madrid press.

LA INCOGNITA AND REALIDAD.   Denah Lida,
"Galdós, entre crónica y novela, " Anales galdosianos, 8
(1973), 63-77, has the following sections: Los corresponsales,
Interés en los crimenes, Crimen y novela: La incognita, La
incognita y lo fundamental del crimen, Realidad, novela dialogada, Crimen y "crimencito, " and Apariencia y verdad.
Galdós was somewhat fascinated by a rather terrible crime
on Fuencarral Street in 1888.   Between July 19 and Aug. 15,
1888 he sent to La Prensa (Buenos Aires) a series of three
articles on this subject.   La incognita and Realidad were
inspired by this crime.   Lida writes: "...valdría la pena
ver en que medida estan presentes en estas novelas el
corresponsal de La Prensa y lo que el transmite a Buenos
Aires" (p. 63).   Lida's article deserves careful reading and
will give the reader new insights into these two novels.

LA DE BRINGAS.   Suzanne Raphael, "La de Bringas,
¿La de todos?" Hommage à André Joucla-Rua, Aix-en-Pro-
vence, Université de Provence, Department d'études hispaniques, 1974, pp. 196-207, finds in chapter eight of this

novel a "filiation résolument quévédesque par le ton, le mouve-
ment, le vocabulaire et les thèmes" (p. 197). Raphael compares several passages of this novel with passages found in
Quevedo's Sueño del infierno. This is one of the few studies
that attempts to show in some detail Quevedo's direct influence on Galdós.

MARIANELA. Brian J. Dendle, "Galdós, Ayguals de
Izco, and the Hellenic inspiration of Marianela," Galdós Studies II, pp. 1-11, discusses the different ideas that leading
critics have had concerning this novel and its sources. This
article develops the theme that "The initial inspiration for
Marianela was almost certainly Ayguals de Izco's 'La belleza
del alma'" (p. 10).

MISERICORDIA. Sara E. Cohen, "Almudena and the
Jewish theme in Misericordia," Anales galdosianos, 8 (1973),
51-61, feels that "it is vital, therefore, to examine the religion of Almudena, to establish once and for all the nature
and origin of his convictions, and to evaluate his moral and
personal worth in order to appreciate the crucial role that
he and his faith play in the novel. In the process we will
see how carefully and poignantly Galdós introduces the beggar
to us and how he transforms him from a secondary character
into a principal figure in the work" (p. 51).

TRISTANA. Raymond Durgnat, "Tristana," Film
Comment, 10, 5 (Sept.-Oct. 1974), 54-62, is one of the
fullest discussions of this Buñuel film in English. His treatment is especially valuable for remarks concerning certain
of the minor characters such as Horacio, Saturna and Saturno
as well as the major protagonists: Don Lope and Tristana.
Durgnat's remarks concerning Buñuel's use of symbolism in
the film are worthy of careful attention.

Linguistic studies

Denah Lida, "El habla de los sefardíes en Galdós,"
Galdós Studies II, pp. 29-33, is a brief note on the speech
of the Sefardíes as found in Gloria, Misericordia, Aita
Tettauen and Carlos VI, en la Rapita.

Emilio Náñez Fernández, "Don Benito Pérez Galdós,"
El diminutivo: historia y funciones en el español clásico y
moderno, Madrid, Gredos, 1973, pp. 293-302, 426-432
(Biblioteca románica hispánica. Estudios y ensayos 196),

studies the diminutives found in Fortunata y Jacinta, Marianela and Gloria.   On p. 293 Náñez writes that "La abundancia
de diminutivos en Galdós es abrumadora.   La importancia,
pues, de este derivado dentro de su obra es grande no sólo
por su frecuencia, sino por su expresividad." Pages 426-
432 list the diminutives found in these three novels.

Stylistics

REALITY.   Leon Livingstone, "On significant reality:
Robbe-Grillet, Celaya, Galdós," Galdós Studies II, pp. 35-47,
deals with the idea of reality as found in these three authors.
He notes that "the concept of total reality ... underlies the
novelistic art of Benito Pérez Galdós" (p. 40).   On p. 47,
he notes: "But the constant lesson of life teaches is that if
reality is there for us to recognize--and Galdós is in all
probability the greatest Spanish realist since Cervantes--
reality is also an act of faith."   His comments are based
on Gloria, Marianela, Doña Perfecta, Misericordia and
Fortunata y Jacinta.

Episodios nacionales

Douglas Hilt, "Galdós: the novelist as historian,"
History Today, 24, 5 (May 1974), 315-325, is an extremely
interesting article.   On p. 315 Hilt writes: "The immediate
question is whether the novelist can claim to be a dispassion-
ate historian, or whether the creative--element the imaginative and artistic components--preclude any factual recounting
of past events.   Many historians reveal biases, openly or
unwittingly, so that the presentation of 'facts' is often dis-
torted or prejudged.   Galdós is certainly not immune from
such criticism, but he made a determined effort to present
an objective picture of nineteenth-century Spain--no easy
task in an era more given to emotion than clear reasoning.
More importantly, he regarded history as a whole, compris-
ing the widest possible spectrum of human activity, including
aspects of everyday life that many professional historians
considered beyond their province."

Despite the shortcomings of the Episodios nacionales
that Hilt points out on pp. 324-325, Hilt concludes in his
last paragraph that "one is still astounded at the magnificent
panorama presented, the fertile imagination wedded to a
shrewd intelligence, the vast erudition and firm grasp of the

copious material.   Above all, there is a generosity of outlook,
a spirit of compromise and understanding rare in nineteenth-
century Spain, a comprehensiveness of vision that perhaps
makes Galdos the best interpreter of his country" (p. 325).

The illustrations and photographs add to the article's
overall interest.

CADIZ.   Daniel Devoto, "Novela, historia y alegoría
en Cádiz, " Revue de littérature comparée, 45 (1971), 145-
158, is of great interest for its discussion on pp. 154-158 of
Byron's Don Juan as the model for Lord Gray, a character
in Cádiz.   The last sentence of this article follows: "Las
imágenes augustas que, semiocultas, se mueven en Cádiz, las
que atraviesan toda la primera serie de los Episodios Na-
cionales--Otello, Romeo y Julieta, Shylock, el alucinante Napoleón de las ratas de Gerona, Don Juan, Don Quijote--no
pertenencen ni a la historia del siglo XIX y ni siquiera tampoco a la novela: son arquetipos sobrehumanos que conducen
estas 'novelas históricas' a las mismas alturas de la alegoría
que recorre El caballero encantado, y que muestran cómo la
genialidad de Galdós sabe siempre evadirse de cualquier jaula
en que queramos clasificarlo" (p. 158).

Theater

Stanley Melvin Finkenthal, "The theater of Pérez
Galdós: the artist as social critic, " New York University,
Ph.D. dissertation, 1972, x, 257 leaves (Dissertation Abstracts International, 33 [1973] 6354) examines "Galdós'
theater in terms of the social reality that lies at the core of
realistic drama.   The plays will be studied in terms of their
historical setting in an attempt to understand the effect on
the audience and their appreciation of the plays" (iii).

The table of contents follows: I.   Galdós sociological
approach to the theater.   II.   Review of the plays of the first
period 1892-1896.   III.   The will and consciousness as social
realities: Realidad (1892).   IV.   Good and evil as social realities: La loca de la casa.   V.   The manuscripts.   VI.
Galdós returns to the theater: the second period 1910-1910.
VII.   The social reality of clericalism: Electra (1901).
VIII.   Reviews of the plays of the third period: 1913-1918.
IX.   The legacy of Spanish history: Santa Juana de Castilla
(1918).   X.   Galdós and modern drama.   Conclusion.   Appendix A: Genealogy of characters Ms. 10 La de San Quintin.
Appendix B: Dramatis personae Ms. 10.   Appendix C: Word

association Ms. 10.   Appendix D: Reverse side of page Ms.
10. Bibliography.

ELECTRA.   Lily Litvak, "'Los Tres' y Electra: la
creación de un grupo generacional bajo el magisterio de
Galdós, " Anales galdosianos, 8 (1973), 89-94, notes that
around 1900 "Azorín, Baroja y Maeztu se habían asociado
en un nucleo generacional con una viva conciencia del problema de España" (p. 89).   Litvak notes that "Este grupo no
acudió a Unamuno al parecer, ni como guía ni como compa-
ñero.   Se caracterizaron por su virulencia anticlerical, y su
guía la encontraron en Galdós" (p. 89).   She states that "Nos
reduciremos a citar y comentar algunos textos olvidados que
tienen bastante interés histórico y a reproducir fragmentos
de artículos de los jóvenes del 98 imprescindibles para comprender su postura política" (p. 99).   Her article allows us
to get a better view of the reactions of these three writers
to Galdós' play Electra.

Special Topics

INDIVIDUAL AND SOCIETY.   John H. Sinnigen, Individual and society in the Novelas contemporáneas of Benito
Pérez Galdós, Johns Hopkins University, Ph. D. dissertation,
1971, 237 leaves.   "Ultimately this study involves an inquiry
into the relation of the Galdosian novel, in terms of both
form and content, to social reality" (abstract that precedes
the dissertation).   It has the following parts: Introduction, 1 El
doctor Centeno, Tormento, and La de Bringas. 2 Fortunata y
Jacinta. 3 The Torquemada series. 4 Nazarin, Halma and
Misericordia.   Conclusion. Works cited in this study.

RELIGIOUS SYMBOLISM.   O. W. Key, Galdosian
symbolism in three spiritualist and one non-spiritualist novels, University of New Mexico, Ph. D. dissertation, 1972,
309 leaves (Dissertation Abstracts International, 33 [1973]
5729) states that its purpose is "two-fold: to study the complex symbolism of these novels, and to show that the religious
symbolism, characteristic of the novels written during the
spiritualistic period is already clearly evident in at least one
of Galdós's early novels, Zaragoza.   This characteristic,
consequently, cannot be traced to the influence of the Russian
spiritual writers.   Galdós was therefore, basically sincere
when he denied the influence of these writers in the composition of his spiritualist novels. "   His first appendix indicates
"a very probable use of Josephus' history for the novelistic
portrayal of the siege of Zaragoza. "

The table of contents of this dissertation follows:
Galdós' spiritualist novels and symbolism.   II.   Nazarin,
incarnate logos of Christ.   III.   Halma; goddess of love.
IV.   Misericordia, the humanization of charity.   V.   Zaragoza: a religious war.   VI.   Conclusion.   Appendix I: Zaragoza and the siege of Jerusalem.   Appendix II: The use
of irony in Nazarin.

SUICIDE.   Serafin S. Aleman, El suicidio en la novela de Benito Pérez Galdós, New York University, Ph. D. dissertation, 1972, 229 leaves with an unpaginated bibliography
(Dissertation Abstracts International, 33 [1973], 6289) is the
fullest treatment yet written on Galdós'' treatment of suicide
and attempted suicide.   The conclusions deal with several
novels to which extended treatment is now given in the body
of the dissertation.

The table of contents follows: Breve exposición del
suicidio en la historia.   I.   Suicidios no consumados en la
narrativa galdosiana.   II.   Estudio del suicidio de Federico
Viera en La incognita y Realidad.   III.   Estudio del suicidio
de Rafael del Aguila en Torquemada en la Cruz y Torquemada en el Purgatorio.   IV.   Estudio del suicidio de don Ramón
Villaamil en Miau.   Conclusiones.

Other works

VIAJES Y FANTASIAS.   Anson C. Piper, "Galdós and
Portugal, " Anales galdosianos, 8 (1973), 79-87, comments on
two letters which are best found in volume 6 of his Obras
completas.   His "Excursión a Portugal" was published under
the general heading of Viajes y fantasías.   Galdós and Pereda
visited Portugal together in the spring of 1885 and Piper
analyzes Galdós' views concerning Portugal as found in these
letters of May 28, 1885 (Lisbon) and Oct. 30, 1888 (Santander).
Piper also takes into account Galdós' views on Portugal as
found in "Pereda y yo, " part of his Memorias de un desme-
moriado.

EL 1º DE MAYO.   Leo J. Hoar, Jr. , "Benito Pérez
Galdós and May day, 1907, " Romance Notes, 15, 2 (1973),
238-245 analyzes and discusses the significance of the article
"El 1º de Mayo" published as "his contribution to the com-
memoration of the workers' holidays in Spain" (p. 238).   The
text of this article is reproduced in pp. 244-245 from España
nueva, año II, número 335, p. 1.

EL DOS DE MAYO. Leo J. Hoar, Jr., "More on the pre- (and post-) history of the Episodios nacionales: Galdós' article 'El dos de Mayo' (1874)," Anales galdosianos, 8 (1973), 107-120 insists that this article, the text of which is reproduced on pages 114-117, "is a significant addition to galdosiana, not only 'archeologically' speaking, but also because it represents a rather peculiar piece of evidence of the existence of a special preparatory ur-quell in his creative process on this theme, extending toward its later and fuller development in his major works" (p. 107).

As this volume was ready to go to press early in 1975 the Dec. 1974 Insula announced as forthcoming Roberto Sánchez, El teatro en la novela: Galdós y Clarín, prólogo de Antonio Sánchez-Barbudo, 210pp. A fourth enlarged edition has appeared of Casalduero's Vida y obras de Galdós (Madrid, 1974), 312pp.

Rodolfo Cardona wrote an introduction and provided notes to an edition of Doña Perfecta based on the Madrid edition of 1907 ([New York]: Anaya-Las Américas, [1974]) pp. 17-47. This introduction is divided into "Biographical sketch," "The manuscript" and "The novel." It is an excellent brief discussion of the novel. Its discussion of the manuscript is the fullest yet published. He is quite willing to discuss the views of other critics. For example, he denies that the novel is a melodrama. His remarks on plot and characters are well-worth consideration.

Late in 1974 there appeared two reviews of Buñuel's Tristana: Teresa Barbero, "Mujeres en el mundo novelístico: Tristana," La Estafeta literaria, no. 551 (1 de nov. de 1974) 18-19 and Beth Miller, "La Tristana feminista de Buñuel," Dialógos, 10, 6 (nov.-dic. 1974) 16-20.

The Barbero article develops the theme expressed in its first paragraph: "La historia de Tristana, una de las creaciones más lúcidas no sólo de Pérez Galdós, sino de la femenina iconografía literaria española, es, fundamentalmente la historia de una mujer que libró--y perdió--la batalla de su identidad. Es también, a pesar de todo, la historia de una liberación, porque hay batallas que, aun perdiéndose, o acaso por perderse, liberan, como hay ilusiones que, al alejarse, depurar. Tristana es un enorme contrasentido como ser humano, pero envuelto en la perfecta e irritante coherencia de una mujer en la sociedad crepuscular del XIX. Vista desde hoy, no sabría decirse si Tristana es una valiente precursora de las "women-lib" o una pobre sirvienta con imaginación, incapaz de luchar en profundidad contra su condición" (p. 18).

Miller writes that "Una de las diferencias más importantes entre la Tristana de Pérez Galdós y la película del mismo título de Buñuel es la localización temporal y geográfica: el escenario del libro es el Madrid de fines del siglo XIX, el de la película el Toledo provincial entre los años 1929 y 1935. Ambas Tristanas pueden considerarse personajes literarios y personifican temas feministas. En este ensayo exploraré las complejidades e implicaciones de la Tristana de Buñuel (representada por Catherine Deneuve) con solamente algunas casuales referencias al personaje creado por Galdós. La Tristana del celuloide deslumbra con la múltiple variedad de imágenes femeninas que en ella se combinan y con los sutiles matices contextuales (socio-políticos, sico-ideológicos) de estas imágenes. La ironía subversiva de Buñuel, los excelentes detalles y la riqueza temática contribuyen a la viveza y la particularidad del personaje. La 'imagen de la mujer' de la obra surge principalmente de la conducta y enérgico desarrollo de Tristana en sus relaciones sociales y en su interacción con los demás (Lope, Horacio, Saturna, Saturno, la Guardia Civil, el cura) (p. 16).

Madeleine de Gogorza Fletcher, "Galdós," The Spanish historical novel 1870-1970 (London, Tamesis, 1973), pp. 11-50 (Colección Tamesis, Serie A - Monografías 32) is divided into a biographical sketch of Galdós: The first two Series, Series III, Series IV and Series V. She writes: "This chapter will attempt to confront these stylistic changes with the historical background which was an important factor in their development, as Galdós' changing attitude towards the present direction of historical events is reflected in the different characters he uses to describe the past. In this process we notice that the historical aspect of the Episodios nacionales is not only their historical content (described historical events) but also their historical intent, which is most visible in the number of occasions outlined here in which Galdós projects the present upon the past and indulges in predictions and didactic-hortatory messages" (p. 14).

The final paragraph of this chapter is: "The deep political and moral concern for Spain evident in Galdós first novels continues to motivate him throughout his career. This concern first influences him to seek lessons for the present in the past conflicts which he outlines with representative characters in Series I and II. Twenty years later he criti-

cizes contemporary defects in the context of the past in Series III and symbolizes the positive characteristics of the
eternal Spain of the intrahistoria made fashionable by the
Generation of '98 in the allegorical Ansúrez family in Series
IV.   Finally, he presents both the bitterness and the hope of
this lifelong concern in the satire and allegory of Series V"
(p. 50).

NOTES

1. Movie versions of Galdós' works: E. D., "Nuestro cinema y Galdós," Insula, no. 82 (Oct. 15, 1962), 11, regrets that Spanish film makers have not made more and better use of Galdós' novels as sources for their films. He points out that many of Galdós' novels would make excellent movies. He lists those films made based on Galdós' novels and declares that "Ninguna de ellas tienen verdadera importancia." Three versions exist of El abuelo (Spanish, 1925; Mexican, 1944; Argentine, 1951), two of La loca de la casa (Spanish, 1926; Mexican, 1950) and one of Marianela (Spanish, 1940). E. D. states that the film Agustina de Aragón was based on Zaragoza. He finds similarities between Miau and El último which he says "es probablemente uno de los films más importantes que ha producido el cine universal."

   Students interested in the screen credits for Mexican films based on Galdós' novels should examine María Isabel de la Fuente, Indice bibliográfico del cine mexicano, 1930-1965 (Mexico, 1967). This Indice presents data on La loca de la casa (entry 935), Doña Perfecta (entry 981), Misericordia (entry 1169) and Nazarín (entry 1720). It also states that the scripts of Adulterio (entry 408) and La mujer ajena (entry 1317) are based on some work by Galdós.

   It would seem that the movie versions of Nazarín and more recently of Tristana are those to which the critics have devoted the most attention.

   Among the reviews of Fortunata y Jacinta found in the Madrid press are the following: Conde Duque, "Fortunata y Jacinta: nada menos que Galdós," Pueblo, April 8, 1970, p. 25; Ignacio de Montes Jovellar, "Allí donde nació Pérez Galdós ha sido la 'premiere' mundial de Fortunata y Jacinta," Madrid, April 4, 1970, p. 13 (this page also contains an advertisement for the movie which occupies about three-fourths of a page); Antonio de Obregón, "Fortunata y Jacinta," ABC, April 8, 1970, pp. 74-75; Juby Bustamante, "Precedida de tres premios la Fortunata de Galdós y Fons, en Madrid," Madrid, April 7, 1970, p. 28.

J. Francisco Aranda, Luis Buñuel: biografía crítica, Madrid, Lumen [1970], is of interest for its comments on Buñuel and Galdós. For example, pp. 388-92 are "Tristana: sinopsis de la novela." Pages 393-97 are "Primer guión de Tristana (época 1923)." The "filmografía" provides data on Nazarín, pp. 412-413, and Tristana (ficha provisional), p. 418.

2. It might be well here to summarize the data on Galdós, Chile and 1943 provided me by Arístides Bocaz Concha. Atenea noted this centennial with the publication of 11 articles; this issue was commented upon as follows: "Un número extraordinario de Atenea," La Nación (Santiago), May 16, 1943, p. 5; "Atenea y Galdós," El Mercurio (Valparaíso), June 9, 1943, p. 3; "El centenario de Galdós. La revista Atenea," España libre. Suplemento de literatura y arte (Santiago), June 19, 1943, pp. 5, 7. España libre ... published five articles on Galdós during this year. As most of these articles are annotated in the body of this bibliography, their data will not be repeated. Latcham's review of Doña Perfecta has been mentioned under Obras completas; his "El centenario de Galdós" appeared in La Nación, May 9, p. 5. La Nación also published "Galdós" by A. R. R., May 11, p. 3, and Rodrigo Soriano, "Galdós," May 23, p. 3. El Mercurio published at least two other articles on Galdós: X, "Centenario de Pérez Galdós," May 10, p. 3; and J. de la Cruz Vallejo, "Hace cien años," May 11, p. 3. Hoy reprints from La Prensa (Buenos Aires) Ramón Pérez de Ayala, "El centenario de don Benito Pérez Galdós o Galdós y la fecundidad creadora," 12, no. 602 (June 3, 1943), 56-59.

There would be little reason to doubt that this centennial did not produce a rather large number of journal and newspaper comments in other parts of Spanish America.

3. I have not located the Colección Austral edition of Libros y autores españoles contemporáneos mentioned by

Gómez Ortiz. However, Unamuno's Obras completas, V (Madrid, Afrodisio Aguado, 1960), is entitled De esto y de aquello and has a section with this title. The three essays are: "La sociedad galdosiana," pp. 465-467; "Galdós en 1901," pp. 468-470; and "Nuestro impresión de Galdós," pp. 471-474.

4. Students interested in a comprehensive bibliography of the Galdós-Balzac relationship should examine William Hobart Royce, A Balzac bibliography (Chicago: University of Chicago Press, 1929), items 12, 594, 600-01, 893, 936-37, 1042, 1329, 1412, 1424, 2725, 2729, 3148, 3300-01, 3485, 3491, 2633 and 3877.

5. Because of Lida's extensive documentation, the reader's attention is called only to the following studies on Spanish krausismo: Vicente Cacho Viu, La institución libre de Enseñanza (Madrid: Rialp, 1963), 2 vols.; Pierre Jobit, Les éducateurs de l'Espagne contemporaine. I. Les Krausistas (Paris: Bibliothèque de l'Ecole des Etudes hispaniques, 1936), 2 vols; Notas sobre el moderno pensamiento español (Quito: Casa de la Cultura Ecuatoriana, 1959), 92pp.; and his "Sanz del Río et ses récents biographes," Mélanges à la mémoire de Jean Sarrailh (Paris: Centre de Recherches de l'Institut d'Etudes Hispaniques, 1966), 1, 437-43; Juan López-Morillas, El krausimo español, perfíl de una aventura intelectual (México: Fondo de Cultura Económico, 1956), 218pp. The index to Sackett has 33 references to krausismo.

COLLECTIONS ANALYZED

The vast majority of articles or chapters in the following works have been listed, classified and annotated in this bibliography. They have usually been referred to by author and title.

Benito Pérez Galdós, edición de Douglass M. Rogers. Madrid, Taurus, 1973. (El escritor y la crítica, 1). Referred to as Benito Pérez Galdós (1973).

Correa, Gustavo, El simbolismo religioso en las novelas de Pérez Galdós. Madrid, Gredos, 1962.

Galdós Studies, ed. J. E. Varey. London, Tamesis, 1970.

Galdós Studies II, edited by Robert J. Weber. London, Tamesis Books Limited, 1974, 68pp. (Colección Tamesis. Serie A - Monografías, XXXIX). Cited as Galdós Studies II.

Gullón, Ricardo, Galdós, novelista moderno: tercera edición revisada y aumentada. Madrid, Gredos, 1973. (Biblioteca románica hispánica).

Gullón, Ricardo, Técnicas de Galdós. Madrid, Taurus, 1971.

Ricard, Robert, Aspects de Galdós. Paris, L'Institut d'Etudes hispaniques, 1961.

Río, Angel del, Estudios galdosianos. New York, Las Américas, 1969.

Rodríguez, Alfred, Aspectos de la novela de Galdós. Almería, Estudios literarios, 1967.

Shoemaker, William H., Estudios sobre Galdós. Madrid, Castalia, 1970.

AUTHOR INDEX

TITLE INDEX

SUBJECT INDEX

Alarcón, Pedro de 201
Alas, Leopoldo 17-18, 28, 146, 201
Alcaide Ibieca, Agustín 243
Alemán, Mateo 136
Allegory 294
Almudena 122, 123-4, 180
Alvarez Quintero, Joaquín 112, 254, 263, 272
Alvarez Quintero, Serafín 112, 254, 263, 272
America in Galdós' works 166-7
Angulo, Pauly 238
Anticlericalism 61, 229, 275
Aparisi y Guijarro, Antonio 240
Appearance-reality contrast 144
Araceli, Gabriel 242
Art 290
Art and society 167
Arte pictórico 205
Augusto 199
Azcárate, Gumersindo de 84
Azorín 16, 18, 28, 268-9, 295

Balzac, Honoré de 47, 91-2, 115, 149, 302
Baroja, Pío 17, 18-19, 28, 58, 96-7, 225-6, 240, 248, 249, 288, 295
Beauvoir, Simone de 153
Benavente, Jacinto 16, 254, 255, 260
Benefactor 190, 191
Benina 121, 124
Bible 44-5, 120
Bibliographies 1-4
Blanco-Fombona, Rufino 146
Blasco Ibáñez, Vicente 28, 98
Blindness 172
Boada, Vicente 28
Borcino, Luciana 277
Bourget, Paul 139

Bringas, Rosalía 109
Bromfield, Louis 83
Buñuel, Luis 152, 154-65
Bushee, Alice H. 28
Business in Galdós' novels 99

Caballero, Fernán 231
Calderón de la Barca, Pedro 51
Camara, Miguel H. de la 19
Camila 199
Camus, Alfredo Adolfo 9-10
Caricatures 205
Carlist wars 248, 249-50
Castro, Adolfo de 235
Celaya, Gabriel 293
La Celestina 258
Centeno, Felipe 143
Cervantes, Miguel de 51-3, 98-9, 118, 145, 153, 154, 242, 262, 271
Characters, abnormal 166, 168-9; blind and handicapped 167-8; census of 113; children and adolescents 169-70; interdependence of 168-9
Charity 190-1
Chil, Gregorio 28
Cholera 173
Christ figure 120-1, 128-9, 290
Classification of novels 55
Clothes (as symbols) 146
Cobián, Lorenza 289
Color symbolism 135-6, 170
Comella, Luciano Francisco 236
Comte, Auguste 33, 111
Concept of life as organic process 171
Congreso internacional galdosiano (1973) 15, 289-90
Coronado, Pío 262